DANGEROUSNESS, RISK AND THE GOVERNANCE OF SERIOUS SEXUAL AND VIOLENT OFFENDERS

Karen Harrison

LONDON AND NEW YORK

First edition published 2011
by Routledge
2 Park Square, Milton Park, Abingdon, Oxon OX14 4RN

Simultaneously published in the USA and Canada
by Routledge
711 Third Avenue, New York, NY 10017

Routledge is an imprint of the Taylor & Francis Group, an informa business

British Library Cataloguing in Publication Data
A catalogue record for this book is available from the British Library

Library of Congress Cataloging in Publication Data
Harrison, Karen, 1974-
Dangerousness, risk and the governance of serious sexual and violent offenders/by Karen Harrison.
p. cm.
1. Corrections. 2. Sex offenders. 3. Violent offenders. 4. Crime prevention. I. Title.
HV8665.H375 2011
364.15–dc22 2011000180

ISBN: 978–0–415–66862–0 (hbk)
ISBN: 978–0–415–66863–7 (pbk)
ISBN: 978–0–203–80921–1 (ebk)

Typeset in Bembo and Stone Sans by
Florence Production Ltd, Stoodleigh, Devon

Printed and bound in Great Britain by
CPI Antony Rowe, Chippenham, Wiltshire

In loving memory of Janet Harrison,
although you are no longer with us,
your influence and encouragement live on

CONTENTS

ILLUSTRATIONS

Figures

Tables

PREFACE

Notwithstanding changing social constructions and understandings, the dangerous offender is arguably one of the most persistent moral panics (Cohen 1972) of the late twentieth and early twenty-first centuries. While there are comparatively few dangerous offenders in terms of the total offender population, the potential harm and subsequent long-term impact that their offences can cause have the potential to be disproportionately high, especially when compared to property offences and crimes not committed against the person. Public protection, governance and the sentencing of these offenders is consequently of prime importance, and due to the high stakes involved, it is imperative that both policies and systems set up to deal with this risky group of offenders are both appropriate and effective. With this backdrop in mind, the aim of this book is to assess the governance of dangerous offenders within England and Wales by providing a critical evaluation of the policies, procedures and institutions involved. In short, it questions whether dangerous offenders are appropriately labelled, detained and managed within the penal system, and whether enough is being done to not only effectively reduce the risk of reoffending but also to ensure public protection.

The first issue that must be decided upon in a book of this nature is who the dangerous offender is and, indeed, this was not an easy task. When the book was first conceptualised, it was intended that it would cover a number of different 'types' of dangerous offender including, but not limited to, terrorists, would-be terrorists (especially due to the significant problems of assessing the risk that would-be terrorists pose), prolific offenders (based on the number of offences that they commit) and the more traditional serious sexual and violent offenders. As the book began to take shape, however, it was realised that, due to space, it would be impossible to include all of these different types. For this reason, it was therefore decided to concentrate solely on serious sexual and violent offenders, although it is freely acknowledged that other dangerous offenders exist and, in some cases, these types may actually pose more of a risk to the public.

By concentrating on just serious sexual and violent offenders, it is thought that this gives the book a better structure and a clearer purpose. Indeed, as each chapter was embarked on, it was realised that, in many cases, a whole book could have been written on each chapter heading, rather than a mere 10,000–14,000 words. Although it has therefore been necessary to be brief in some areas, it is nevertheless hoped that the book still provides sufficient material to not only explain and begin to evaluate the issues involved, but also to provoke thought, discussion and further reading on this important subject. In order to ensure that sufficient breadth was covered, the book is divided into nine chapters. Chapter 1 begins by considering what a dangerous offender is and provides a brief historical account of how the label has been used for different types of offender over the last three or four centuries. It further explains why the book concentrates solely on serious sexual and violent offenders, although notes the many other different types that exist. This is then followed by Chapter 2, which considers sentencing policy in addition to early and current dangerousness legislation. In particular, it evaluates the available sentences specifically designed for dangerous offenders and assesses their use and appropriateness. In order to come within current dangerousness legislation, the offender must have been 'assessed as dangerous' and, following on from sentencing policy, Chapter 3 looks at the role of risk-assessment tools, considering what risk assessment is, the way in which it works and how, over recent times, it has become more reliable and valid.

Chapters 4 to 6 then look at the practical realities of how serious sexual and violent offenders are dealt with by the penal system in England and Wales. This includes a chapter on the use of imprisonment, a chapter on strategies of risk management and a chapter on interventions designed to reduce risk. Within each chapter, specific methods, regimes, programmes and strategies are outlined, with efficacy evaluated and commented on. Gaps within the system are also identified. Finally, within Chapters 7 to 9, specific offender groups are considered, including female offenders, children and young people, and mentally disordered offenders (MDOs). Each chapter considers whether there are any differences in terms of policy, assessment and management strategies when sentencing and managing each distinct group; and, if not, whether any such modifications are required. In all three of these final chapters, the general theme is the same: if the individual is not a sane adult male, then there needs to be recognition of this in every process and procedure undertaken.

Every effort has been made to ensure that this book details the most up-to-date processes, procedures and interventions, and HM Prison Service has been particularly helpful in this regard. The law is stated as at 10 December 2010.

Karen Harrison
Hull
December 2010

LIST OF ABBREVIATIONS

AIM	Assessment, Intervention, Moving-on
ATC	Association of Therapeutic Communities
AUC	area under the curve
CALM	Controlling Anger and Learning to Manage It
CARAT	Counselling, Assessment, Referral, Advice and Throughcare
CARE	Choices, Actions, Relationships and Emotions
CDA	Crime and Disorder Act
CEOP	Child Exploitation and Online Protection
CJA	Criminal Justice Act
CJIA	Criminal Justice and Immigration Act
COSA	Circles of Support and Accountability
CPA	cyproterone acetate
CPS	Crown Prosecution Service
CSC	close supervision centre
CSCP	Cognitive Self-Change Programme
C-SOTP	Community Sex Offender Treatment Programme
CTO	community treatment order
DPP	Detention for Public Protection
DSPD	Dangerous and Severe Personality Disorder
ECHR	European Convention on Human Rights
ECtHR	European Court of Human Rights
ERASOR	Estimate of Risk of Adolescent Sexual Abuse Recidivism
ERU	Exceptional Risk Unit
FTO	Foreign Travel Order
GPP	Generic Parole Process
GPS	Global Positioning System
GSM	Global System Mobile

HCR-20	Historical, Clinical, Risk Management-20
HMCIP	Her Majesty's Chief Inspector of Prisons
HMIP	Her Majesty's Inspectorate of Prisons
IDAP	Integrated Domestic Abuse Programme
IMB	Independent Monitoring Board
IPP	imprisonment for public protection
i-SOTP	Internet Sex Offender Treatment Programme
J-SOAP	Juvenile Sex Offender Assessment Protocol
LHRH	Luteinizing Hormone-Releasing Hormone
LISP	Life and Indeterminate Sentence Plan
LS/CMI	Level of Service/Case Management Inventory
LSI-R	Level of Service Inventory-Revised
LSP	life sentence plan
MAPPA	Multi-Agency Public Protection Arrangement
MAPPP	Multi-Agency Public Protection Panel
MBU	Mother and Baby Unit
MCBS	Managing Challenging Behaviour Strategy
MDO	mentally disordered offender
MHA	Mental Health Act
MHTR	mental health treatment requirement
MPA	medroxyprogesterone acetate
NO	Notification Order
NOMS	National Offender Management Service
NPS	National Probation Service
N-SOTP	Northumbria Sex Offender Treatment Programme
OASys	Offender Assessment System
OGRS	Offender Group Reconviction Scale
OMA	Offender Management Act
OVP	OASys Violence Predictor
P-ASRO	Prison-Addressing Substance Related Offending
PCL-R	Psychopathy Checklist-Revised
PTD	personal tracking device
RHSO	Risk of Sexual Harm Order
RM2000	Risk Matrix 2000
SARN	Structured Assessment of Risk and Need
SAVRY	Structured Assessment of Violence Risk in Youth
SFO	serious further offence
SOA	Sexual Offences Act
SOPO	Sex Offences Prevention Order
SOTP	sex offender treatment programme
SSRI	Selective Serotonin Reuptake Inhibitor
STC	secure training centre
TC	therapeutic community
TV-SOTP	Thames Valley Sex Offender Treatment Programme

UN	United Nations
ViSOR	Violent and Sex Offender Register
VOO	Violent Offender Order
WCP	Women's Community Project
YJB	Youth Justice Board
YOI	young offender institution
YOT	Youth Offending Team

Publications

Acta Neurochir Suppl (Wien)	Acta Neurochirurgica Supplement (Wien)
Ann. N.Y. Acad. Sci	Annals of the New York Academy of Sciences
Arch. News	Archbold News
Bull. Am. Acad. Psychiatry Law	Bulletin of the American Academy of Psychiatry and the Law
Crim L.R.	Criminal Law Review
J. Forensic Sci.	Journal of Forensic Sciences

1

DANGEROUSNESS AND THE DANGEROUS OFFENDER

Introduction

Although the terms danger, dangerous and dangerousness are used in common parlance, their actual precise meanings in criminal justice terms is much more elusive, with Shaw arguing that 'the problem of "dangerousness" is [in] its definition' (1973: 269). Considering the nature of this book, it would seem appropriate that the first task is to decide on, or at least attempt to define, what such concepts mean and appraise their use in the context of historical, political, legal and social perspectives. Such an assessment, albeit in brief, is the main aim of this chapter (for a fuller discussion, see Rennie 1978; Pratt 1997, 2000).

Existing definitions

The *Oxford English Dictionary* (2009a) currently defines dangerous as 'fraught with danger or risk; causing or occasioning danger; perilous, hazardous, risky, unsafe', and danger as 'power (of a person, weapon, or missile) to inflict physical injury' (*Oxford English Dictionary* 2009b). *Webster's New World College Dictionary* (2009a, 2009b) correspondingly defines dangerous as 'involving an active threat' and danger as 'the general term for liability to injury or evil, of whatever degree or likelihood of occurrence'. It is worth noting that, while contemporary definitions appear to focus on physical concepts, this is not where the term danger originates from. Rather, its linguistic roots come from the Latin derivative *dominium*, which meant lordship or sovereignty. Sarbin therefore argues that the real meaning of danger is power, where danger is 'a symbol denoting relative power in a social organisation' (1967: 286).

Over the last half century, there have been a number of reports and studies that have attempted to define these terms, particularly for legal and clinical purposes. One of the first looked at the difference between violence and danger, arguing that, while 'violence denotes action; danger denotes a relationship' (Sarbin 1967: 285). Dinitz and Conrad note that, although violence can occur from organic, psychological or situational factors, 'danger is a function of social structure' (1978: 100). Furthermore, Sarbin argues that danger and violence are connected, as an offender will often 'use violence to change the [social] system when no other alternatives are available for maintaining an acceptable social identity' (1967: 293). This, he argues, is dangerous conduct because it threatens the *dominium*.

For policy purposes, however, reference is more commonly made to the term dangerousness, although we still refer to offenders as dangerous. In 1975, the Butler Report argued that dangerousness was 'a propensity to cause serious physical injury or lasting psychological harm' (Home Office and Department of Health and Social Security 1975: xiii), equating dangerousness with a physical disease, but not further defining what it meant by either 'serious' or 'lasting'. Consultant Forensic Psychiatrists in the same report argued that it was 'unwanted behaviour which is threatening or disturbing to the public and may require that the offender be placed in custody to protect the public' (ibid.: 59). Earlier, but in the same year, the Scottish Council on Crime provided a slightly tighter test, defining dangerousness as 'the probability that he will inflict serious and irremediable personal injury in the future' (Scottish Council on Crime 1975: para. 122). Two years later, it was held to be 'an unpredictable and untreatable tendency to inflict or risk serious, irreversible injury or destruction or to induce others to do so' (Scott 1977: 128), and a year after this the dangerous offender was viewed to be that 'repetitively violent criminal who has more than once committed or attempted to commit homicide, forcible rape, robbery or assault' (Dinitz and Conrad 1978: 99). In the 1980s, dangerousness was defined as 'a pathological attribute of character: a propensity to inflict harm on others in disregard or defiance of the usual social and legal constraints' (Floud and Young 1981: 20), with an acknowledgement that 'violence is almost universally regarded as the hallmark of dangerousness' (ibid.: 7). Interestingly, it was also recognised that 'dangerousness inheres in situations, not in persons; that there are no "dangerous persons", but only dangerous situations, harmful behaviour and unacceptable (or, at least, unaccepted) risks' (ibid.: xvi). This was further emphasised by Floud, who argued that 'there is no such psychological or medical entity as a "dangerous" person and that "dangerousness" is not an objective concept' (1982: 213). Furthermore, Gunn, a year later, argued that dangerousness is made up of a number of elements, of which he felt three stood out the most: 'destructiveness, prediction and fear' (1982: 7).

Current academic interpretations include Holmes and Soothill (2008), who state that it is a pathological attribute of character (although, as offenders labelled in this way are rarely constantly dangerous, they warn that it should not be viewed as a character trait), and Thompson, who classifies it as 'a concept that hints at an inherent and immutable individual characteristic' (2007: 85). In fact he argues that the term no longer actually exists, being replaced rather by the concept of 'risk of serious harm' (ibid.). Additionally, a more recent interpretation is that dangerous offenders are 'those who commit the most serious acts of physical and sexual violence'

(Hebenton and Seddon 2009: 343). Recent policy and strategy documents also contribute to, or perhaps further muddy the water when seeking, a clear definition. HM Prison Service's Dangerous Offender Strategy, for example, states that a dangerous offender is

> someone with convictions for sexual or violent offences who is assessed as presenting a high or very high risk of serious harm . . . a risk which is life threatening and/or traumatic and from which recovery, whether physical or psychological can be expected to be difficult or impossible.
>
> (HM Prison Service 2004: para. 2)

Likewise, the Criminal Justice Act (CJA) 2003 states that an offender is dangerous if he has previously been convicted of a specified offence (which can include any one of 88 sexual offences and 65 violent offences), and the court decides that there 'is a significant risk to members of the public of serious harm occasioned by the commission by him of further such offences' (s. 229 CJA 2003). Serious harm is categorised as 'death or serious injury whether physical or psychological' (s. 224(3) CJA 2003).

There are consequently several definitions from which to choose from, although with little consensus between them they do not really help to decide what category of person is or should be seen as dangerous, although clearly the more modern definitions appear to concentrate on just sexual and violent offenders. Perhaps, then, the task for this chapter is not so much about how dangerousness is defined, but rather what is meant by the term dangerous offender. As outlined in more detail below, the meaning and understanding of the term has changed over time, with changing notions and hence constructions of who is perceived to be dangerous. The next section, therefore, looks at the historical and sociological constructions of the dangerous offender.

Historical and sociological constructions of the dangerous offender

The concept of dangerous types is not new. For example, in biblical times, the first Christians were seen as dangerous, as too were thousands of women who were accused of being witches in the late Middle Ages (Rennie 1978). Furthermore, in medieval times, the label was given to the landowner, who had power over slaves, peasants and vassals and the authority to control every aspect of their lives. Dangerousness, in this sense, was therefore connected with ownership and power (Dinitz and Conrad 1978). Elizabethan times, however, saw the dangerous offender being defined for the first time. This included:

> scholars going about begging; all seafaring men pretending losses of their ships and goods on the sea; all idle persons going about either begging or using any subtle craft or unlawful games and plays, or feigning to have knowledge

> in physiognomy, palmistry or other like craft science; . . . all jugglers, tinkers, pedlers and petty chapmen; all wandering persons and common labourers refusing to work for the wages commonly given; . . . [and] all persons who wander abroad begging.
>
> (An Act for the Punishment of Rogues, Vagabonds and Sturdy Beggars, 39 Elizabeth c. 4 (1597–98), cited by Rennie 1978: 7)

A clear shift was thus seen from the all-powerful, to those classified as members of an underclass, 'feared not because of their power but because of the lack of it' (Dinitz and Conrad 1978: 129). The dangerous were henceforth seen as the poor: beggars, vagabonds, escaped servants, strangers and gypsies, and, although previously seen as just a social nuisance, those who could be viewed as wanderers were additionally classified as dangerous by the sixteenth century (Rennie 1978).

In the eighteenth and nineteenth centuries, the dangerous were those who were challenging authority's power, with examples including French revolutionists, the Italian Carbonari and, in England, working men's associations created at the time of the Industrial Revolution (Rennie 1978). These people were thought to possess a power of destruction, not just of property, but, more worryingly, against tradition, order and the law. Categorisation of dangerousness was therefore based on civil disobedience rather than any other maxim (Pratt 1997). Individuals thought to be dangerous at this time were people such as Karl Marx, Friedrich Engels (Marxism) and Mikhail Bakunin (anarchism). Indeed, in modern-day China, dangerous offenders are still defined to include political activists and counter revolutionists (Epstein and Hing-Yan Wong 1996).

Other mentions of dangerousness in the nineteenth century related not to dangerous offenders per se, but rather to the dangerous classes. These included dispossessed agricultural workers, trade unionists, political agitators, criminals (Pratt 2000) and the poor. These were often referred to as the proletariat, being only fit to reproduce (Rennie 1978). In 1840, Fregier, for example, spoke about an underclass that included both the virtuous (working) poor and the vicious (idle) poor, of which it was the latter who were the objects of fear (Dinitz and Conrad 1978). Brace, moreover described them as the 'ignorant, destitute, untrained and abandoned youth' (Rennie 1978: 4). Membership of the dangerous classes was based on a lack of wealth rather than behaviour, with the premise being that the labouring class, a term used synonymously with dangerous, would inevitably have some lapse in moral integrity due to their economic state and dispossess honest citizens of their money (Rennie 1978). This was also seen in literature, with Dickens, in *Oliver Twist*, describing the criminal poor as the dangerous classes of Victorian London, with similar references made by Victor Hugo in *Les Miserables*.

Radzinowicz likewise describes the portrayal of the dangerous classes as 'a race apart, morally depraved and vicious, living by violating the fundamental law of orderly society, which was that a man should maintain himself by honest, steady work' (1966: 38–9). Brace argued that:

> The cheapest and most efficacious way of dealing with the 'Dangerous Classes' of large cities is not to punish them, but to prevent their growth; to so throw the influences of education and discipline and religion about the abandoned and destitute youth of our large towns; to so change their material circumstances, . . . that they shall grow up as useful producers and members of society.
>
> (1872, cited by Dinitz and Conrad 1978: 101)

Dangerousness was therefore a biological factor rather than an actual physical threat, with emphasis given to wealth rather than actual danger. As Dinitz and Conrad (1978) note, while the poor and dangerous were viewed as dangerous, the rich and dangerous were viewed simply as rich. This would appear to be apparent even today, where street crime is always held to be a crime, but in some circles white-collar crime is classified as 'an aberration of the free enterprise system' (102).

The collection of criminal statistics in the mid 1800s, however, began to change this view of the poor, with statisticians realising that being poor was not, on its own, a good indicator of criminality. Crime was actually more likely to take place in the affluent cities than the impecunious rural areas, and an individual was more likely to commit crime if he had seen a downturn in his economic state rather than because of long-term poverty (Rennie 1978). While dangerous people still existed at this time, they were seen more as representatives of a dangerous class rather than as an individual threat to fellow man.

In the second half of the nineteenth century, concern began to shift from the dangerous classes to individual people, and thus the penal concept of the dangerous offender was born. The move from the dangerous classes to the dangerous individual was largely due to a social change in risk and to whom or what these levels of risk affected, including a transition in the political economy of dangerousness.

> It is a quality that is no longer possessed by a class but by individuals or small groups of criminals; it is a quality that no longer threatens to tear down the portals of the state itself in an orgy of blood and destruction; instead, it is targeted at the quality of life of its individual subjects; it is not a quality that threatens their physical existence, but insidiously puts at risk all by which their worth as citizens is judged – their property.
>
> (Pratt 1997: 17)

Centred largely on repeat offenders, dangerous offenders were property recidivists and fraudsters, including those who would commit crime and then move on to the next town with a different name and identity (Pratt 2000). The terms repeat or habitual offender began to be used synonymously with the idea of the dangerous offender. Originally, fear of such offenders was just experienced by the upper classes but, as the romance of the highwayman who only stole from the rich disappeared, criminality became a threat and a reality for all. Therefore, the risk to the state as experienced in the nineteenth century was now being replaced by a risk to all individuals who owned property. Consequently, in 1895, the habitual prisoner, who was constantly in prison for minor offences, was seen as one of the most dangerous classes of offenders (Radzinowicz and Hood 1980).

Interestingly, at this stage in history, violent and sexual offenders were perceived to be less dangerous than property offenders. This was so even though violence in private (that is, against women and children) was prevalent, and crimes of a sexual nature were actually on the rise (Pratt 1997). In all likelihood, this was due to the fact that insurance was not freely available and so once property had been stolen it was often irreplaceable (Pratt 2000), making it more valuable than personal self. It is also worth noting that it was only men who could hold property, and women who wanted to avoid being 'ruined' could not talk about offences of a sexual nature (Pratt 1997).

This duality in offences can also be explained by the fact that English Law paid more attention to property crimes, considering violent and sexual crimes as mere torts that could be made right through compensation. So, while the feudal classes would often engage in acts of violence, it was the crimes of theft and robbery committed by the lower classes that were feared the most (Rennie 1978). Property offenders were therefore given what we may now consider disproportionate sentences of imprisonment for their crimes, especially when compared to those handed out for physical assaults. For example, in 1877, a man who had kicked his 13-year-old stepdaughter into unconsciousness, causing a one-and-a-half-inch wound to her abdomen and partial paralysis to her leg, received a four-month custodial term. Another man who was convicted of stealing five silver spoons was sentenced to seven years of penal servitude (Pratt 1997).

It was not until the 1880s, therefore, that the dangerous offender was labelled in such a way that we might now be acquainted with. Garofalo, an Italian criminologist working with Lombroso, was the first to divide criminals into groups, with one known as *temibilita*, meaning fearsomeness or frightfulness. Ferri, another criminologist and colleague of Lombroso, took the groupings one step further, converting it to the related term of *pericolosita*, or dangerousness. Both terms were used to suggest that these were offenders who were likely to reoffend in the future, and so the labelling of recidivists in this way was to demonstrate their capacity for future offending. All three men were from the positivist school of criminology, which argued that the key question regarding criminals was not what they had done in the past but the extent to which they posed a danger to society in the future (Rennie 1978). Contrary to classical jurisprudence, where punishment is sought to fit the crime, positivists believed that the punishment should fit the offender and should be whatever was needed to protect society from danger. Positivism is based on the belief that science can predict dangerousness and that, if possible, a person should be treated and cured; but if this is not possible, he should then be confined (Bottoms 1977). This was the beginning of sentencing the offender rather than the offence and the creation of indeterminate sentencing based on public protection. In 1910, this belief was also held by Prins, who categorised two types of dangerous individuals: the mentally deficient and the recidivist (Rennie 1978), with other early positivists viewing the dangerous offender as 'falling somwhere between the healthy and the psychotic, the resposible and irresponsible, the doomed and the far from hopeless. The dangerous offender was *both* mad and bad' (Dinitz and Conrad 1978: 105, emphasis in original).

Membership again changed in the 1930s, as children became to be viewed as more valuable, being members of the family rather than mere commodities of them. With more families having to move in order to find work, children were often being cared for by relative strangers, which gave rise to more opportunities for people to commit sexual crimes against them. As this began to be acknowledged, such offenders were additionally labelled as dangerous, with the concept of dangerousness being, for the first time, sexualised (Sutton 2000). For example, the *Report of the Departmental Committee on Persistent Offenders* defined the dangerous offender as including 'certain sexual offenders . . . particularly those who commit repeated offences against children or young persons and those who corrupt children' (Home Office 1932: 18). The 1950s also saw a change to the definition with the removal of repeat property offenders, the first titleholders of the term. This was largely due to the increased usage of insurance and an increase in individual wealth, with property being more readily replaceable than ever before (Pratt 2000). The 1960s saw an emphasis on managing those offenders who were deemed to have personal inadequacies (Sutton 2000), with membership again extended in the 1970s to include those who engaged in domestic violence and sexual abuse against women. Additionally, for most of the twentieth century, those deemed to be mentally disordered were also classified and labelled as dangerous (Thomas 2005). What can be seen here then is a changing notion and construction of what and who the dangerous offender is, changing with time, place and popular belief. As explained by Rennie, the 'dangerous offender is a protean concept, changing its color and shape to suit the fears, interests, needs, and prejudices of a society. It is an *idea*, not a person' (1978: xvii, emphasis in original). Pratt, likewise, contends that 'dangerousness is neither a statistical artefact nor a political property' (1997: 6), but rather a creation of modernity, beginning when risk and risk management were formed. Understandings and constructions of dangerousness are therefore constantly changing, being influenced by society's fears and anxieties, and governmental responses to such concerns.

Current constructions of the dangerous offender

This, for some, would bring us to our more modern-day interpretations of who the dangerous offender is. Pratt therefore argues that it is 'that group of offenders whose propensity to repeatedly commit crimes of a non-capital but otherwise serious nature puts the wellbeing of the rest of the community at risk' (2000: 35). While, in the 1970s, it may only have been perceived to include those who committed violent and/or sexual offences, and, in particular, violent and/or sexual crimes against women and children, this has now changed. The traditional idea of the dangerous offender was the rapist, the child abuser, the bank robber, the serial killer and the alcohol-fuelled domestic violence perpetrator, but, as Pratt argues, this is a very simplistic view of what the term dangerous could, and importantly should, entail. Rather, he argues, there has been yet another shift in the concept. 'From being largely confined to those who would put at risk the well being of women and children the concept now comes to have the potential to remove an increasingly broad range of the socially undesirable' (2000: 47).

Taking the term dangerous offender literally, it could include all those offenders who pose a danger, whether that danger is to individuals, society as a whole or even the environment. Historically and socially, the definition of a dangerous offender has often excluded

> many persons responsible for death, serious and lasting injuries and extensive loss and destruction of property, either because the harmful conduct of such persons is not made punishable or because though punishable it is viewed and treated leniently so that even a substantial risk of repetition does not make them eligible to be classed as 'dangerous'.
>
> (Floud and Young 1981: 10)

There is no valid reason why this should be the case. Examples of those described above include the habitually drunken driver, keepers of unsafe factories, health and safety violators, and environmental polluters. There are also those people who should be classed as dangerous even though they have not actually committed previous offences, such as would-be terrorists or those who carry knives. Moreover, the environmental polluter and/or the corporate criminal actually have a greater potential to cause more widespread harm, and are potentially more dangerous than the worst serial killer; even though, as a society, we are more reticent to include such people in our definitions of what we perceive to be dangerous and more taciturn to sentence them as such. While there is a distinct social difference and level of anxiety between, for example, violent acts and white-collar criminal activity, there is no reason why one should be seen as more dangerous than the other. Indeed, Bennett argues that

> the reason for the differential level of concern and attention is that while employers and other powerful economic groups can avoid scrutiny, it is the harms caused by the marginalised and powerless that are targeted for control rather than those of the powerful.
>
> (2008a: 19)

Bottoms (1977) too talks about the distribution of power, arguing that punishment is often used against petty criminals rather than those in society who have considerable power, but also considers the intentionality versus negligence argument. He and others (Smith 1974; Hart 1961, both cited by Bottoms 1977) contend that there is a difference between when an act is done intentionally as opposed to when it has been carried out negligently, with the former being considered more morally wrong. While it is accepted that this difference in *mens rea* may be relevant to sentencing decisions, it does not bear any relevance as to whether or not that act or actor is dangerous. Therefore, a factory owner who negligently or even recklessly contravenes health and safety regulations is just as dangerous to his employees as one who acts intentionally, and just as likely to risk death or serious injury. While *mens rea* may therefore affect moral blameworthiness, it does not affect actual consequence. This arguably takes us into the realms of sentencing, which is discussed in Chapter 2, but again there would appear to be no logical explanation as to why the factory owner who risks hundreds of lives is any less dangerous than the individual who takes part in a fist fight with another individual. Indeed, the Floud Report acknowledged that 'corporate offenders must be judged "dangerous" on the same moral terms as individual offenders' (Floud and Young 1981: 15).

Those who could be viewed as dangerous therefore include traditional violent and sexual offenders, but could also arguably encompass reckless, tired, inexperienced and/or alcohol/drug impaired drivers; environmental polluters, financial and other corporate and white-collar criminals; those involved in organised crime; terrorists and would-be terrorists; people who neglect their children; arsonists; people who incite others to commit crime; those who incite racial and religious hatred; cult leaders and members, especially those with aggressive recruitment policies; those who flout health and safety regulations; human traffickers and pimps; and, from a fear factor: those who suffer from personality disorders and other mental health problems, refugees, immigrants and young people. Indeed, it would seem appropriate to once again include the repeat or habitual offender (the first titleholders of the term dangerous offender) or, as they are more commonly referred to now, the persistent or prolific offender. While it is accepted that, taken independently, low-level criminal acts are probably not dangerous, there comes a point whereby 'individually non-dangerous offences, if repeated sufficiently often, achieve dangerousness by their threat to the rule of law' (Scott 1977: 128). The above-suggested list, while lengthy, is by no means definitive and to an extent is infinite, especially when we bear in mind changing social notions and constructions. While it may therefore be sensible to keep such a list open, this does not provide the law with any certainty or transparency, especially when sentencing and risk-management decisions are based on the use of such concepts. Moreover, care must be taken concerning to whom or to what we attach the term, as dangerousness is a label that, while easy to append, is extremely difficult to eradicate (Scott 1977).

Furthermore, there is no reason why the concept of an offender needs to be limited to an individual person, with companies and even governments being able to commit dangerous acts.[1] Christie (2000), for example, argues that a government can be dangerous to its citizens by incarcerating them, which can cause risks to their physical and mental well-being. Likewise, a government could be dangerous by causing citizens to experience perilous situations such as sending them off to war and subjecting them to the risks of death, physical injury or psychological harm.

Moreover, Christie maintains that a state can be dangerous to its citizens at large if it is 'preoccupied with crime in general, rather than the danger of some individuals selected due to their peculiarly dangerous crimes' (190), with Bennett (2008a) arguing that recent governments in England and Wales have indeed acted in this way. This has been done by overemphasising the dangerous offender problem and thus creating an ever-increasing prison population, which has consequently exacerbated social inequality and legitimised attitudes that encourage more punitive sentences and conditions.

It may also be the case that we are returning to the idea of the dangerous classes, although reference is now made to an underclass rather than to a dangerous class. This revival arguably began in the late 1970s with the term underclass being used to denote 'society's losers' (Dinitz and Conrad 1978: 103).

> They are welfare clients and the unskilled, socially immobilized people who have received little from society and feel that they have as little to lose . . . More and more the underclass is seen by a hostile and fearful public as characterized by uncontrolled juvenile gang violence, unrestrained use of dope and booze, and rioting, looting and vandalism.

Dinitz and Conrad explain that 'by threatening personal and property rights, much of the American underclass is labelled as dangerous' (1978: 104). Indeed, the term underclass became a mainstay in the media concerning discussions on changing values and morals, social welfare, and crime and disorder in the late 1980s and early 1990s, with the concept used to focus on 'the social causes and consequences of mass unemployment and shifting behavioural norms among the lower classes' (Hayward and Yar 2006: 10). While the use of the term underclass has recently declined, particularly regarding media usage, this seems to have been replaced with the word chav, a rise and fall that is arguably connected, with chav representing 'a popular reconfiguration of the underclass idea' (ibid.). Defined by the *Oxford English Dictionary* (2009c), a chav is 'a young person of a type characterized by brash and loutish behaviour and the wearing of designer-style clothes (esp. sportswear); usually with connotations of a low social status'. Other definitions or origins include Council Housed And Violent; Council House Vermin and Cheltenham Average (i.e. not having the intelligence to be educated at Cheltenham College) (Hayward and Yar 2006). Different to previous underclasses, however, chavs are not necessarily impoverished and it is not a simple divide between the rich and the poor. Social status is rather linked with consumerism, with chavs denoted not by the fact that they do not have the means to be consumers, but by their choice of what they consume; for example, 'clothing (branded or designer "casual wear" and "sportswear"), jewelry ("chunky" gold rings and chains), [and] cosmetics ("excessive" make-up, sunbed tans)' (ibid.: 14), and as such are flawed. This preoccupation with chavs is therefore a reconfiguration of the underclass but this time through the lens of a consumerist society. Chavs have additionally been linked to aggressive teens and young adults who engage in antisocial behaviour and petty criminality, with items of clothing such as hoodies and baseball caps seen as signifiers of deviance. This has subsequently led to them being viewed by the media and the public as a dangerous underclass of offenders. As one commentator writes,

> These sub-human runts have Burberry caps and Adidas trousers tucked into red Reebok socks. But the worst thing about the chav is that they have genitalia thus being allowed to procreate and birth new runtish chavs. Soon like a cancer they will spread and take over the whole of England.
>
> (cited by Hayward and Yar 2006: 17)

It would therefore appear that there has been a cyclical return to a dangerous/underclass, whereby membership of a determined group or mere labelling of someone as coming from a lower or different social status is sufficient to further label them as dangerous.

Conclusion

The term dangerous offender is therefore very difficult to define and it is not helped by the fact that it is not a scientific or medical term and not necessarily linked with mental abnormality. As Morris (1999a) contends, it is society and not medical personnel that determines when the gravity and risk of harm is unacceptable. Floud and Young also argue that 'harmful behaviour and unacceptable risks are socially constructed and people are socially defined as dangerous accordingly' (1981: 20). People are hence dangerous if they are dangerous to us (that is, they threaten our security, our property or those we care about). It is thus usually a fear that something is going to be taken from us, although this is highly subjective and can change from person to person. So, for example, while one person may consider a group of loitering young people as dangerous, another may recognise them as bored and harmless teenagers. Brown and Pratt (2000) likewise argue that the way in which we classify offenders as dangerous tells us more about ourselves than about that particular offender, in that it shows what types of offending we fear the most and also what we place the most value on. Moreover, when we talk about sentencing dangerous offenders, it shows the lengths to which we are prepared to go to reduce the risk of us having to encounter them.

People are additionally considered to be dangerous if we misunderstand or feel threatened by them. The term is therefore usually defined by those who are in fear and see themselves as the potential victims, and consequently this can change over time. Examples include previous preoccupations with mods, rockers (Cohen 1972), 'yobs' and 'neds'[2] (Brown 2005). It may be the case then that danger is only in the eye of the beholder: 'risk is a matter of fact; [but] danger is a [mere] matter of opinion' (Floud and Young 1981: 4). While it is possible to evaluate whether a given thing is risky (fact), it is then up to the individual to decide whether it is an acceptable risk or not, and what is acceptable to one, as discussed above, will be dangerous to another. When assessing or trying to establish who the dangerous offender is, a definition of dangerousness may therefore be impossible, as any definition would also need a social context. Perhaps, instead, we should focus on risk. Otherwise, understandings and constructions will almost inevitably be based on fear, which can convert factual risk into danger, but can also be over-inflated by the media, pressure groups, the government[3] and the public at large.

Another factor to take into account is that, even if we could pinpoint who was dangerous and who was not, would this actually be helpful? Are all dangerous offenders harmful and, conversely, are all those offenders not considered to be dangerous safe? Indeed, such a suggestion is too simplistic:

> No one is totally primitive – concerned only with the immediate satisfaction of limited goals – or totally mature – maintaining judicious control of all impulses. The dangerous potential may be fixed and habitual, episodic, or sporadic. People cannot be divided into the dangerous and the non-dangerous – the bad guys and the good guys. The spectrum is wide, with the extremely dangerous at one end and the absolutely non-dangerous at the other.
>
> (Kozol *et al.* 1972: 379)

So perhaps rather than clarifying who the dangerous offender is, this chapter only further muddies the waters by creating an extensive and non-exhaustive list of possibilities. For the purpose of this book, however, it is necessary to be somewhat more precise. While it is true to say that the environmental polluter has the potential to cause monumental levels of harm, it is probably not true to simplistically equate danger and harm, and thus the degree of harm caused and how dangerous an individual is are different concepts. While the lists above may include those who have caused great levels of harm, reconviction rates in areas such as corporate crime are thought to be extremely low, so it would be entirely inappropriate for such criminals to come under public protection agendas. On the basis that this book is concerned with the sentencing, risk and governance of dangerous offenders, it must therefore follow that consideration is limited to those offenders who the government considers are likely to cause the most serious and far-ranging harm.

2

SENTENCING POLICY AND DANGEROUSNESS LEGISLATION

Introduction

While the concept and construction of the dangerous offender has changed over the last 100 years, as outlined in Chapter 1, the need to protect the public from him has always remained. By the end of the nineteenth century, it began to be recognised that one of the state's duties was to protect its citizens from risk, with the argument that crime was not just misfortune, fate or an act of God steadily growing (Pratt 1997). The task of protecting citizens from dangerous offenders is, however, far from easy, with ideas and strategies on how best this can be achieved also constantly changing. How governments in England and Wales have sought to realise this goal is thus the subject of this chapter.

Early dangerousness laws

Dangerousness laws have existed in England and Wales since the late nineteenth century, when they reflected a change in penal policy towards dangerous offenders due to transportation, impression to the navy, corporeal punishment and sterilisation under a eugenics movement being either no longer possible or socially unacceptable. One of the first people to propose longer periods of imprisonment was the penal reformer Matthew Davenport Hill who, in 1846, suggested that lengths of detention should be determined by the time needed for reformation (Radzinowicz and Hood 1980). Containment for purposes of public protection and crime prevention was therefore justified on grounds of utilitarianism. Such views were not universally shared, however, with Sir Joshua Jebb, the then Director of Convict Prisons arguing that indeterminate sentencing was a 'transfer of legal powers to irresponsible hands' (ibid.: 1321), favouring instead the option of determinate sentences of 8 to 10 years for the majority and a system of selective incapacitation to be used in exceptional circumstances for the small minority.

Concern regarding abuse of power, especially by the police, was collective, with penal policy in the early 1850s amounting to the use of cumulative[1] rather than indeterminate sentencing. In the late 1850s, however, the suggestion of a dual-track system was made, whereby punishing penal servitude would be followed by more palatable but indefinite containment. While some commentators were appalled by such repression, others felt that it would at least rid society of its habitual and professional criminals and would act not just to protect the public, but also as a means to reform and deter offenders (Radzinowicz and Hood 1980).

The first legislative attempt at dealing with habitual and professional criminals, therefore, concerned the use of minimum sentences, with the Penal Servitude Act 1864 increasing the minimum period for penal servitude to that of five years. This was followed by the Habitual Criminal's Act 1869, which not only made it mandatory for a judge to impose a period of seven years of penal servitude for those offenders who had three felony convictions, but also created a register of habitual, dangerous and professional offenders. The register included photographs of offenders and attempted to prevent fraudsters from changing their identities in a bid to escape from the authorities (Pratt 2000). This, Pratt (1997) argues, was the first real indication that the state was beginning to protect its citizens and, in particular, protect against certain individual expectations such as the right to life and the right to be protected from certain risks that could threaten or even endanger quality of life. Foucault (1979, cited by Pratt 1997) contends that this protection was another example of the crossover into modernity. While persistent and petty offenders had always existed, they began to be increasingly seen as a threat to this new-found protection, as they were the offenders who could affect a citizen's quality of life. The creation of sentencing and other control measures against such offenders were, as Pratt (1997) maintains, no more than insurance techniques. Notwithstanding the fact that crime decreased under this regime, the mandatory seven years was repealed in 1879 on the basis that it was indiscriminate and unfair (Radzinowicz and Hood 1980).

The notion of preventive sentencing was again suggested in 1895 by the Gladstone Committee, who argued that it was necessary to have longer imprisonment sentences for habitual offenders, which would have a greater deterrent effect and be justified on the incapacitation model (Dinitz and Conrad 1978). The committee recommended that:

> A new form of sentence should be placed at the disposal of the Judges by which these offenders might be segregated for long periods of detention during which they would not be treated with the severity of first class hard labour or penal servitude, but would be forced to work under less onerous conditions.
>
> (Home Office 1895, cited by Home Office 1963: 1)

At the same time, a Departmental Committee on Habitual Offenders in Scotland also recommended the introduction of extended confinement, for those that it labelled as 'persistent petty offenders' (Radzinowicz and Hood 1980: 1355). Correspondingly, in 1890, the International Union of Penal Law recognised that there were some offenders who needed more-than-usual levels of punishment. These offenders (that is, those seen to be degenerate or habitual) were to be sentenced according to the danger that they posed, with the aim being to prevent such future danger occurring (Rennie 1978). Sentencing and sentencing regimes were therefore based on the repression of future harm, rather than just on the specific offence committed (Radzinowicz 1939).

Although an extensive time gap, the Gladstone Committee's recommendations were finally seen in legislation in 1908 through the Prevention of Crime Act, which was the first time that the notion of public protection had been introduced into legislation. Radzinowicz and Hood (1980) argue that the delay was mainly due to problems with how the term 'habitual criminal' would be defined, recognition of which has been previously dealt with in Chapter 1. Part II of the Prevention of Crime Act 1908 focused on habitual criminals and allowed the court to sentence the offender to an additional period of 5 to 10 years of containment, which would follow on from a determinate period of penal servitude. A habitual criminal was defined as one who either had three previous convictions or who, on a previous occasion, had already been found by the court to be a habitual offender. What is interesting is that, once the period of penal servitude had been completed, the prisoner would be moved to another prison or a habitual offender's division for his period of preventive detention. This containment would be under much less rigorous conditions (s. 13(2) Prevention of Crime Act 1908), presumably because the aim was one of public protection and to a lesser extent of reform and rehabilitation, rather than that of punishment. While the period of preventive detention would be decided upon and set by the sentencing court, the Secretary of State had the power to release a prisoner on licence if it was thought

> that there is a reasonable probability that he will abstain from crime and lead a useful and industrious life or that he is no longer capable of engaging in crime, or that for any other reason it is desirable to release him from confinement in prison.
>
> (s. 14(2) Prevention of Crime Act 1908)

Similar legislation was also introduced in Australia, New Zealand and the USA (Pratt 1997), with such acts arguably signalling the emergence of state-governed risk management.

As noted above, once an offender had completed his period of penal servitude and was to commence the preventive part of his sentence, he would be moved to a different prison and regime. HMP Camp Hill on the Isle of Wight was thus built and opened in 1912 as an experimental regime to house such prisoners. Winston Churchill, the then Home Secretary, was critical of preventive detention, arguing that it was being used too frequently and against far too many individuals and, while he was sceptical that a regime of detention could be anything other than punishing, he did welcome the difference in living conditions. The prison rules thus allowed for three grades of preventive detainee:

> Ordinary, Special and Disciplinary (for those guilty of prison offenses). Those in the Ordinary and Special Grades would work at trades or agriculture and earn a small gratuity, part of which they could use to purchase items from a canteen. After eighteen months of good behavior a garden allotment could be cultivated and the products could be consumed or could be sold to the prison. The Ordinary Grade would be allowed to associate at meal times and, after a year, to play chess, draughts, and dominoes in the evenings. But it would take two years to earn entry to the Special Grade, where they could enjoy 'relaxations of a literary and social character . . . and selected weekly papers' and tobacco.
>
> (Radzinowicz and Hood 1980: 1374)

If the purpose of such containment was not to punish but to detain, then such conditions were appropriate, although this view was not universally shared. Indeed, many politicians were concerned that offenders were experiencing better conditions than the honest poor and that these privileges were counterproductive to the aims of deterrence. In one House of Commons debate, Mr Douglas Hall asked:

> Whether the convicts confined in the Camp Hill Prison, Isle of Wight, many of whom are habitual criminals of the worst type, are allowed to dine together and smoke and chat after meals; whether tablecloths and floral decorations are provided for them, and they are allowed, out of the moneys which they earn in prison, to buy confectionery, sardines, and other tinned meats; whether their cells are fitted with electric bells and hot shaving water is supplied to them when they ring for it; whether they are allowed to adorn their cells with photographs; and whether these luxuries and privileges have been granted with the object of deterring other criminals from seeking to qualify for admission to this prison or inducing those at present confined there to do everything they can to remain there?
>
> (HC Deb, 12 December 1912, vol. 4: cc. 758)

Despite such pessimism, it was generally accepted that the only real difference between Camp Hill and other prisons was that those at Camp Hill 'could talk within reason and could buy jam and sweets' (Radzinowicz and Hood 1980: 1375). By 1914, the regime began to be seen in a more positive light, being described as 'a new and better epoch in the slowly moving development of penal reform' (ibid.: 1377). Despite this, usage could only be described as cautious (see *R v Sullivan* (1914) Cr. App. R. 201) and began to diminish further, with only 31 offenders being sentenced to preventive detention per year between 1922 and 1928. This led to the Prison Commissioners concluding that it was having a negligible effect on protecting the public from habitual offenders and Enrico Ferri, head of the positivist school, arguing that the only other available solution was that of indeterminate sentencing (Radzinowicz and Hood 1980). Conversely, there were also concerns that, through a process of net widening, many offenders not originally thought suitable for the punishment were being sentenced to preventive detention. Indeed, in 1911, a memorandum drawn up by the Home Secretary stated how it should only be used for those who were persistent dangerous criminals, rather than for those who were more correctly labelled as social nuisances (Home Office 1963).

Such concerns led to the setting up of a Departmental Committee on Persistent Offenders that reported in 1932. The committee argued that not only had the 1908 Act faulted because of the dual-track system and the excessiveness of the two sentences when put together, but also because professional and dangerous criminals were often escaping the net of prison, which more frequently detained thieves and petty criminals (Home Office 1932). While the regime in Camp Hill was seen as better than that experienced in penal servitude, it was still criticised as being unable to perform the tasks of reform and rehabilitation. In place of preventive detention, the committee recommended 'medium' and 'prolonged' detention schemes, where medium detention was to be used for those offenders under 30 years of age and who were still in the early stages of their criminal careers. For these offenders, the recommended time period in detention was between two and four years. Prolonged detention was a partly indeterminate sentence where the offender was eligible for parole at the one-third stage of the sentence, and could last for up to 10 years (ibid.), although this was extended to 14 years in the subsequent Act. The proposals were contained in the Criminal Justice Bill 1938, which was abandoned at the outbreak of World War II and so did not come into fruition until the CJA 1948. The relevant provisions were labelled as corrective training and preventive detention. For preventive detention, the offender had to be 30 years or above, have been convicted on indictment of an offence punishable with imprisonment of 2 years or more, have been convicted on indictment on at least 3 previous occasions since the age of 17, and have been sentenced to borstal (corrective) training on at least 2 prior occasions. The court also had to be satisfied that it was 'expedient for the protection of the public that he should be detained in custody for a substantial time' (s. 21(2) CJA 1948).

The Home Secretary's Advisory Council on the Treatment of Offenders interpreted this to mean that the sentence should only be used in circumstances where the protection of the public was of more importance than other factors, such as the possibility of reform or the seriousness of the offence, and hence was only really suitable for those where there was little hope for reform (Home Office 1963). Under the 1948 Act, the judge had the power to fix a sentence of between 5 and 14 years with the offender being subjected to supervision within the community if he was released before the end of his term. Intererestingly, the new sentence of preventive detention was stated to be an alternative rather than an addition to any other sentence and, by doing this, the Act consequently brought to an end the dual-track system. The Act also abolished penal servitude, whipping, hard labour and prison divisions (s. 1 CJA 1948).

Despite this abolition, the Prison Rules 1949[2] maintained the need for a different preventive detention regime (although the first stage of the sentence was served in a local prison under ordinary conditions) and accordingly contained 13 special rules. This difference was warranted on the basis that, as the prisoner was being detained for longer than his current offence justified, the conditions under which he should serve his sentence should be less oppressive and superior to ordinary imprisonment. Under the rules, such differences included payment for work at a higher rate, facilities for spending money earned in prison on items such as newspapers and periodicals, the cultivation of garden allotments and the use or sale of the produce, the practice of arts or crafts, additional letters and visits, and association in common rooms for meals and recreation.

Despite the careful planning of the new sentence, it too was met with censure from the judiciary. Indeed, in 1962, the Lord Chief Justice issued a practice direction in the Court of Appeal stating that preventive detention should not ordinarily be used where an offender had proven that he could stay out of trouble and hold down employment for a period of 12 months or more; that long term imprisonment was often more appropriate and that it should 'only be given as a last resort and to those nearing 40 years of age or over' (*Practice Direction (Corrective Training: Preventive Detention)* [1962] 1 WLR 402 at 403). Such disapproval led to the setting up of yet another Departmental Committee that reported on their findings in 1963 (Home Office 1963). The report was critical of the use of preventive detention on the basis that it was mainly being used against property offenders, rather than those who had a 'seriously violent or aggressive type of personality' (ibid.: 8) and noted that, in practice, it was only used for those who were aged 40 and above and who could not prove that they would remain crime free for a period of 1 year or more. The report also stated that, while the conditions under the Prison Rules were being maintained, developments in local prisons meant that, in practice, there was little difference between conditions in preventive detention prisons[3] and ordinary imprisonment. Instead, it described the period of segregation as 'demoralising and embittering . . . [doing] little, or nothing, to prepare most of them for life in the outside world on their release' (ibid.: 19). Due to such concerns, and also those regarding release and aftercare, the report recommended abolishing preventive detention under the 1948 Act and replacing it instead with longer terms of imprisonment.

These recommendations were largely enacted in the CJA 1967, which introduced the extended sentence. This gave the court the power to increase a sentence by up to five years in instances where the maximum was less than five years, and was to be used against delinquents whose character and previous offending were such as to put it beyond all doubt that they were real menaces to society. Notwithstanding such discussion and planning, the extended sentence was used even less frequently than preventive detention, with 129 sentences being imposed in 1970 but only 14 being passed in 1976. Of additional concern was the fact that usage was predominantly for property rather than serious sexual and/or violent offences, with only 16 per cent of all extended sentences being issued for offences against the person between 1974 and 1976 (Dingwall 1998).

This led to a number of reviews and reports including the Scottish Council on Crime (1975), which recommended the creation of a public protection order; the Butler Committee, who suggested a reviewable sentence (Home Office and Department of Health and Social Security 1975); and the Home Secretary's Advisory Council, who, in 1978, recommended a restructuring of maximum penalties (Home Office 1978). While, on the whole, maximum penalties were reduced to more realistically reflect the practice of modern sentencing, a loophole was left whereby those offenders who caused serious harm could be sentenced to an exceptional sentence. The Floud Report, published three years later and after an extensive review of dangerousness legislation, supported the Advisory Council's recommendations, believing that there should be a two-tiered approach to sentencing through which maximum penalties should be reduced for 'normal' offenders but a protective sentence made available for those dangerous offenders who were likely to cause grave harm (Floud and Young 1981). Despite this level of agreement, all proposals were criticised for lacking precision in both definition and prediction of who the dangerous offender was. 'The history of English measures aimed specifically at persistent offenders seems to be widely acknowledged [therefore] to be a history of failure' (Ashworth 2005: 182). Ashworth claims this is due to two factors: the fact that legislation was unclear about which offenders should be included and which should be excluded, and uncertainty surrounding which group or groups of offenders needed such special measures.

More recent committees and Home Office reports include *Making Punishments Work* (Halliday *et al.* 2001), *Justice for All* (Home Office 2002a) and *Protecting the Public* (Home Office 2002b). The Halliday Report, among other things, recommended the introduction of a new 'special' sentence for the dangerous offender, who was defined as 'an offender assessed as having a high-risk of committing a further offence that would cause serious harm to the public' (Halliday *et al.* 2001: 32). The sentence was to be determinate in length, but whereas 'normal' offenders would be released at the halfway stage, dangerous offenders would only be released at the discretion of the Parole Board. Furthermore, when they were released, they would additionally be subject to longer than normal periods of supervision within the community (ibid.). The Home Office debatably went further, arguing that what was needed was an indeterminate sentence whereby dangerous offenders (defined as violent and sexual offenders) would 'remain in custody until their risks are considered manageable in the community' (Home Office 2002a: para. 5.4.1). Offenders assessed and categorised as dangerous would therefore serve a minimum determinate term but would only be released if the Parole Board considered it safe to do so, meaning the offender could be kept in prison for life. New indeterminate sentences for public protection were consequently announced in 2002 through the Criminal Justice Bill.

Current legislation and policy

Current legislation regarding dangerous offenders can therefore be found in sections 224–9 of the CJA 2003 (as amended by the Criminal Justice and Immigration Act

(CJIA) 2008) and applies to offences committed on or after 4 April 2005.[4] Sections 226 and 228 refer to young offenders and are discussed in Chapter 8. Following previous legislation such as the CJA 1991 and the Powers of Courts (Sentencing) Act 2000, the CJA 2003 works on the basis of commensurate sentencing, following a just deserts model of penal policy. Sentences are therefore only justified if the offence before the court is serious enough to justify the severity of the measure. However, also following on from previous Acts, the CJA 2003 provides provision for the sentencing of offenders to lengths of imprisonment and/or supervision within the community that, while deemed to be incommensurate to the offence, are justified on the basis of the 'serious harm' that the offender is likely to cause in the future, hence defensible under public protection and crime prevention rationales.

For sentencing purposes, section 224(3) defines 'serious harm' as 'death or serious personal injury, whether physical or psychological'. The legislation applies to all those who have committed either a 'specified violent or sexual offence', which are listed in Schedule 15 of the Act,[5] or a 'serious specified offence', which are specified violent or sexual offences punishable either by life imprisonment or by a custodial sentence of 10 years or more. If an offender is 18 or over, has been convicted of a serious specified offence and 'the court is of the opinion that there is a significant risk to members of the public of serious harm occasioned by the commission by him of further specified offences' (s. 225(1)(b) CJA 2003), he will receive either a discretionary life sentence or a sentence of imprisonment for public protection (IPP). For a life sentence, the offence must be punishable by life and the court must be of the opinion 'that the seriousness of the offence, or of the offence and one or more offences associated with it, is such as to justify the imposition of a sentence of imprisonment for life' (s. 225(2)(b) CJA 2003). When deciding on this, the court following *Kehoe* ([2009] 1 Cr. App. R. (S.) 9), must consider whether the culpability of the offender is particularly high or whether the offence in question is particularly serious. In essence, imprisonment for life should only be used when it is essential to do so (Sentencing Guidelines Council 2008). Unless the court feels that a whole life tariff is suitable, it must set the notional determinate term, from which the court will also identify the minimum term (that is, the minimum period that the offender has to serve in custody before he can be considered for release by the Parole Board). The minimum term is often set at half the notional determinate term.

If the offence is not punishable by life or does not warrant a life sentence, but is punishable by 10 years or more (and there are 95 offences that fall into this category), the court, as long as two statutory conditions are met, has the option of a sentence of IPP. The conditions are *either* that the offender has a previous conviction for an offence specified in Schedule 15A of the Act (such as murder, manslaughter, soliciting murder, wounding with intent to cause grievous bodily harm and rape) *or* that the notional determinate term, if the offender was not classified as dangerous, is at least four years. This equates to a minimum custodial term of at least two years on the basis that offenders only serve one half of their custodial sentence in prison. The notional determinate sentence should not exceed the maximum penalty for the offence and should be in proportion to the seriousness of the offence. This is justified on the basis that the indeterminate nature of the sentence covers the needs of public protection (Sentencing Guidelines Council 2008), as the offender will not be released until it is deemed safe to do so. These statutory conditions, inserted in 2008 by the CJIA, were enacted largely to appease critics (for example, the Howard League) and to limit the sentences' use, as, prior to the reform, minimum tariffs (that is, the minimum time an offender had to serve in custody before being eligible for parole review) were often set at very low levels. For example, in March 2006, the average term was 30 months, which reduced to 20 months in May 2007, with one sentence in 2007 having a minimum tariff of only 28 days (HM Chief Inspector of Prisons and HM Chief Inspector of Probation 2008).

In practice, the statutory condition regarding previous offending means that the court can impose an IPP even where the offence under consideration is not that serious, meaning that, despite the intention to avoid short minimum tariffs, these can still be imposed where the offender has a previous conviction of an offence contained within Schedule 15A (Thomas 2008a). It also affirms the fact that, despite risk-assessment tools being used to aid in the prediction of dangerousness (see Chapter 3), the CJA 2003 relies heavily on using an offence-based classification where previous offending is a predominant predictor in serious further offending. While this makes the system less complex and arguably easier to follow, it also erodes the court's discretion and could include in its dangerousness classification those people who have been involved in one-off dangerous incidents, thus risking confusion and similarity between dangerous incidents and dangerous people. It may also miss those whose previous offending has not brought them into the dangerousness fold (Nash 1992). Indeed, Nash argues that, while offence-based classification systems can work as a starting point, they are limited 'as much by what they omit as by what they include' (341).

Current legislation and the choice of the 'serious harm' test also creates a real risk that the court will equate seriousness with dangerousness, meaning that all serious offenders will be brought within its provisos regardless of whether they are dangerous or not. For example, an offender who commits homicide due to morally but not legally justifiable circumstances could, in theory, be brought within these provisions. While he has committed a serious offence, it is doubtful that he is a dangerous offender. Section 225 of the CJA 2003, however, abolishes the need for proportionality and firmly embeds the principle of longer-than-commensurate sentencing into penal policy. On release, an offender will be subject to a period of supervision of at least 10 years and furthermore subject to recall to prison if he breaches any licence conditions. The licence can be terminated by the Parole Board if it thinks it is appropriate to do so but, if it does not, can run indefinitely.

The CJA 2003, in addition to indeterminate prison sentences, also provides for a new extended sentence under section 227. The section applies to all offenders aged 18 or over who have been convicted of a specified offence if the court considers that there is a significant risk that serious harm will be occasioned to members of the public by the commission of further specified offences and the court is not required under section 225 to impose a life sentence. Again, two statutory conditions apply. Either that the offender has a previous conviction for an offence listed in Schedule 15A or the custodial term of the sentence is for at least four years. Prior to the CJIA 2008, the sentence had to be made; now it may be made, although this slight concession has been counterbalanced by the fact that the sentence is no longer restricted to just serious specified offences, encompassing also all specified offences.

Unlike the indeterminate sentences of life and IPP, the extended sentence is a determinate sentence made up of two parts. The first period, known as the 'appropriate custodial term', is the time spent in custody and is for whatever term that is commensurate with the seriousness of the offence, or where there is a previous dangerous offence and the appropriate custodial term would have been for less than 12 months, a term of at least 12 months. The custodial term must not exceed the statutory maximum and cannot be increased to serve public protection concerns, with the offender entitled to automatic release at the halfway stage (s. 247 CJA 2003, as amended by s. 25 CJIA 2008). The second period, known as the 'extension period', is a period of licence that follows the determinate custodial term. At the end of the custodial term, not on actual release, the offender's licence period will be extended by up to five years for violent offenders and by up to eight years for sex offenders. The length chosen will be that which the court considers to be necessary in order to protect the public, although the aggregate length of the entire sentence must not exceed the maximum term allowed. The length of the extension period is not intended to be proportionate to the seriousness of the offence but is rather designed to protect the public from further offending; thus the extension is often set to coincide with the availability and length of treatment and other rehabilitative programmes (Sentencing Guidelines Council 2008).

For this dangerousness legislation to apply, the offender has to satisfy a number of criteria that are set out within the Act. The first is that the offender must have been 'assessed as dangerous'. Section 229 helps to define this by providing a list of factors that the court needs to take into consideration when making its decision regarding whether or not there is a significant risk to members of the public of serious harm occasioned by the commission by the offender of further such offences. When the 2003 Act was first enacted, section 229(3) contained a presumption of dangerousness if the offender had previously been convicted of a specified offence, was over 18 at the time of the crime and the court felt that it was reasonable to conclude that the offender was dangerous. This presumption was repealed by the CJIA 2008. There is now a single test under section 229 which states that, where a person has been convicted of a specified offence, the court, in making its assessment regarding dangerousness, 'must take into account all such information as is available to it about the nature and circumstances of the offence' (s. 229(2)(a)); 'may take into account all such information as is available to it about the nature and circumstances of any other offences of which the offender has been convicted' (s. 229(2)(aa)); 'may take into account any information . . . about any pattern of behaviour' (s. 229(2)(b)); and 'may take into account any information about the offender which is before it' (s. 229(2)(c)). This latter proviso allows the court to take into account pre-sentence reports from the Probation Service, psychiatric reports and any other expert opinion that can inform its decision. The test therefore allows an assessment of dangerousness to be made both where the offender has previous convictions and where he is a first time offender.

When deciding on whether the offender presents a significant risk of causing serious harm through further offending, the court must apply a two-stage test, asking first whether there is a significant risk that the offender will commit further specified offences (whether serious or not) and, if so, whether there is a significant risk that a future victim would suffer serious harm. When assessing significant risk, the sentencing judge, following *R v Lang and Others* ([2006] 2 Cr. App. R. (S.) 3), should take into account the following:

- The risk identified must be significant. This is a higher threshold than mere possibility and could be taken to mean noteworthy.
- The nature and circumstances of the current offence including the offender's history of offending, together with previous sentences; whether the offending indicated a particular pattern; his attitude to offending, supervision and emotional state; and other social and economic issues such as relationship with alcohol and/or drugs, employment, and accommodation.
- A further offence may be serious, but that does not automatically mean that it will necessarily result in a significant risk of serious harm to the public. Indeed, persistent offending at a relatively low level that does not cause serious harm does not in itself suggest there is a significant risk of serious future harm.

Other important factors that have developed through case law include:

- The sentence of an IPP is directed at the future protection of the public. It does not represent punishment for past offending.
- The absence of previous convictions does not preclude a finding of dangerousness.
- The presence of previous convictions assumes dangerousness but this can be rebutted.
- Previous convictions of offences that are not specified offences can still be taken into account.
- It does not automatically follow, from the absence of actual harm caused by the offender to date, that the risk that he will cause serious harm in the future is negligible.
- The inadequacy, suggestibility or vulnerability of the offender may serve to mitigate the offender's culpability but may also serve to reinforce the conclusion that the offender is dangerous.
- The prosecution should describe the facts of previous specified offences.
- The court should not rely on a disputed fact when making the assessment of dangerousness.

- The judge should give reasons for his decision (*Johnson and Others* [2007] 1 Cr. App. R. (S.) 112).
- In assessing whether an offender is dangerous for the purposes of section 229, the court may take into account previous offences committed by the offender, even though he has not been convicted of those offences (*Considine* [2008] 1 Cr. App. R. (S.) 41).
- Any information that formed the case for the imposition of an antisocial behaviour order can be considered (*Hillman* [2006] 2 Cr. App. R. (S.) 85).

These factors have more recently been approved of by the Sentencing Council in their guidelines for sentencers and practitioners regarding dangerous offenders, which additionally provides a useful sentencing flow chart detailed in Figure 2.1.

Despite the minimal use of almost all other dangerousness legislation, there has arguably been a boom in the use of indeterminate sentencing under the CJA 2003. In June 2006, there were 1,100 prisoners serving sentences of IPP, equating to

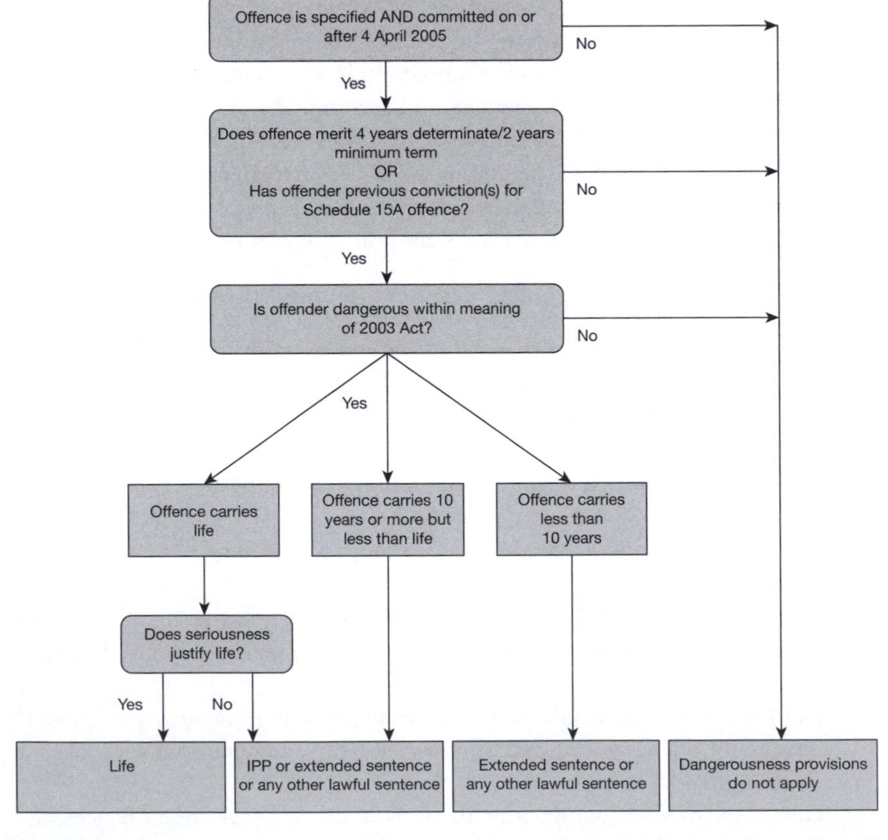

Figure 2.1 Dangerous offender provisions flow chart (Sentencing Guidelines Council 2008).

1 per cent of the total prison population. In June 2007, this had risen to 2,900, or 4 per cent (Hansard 16 Jan 2008, Column 1337 W). On 30 June 2008, there were 9,481 prisoners serving sentences of either life or IPP in prisons in England and Wales, with 2,859 of these offenders detained under an IPP sentence (Ministry of Justice 2009a). By 3 November 2008, the IPP population had increased to 4,863. This reached 5,600 in October 2009 (HL Deb, 28 October 2009, c1253) and stood at over 6,000 in July 2010 (Blunt 2010). Predictions suggest that, by 2012, there will be over 10,000 IPP prisoners (HL Deb, 28 October 2009, c1251) and a staggering 25,000 lifer population (The Howard League for Penal Reform 2007).

Despite this popularity, the sentence has been heavily criticised. Such criticisms have focused on how dangerousness is assessed (see Chapter 3), the lack of rehabilitation programmes that are needed to effect release, and how the sentence disproportionately contributes to an ever-increasing prison population. The Howard League for Penal Reform, for example, was heavily critical of the sentence in its report on IPPs in 2007. Describing the sentence as 'ill-conceived and . . . ultimately flawed' (2007: 3), they argued that it was misguided, unworkable in the long term and prevented offenders from proving their suitability for release. As a result, they recommended that the court should be provided with more discretion when imposing the sentence, changing the situation to one where the court could impose a sentence of IPP rather than it being mandatory. They also recommended that there should be a consistent and effective assessment process so that dangerousness could be accurately assessed, and that the minimum tariff should not be so low so that there is insufficient time for an offender to show a reduction in risk before parole is considered.

Justice has also picked up on the problems with assessing dangerousness, arguing that 'the dangerousness requirements are insufficiently stringent only to catch those offenders who need this kind of sentence' (Justice 2007: 9). This was further emphasised by the Prison Governors Association (2007, cited by The Howard League for Penal Reform 2007) who argued that there were too many occasions where IPPs were being imposed by judges who did not have access to either pre-sentence or psychiatric reports. Such criticisms were also echoed in September 2008 through a joint thematic review of the sentence by both HM Chief Inspector of Prisons (HMCIP) and HM Chief Inspector of Probation. The report criticised how the sentence was being used for offenders who were displaying mental health needs (particularly women who had committed arson); how risk-assessment tools were either not being properly administered or classifications of dangerousness were being too easily made; how many offenders over their minimum tariff were still being detained; and how 'prisoners and staff became increasingly frustrated with their Kafka-esque predicament, unable to access the interventions they needed in order to secure release' (HM Chief Inspector of Prisons and HM Chief Inspector of Probation 2008: 3).

Such criticisms led to a government review, looking in particular at the way in which the sentence was being excessively used. Proposals to reduce its use, and therefore to ensure that it was only being used for those offenders who were truly dangerous, were enacted through the CJIA 2008, as discussed above. As already highlighted, this abolished the presumption of dangerousness in section 229, gave the court more discretion in that the sentence was no longer mandatory and introduced the statutory conditions for both the IPP and extended sentence. It also extended the availability of the extended sentence for all specified offences. While such amendments have been described as 'a vast improvement on the 2003 scheme' (Thomas 2008a: 8), there are still concerns regarding the minimum custodial term for IPP sentences. Courts will have to pay particular attention to the length of the notional determinate sentence to ensure that a length of four years can actually be justified, which can become more complicated if mitigating factors and/or a guilty plea need to be taken into account. The court also has to decide how best public protection can be achieved; is it through commensurate sentencing, the use of IPPs or through an extended sentence? Furthermore, how the sentencing court should make these choices is also arguably unclear. Thomas (2008a) argues that the overriding principle should be that the court should choose the less onerous option that will provide public protection, but also acknowledges that it is a matter that requires Court of Appeal guidance.

Despite these amendments and the obvious limits that they have imposed, total abolition of the sentence was considered by the House of Lords in October 2009. For this reason, the House debated the insertion of a new clause into the Coroners and Justice Bill (Amendment 90): 'Sentences of imprisonment or detention for public protection under section 225 or 226 of the CJA 2003 (c. 44) (indeterminate sentences) shall not be imposed after the date on which this Act is passed' (HL Deb, 28 October 2009, c1247). The amendment would not only have brought to an end the imposition of future indeterminate sentences (where life imprisonment was not a statutory option) but would have secured the release of all offenders serving a sentence of IPP, if this had not already occurred, once the maximum term of imprisonment had been served. The amendment was put forward by Lord Goodhart, but also supported by Lord Ramsbotham (the former Chief Inspector of HM Prisons), Lord Carlile of Berriew (President of the Howard League for Penal Reform) and Lord Hylton, who supported it 'on grounds of certainty, rehabilitation and resettlement' (HL Debate, 28 October 2009, c1251). Despite such opposition to the sentence, the amendment was not included in the Bill, although Lord Hunt of Wirral, Shadow Business Minister, did acknowledge that, while he did not support the amendment, 'We [do] need a fundamental reform of sentencing. If there is to be a Conservative Government – which I strongly believe there will be – I hope that that Government will deliver fundamental reform by introducing honest sentences that spell out minimum and maximum terms' (HL Deb, 28 October 2009, c1251). Whether this is something which the new coalition government will do remains to be seen.

Discussion

The rise of modern-day dangerousness legislation in England and Wales can arguably be attributed to the rise of the new penology: the identification and management of high-risk categories and sub-populations (Simon 1998). Such legislation therefore aims to not only protect the public but also to prevent crime. As Garland notes,

> the new penal idea is that the public be protected and its sentiments be expressed. Punitive segregation – lengthy sentence terms in no frills prisons and a marked, monitored existence for those who are eventually released – is increasingly the penal strategy of choice.
>
> (2000: 350)

This is achieved by punishing the criminal rather than by punishing the actual crime, thus paving the way for sentencing which is longer than commensurate with the offence in question. The length of a custodial sentence is thus determined not upon 'the nature of the criminal offense or upon an assessment of the character of the offender, but upon risk profiles' (Feeley and Simon 1992: 458), that is, those classified as dangerous are selected and incapacitated for longer than those who are deemed to be less risky. Sentencing policy has thus seen a shift from a retributive penal philosophy where the emphasis was focused on what the offender had done to one where the prevention of crime is key. As explained by Feeley and Simon:

> The new penology is markedly less concerned with responsibility, fault, moral sensibility, diagnosis, or intervention and treatment of the individual offender. Rather it is concerned with techniques to identify, classify, and manage groupings of sorted dangerousness. The task is managerial, not transformative . . . It seeks to *regulate* levels of deviance, not intervene or respond to individual deviants or social malformations.
>
> (1992: 452, emphasis in original)

This change is justified on a non-retributive, utilitarian theory of social defence, where the greater good (detaining a few dangerous offenders) is achieved for the greater number (the public at large) by maximising the amount of aggregate pleasure and minimising the amount of aggregate pain (Bentham 1781, cited by Haist 2009). On the basis that we expect the state to protect us against the criminal actions of others, it is felt that if a person harms others then he gives society the right to interfere in his life, even if this amounts to indefinite containment. Walker (1996) argues that this interference is not retribution but rather the loss of that person's immunity to such interference. In the nineteenth century, definite periods of imprisonment followed by further periods of imprisonment had had no deterrent effect on habitual, persistent or professional offenders and so the new penology had to produce something that attempted to solve this problem. Indeed, Ashworth recounts how the Gloucestershire Magistrate Barwick Lloyd Baker believed in the cumulative principle whereby further offending would produce longer and more severe periods of imprisonment:

> In 1863 he proposed that for a first felony conviction the punishment should be one week or ten days' prison on bread and water; for the second

> conviction 12 months' imprisonment; for the third, seven years' penal servitude; and for a fourth, penal servitude for life or for some very long period which would allow surveillance on ticket-of-leave for the greater part of the criminal's life.
>
> (Ashworth 2005: 185)

The rationale was, therefore, if offenders were going to continue offending, especially if this was going to cause serious harm, then such offenders should be kept in prison so that the public would be protected and such offending would be avoided (Pratt 1996a). As Ashworth (2005) correctly states, this, however, assumes not only that preventive detention can work to deter and prevent future offending but also that it does not actually make the offender's life, and hence chances of reoffending, actually worse. Indeed, in an earlier article, Ashworth (1989) contends that 'public protection requires public policies aimed specifically at crime prevention and generally at reducing criminogenic circumstances' (342). While the government has focused on the former, its attention to the latter has arguably not been as determined, with this omission often cited as one of the reasons why current dangerousness legislation is criticised. Rehabilitative programmes do, however, exist and have had varying degrees of success, with such risk-reduction strategies assessed in more detail in Chapter 6.

Dangerousness legislation has also been influenced by populist punitiveness (Bottoms 1995), which adopts a zero tolerance policy in an effort to eliminate all offending behaviour. Although this is different to the new penology, which accepts that crime is the norm and thus concentrates on methods of managing it, it has nevertheless been argued that the two concepts still appear to coexist (Simon 1998). Recalling the quote by Garland (2000) above, the new penal idea is not just about public protection but is also about expressing the sentiments of the public. So, when new penal measures such as the sentence of IPP are brought into existence, often this is due to the need to satisfy a public who perceive, often wrongly, that society is plagued by dangerous offenders, even though these same politicians proudly state how crime 'on their watch' has decreased. The introduction of new penal measures is therefore largely due to 'the feeling that "something must be done" and "someone must be blamed" [which] increasingly finds political representation and fuels political action' (368). Garland (2000) also notes that, while policy used to be influenced and formulated by researchers and civil servants, this role has increasingly been taken over by political action committees and political advisors, who are seeking to please the voting public. This change has occurred since the 1960s, when the middle classes became less tolerant of criminals, no longer believing it was something that just affected the poorer classes, and consequently became less supportive of rehabilitative responses. Instead, the 'elite' wanted 'expressivity, punitiveness, victim-centredness and public protection' (Cesaroni and Doob 2003: 435). This is demonstrated through mandatory sentencing laws, victims' families spearheading new sentencing regimes or taking on the role of the victim's champion[6] and, as discussed above, preventative incapacitation.

The life of the dangerous offender and dangerousness legislation has additionally seen a shift from welfare to neo-liberal rationality.[7] Originally, the need for protection against such offenders was based on the belief that it was the state's duty to protect its citizens in some way to provide them with a form of insurance against petty thieves and habitual offenders. As discussed in Chapter 1, this was important because insurance in other forms either did not exist, or was too expensive for the everyday man to contemplate purchasing. Property thus took on importance, with the loss of it often resulting in it not being replaced. The state was thus the protector of its people. Neo-liberalism, however,

> constitutes a mentality of government, a conception of how authorities should use their powers in order to improve national wellbeing, the ends they should seek, the evils they should avoid, the means they should use and, crucially, the nature of the persons upon whom they must act.
>
> (Rose 1992: 145)

As Pratt explains, one of the major differences between the two eras was the fact that penal resources 'came to be distributed according to an economy of scarcity' (Pratt 1996a: 30). While welfarism wanted to widen the net and include as many people as possible into definitions of dangerousness, neo-liberalism wants the opposite (that is, for it to only include the critical few so that expense can be lessened). This, consequently, demands that the classification and prediction of dangerousness is accurate and thus demands effective risk-assessment techniques. Similarly, whereas welfarism offered a sense of protection to its citizens, neo-liberalism expects us to protect ourselves from risk through strategies such as security alarms, insurance, preventative architecture and private security firms. Under neo-liberal rule,

> The wellbeing of both political and social existence is to be ensured not by centralizing planning and bureaucracy, but through the 'enterprising' activities and choices of autonomous entities – businesses, organisations, persons – each striving to maximise its own advantages by inventing and promoting new projects by means of individual and local calculations of strategies and tactics, costs and benefits.
>
> (Rose 2007: 19)

Despite such a change, 'one right . . . that the state owes to its subjects still lives on: the "right to protection" from the dangerous' (Pratt 1996b: 255). Thus, from the 1970s onwards, a true bifurcatory system emerged whereby only the really dangerous offenders were picked out as needing special and thus expensive forms of containment and punishment. However, whereas the judiciary had once made this classification, this determination is now largely made in advance by the state (Pratt 1996b). Such justifications are largely why, in England and Wales, dangerousness legislation is mainly focused on sexual and violent offenders, as these are deemed by most to commit the most serious offences and cause the most debilitating harm. This targeting of groups of offenders, rather than individualised attention, is arguably another attribute of the new penology (Feeley and Simon 1992).

The rationale for dangerousness legislation

While it can be argued that dangerousness legislation is needed, the obvious and indeed most persuasive argument against the use of sentencing offenders to longer than commensurate terms of imprisonment is that you are punishing offenders for what they may do in the future rather than for what they have done in the past. Indeed, Lord Justice Denning stated that it 'would be contrary to all principle for a man to be punished, not for what he has already done but for what he may hereafter do' (*Everett v Ribbands* [1952] 2 QB 198, at 206). If an offender is placed into the dangerous offender category, then arguably a preventive sentence is being imposed because of who the offender is rather than based on what he has done. Walker argues that this was the approach taken by the Floud Report:

> When a person is proved to have done violence to someone else he can no longer claim the benefit of the presumption of future harmlessness. He cannot complain if the State (acting judicially) decides not to sentence him in the normal way but to impose precautions. This is not to say that the State is obliged to do so: only that it should have a discretionary power to do so.
>
> (1982: 282)

However, as acknowledged in the report, this arguably creates a notion of the offender being a second-class citizen who is judged as guilty before even an act has been performed, let alone an investigation, trial and finding of guilt (Floud and Young 1981). Additionally, as von Hirsch (1976) contends, this takes the fate of responsible individuals out of their own hands and abrogates their right to be viewed as harmless and innocent, although it is recognised that for the critical few this may still be appropriate.

Interestingly, fathers of jurisprudence such as Beccaria and Bentham held that punishment should fit the crime and not the criminal, believing that proportionality should be measured against what the offender had done rather than what he might do in the future. Thus, detainment for public protection purposes was considered by them to be unlawful. Based on ideas of liberalism, they believed that the law should place no more restrictions on an offender than was necessary to promote the welfare of society (Rennie 1978). More recently, this has been emphasised by Cavadino (1990):

> Once sentencers abandon this principle [of desert], they are no longer applying justice but a form of social engineering devoid of moral content. Such sentencing decisions would be highly subjective, based not on what the offender has done but on the Judge's guess as to what he might do in the future,
>
> (cited by Nash 1992: 345)

The obvious response to the public protection argument is that detention warranted on this basis should not be viewed as punishing the offender for something that he might do in the future but as a preventive measure for the public against what he may do in the future. This argument also has judicial authority, with Blackstone praising preventive detention as 'an honor . . . to our English Laws . . . since *preventive* justice is, upon every principle or reason, of humanity, and of social policy, preferable . . . to *punishing* justice' (Blackstone 1765–69, cited by Dershowitz 1973, emphasis in original). As Floud and Young (1981) contend, it is about the redistribution of risk between an already convicted offender and his potential future victims.

If public protection is truly the aim of indeterminate sentencing rather than more sinister punitive goals, then once the retributive element of the custodial sentence has been completed (that is, the minimum period in the case of an IPP) and the offender enters into the public protection phase of his sentence, should he then be moved to a less punitive regime? While it is accepted that modern imprisonment works on the basis that it is the lack of liberty that is the punishment and that the prison regime should not be such as to contribute to this, in reality the vast majority of prison regimes are punitive and detrimental. Following history and the rationale for different regimes in the early twentieth century, separate prisons or wings of prisons could be created that foster a more rehabilitative way of life, including a greater focus on education and the learning of life skills. This would support the argument made by Ashworth (1989) above. If offenders remain within the normal prison estate, which, for all those within it, is for punishment purposes, then the rationality of IPP not being about punishment does not stack up. While open prisons may offer this less punitive and rigid way of life, it is unlikely that many offenders being held under sentences of IPP will find themselves in such environments. As discussed in more detail in Chapter 4, the vast majority of offenders being held in prison after the completion of their minimum terms are detained in punitive closed prisons, emphasising the belief that they are being detained for punitive rather than for public protection purposes.

Efficacy

The most credible argument for having dangerousness legislation would obviously be that it worked (that is, it prevented future crime and hence kept the public protected). A number of research studies focused on this issue have, however, reported rather cautious and unimpressive findings. For example, *Taking Offenders out of Circulation* concluded that, regarding preventive detention, 'it seems safe to say that the effect on the recorded crime rate would be negligible' (Brody and Tarling 1980: 35). This has also been asserted by van Dine *et al.*, who found in the USA that the effectiveness of its incapacitation strategy 'would have prevented no more than 4.0 per cent of the violent crimes in Franklin County in 1973' (1977: 22). Such pessimism has also been supported by Bottoms (1977) in the UK and Megargee (1976) in the USA. These studies are obviously quite old and so perhaps their conclusions should be read with some caution, although more recent studies show similar negativity (see Appendix 6 of the Halliday Report (Halliday *et al.* 2001) and von Hirsch *et al.* 2000). For example, the Carter Review states that, while 'prison does reduce crime . . . there is no convincing evidence that further increases in the use of custody would significantly reduce crime' (Carter 2003: 15). So, while it is true to say that preventive detention prevents the individual from offending, there is no reliable evidence to suggest that its deterrent effect works to adequately protect the public from other offenders within society. Such findings are therefore why Ashworth (2004a) concludes that, 'even in official circles, there is no confidence that the increased use of prison sentences has had a substantial impact on crime rates, let alone on public protection from serious offences' (521). Why the government continually persists in its endeavours to create and update dangerousness legislation returns us to the previous discussion concerning the new penology, neo-liberalism and populist punitiveness.

Conclusion

Dangerousness legislation has thus existed, in one form or another, for many centuries, with current policy focused on containing serious sexual and violent offenders for longer than commensurate periods under rationales of deterrence and public protection. While such policies may be sound in theory, current legislation is arguably too wide and brings too many within its dangerousness net. Not only is this adding to an ever-increasing prison population, but of more concern is the fact that there is no evidence that indeterminate sentencing actually contributes to public protection. Despite this acknowledgement, it would appear that dangerousness legislation is here to stay, with the remainder of this book looking at how offenders are first assessed as dangerous and thus brought within the dangerousness net, but also how they are then subsequently treated while held and managed within this system.

3

FROM DANGEROUSNESS TO RISK AND RISK ASSESSMENT

Introduction

In order for current dangerousness legislation to apply, an offender must first be 'assessed as being dangerous' (s. 229 CJA 2003). This is the case even though it has been recognised that people are rarely dangerous per se, rather it being the situations that they find themselves in that are the cause of their dangerousness (Floud and Young 1981). Also, as Castel (1991) notes, dangerousness is a feeling that can only be reliably predicted after an event has taken place, and so, in order to predict dangerous behaviour, it is necessary to focus on something other than mere dangerousness. In terms of penal policy and practice, it is therefore more correct and practical to refer to the likelihood that the offender will reoffend and cause serious harm, and, indeed, this is the basis of the dangerousness test in the CJA 2003. The main question, therefore, is how likely it is that a given offender will commit further serious offences. In penal circles, this is assessed through a reliance on risk and the presence of risk factors, which are used to determine whether or not someone is likely to be dangerous. This, therefore, sees the focus changing from dangerousness to risk. This is because risk of reoffending is not the same as dangerousness, with the former relating to imminence of behaviour and the latter to severity (Craig *et al.* 2008). Risk of recidivism and the assessment of this is therefore the main subject of this chapter. In particular, it addresses what is meant by the concept of risk, how risk assessments are made and, importantly, whether such methods are reliable and effective.

Risk and its importance in penal practice

Until fairly recently, the term risk was used as a neutral word, customarily within the insurance industry, to categorise the likelihood of a certain event occurring and was used to refer to both loss and gain (Kemshall 2001). Of late, however, risk has become the 'world's largest industry' (Adams 1995: 31), with a growing emphasis on what has become known as the 'risk society' (Beck 1992). As Bennett (2008a) explains, risk now dominates our view of the world, which has led to an obsession with how such threats are controlled. This has been categorised as 'dangerization', which is defined as

> the tendency to perceive and analyse the world through categories of menace. It leads to continuous detection of threats and assessment of adverse probabilities, to the prevalence of defensive perceptions over optimistic ones and to the dominance of fear and anxiety over ambition and desire.
>
> (Lianos and Douglas 2000: 267)

Risk in late modernity is therefore associated with hazards and dangers (Douglas 1992) to such an extent that risk, as a criminal justice concept, is often expressed in terms of an offender's perceived danger to the public (see Beck 1992; Douglas 1992; Adams 1995; Kemshall 2003). It is thus commonly understood as an 'uncertain prediction about future behaviour, with a chance that the future outcome of the behaviour will be harmful or negative' (Kemshall 1996: v). Risk can also be viewed as wider than dangerousness, as dangerousness only suggests 'dispositional personality traits', while risk also includes 'a wider consideration of contextual and circumstantial factors' (Kemshall 2002: 12). This again emphasises the belief that it is not, in the majority of cases, the offenders themselves who are dangerous, but the risky situations that they find themselves in. The acceptance of such knowledge has thus seen a rise in the interest in risk in criminal justice, with many decisions now based on risk and its assessment.

This interest also feeds into the rise of populist punitiveness and the emphasis on public protection as described in the previous chapter. With public protection being the key objective of legislation and penal policy, especially for serious sexual and violent offenders, there has thus been a consequent increase in restrictions, surveillance and monitoring. On the basis that it is necessary to know who these dangerous offenders are in order to channel them through the correct legislative and sentencing routes, risk assessment and its effectiveness has taken on a new importance. Kemshall (2009) argues that this has resulted in risk and its assessment within offender management taking place within a 'climate of public blame, community anxiety and challenge to the expertise of professionals if "things go wrong"' (331). Carson (1996) similarly talks about 'defensibility' on the basis that risk prediction will never be 100 per cent accurate, and so the main criteria for practitioners must be whether their decisions regarding risk are reasonable. Kemshall hence argues that risk in offender management is now better categorised as '"taboo" risk, unwanted, carrying the perception of high costs with limited benefits, and with risks often distributed inequitably towards the most vulnerable and least able to manage or avoid such risks' (2009: 331).

The assessment of risk

The assessment of risk can be classified as the act of estimating the probability of an outcome occurring for any given individual (Towl and Crighton 1997) and 'involves an assessment about the frequency of the behaviour/element, its likely impact and who it will affect' (Kemshall 1996: v). Risk assessments are therefore generally broken down into two components: the estimation of the likelihood of a specified event occurring and a judgement about the acceptability of the level of risk estimated (Towl and Crighton 1997), although to be useful, risk assessments should additionally specify:

- The *behaviour* of concern;
- The *potential damage or harm* likely from that behaviour; and
- The *probability* that it will occur and under what circumstances.

(Scott 1977, cited by Kemshall 2001: 11, emphasis in original)

In penal terms, therefore, it is usually the assessment of how likely it is that an offender will reoffend, the nature of this reoffending and, from this, a calculation of how great a danger the offender is to the public. As discussed in Chapter 2, such practice is articulated in dangerousness legislation, with the test of dangerousness being whether the court believes that there is a significant risk that the offender will go on to commit further offences that will result in serious harm to members of the public. Thus, for risk-assessment purposes, the court needs to know not only how likely it is that the offender will reoffend, but also if he does go on to do so, what the nature or severity of this reoffending will be.

To aid with such distinctions, offenders are classified into groups and labelled as being low, medium or high (and sometimes very high) in risk. In respect of sex offenders (although they can easily be applied to violent offenders), O'Hare *et al.* explain these categories in the following way:

- Low risk: someone whose behaviour gives no current cause for concern with regard to their capacity to seriously harm other people or carry out a contact sexual offence.
- Medium risk: someone whose behaviour gives clear cause for concern with regard to his or her capacity to carry out a contact sexual offence.
- High risk: someone whose sexual offending has been assessed as currently likely to lead them to seriously harm people.

(2008)

Castel (1991) argues that this grouping of individuals is reminiscent of the new penology whereby strategies are employed that 'do away with the subject (a concrete individual) and replace him with a factor or combination of factors (otherwise known as risk factors)' (281).

In addition to classifying offenders into groups, risk assessment is also used to identify the high-risk cases that require the most intensive supervision (Andrews *et al.* 1990). Risk assessment is therefore additionally useful for resource allocation reasons; if an offender is assessed as being dangerous, then it is likely he will need a number of expensive interventions in order to manage this risk. Risk can therefore work as 'both a rationing and a targeting mechanism within an economic discourse of probation practice' (Kemshall 2003: 99). It is also used in a clinical sense to aid the accuracy of clinical decisions regarding the type, quality or quantity of the treatment needed and to ensure that the right offender is matched with the right programme or level of supervision. Kemshall (2002) additionally remarks how risk assessment should be viewed as a continuing process, involving not just the initial assessment but also involving re-evaluations, with risk being capable of increasing and decreasing over time. She also notes how a risk assessment is only ever a prediction based on estimates and probabilities, and thus can never provide a 'certain result' (12).

Methods of risk assessment

The two main methods for predicting and assessing human behaviour are based on clinical and actuarial techniques. In the area of criminal behaviour, a clinical assessment involves an expert, for example a probation officer or psychiatrist, interviewing an offender for the purposes of determining how likely it is that that person will reoffend, with the end result based on the person's wisdom, experience and intuition (Gendreau *et al.* 1996a). Pollock *et al.* (1989) describe it as 'a theoretically based decision-making process which proceeds by posing and testing clinical hypothesis derived, at least implicitly, from a theoretical model of human personality and behaviour' (ibid.: 97). To aid with accuracy, a number of checklists have been developed for practitioners that, for sex offenders, could include factors such as predisposing preconditions, the cycle of assault, the role of cognitive distortions and denial (Kemshall 2002). Due to the nature of the method, it is highly subjective, has poor inter-rater reliability (Menzies *et al.* 1994) and thus is often criticised for inaccuracy and unreliability (Quinsey *et al.* 1995). Monahan (1981), for example, claims that clinical assessments have a poor record of accuracy when used to predict recidivism, risk of violence or dangerous behaviour. Moreover, the method is thought to be more unreliable than any other method of assessment and more likely to result in a prediction of dangerousness (probably because of the possible consequences to the assessor if the person does go on to commit further serious offences and was assessed as being low in risk). It is also thought to be unsuitable for criminal justice agencies, where assessors often work in time- and resource-pressured environments (Mandeville-Norden and Beech 2006). Despite such comments, clinical assessments can be useful in assessing and understanding why an individual offender behaves in such a way and can help the assessor to decide how the offender's behaviour should be addressed (Kemshall 2001). Moreover, Craig *et al.* (2008) argue that psychological assessments can be imperative as a precursor to actuarial methods, in that they can aid with the decision of which risk-assessment tool should be used.

Actuarial assessment, on the other hand, has its roots in the insurance industry and is based on 'empirically established correlations between a standardized objective risk measure and recidivism' (Gendreau *et al.* 1996a: 65) and is thus a 'statistical calculation of probability' (Kemshall 2002: 15). Factors that are known to statistically relate to risk are selected and the offender is measured against these. Such factors, known as the offenders' risk factors, are often described as the personal attributes and circumstances that can be found out about an offender and can be used to predict the offender's future criminal behaviour (Andrews *et al.* 1990). These commonly derive from static demographic or historical factors and, therefore, rarely change over time (Kemshall 2002), with examples including age, gender, number of youth custody sentences, total number of court appearances, time in years since first conviction and type of offence (Copas and Marshall 1998). Known facts about categories of offenders will thus be collected, with an individual offender being measured and his risk of reoffending calculated against such information. The tool will therefore produce an estimate of what rate of reconviction might be expected from a group of offenders who match an individual on a set of factors used in the model, with the probability score representing the average reconviction rate from a group of offenders who match the individual offender on the factors used in the model (ibid.). For example, if a risk score is 56 per cent, it means that an average of 56 out of every 100 offenders with the same characteristics would probably be reconvicted for a further offence within a two-year period.

While early assessment tools used static factors, over the past few years it has been accepted that it is far more productive and accurate to additionally include dynamic factors. There are two types of dynamic risk factors, namely stable and acute. Stable dynamic factors are those that can change over time, or those that can be changed through treatment programmes or other forms of intervention, but change tends to occur relatively slowly (that is, over periods of months or years). Examples include levels of responsibility, cognitive distortions and sexual arousal (Craig *et al.* 2008). Acute dynamic factors, on the other hand, are those that change much more quickly, over periods of minutes, days or weeks, and include issues such as substance misuse, depression, isolation, victim acquisition behaviours and negative emotional states (Hanson *et al.* 2003). Acute risk factors are said to often appear at the time of the offence and, as such, can be seen as warning signs that reoffending behaviour is imminent. While intervention planning is often focused on stable dynamic risk factors, information regarding the offender's acute factors is useful in community supervision settings, where sharp increases in risk need to be readily and, more importantly, accurately identified (ibid.).

Andrews and Bonta identify the most important stable dynamic risk predictors as criminogenic needs. These are defined as

> a subset of an offender's risk level. They are dynamic attributes of the offender that, when changed, are associated with changes in the probability of recidivism. Non-criminogenic needs are also dynamic and changeable, but these changes are not necessarily associated with changes in recidivism.
>
> (1998: 243)

In essence, they are why offenders offend and can include such factors as unemployment, too much leisure time, poverty, and destructive relationships. Once such factors are identified and assessed, interventions that work to change attitudes and behaviour can be employed, with the overall goal being the lowering of risk. Due to the link with treatment and intervention planning, it has been accepted that the term dynamic risk factor can be used interchangeably with criminogenic needs and treatment needs (Ogloff and Davis 2004). For the purposes of simplicity, the remainder of this chapter will refer to dynamic risk factors.

A number of studies have attempted to discover the predictive accuracy of dynamic risk factors, with Gendreau *et al.* (1996b) contending that they are as effective as static factors in predicting recidivism. Kemshall (2002) disagrees, although notes that, while dynamic factors are not thought to be as good as predictors as static factors, they do nevertheless still have an important role to play in risk assessment. For example, May (1999) contends that factors such as drug misuse, unemployment and accommodation all have clear links with recidivism and reconviction and, while dynamic risk factors on their own may only aid in risk assessment, their greater utility is in intervention planning. Therefore, it is now widely acknowledged that the best and most effective risk-assessment tools will combine both static and dynamic risk factors because of 'an important "value added" component by identifying behavioural traits, environmental stressors, personal characteristics and social variables which can trigger offending or exacerbate risk' (Kemshall 2002: 21). This is further emphasised by Beech *et al.* (2002), who suggest that it is through the use of tools that take into account both static and dynamic factors that the best predictive accuracy is obtained. Therefore,

> the prediction of recidivism is best accomplished by employing a measure that assesses static *and* dynamic risk factors. The measure should be composed of at least as many, if not more, dynamic risk factors to ensure the assessment is as sensitive as possible to initial risk level and future changes in risk level.
> (Gendreau *et al.* 1996a: 66, emphasis in original)

On the basis that this combination of static and dynamic risk factors can provide not only a risk score, but can also aid in risk management and risk-reduction planning, such assessment tools are now known as multi-variant analysis.

In the actuarial method, the assessor's subjective opinion and judgement is only used when there are compelling reasons to divert from the results of the assessment. The tool cannot, however, predict possible seriousness, nature, or extent of the offence, nor can it predict actual or potential reoffending. Despite this, after looking at several North American studies that used both clinical and actuarial approaches, Gendreau *et al.* (1996a: 65) concluded:

> with the exception of situations where reliable predictive data are lacking, there is simply no justification whatsoever for the continued use of the clinical model of assessment considering what is at stake in our line of work.

> Nonetheless, the clinical method is well ingrained in human service fields. It is still adhered to even among the most highly trained of scientists.

In addition to the two main methods of assessing risk, developments in risk-assessment tools have led to what Bonta (1996) describes as first-, second- and third-generation assessment. First-generation assessment involves the collection of information about the offender and his situation, and the use of this information to assess the offender's risk of reoffending. In essence, it is the use of the clinical model as discussed above. Second-generation assessment tools are more objective and empirically based (that is, actuarial, but still only contain static factors in their assessment). Due to the limitations of both of these forms of assessments, as discussed above, Bonta (1996) argues that the rehabilitation of offenders is largely based on the assumption that people can change and that any effective assessment tool, therefore, has to be able to measure any such change. The ability to measure change in an offender is the fundamental difference between second- and third-generation assessment tools. Third-generation assessment tools are therefore 'risk-needs assessments' (22). These go further than just measuring risk using static indicators, in that they also measure and recognise the criminogenic needs of the offender. As previously mentioned, dynamic factors are therefore included in the assessment process so that decisions can be made about the offender's level of freedom and suitability for offending behaviour programmes. Dynamic risk factors, therefore, serve as targets, in that they show what must be changed about either the offender or his situation in order to minimise the risk of recidivism. Bonta (1996) argues that third-generation tools are 'inextricably linked to rehabilitation and control efforts' (27–8), as they are able to identify who warrants the investment of scarce probation resources (Robinson 1999), which, as discussed in Chapter 2, is imperative to the new penology.

Further work has recently resulted in the development of fourth-generation assessment tools. Campbell *et al.* describe these as 'Those specifically designed to be integrated into (a) the process of risk management, (b) the selection of intervention modes and targets for treatment, and (c) the assessment of rehabilitation progress' (2009: 569). Assessment scales that adhere to this generation of development are designed to be used on multiple occasions, so that changes in dynamic risk factors can be recorded and risk-management plans can be accordingly altered, either because risk has decreased or increased. Other important additions and added developments include looking at the responsivity of the particular offender. This works on the basis that each offender is different regarding personality, motivation and cognitive/emotional abilities. All of these can affect the offender's responsiveness to various risk-reduction programmes and it is thus essential, for the purposes of effective supervision and intervention, to match the offender's responsivity to the correct programme. This links in with Andrews and Bonta's risk–need–responsivity principles (1998, 2006). Mandeville-Norden and Beech (2006), moreover, state that, in addition to historical and dynamic factors, it is also important to consider 'contextual antecedents to crime' (258). These relate to factors that either motivate the offender or contribute in some other way to the possibility of the offender reoffending, such as feeling emotionally isolated.

Marshall and Barbaree (1990) additionally argue that risk scales should also include developmental factors, to further aid predictive validity. In relation to sex offenders, they argue that factors such as poor parenting, inconsistent and harsh discipline, and physical and sexual abuse can all result in increased vulnerability to recidivism. Indeed, by looking at the relationship between developmental factors and risk, Craissati and Beech (2005) found that the existence of two of more childhood adaptive difficulties (plus never having been in a long-term relationship) correctly identified 87 per cent of offenders who had poorly attended treatment programmes. Moreover, childhood difficulties plus contact with mental health services as an adult correctly identified 83 per cent of treatment dropouts. Marshall and Barbaree (1990) therefore argue that, in order to obtain the most accurate risk scores, developmental factors should be routinely included in all risk-assessment scales. This has become known as the 'risk-aetiological model' (Craig *et al.* 2008: 144), although, to date, developmental/aetiological factors do not appear to be widely included in the majority of risk scales, probably because it has yet to be empirically tested on a large enough scale. Whether this will change in the near future is unclear, but perhaps here we can see the beginnings of a fifth generation of risk-assessment tools.

Problems with risk assessment

While the necessity to assess risk is rarely disputed, one of the biggest problems regarding the use of risk-assessment tools, especially when it is the determining factor in decisions regarding sentencing and prison release, concerns accuracy. While the actuarial method is thought, in general, to have greater predictor reliability over the clinical method, it works by comparing similarities between the profile of an individual and aggregated knowledge of past events of a cohort of convicted offenders. This, therefore, assumes that information from one offender population can be easily generalised and transferred to an individual placed under assessment – an issue commonly known as statistical fallacy (Dingwall 1989). This, however, is rarely the case, and is problematic when an individual has different characteristics to the cohort data. This is especially so when transferring data based on white male offenders to either ethnic minorities or female offenders (Grubin and Wingate 1996). Furthermore, Quinsey *et al.* (1995) found that offenders who sexually offended against children were less likely to reoffend than rapists, and so data collected on one group did not have the same predictive validity for the other group. This has led Craig *et al.* (2008) to argue that actuarial scales should be restricted to those individuals who share all characteristics with the original cohort, on the basis that to do otherwise would affect the predictive accuracy of the results. Whether this is a practical and realistic suggestion, however, is unlikely. Classification profiles are also liable to change over time, so scales designed on a particular offender group will, at some point, become outdated and redundant. Another problem relates to the original cohort size, with better predictor reliability occurring when the cohort is larger rather than where it is small (ibid.).

An additional problem is the occurrence of low base rates. The base rate is the 'known frequency of a behaviour occurring within the population as a whole' (Kemshall 2002: 16) and is thus what any given offender is measured against to determine his risk. When the base rate in the general population for a particular offence is low, such as sexual offending (for example, Hanson and Bussière (1998) reported an overall recidivism rate of 13 per cent, while Hood *et al.* (2002) claimed that it was only 8.5 per cent even after a 6-year follow-up period), predicting behaviour based on this low base rate can cause obvious problems and lead to errors, especially when we know that child sexual abuse occurs at a much higher unrecorded rate. Artificially raising base rates to try to compensate for this can also lead to problems, and will often lead to false negative predictions. This leads Pollock *et al.* (1989) to argue that, in such instances, the most accurate thing to do would be to declare that everyone was not dangerous, as this is likely to be more accurate than claiming that some are dangerous and some are not. However, they also acknowledge that, while this may be theoretically sound, it does not offer any practical assistance for legal or clinical purposes, especially considering that, while recidivism rates may not be particularly high, in many instances when reoffending does occur it has the potential to cause significant levels of harm (Hood *et al.* 2002). Moreover, some academics believe that however high or low the particular base rate is, using it as the predictive basis of risk-assessment tools is still problematic. Koehler, for example, describes the use of base rates as 'inherently ambiguous, unreliable and unstable' (1996, as cited in Craig *et al.* 2008: 38). Craig *et al.* (2008) therefore warn that risk scores and consequential classifications should be used with caution and with a common-sense approach.

Another significant difficulty is the high incident of both false positives and false negatives. False positives occur when a person is assessed as being 'risky' but, in actual fact, is not; and, conversely, a false negative is where the assessment of risk is classified as low, but reoffending occurs at a serious level. One study that looked at this was carried out by Hood *et al.* (2002), which followed 162 released sex offenders for 4 years and 94 for 6 years. Working out reconviction rates, these were then compared to Parole Board risk classifications at the time of release or at the last parole review. The research found that, while there were many true positives (that is, where offenders were classified as 'risky' and this turned out to be true), there were also many false positives. Over a 4-year follow-up period, for sexual and violent offences the false positive rate was 87 per cent. At the 6-year follow-up stage, for the same category of offences, this had only fallen to 72 per cent; so, in nearly three quarters of the cases, the Parole Board had overestimated the seriousness of the offender's risk. Similarly, the study found a high true negative rate (that is, where the classification was one of low risk and this turned out to be true), but a low false negative rate. In the six-year follow-up study there was only one case where the offender was classified as being low in risk and then went on to reoffend. All of this would suggest that the Parole Board too easily attach the label of high-risk to convicted sex offenders, although the authors did acknowledge, as discussed above, that risk prediction for categories of offences where the base rate is particularly low is especially hard. They did, nevertheless, think that better prediction could be achieved through the use of actuarial risk-assessment tools that combined both static and dynamic risk factors rather than exclusive reliance on prisoner files.

Grubin and Wingate (1996) argue further that actuarial risk scores are limiting because, while they can predict risks, they do not understand or explain the involved behaviour. This is imperative when risk-management and risk-reduction decisions need to be made, as, if practitioners do not understand why an offender is behaving as he is, they will not know which strategies and interventions are needed in order to manage and reduce that risk. Furthermore, they contend that the most crucial difficulty is the fact that, as mentioned above, prediction is based on information of groups of offenders and, therefore, can tell very little about any given individual. Even though, in the 1970s, Dworkin (1977) cautioned against this,[1] it is yet another reminder that current penal practice is based around the classification of groups into categories of risk rather than more individualised, and consequently more resource intensive, approaches. Such notes of caution have led to the argument that actuarial tools should primarily be used for risk-management plans and resource allocation, rather than for predicting actual recidivism.

Despite such criticism, Craig *et al.* (2008) accept that actuarial risk-assessment tools are presently the most cost-effective way of dividing offenders into groups based on long-term risk and thus are currently used to:

- Establish those risk predictors which have a proven track record;
- Establish the relevant base rates for clinical assessment;
- Increase the accuracy of risk assessments; and
- Increase levels of consistency and reliability.

(Kemshall 2002: 17)

Current risk-assessment tools

As the assessment of risk is such an important issue for those in offender management, the choice of which risk-assessment tool to use is crucial. Even though it is widely assumed by the majority of the public that all sexual and violent offenders are dangerous, this is not actually true. Both categories of offender are heterogeneous in nature (Kemshall 2001) and thus display different levels of risk, be it low, medium, high or very high. Such diversity therefore means that it is imperative that risk-assessment tools are specific enough to the given offender group, in order for the best and most accurate conclusions concerning risk to be reached. Despite this acknowledgement and note of caution, Grubin still argues that offenders can nevertheless be classified according to their 'choice of victim, criminal background, sexual arousal patterns, social functioning, and risk of reoffending' (1998: 4). While there is not room here to fully describe how risk-assessment tools are designed, many will start with known risk factors for the given set of offenders that the tool is being specifically designed for. For the purposes of risk-assessment tools designed exclusively for sexual and violent offenders, Powis (2002) carried out a meta-analysis of known research into the factors associated with both violent and sexual offending. From her findings, she set out risk factors for both categories. For violent offending, these are listed as: a history of previous violent offending and aggression; male; youth; coming from a lower social class and living in poverty; unemployed; low IQ, particularly if associated with psychopathy; parental criminality and family violence; drug and alcohol misuse; mental disorders; availability of weapons; proximity to victims; levels of environmental stress; a history of impulsive behaviour; a lack of remorse and insight into crime; a lack of victim empathy and sado-masochistic tendencies. More specific risk factors are also identified for different categories of violent offenders, including those for domestic violence offenders and stalkers (see Powis 2002). For sex offenders, risk factors are identified as: a previous history of sexual offending; male; unmarried; unemployed (although this has been debated by Grubin and Wingate 1996); low educational achievements; substance misuse; choice of victim and type of crime; low victim empathy; personality disorders; sexual deviancy; treatment completion and sadistic fantasies. More specific risk factors are also given for rapists, child sexual offenders and female sexual offenders (see Powis 2002). The above static and dynamic risk factors are therefore important when designing risk-assessment tools for sexual and/or violent offenders.

There are currently a plethora of assessment tools on the market for the assessment of risk in both sexual and violent offenders. Space, unfortunately, precludes a consideration of all of these tools, thus the remainder of this chapter will concentrate on one example of a static-risk tool and one example of a dynamic-risk tool for both serious sexual and violent offenders.

Risk-assessment tools for serious sexual offenders

Risk Matrix 2000

Risk Matrix 2000 (RM2000) (Thornton *et al.* 2003) is currently the most commonly used static risk-assessment tool for sex offenders in England and Wales and is used by police, prison and probation (Mann 2009). Developed for use in the UK, it arose out of modifications made to the already existing tool, Structured Anchored Clinical Judgement (Hanson and Thornton 2000) and is evidence-based. It is suitable for use with male adults who have had at least one prior conviction for a sexual offence committed after the age of 16 and can predict the likelihood of sexual reoffending for up to 15 years (National Offender Management Service (NOMS) 2007a). It is not suitable for female or adolescent sex offenders, and should be used with caution with other marginal groups such as mentally disordered and low-functioning sex offenders (Thornton 2007). For offender management purposes, it is used for:

- All pre-sentence and parole reports on sex offenders.
- As part of the assessment of offenders for accredited sex offender programmes.
- As the first part of the Structured Assessment of Risk and Need.

(NOMS 2007a: 2; also, see the following)

The tool consists of three scales: RM2000/S, which predicts sexual reoffending; RM2000/V, which predicts non-sexual violence, although the offender still needs to have had a prior sexual conviction; and RM2000/C, which combines the two and predicts sexual or other violent reoffending (NOMS 2007a). As RM2000 is being used as an example of a static tool for sex offenders, only RM2000/S will be considered further. RM2000/S is made up of two parts. Part one contains three factors, with the first being the 'age at commencement of risk', which is taken either from prison release or at the start of a community order. Age is categorised into the ranges of 18–24 (2 points), 25–34 (1 point) and older (0 points). The second factor measures 'sexual appearances' in court, which are differentiated into four levels of 1 previous appearance (0 points), 2 appearances (1 point), 3–4 appearances (2 points), and 5 or more (3 points). Finally, the third factor looks at total 'criminal appearances', where less than 4 amounts to 0 points and 5 or more equals 1 point. The total score thus ranges from 0 to 6, with 0 equalling a low-risk classification; 1–2 amounting to medium risk; 3–4 being a sign of high risk; and 5–6 representing a very high risk (Thornton *et al.* 2003).

Part two then contains a list of four aggravating factors: 'any conviction for a sex offence against a male'; 'any conviction for a sex offence against a stranger'; being 'single'; and, 'any conviction for a non-contact sex offence' (Thornton *et al.* 2003). These are scored either with a yes or no response. If two are present, this will have the effect of increasing the risk classification by one level. If all four are present, this will increase the classification by two levels. Based on reconviction data from a 15-year follow-up study on 429 men released from prison in 1979, the risk classification is then converted into a percentage chance of reconviction, with low risk amounting to a 7 per cent chance; medium risk meaning a 19 per cent chance; high risk equalling a 36 per cent chance; and very high risk representing a 59 per cent chance of reconviction (Grubin 2008a). When we know that there is a gap between reconviction and actual reoffending, it is likely, however, that the percentage chance of actual reoffending is significantly higher than that stated above. Indeed, Hanson *et al.* (2003, cited in Thornton 2007) estimate that, with regards to sexual reoffending, the detection probability is only 0.10 (that is, only 10 arrests are made for every 100 offences). Taking this into account, it is therefore possible that the actual chance of reconviction for each risk classification over a 15-year period amounts to: 11 per cent for low-risk offenders; 29 per cent for medium risk; 55 per cent for high risk and a staggering 91 per cent for very high risk (Thornton 2007). Depending on which risk classification is reached will obviously have a significant effect on decisions concerning risk management, intervention programmes and the applicability of dangerousness legislation.

The validity of any assessment tool is obviously of prime importance, not just because of the possible consequences for the offender in terms of containment, monitoring and surveillance, but also because of the offender's impact on the public at large. One way in which to assess predictor validity is through the receiver operating characteristics analysis's area under the curve (AUC) statistic (ibid.). The strength of using this method of analysis is that the AUC is a single statistic that is not affected by discrepancies in the base rate of recidivism and thus can be used to compare a number of different tools (ibid.). This means that the most reliable and accurate tool can be determined for any given group/type of offender (Howard 2009a). The AUC score ranges from 0–1, with a score of 0.5 equalling chance (that is, no predictive accuracy) and a score of 1 representing absolute certainty. As no risk-assessment tool can ever offer certainty, but should provide data better than that of chance, a score of 0.7 is held in practice to be generally good (ibid.). Howard describes the AUC statistic as:

> equal to the probability that a randomly chosen reconvicted offender will have a higher score on the predictor than a randomly chosen non-reconvicted offender. For example, an AUC of 0.65 implies that when 100 pairs of offenders are checked, the reconvicted offender will (on average) have a higher score on the predictor than the non-reconvicted offender in 65 cases.
>
> (2009a: 85)

Testing of RM2000 has resulted in moderate predictive accuracy. Thornton (2007) found AUC scores for RM2000/S to range from 0.75–0.77, which is just above the 0.7 marker of moderately good. RM2000/V and RM2000/C were slightly better, with AUC scores ranging from 0.78–0.85 and 0.74–0.81 respectively. Hanson (2006, cited by Thornton 2007) also carried out a meta-analysis of a number of static risk tools, of which RM2000/S was one. The average AUC score for RM2000/S was found to be 0.82, which was the highest when compared to the other four tools included in the analysis. A cross-validation of the predictive accuracy of the RM2000 was also carried out by Craig *et al.* (2006), when they compared RM2000 with four other risk scales. In terms of predicting sexual and violent offending, the best predictor was the RM2000/V, with RM2000/S being the second best. Interestingly, this validity was consistent at the 2-year, 5-year and 10-year follow-up stages. For violent offending, the RM2000/V had relatively high AUC scores – 0.87 at the 2-year follow-up stage and 0.86 at the 5- and 10-year follow-up points. When it is thought that 0.90 is the best that can be feasibly achieved (Craig *et al.* 2008), this would suggest that RM2000/V is as near to perfection as it is ever going to be. If this is the case, and indeed more evaluation studies would be needed in order to verify this, it may be that RM2000 becomes the static risk assessment of choice for not just sex offending, but for violent offending as well.[2]

Despite such results, other academics have criticised the testing of the tool. Grubin, for example, argues that it 'has not been subject to any form of rigorous evaluation, and its empirical foundation is thin' (2008b: 3). He therefore contends that, as the tool cannot predict either the severity or imminence of reoffending, it 'should be seen as the first step in an assessment process, not [as] a substitute for the assessment process itself; to be effective, it must form part of a wider package' (ibid. 2008b: 28). While there is no evidence that NOMS acted directly upon this advice, this is how the tool is currently used (that is, as part of the Structured Assessment of Risk and Need (SARN)).

The Structured Assessment of Risk and Need

The Structured Assessment of Risk and Need (SARN) is a risk-assessment tool designed specifically for sex offenders, and has been used by prison and probation personnel in England and Wales since 2000 (Mann 2009). It originally began as the Structured Risk Assessment (Thornton 2002) instrument, but was later renamed SARN to emphasis the important link between assessment and treatment (Webster *et al.* 2006). SARN is made up of both static and dynamic risk factors and so is able to assess not just static risk, but also treatment needs as separate concepts (Mann and Attrill 2006). The tool is divided into three parts, with the first being RM2000, which can predict risk of sexual reoffending, violent recidivism or a combined risk. Part two of the tool contains a treatment needs analysis that is made up of 16 dynamic risk factors divided into the four domains of: sexual interests, distorted attitudes, social and emotional functioning, and self management (Webster *et al.* 2006; for more information on each domain, see Thornton 2002). Existence of problems in at least two of these domains is classified as high deviance; moderate deviance is where there are problems occurring in one domain; and, where there are no discernable problems, this is classified as low deviance (Thornton 2002). Examples of known risk factors include sexual preoccupation, child abuse supportive beliefs, distorted intimacy balance, and poor problem-solving (Webster *et al.* 2006). Finally, part three is the risk report, which considers the offender's progress while in treatment (Mann and Attrill 2006).

Each risk factor is scored out of 2, where 0 means the factor is 'not present', 1 means it is 'present but not a central characteristic', and 2 means it is 'a central characteristic' (Webster *et al.* 2006: 440). Presence of the factor is also assessed not just in the offender's general life, but also in the lead up to the actual offence. This is known as the 'offence chain' (ibid.). There is also a 'not possible to score' option where there is not enough information available. Any dynamic risk factor that has a score of 2 in both the offence chain and in the offender's general life is considered to be a relevant treatment need (Webster *et al.* 2006). This evidences how assessment of risk and treatment need to be linked together to better inform risk-management practice.

On the basis that the tool contains some dynamic risk factors (that is, those that can change over time), the main purpose of using SARN is to evaluate whether risk factors have decreased and/or increased following completion of intervention programmes. Prior to the introduction of SARN into England and Wales, once an offender had completed an accredited sex offending behaviour programme, the programme tutor would need to complete an end-of-programme report that would comment on changing risk factors. SARN now replaces this report (NOMS 2007a). SARN is therefore used to not only measure progress through treatment, and therefore assess its effectiveness, but also to identify any future treatment needs. It is also worth noting that the author of the scale stated that the 'model is intended to be a framework for organizing judgement . . . not a prediction scale' (Thornton 2002: 151).

Although the tool is being used in prison and probation throughout England and Wales, there appear to be few validation studies concerning its predictive accuracy, although Thornton (2002) has carried out two studies looking at the predictive validity of the four domains of dynamic risk factors as described above. The studies, which looked at 158 and 117 adult male sex offenders imprisoned in England and Wales, found that the inclusion of dynamic risk factors in the assessment significantly increased the accuracy of predicting recidivism risk. Moreover, Mandeville-Norden and Beech describe SARN as 'one of the most comprehensive methods of evaluating risk of sexual recidivism' (2006: 264). Despite such high praise, more analysis on larger sample groups and over longer follow-up periods would be useful and would provide the tool with even greater validity.

Risk-assessment tools for serious violent offenders

OASys and the OASys Violence Predictor

The Offender Assessment System (OASys) is currently the principal risk-assessment and -management system used by NOMS in England and Wales for general offending behaviour (Howard 2009b; see Howard 2006; Howard *et al.* 2006; Debidin 2009). By using a combination of static and dynamic risk factors, the tool is able to assess the risk of reoffending and the severity of this reoffending, as well as propose necessary interventions for offender management and sentencing planning purposes. The main body is divided into 12 scored sections,[3] with a total of 73 practitioner-completed questions. Each section varies in terms of its accuracy in predicting reoffending, and so is weighted according to its predictive validity (Debidin and Fairweather 2009). Each offending-related factor also produces a yes/no dynamic risk-factor measure, with the need being present if the score goes above a certain threshold. For example, accommodation is deemed to be a risk factor if the offender scores at least two out of a maximum eight points (Howard 2009a). Final scores can range from 0–168, with risk of reoffending classification based on this score: 0–40 = low risk; 41–99 = medium risk; and 100–168 = high-risk (Debidin and Fairweather 2009). In addition to the main body, the tool also has an additional risk of serious-harm assessment. This works by drawing together pertinent information from the main body of the tool, with a number of additional questions relevant to the risk an offender presents not just to others, but also to himself. Practitioners, based on this information, are then required to make judgements as to whether risk of serious harm is present at either a low, medium, high or very high level. Risk-management plans are then required to be completed, which will contain specific information on how risk-reduction strategies are to be employed in an attempt to reduce or at least manage the presented risk (ibid.).

While OASys works 'moderately well' (Howard 2009b: 1) and is a 'reasonable predictor of general reoffending' (Howard 2009a: 78), it does not provide a calculation of future violence, with recent improvements added to increase its predictive validity for serious violent offenders. This has resulted in OASys Violence Predictor (OVP), which has been designed to be able to foresee the likelihood of 'violent-type' reoffending. This has been defined to include: homicide (non-motoring) and assaults, threats and harassment, robbery and aggravated robbery, possession of offensive weapons (not use), criminal damage (not arson), and, public order offences (Howard and Seaton 2008). Based on the data of 26,619 violent offenders (Howard 2009a), OVP is made up of static and dynamic risk factors. Static factors include previous violent offending, age, sex, and any other previous offending. The dynamic factors cover drug and alcohol misuse, thinking and behaviour, accommodation, employability, temper control, and attitudes towards offending (Howard 2009b). In addition to normal OASys questions, the OVP covers demographic questions and separates previous violent-type offences from non-violent type offending (Howard 2009a). The dynamic factors therefore help assessors to identify key risk-reduction interventions, with change in such factors being noticed in further re-assessments (although, as noted above, these factors can increase as well as decrease). Offenders receive a risk score out of 100, which is then translated into predictions of proven reoffending within 12 or 24 months of either community order commencement or prison release (Howard and Seaton 2008); although, in theory, predictions for reoffending within 1 to 24 months is also achievable (Howard 2009a).

Validity checks have, so far, shown that not only is OVP the best predictor for future violent offending (Howard 2009a), but it also represents a significant improvement on what are considered to be the next best two: OASys and the Offender Group Reconviction Scale (OGRS) 3 (Howard *et al.* 2009). For general violent offending, OVP has an AUC score of 0.74, which can be compared to AUC scores of 0.68 for OASys and 0.70 for OGRS 3 (Howard 2009a). This improvement in validity can also be seen for specific types of violent crime; for example, for homicide and wounding, the AUC score for OVP is 0.74, while for OGRS 3 it is only 0.68 (Howard 2009c). OVP will thus help assessors to identify those offenders who are at the highest risk of violent reoffending and are presenting a significant risk of causing serious further offences (SFOs) (Howard and Seaton 2008; Howard 2009b). The risk score is also thought to be important in parole and other supervised licence decisions, with detailed tables being supplied to the Parole Board that will translate scores out of 100 into likelihoods of violent-type reoffending across a range of follow-up periods (Howard and Seaton 2008).

The first pilots of OVP took place in 2007 and 2008, with national roll-out occurring in August 2009 (Howard 2009a). Also, from August 2009, OASys assessments are now either Full or Standard, with OVP scores included in both versions. The Full OASys includes the majority of the questions in the previous version of OASys, while the Standard version is much shorter. The predictive validity of Full OASys OVP is identical to that of the version noted above, although that of the Standard OASys OVP is slightly lower (Howard 2009c). Obviously, the tool is still very much on trial, although, as mentioned above, initial evaluations would suggest that it is a valuable addition to the assessment package of tools for violent offenders.

The Historical, Clinical, Risk Management–20 risk-assessment scheme

The last risk-assessment tool under consideration is Historical, Clinical, Risk Management-20 (HCR-20), version 2 (Webster *et al.* 1997). This is a dynamic risk-assessment scheme, designed specifically for violent offenders and currently used in and outside prison in England and Wales for known violent offenders (Mann 2009). As it is dynamic and thus assesses risk factors that can change over time, it can be used in the continual assessment of offenders to assess change and any subsequent decrease and/or increase in risk. The tool was originally made available in 1995, although version 2, which is used today, was quickly developed in light of clinical experience gained from the initial pilots of the tool's use. This became available in 1997 (Webster *et al.* 1997). A third version is currently being developed and tested (Webster and Hucker 2007).

HCR-20 is made up of 20 items: 10 deal with historical factors; 5 with clinical aspects and 5 with risk-management variables (which is how the tool got its name). The historical factors obviously deal with past static events, the clinical aspects are designed to cover dynamic risk factors and the risk-management section is there to attempt to assess future 'situational post-assessment factors that may aggravate or mitigate risk' (Douglas *et al.* 2006: 2). Historical factors include: 'previous violence; young age at first violent incident; relationship instability; employment problems; substance use problems; major mental illness; psychopathy; early maladjustment; personality disorder; and prior supervision failure' (Webster *et al.* 1997). The clinical aspects include: 'lack of insight; negative attitudes, active symptoms of major mental illness; impulsivity; and unresponsiveness to treatment' (ibid.). Finally, through the risk-management section, HCR-20 has a 'value-added' element that helps towards structuring intervention and treatment plans (Kemshall 2001). Risk-management factors therefore include: 'plans lack feasibility; exposure to destabilizers; lack of personal support; noncompliance with remediation attempts; and, stress' (Douglas *et al.* 1999: 918). Each item is scored on the basis of not being present (0); possibly present (1); and definitely present (2), with the maximum score being 40. Offenders are then assessed as being low, moderate or high in risk (Webster and Hucker 2007).

Since the tool's invention and the initial pilot studies, much research has been carried out regarding its predictive validity. In civil psychiatry, AUC scores have ranged from 0.65 to 0.80, while for forensic psychiatry, the AUC score has been recorded to be as high as 0.85. For offender management purposes, the range has been found to lie between 0.65 and 0.82 (Douglas *et al.* 2006). Bearing in mind that scores of 0.7 are held to be generally good (Howard 2009a), scores that are reaching the mid-0.8s would appear to suggest that the validity of HCR-20 is extremely high. Looking at its use in correctional settings in more detail, HCR-20 has been found to be capable of separating violent from non-violent prisoners and thus can predict violence by incarcerated offenders (Belfrage *et al.* 2000). Cooke *et al.* (2001), in their retrospective study carried out on 250 Scottish male adult prisoners released from prison, not only found that HCR-20 as a whole was a good predictor of institutional violence, but also that the historical section (the H Scale) was found to be the strongest predictor of violent reoffending that resulted in a return to prison. In their conclusion, they stated that HCR-20 'remains the instrument of choice because it provides guidance on how to *manage* risk not merely how to *predict* risk' (3, emphasis in original). Furthermore, Douglas *et al.* (1999) noted in psychiatric patients how those 'scoring above the HCR-20 median . . . [were] six to thirteen times more likely to be violent than those scoring below the median' (917). Interestingly, and convenient for the new penology, Logan and Watt (2001, cited in Douglas *et al.* 2006) found that HCR-20 is as accurate when administered in a group environment as it is when used on an individual basis.[4] Kemshall therefore states that 'the HCR-20 provides both prediction, and identification of areas pertinent to the formulation of treatment interventions and risk-management strategies, particularly for forensic and prison populations' (2001: 37). Moreover, Farrington *et al.* contend that 'on the basis of currently available evidence, the HCR-20 seems the most useful of . . . instruments' (2008: 49).

Conclusion

While the focus in previous chapters has been on the concept of the dangerous offender and dangerousness, this chapter has argued that, for practical purposes, there must necessarily be a shift from this to risk and risk assessment. Current penal risk assessment in England and Wales, and indeed around the world, is centred on classifying individuals into groups based on static and dynamic risk factors. Such information is then used to decide how risky any given individual is, with a number of factors described above that may affect the predictive reliability of this. While there are several risk-assessment scales currently in use for serious sexual and violent offenders, some of which have high predictive validity, they cannot help any further in preventing that risk. What is done with the offender once risk and need has been identified is, therefore, important and will ultimately determine whether prison or a community intervention is a success. To secure this success, offenders therefore need to be treated as individuals, matched with the most appropriate behaviour programmes and continually assessed for change so that the appropriateness of treatment and other interventions can also be continually re-assessed. What is done with serious sexual and violent offenders once their risk has been assessed and dangerousness legislation has been applied is therefore the focus of the remainder of this book.

4

THE USE OF IMPRISONMENT

Introduction

Although sentencing policy for dangerous offenders has changed quite considerably over the last century, a common thread throughout this time has been the use of imprisonment and the desire to contain and segregate serious sexual and violent offenders from the general population. Policies have focused on initiatives such as preventative detention, extended sentences, longer-than-commensurate sentencing and, more recently, IPP. While it is not suggested that confinement is the only way in which serious sexual and violent offenders are currently managed (other techniques are considered in Chapters 5 and 6), this chapter considers the use of imprisonment in the governance of these high-risk offenders. In particular, it looks at indeterminate-sentenced prisoners, the high security estate, close supervision centres (CSCs), therapeutic communities (TCs) and the role of the Parole Board in relation to release and recall.

Sentences of the court

Any individual can be sentenced to imprisonment if their convicted criminal offence is considered serious enough to warrant a custodial term. While imprisonment is used for many offences and for all categories of offenders, since this book is concerned with the governance of serious sexual and violent offences, this section will limit its discussion to these offenders. Although there are, of course, exceptions, many who commit such serious offences will be sentenced to indeterminate periods of imprisonment, and so this chapter focuses on those who have been sentenced to imprisonment for life. This is an indeterminate sentence and includes mandatory life (used in cases of murder), discretionary life and sentences of IPP.

As discussed in Chapter 2, since the introduction of IPPs in 2005, the use of them has been dramatic. In June 2006, there were 1,100 prisoners serving sentences of IPP in England and Wales. This rose to 2,900 in June 2007 (Hansard 16 Jan 2008, Column 1337 W), stood at 4,863 in November 2008 (HC Deb, 10 November 2008, c872W) and continued to increase to 5,600 in October 2009 (HL Deb, 28 October 2009, c1253) and to over 6,000 in July 2010 (Blunt 2010). In March 2009, the entire lifer population stood at 12,090, which was higher than the total lifer population (11,477) in all other 46 Council of Europe countries[1] (The Howard League 2009).

The majority of life-sentenced prisoners will, at some stage, be released on licence into the community, although the last decade has seen the average term spent in prison for lifers steadily increase. In 2000, for example, the average length of tariff served was 14.32 years. This dipped in 2002 to 13.19 years but, since then, has steadily increased to 14.52 in 2004, 15.91 in 2007 and 17.54 in 2009 (HC Deb, 22 February 1010, c256W). There are also a small number of prisoners who have been deemed to be so dangerous that whole-life tariffs have been imposed (that is, for them, life will mean life). There are currently 35[2] inmates sentenced to whole-life tariffs, including notorious figures such as Ian Brady, Dennis Nilsen, Donald Neilson, Jeremy Bamber and Colin Ireland. The only woman is Rosemary West (Penrose 2009). Such sentences have been held not to breach either Article 3 (torture) or Article 7 (retrospectivity) of the European Convention on Human Rights (ECHR) (*R. v Jeremy Bamber* [2009] EWCA Crim 962).

Prison categorisation

Once an offender has been sentenced to imprisonment, he will be assessed on two matters: the likelihood that he will escape and, if he did, the level of risk to the public he would then pose. This is known as categorisation.[3] Male offenders are therefore categorised as being either:

> Category A: prisoners whose escape would be highly dangerous to the public or the police or the security of the State, no matter how unlikely that escape might be, and for whom the aim must be to make escape impossible.
>
> Category B: prisoners for whom the very highest conditions of security are not necessary, but for whom escape must be made very difficult.
>
> Category C: prisoners who cannot be trusted in open conditions, but who do not have the resources and will to make a determined prison escape attempt.
>
> Category D: prisoners who can be reasonably trusted in open conditions.
>
> (HM Prison Service 2000: para. 1.1)

Allocation to a category is based on the offender's main index offence. Indeterminate prisoners used to be automatically categorised as Category B and were only labelled as Category A if, for example, the main index offence involved extreme, sadistic or frenzied violence; extreme sexual violence; or robbery with the use of potentially life-threatening violence. Since February 2008, however, this is no longer a requirement for IPP prisoners, although remains for other indeterminate inmates. Now, those serving minimum terms of three years or less are usually classified as Category C, and allocated to a local training prison (HM Prison Service 2008a). IPP prisoners can still be classified as being suitable for Category A status, although this will be extremely rare. Once an offender has been categorised, he will be placed in a prison of that category. The regime of the prison will obviously depend on the type of prison it is, with more punitive and restrictive conditions found in Category A and B wings.

Review of an offender's categorisation will depend on the length of his sentence. For those serving less than 12 months (short-term prisoners), categorisation will be reviewed if and when circumstances change. For those serving 12 months but less than 4 years (medium-term prisoners), review will be every 6 months, and for those serving 4 years or over (long-term prisoners), review takes place on an annual basis (Bennett 2008b). For Category A offenders, review will take place 2 years after conviction and then every 12 months thereafter (Bennett 2008c).

Serving a life sentence

While in prison, an indeterminate prisoner will usually go through a number of stages before he is considered for release, and, although no two life sentences are the same, the typical structure is divided into three stages. On conviction and on receipt of an indeterminate sentence, an inmate will initially be held at a local prison so that categorisation, as explained above, can take place. The inmate's life sentence plan (LSP) will also begin to take shape with the local prison responsible for deciding which type of prison is required. For example, if the prisoner is categorised as being a Category A offender, then a request will be made to the high-security estate, and, where the offence is sexual in nature, allocation should be to a prison where the offender can be assessed for and take part in a Sex Offender Treatment Programme (SOTP). All prisoners serving indeterminate sentences are additionally encouraged to participate in an induction programme (HM Prison Service 2008b).

The first stage of the offender's sentence will start once he has reached his allocated prison, where a detailed LSP will be developed. The LSP will contain clear and detailed information regarding the inmate's offence, a summary of the main risk factors, a projection of offending behaviour targets, a system for sentence planning and progress review, and a record of the prisoner's accomplishments. The purpose of the LSP is thus to

> plan, monitor and record the means by which each lifer is supported in the process of achieving a reduction in risk during sentence such that he or she may safely be released on licence into the community at tariff expiry.
>
> (HM Prison Service 2008b: para. 8.2)

Under principle one of the Prison Service Vision (to deal fairly, openly and humanely with prisoners), whenever practicable, the LSP must be disclosed to the prisoner, although sensitive information such as that contained in the confidential summary dossier or medical information that healthcare staff have decided not to disclose, or security-sensitive information can be kept from the inmate (HM Prison Service 2008b). Work will then be undertaken to not only manage risk, but also to reduce it, with the overriding factor in determining whether a lifer progresses through the system being that he has demonstrated a reduction in his risk. Progression will therefore depend on factors such as displaying a willingness to provide an open and active account of the index offence, showing a motivation to change, achievement of sentence planning targets, participation in offending behaviour programmes and conformity with the custodial regime (Harrison 2007a). Stage one of a life sentence usually lasts from 18 months upwards, although this can be reduced for those who have short tariffs under sentences of IPP, or for those who are making 'exceptionally good progress' (HM Prison Service 2008b: para. 4.4.2).

The second stage of a lifer's sentence will take place in a high-security prison, a Category B training prison or a Category C local prison, and it is this stage that will make up the bulk of the offender's sentence, with much of the necessary offending behaviour work occurring at this stage. As with progression from stage one, the inmate needs to show that he is making 'significant and sustained progress' (HM Prison Service 2008b: para. 4.5.1) and within stage two he can be transferred to Category B and C establishments. The inmate may be held in a number of prisons during stage two, with some transfers specifically made to enable the prisoner to undertake offending behaviour programmes. Stage two can often last upwards of 6 to 8 years (Harrison 2007a), although this will obviously depend on the inmate's progression and evidence of risk reduction. Finally, the offender has the opportunity to progress to stage three, which takes place in open or semi-open conditions. To graduate to this status, inmates have to show that 'their risk of reoffending or of escaping/absconding has reduced to such an extent that they can reasonably be trusted in conditions of minimum security without placing members of the public at risk' (HM Prison Service 2008b: para. 4.6.3). This assessment is carried out by the Parole Board, with most lifers spending up to two years in open conditions before being considered for release into the community. There is no set time period for each stage of the sentence, and so offenders will progress at their own individual pace, although, as stated above, the average length of a life sentence in 2009 was just over 17.5 years. It is also worth noting that offenders can move in both directions through the stages; so, if it is perceived that risk has increased, or the inmate has behaved disruptively, he will be transferred to a higher-category establishment and regress back a stage.

Currently, nearly half of the lifer population is made up of those serving sentences of IPP. To reflect the fact that many of these inmates will be serving life sentences with tariffs of less than five years (and, in some cases, considerably less), there is an additional policy for short-tariff lifers. The different stages of the LSP remain, although importantly, and as emphasised in bold in the *Indeterminate Sentence Manual* (HM Prison Service 2008b), short-tariff lifers 'must be prioritised for offending behaviour programmes according to the length of time left till tariff expires . . . [and] lifers must be given every opportunity to demonstrate their safety for release at tariff expiry' (ibid.: para. 4.13.2). Whether this is actually taking place will be discussed in more detail below.

The high-security estate

As mentioned above, Category A offenders, those who pose the greatest risks in terms of escape and subsequently public protection, are held under the most severe control regimes in high-security prisons, previously known as dispersal prisons. Managed centrally by a Director of High Security, these are currently HMP Belmarsh, HMP Frankland, HMP Full Sutton, HMP Long Lartin, HMP Manchester, HMP Wakefield, HMP Whitemoor and HMP Woodhill. In 2007, there were 5,895 men held within the high-security estate (The Howard League 2008). Due to the fact that it is these prisoners who are considered to be the most dangerous, it is unsurprising that HM Prison Service has a target to ensure that there are no Category A escapes and, since 1995, there have been none (HC Deb, 20 July 2009, c1076W). In 2006/07, it cost the taxpayer £52,037 to keep a prisoner within the high-security estate. This can be compared to the cost of £25,265, which was the service-wide prisoner average for the same period of time (HM Prison Service 2007).

To differentiate the high risk from the extremely high risk, Category A is divided into three further classifications: standard, high and exceptional risk. Standard Category A prisoners make up the bulk of the high-security estate and include those who have no history of escape planning, are not considered to have the skill or determination to escape and/or do not have access to outside resources to assist with such an escape. High-risk escape prisoners, however, do have such a history and are perceived to have both the skill and determination to overcome the security measures applied to them, or have links with associates who possess the resources (explosives and/or firearms) to affect an escape. Finally, exceptional-risk prisoners have the same characteristics as the high-risk escape prisoners but are thought to be even more risky in terms of escape (Bennett 2008c).

Due to the function of containing the most dangerous of offenders, the regime in a high-security prison is therefore the most severe in terms of security measures. This can include frequent cell and personal searches, control of movement, restrictions on communications, limitations on visits, closer observations and special measures for outside transfers (Bennett 2008c). Much of this can result in inmates being locked up in their cells for long periods of time. For example, in 2005, one third of all prisoners in HMP Wakefield spent more than 20 hours per day locked in their cells (The Howard League 2008). More stringent measures are used for those who pose a high risk, as opposed to just a standard risk, and all exceptional-risk inmates are kept within special security units (Bennett 2008c). Despite the regime being more severe in terms of security, in terms of the general environment, those in the high-security estate are likely to experience better conditions. For example, high-security prisoners are often allowed to cook their own meals and wear and launder their own clothing. They often have better educational and work opportunities and are allowed to possess more personal items (Creighton *et al.* 2005).

Despite this better regime, Category A prisoners can be, by their nature, violent and disruptive, and if a prisoner is thought to be too troublesome for even the high-security estate, the final option is transfer to a CSC. Before this last resort, however, and since August 2007, the Prison Service has being using a national strategy for managing difficult prisoners called the Managing Challenging Behaviour Strategy (MCBS). This aims to manage disruptive prisoners locally rather than transferring them to other prisons, and uses devices such as the Incentives and Earned Privilege scheme, anti-bullying systems, violence reduction strategies, internal re-location, adjudication awards, positive dialogue, in-area transfer, and segregation (HM Prison Service 2005). A prisoner will be included in the strategy if he has been violent towards staff, other prisoners or self-harmed, with the latter signifying that clinical assistance is additionally required. Referral will also occur if the inmate has damaged property or committed arson, is found in possession of or used a weapon, has committed repeated disciplinary offences, or made dirty protests (Brittles 2009). There are four structural components to the MCBS, although in essence it is a multi-disciplinary approach to managing disruptive offenders, bringing together the expertise of mental health support and custodial care to try to prevent long-term segregation. Inmates within the strategy will be given an individualised management plan that focuses on 'timely and appropriate exit strategies from segregation' (ibid.: 39). Brittles (2009) states that the MCBS, in place across the entire high-security estate, is showing promise and is delivering improvements in the task of managing challenging prisoners.

Close supervision centres

Despite the existence of the MCBS, if an inmate, either within the main or the high-security estate is being exceptionally violent and/or disruptive, under Prison Rule 46,[4] the Secretary of State can direct a prisoner's removal from association and assign him to a CSC. This is for reasons of maintaining good order or discipline, or to ensure the safety of prison staff or other prisoners, and is used for a small number of extremely dangerous offenders. Adams describes these as the '3Ds prisoners' (10): dangerous, difficult and disruptive. CSCs have existed in the prison estate since February 1998 and replace special security units and the Continuous Assessment System (for more on these, see Walmsley 1989; Ditchfield 1990; Bottomley and Hay 1991; Walmsley 1991; King 2007). The CSC system is a national strategy with its aim being to remove 'the most significantly disruptive, challenging and dangerous prisoners from ordinary location, and manage them within a small and highly supervised unit' (HM Prison Service 2009a: 6). Such inmates are likely to suffer from mental illnesses and personality disorders, but are held not to be suitable for transfer to either a high secure hospital or to a Dangerous and Severe Personality Disorder (DSPD) unit (see Chapter 9).

There are currently three CSCs in England and Wales located at HMP Wakefield, HMP Woodhill and HMP Whitemoor (Walls 2010). The unit at

Wakefield operates as the Exceptional Risk Unit (ERU) and is designed to contain the most dangerous of prisoners held within the CSC system. Inmates held within the ERU are kept segregated from other prisoners, but do have access to a singular unlock regime that includes one-to-one therapeutic care (ibid.). Woodhill is the main assessment centre and houses those who have been accepted for pre-selection assessment. It also operates a 'step-down' location for those who have been downgraded from the ERU and a regime for long-term prisoners. Finally, the units at Whitemoor offer two regimes: one that is open and progressive and thus suitable for those who have progressed through the system and are working towards deselection, and one that is more restricted and suitable for those who have made minimal progress (ibid.). Funding for these units amounted to £308 million in 2006/07 and £336 million in 2007/08 (HC Deb, 14 October 2008, C1025W). Designated CSC cells also exist on the segregation units at Wakefield (2), Whitemoor (2), Long Lartin (4), Full Sutton (2), Frankland (2), Manchester (2) and Belmarsh (2) (ibid.). On 1 January 2006, there were 29 prisoners held within the CSC system. 83 per cent were serving life sentences, 10 per cent had sentences of more than 10 years and 3 per cent were serving less than 10 years. 52 per cent had already spent more than 10 years in custody (HM Inspectorate of Prisons (HMIP) 2006a). In May 2006, this number had fallen to just 24 (King 2007).

Referrals for a transfer to a CSC can be made following either a single serious event or where attempts to manage the inmate under the MCBS have failed. Referral criteria, defined by HM Prison Service, are:

- Demonstrating violence towards others on a regular basis.
- Carried out, or orchestrated, a single yet extreme or significant act of violence or disorder.
- Causing significant day-to-day management difficulties by undermining the good order of the establishment.
- Threatening and/or intimidating behaviour, directed at staff and/or prisoners.
- A long history of disciplinary offences.
- Repeated periods of segregation under Prison Rule 45 – Good Order or Discipline.
- A continuous period of segregation exceeding six months.

(2009a: 7)

Morris (2006) therefore defines those suitable for referral as 'ferocity-type prisoners' (92), those who have killed in prison and those involved in organisational violence. In essence the CSC system is appropriate for those inmates where everything else has been tried, but has failed (including the new Case Management Protocol for Difficult to Manage Prisoners, see Jonah 2009). The CSC system is therefore seen as the last resort.

The referral process is made up of four stages. Stage one is when an inmate is identified as needing CSC supervision and information will be sent to the CSC unit at Woodhill. A selection committee will then meet to discuss the referral and make recommendations to the CSC Management Committee. It is this committee that will either accept or decline the application. If accepted, the inmate will be moved to Woodhill and placed under Rule 46 for four months. The first three months will involve detailed risk and needs assessment, with the final four weeks used for report writing. A local assessment case conference will then be held to accurately determine whether the CSC system is suitable, with recommendations on this passed to the CSC Management Committee. Again, this committee will decide whether the inmate is to be accepted or whether he should be handled in the high-security estate under the MCBS. If accepted, the inmate will then enter into the CSC system (HM Prison Service 2009a).

Deselection from the system will occur only when the team believes that the intensive supervision and controlled environment is no longer needed. The inmate will then be transferred either to a high-security prison or back to the main prison estate (HM Prison Service 2009a). The decision to hold an inmate under Rule 46 must be reviewed on a monthly basis, but can be extended without independent scrutiny for indefinite periods of time (Lloyd 2008). For example, Charles Bronson has been held in solitary confinement under Rule 46 (or its prior equivalent) for over 30 years.

Since 1998, there have arguably been three phases in the development of the CSC system. The first phase was based on the Prison Service's Incentives and Earned Privileges scheme, whereby responsible behaviour was rewarded and disruptive behaviour punished. At this time, there were six CSC units: four wings at Woodhill, one at HMP Durham and one at HMP Hull. If a referral had been accepted, the inmate would enter the CSC system and be placed on the induction and assessment 'B' wing at Woodhill (level two). Progression was then possible to 'C' wing, known as the programmes unit (level three) and then to a standard activity regime (level four) to prepare the inmate for a return to the normal estate; this was initially at Hull, and then, in March 1999, located on 'G' wing at Durham (King 2007). If the inmate continued to behave badly, rather than progressing on to 'C' wing he would be regressed to 'A' wing at Woodhill (level one), which offered a 'highly structured and safe regime' (Morris 2006: 89). Further disruptive behaviour earned the inmate a transfer to 'D' wing, also at Woodhill, an intensive care unit for exceptionally high-risk inmates (that is, solitary confinement). Morris notes how inmates described 'D' wing as 'CSC seg or the superseg (Segregation Unit)' (ibid.). 'I' wing at Durham (level four) was also available for prisoners who needed specialist care due to clear psychiatric difficulties. The regime in phase one of development was therefore control orientated.

In 1999, both Woodhill and Durham were inspected (HMCIP 2000). At the time of the inspection, 36 prisoners were being contained within the CSC units (ibid.). Approximately one quarter of the 36 were progressing through the system, while three quarters were regressing and thus being held in sub-basic segregation units (Lloyd 2008). All of the wings at Woodhill were described as 'sterile and void of stimulation' (HMCIP 2000: para. 2.2), with views from the cells being of coiled razor wire or caged exercise yards. Cells on 'D' wing were found to contain a toilet and sink, a mattress and a cardboard table and chair. Prisoners were kept segregated in their cells at all times, except for one hour of solitary exercise each day and three showers per week. All face-to-face contact with staff was with a 'helmeted figure' (ibid.: para. 2.24). Inmates were allowed two 30-minute visits per month, although few took up this right:

> This meant that, prisoners were hardly at all exposed to the humanising influence of people who cared for them and who might motivate them to modify their behaviour. Staff inevitably, therefore, saw them as social isolates rather than as people with families like themselves who could be damaged by dehumanising regimes.
>
> (ibid.: para. 2.20)

The report further stated that many of the CSC prisoners had both emotional and behavioural problems that were further exacerbated by the isolation and lack of mental stimulation. At least 60 per cent of the inmates had previously been referred to a special hospital and therefore needed a regime focused on control and treatment, rather than control alone. Regarding the sub-basic regime on 'D' wing in Woodhill, the inspectors argued that such 'punishment conditions for unlimited periods [was] unacceptable' (HMCIP 2000: para. 5.2). Instead, they recommended that prisoners should be returned to normal conditions, if appropriate, as soon as possible; that 'unlimited use of isolation in punishment conditions should cease' (ibid.: para. 5.10) and that those in solitary conditions should be provided with in-cell activities (see also Clare and Bottomley 2001).

The second phase of CSC development therefore followed this damming report. As a result, the punishment regime was ended and progressively less controlling and segregating systems were introduced. Two major changes therefore took place: geographical expansion and the introduction of 'individualised care planning' (Morris 2006: 89). In terms of expansion, new units were created at Long Lartin and Wakefield, and cells were made available at all high-security estate prisons for Rule 46 respite stays, with the whole system managerially controlled by the governor at Woodhill. Due to Durham being reclassified as a Category B prison in 2004, the specialist intensive care unit on 'I' wing was transferred to Whitemoor and 'G' wing was closed. This expansion of the system allowed for the separation of prisoners who were undermining the progression of others, as well as giving the system enough flexibility so that individual specialist needs could be met (Morris 2006). All inmates held under Rule 46 were explicitly told what they had to do in order to return to the normal estate and progression paths were planned to enable this.

Phase three of development has again centred on treatment, with the biggest change being the introduction of the 'Violence Reduction Programme' (Wong and Gordon 2003, cited by Morris 2006). This was initially piloted at Woodhill in 2004 and is now run at Whitemoor (King 2008). The third phase of the CSC system has thus seen an increased emphasis on treatment rather than mere containment, with Lloyd (2008) describing the present CSC system as a 'violence reduction strategy for disruptive prisoners' (47). As summed up by Morris,

> The CSC system discharges its duty to these most difficult prisoners by working to enable them to de-escalate their dangerous behaviour by exploring its causes; managing them while they are in the grip of it; and all the while creating pathways out of the higher-security setting.
>
> (2006: 98)

A further inspection in June 2006 (HMIP 2006a) evaluated whether such changes had improved conditions, with the inspectors noting that, while the punishment regime had ended and there were more opportunities for prisoners to engage in educational and therapeutic activities, there were still a number of concerns. For example, they found that the quality of exercise and visits were poor; prisoners were unhappy and complained of boredom; in-cell activities for those held in solitary confinement were still inadequate; and out-of-cell time was inferior. Furthermore, the report recommended that more use should be made of occupational therapy in supporting the mental health needs of the inmates involved and, for those whose mental health conditions were likely to deteriorate due to the solitary conditions, speedy transfers to secure hospitals should be made (ibid.).

Conditions within the CSC system would thus appear to be improving, although arguably there is still a way to go in ensuring that the treatment ethic is maintained rather than being one of just mere containment. Even if the above recommendations are implemented, it must still be borne in mind that keeping offenders in solitary conditions can be extremely detrimental to their mental health (see Haney 2003; Scharff Smith 2006). When CSCs at a sub-basic level are required, an inmate should only be kept in these conditions for as little time as possible, and should be given every support to progress to the other regimes and finally back to the main prison estate. Thankfully, the number of prisoners subject to the CSC system is small and, over the last decade, there has been a steady decrease, with 36 detained in CSC units in 1999 but only 24 in May 2006. When this is compared to the 85,000 currently held by HM Prison Service, this is a miniscule amount, although of course does not mean that such offenders should not be shown care and respect by the prison authorities or should not be supported to progress through the system like all other offenders.

Therapeutic communities

In sharp contrast to the CSC system and the use of solitary confinement is the existence of therapeutic communities (TCs). These are defined as 'psychologically planned environments . . . where the social relationships, structure of the day and different activities together are all deliberately designed to help people's health and well-being' (Association of Therapeutic Communities (ATC) 2010a). TCs designed for the treatment of offenders have existed in England and Wales since 1962, when HMP Grendon in Buckinghamshire opened. Although Grendon was originally set up as a psychiatric experiment under the control of a Medical Superintendent, it came under the control of the main prison estate in 1985 and is now run by a prison governor, assisted by a Director of Therapy. Its original purpose was 'To investigate and treat mental disorders generally recognised as responsive to treatment, to investigate offenders whose offences in themselves suggest mental morbidity, and to explore the problems of dealing with the psychopath' (Commissioners of Prisons 1963, cited by Genders and Player 1995: 6).

As discussed below, Grendon has largely been held to be successful and, consequently, a number of other TC units have been opened within the prison estate. For example, there have been therapeutic units at HMP Glen Parva, the Max Glatt unit at HMP Wormwood Scrubs, Albatross House at YOI Feltham and a wing at YOI Aylesbury, although, for a number of reasons, these have now all been closed. Currently there are 12 democratic TCs in England and Wales: 5 at Grendon, 4 at HMP Dovegate in Staffordshire, 1 on the lifer unit for indeterminate prisoners at HMP Gartree, 1 at HMP Blundeston and 1 for women offenders at HMP Send[5] (Turner 2010). As it is Grendon and Dovegate that make up three quarters of the TC estate, it is these that will be discussed further.

Grendon is a Category B (medium-security) prison with an operational capacity of 235 male offenders across 6 wings; 5 of which hold approximately 40 offenders each and one, the assessment and induction wing, that has space for 25 (HMIP 2007a). Although each wing works as an independent TC, typical staff on each unit consists of uniformed prison officers, a therapist, a probation officer and a psychologist (Morris 1999b). The TC at Dovegate was opened in November 2001 and is a unit attached to a Category B training prison. Despite not being independent like Grendon (inmates from both sites share central services), it still houses 200 offenders in the TC unit, being made up of 4 wings of 40 beds each, an assessment and resettlement wing, and a high-intensity programme wing (both having 20 beds each). The high-intensity programme is used for those prisoners who have special psychological needs and who need to undergo pre-treatment before commencing therapy on a normal TC wing (Smartt 2001). Dovegate accepts Category B and C offenders and is a private prison operated by Serco Home Affairs.

Over the last few years, the typical 'Grendonite' (Smartt 2001: 9) has remained fairly stable in terms of main index offence (see Table 4.1), although there have been significant increases in indeterminate sentences. In fact, in terms of those serving life, as shown in Table 4.2, there has been a 232 per cent increase at Grendon between 1995 and 2009. On 30 June 2010, 92 per cent of the population at Grendon were serving indeterminate sentences, with 48 per cent of these serving sentences of mandatory life (Brookes 2010). From these statistics, it can be gleaned that Grendon is predominantly made up of serious sexual and violent offenders. While the results may also suggest that, over time, it has taken in more serious offenders, based on the increase in the length of the inmate's sentence and the increase in life sentences, this may be more illustrative of the up-tariffing of dangerous

Table 4.1 Prisoner population profile at Grendon (1994–2009) in terms of main index offence

Year	*Total of men admitted into Grendon*	*Violence against the person*	*Robbery*	*Sexual offences*
1994–95	229	38%	28%	27%
1995–2000	607	50%	28%	15%
2004	220	46.4%	18.6%	18.2%
2007	222	48%	17%	20%
2009	185	65.4%	12.43%	17.29%

Source: Hobson and Shine 1998; Shine and Newton 2000; HMIP 2004, 2007a, 2009

Table 4.2 Prisoner population profile at Grendon (1995–2009) in terms of sentence

Year	*Total of men admitted into Grendon*	*2 years but less than 4 years*	*4 years but less than 10 years*	*10 years and over but not life*	*Life*
1995–2000	607	Data not available	Data not available	Data not available	25%
2004	220	0.4%	30.5%	18.6%	50%
2007	222	0%	20%	21%	59%
2009	185	0%	4.3%	12.4%	83.2%

Source: Shine and Newton 2000; HMIP 2004, 2007a, 2009

offenders under populist punitiveness and the introduction of IPPs (as previously discussed in Chapter 2). Such results are also true for Dovegate. For example, in 2006, 43 per cent of inmates had been imprisoned for violence, 9 per cent for sexual offences and 19 per cent for robbery (HMIP 2007b). This had not significantly altered in 2008, when 46 per cent were in custody for violent offences, 6 per cent for sex crimes and 26 per cent for robbery (HMIP 2008a). However, while in 2006 there were no lifers (HMIP 2007b), in 2008 those serving life made up 42 per cent of the population, with an additional 10 per cent sentenced to IPPs (HMIP 2008a).

The referral process

To gain a place on a TC, inmates must be motivated to participate in the group therapy process, as well as having the ability 'to communicate openly within a group without recourse to physical violence' (Home Office 1987: para. 4). Arguably, this is the major difference between those who progress to a TC and those who regress to a CSC. To be accepted at Grendon, for example, the offender should have at least 12, if not 24, months left on his sentence (at Dovegate, it is more than 18 months (HMIP 2007b)); have volunteered to be there; not be a drug abuser; be classified as Category B or lower; and be under 40 years of age, although this last criterion appears to be somewhat flexible. There are no restrictions regarding the type of offence or behavioural characteristics, with the main criterion being a 'genuine motivation to change' (Genders and Player 1995: 48). Typical residents include: 'explosive aggressive individuals, arsonists, sex offenders, unusual murderers, those who deliberately self mutilate and the isolated and hostile individuals who prove difficult in other prisons' (Home Office 1987: para. 3). Shine and Newton, unsurprisingly, describe these men as 'damaged, disturbed and dangerous', who show:

> high levels of psychological disturbance on psychometric assessments and often have histories of self harm and suicide attempts. Their offending behaviour is usually serious and chronic and a substantial number have histories of pronounced institutional misconduct, sometimes severe, prior to admission. The men also show elevated scores on measures of dangerousness and often have a high risk of reconviction.
>
> (2000: 33)

It is therefore not uncommon for men to experience Category A/high security and CSC conditions before being accepted on to a TC unit.

With such inmates in mind, and over a period of consultation, the ATC has identified 10 core values that underpin and shape the TC approach. These include:

- attachment (healthy attachment is a developmental requirement for all human beings, and should be seen as a basic human right);
- containment (a safe and supportive environment is required for an individual to develop, to grow, or to change);
- respect (people need to feel respected and valued by others to be healthy);
- communication (all behaviour has meaning and represents communication that deserves understanding);
- interdependence (personal well-being arises from one's ability to develop relationships that recognise mutual need);
- relationships (understanding how you relate to others and how others relate to you leads to better intimate, family, social and working relationships);
- participation (the ability to influence one's environment and relationships is necessary for personal well-being);
- process (there is not always a right answer and it is often useful for individuals, groups and larger organisations to reflect rather than act immediately);
- balance (positive and negative experiences are necessary for healthy development of individuals, groups and the community); and
- responsibility (each individual has responsibility to the group, and the group in turn has collective responsibility to all individuals in it).

(ATC 2010b)

Smartt argues that the two central aims of TCs are

> to help psychologically disturbed and difficult-to-handle prisoners to adjust better to prison life and . . . to change their anti-social behaviour and criminal attitudes in order for them to adjust better to mainstream prison life before they can be fully released.
>
> (2001: 20)

Genders and Player (1993) similarly state that 'the most dominant theme of the therapeutic process is that of personal relationships, whereby the men are encouraged and expected to assume liability for their own actions and not to blame others for their shortcomings' (240).

Prisoners are commonly referred to Grendon and Dovegate by a prison doctor (although actual acceptance will be decided by the Director of Therapy), and, depending on availability, may have to wait a period of time before a place becomes vacant, especially because the waiting list works on how long is left on an inmate's sentence rather than on a first-come, first-served basis. For some prisoners, in 2000, this meant a wait of up to five years (although, since the addition of Dovegate, such time periods are now extremely rare (Smartt 2001)). This may mean that inmates who are committed to the TC experience may find themselves choosing Grendon or Dovegate over possible early parole release (Morris 1999b). Other routes of entry include recruitment drives (medical officers visit other prisons and interview prisoners), rescue cases (a prison may ask the TC to take a particularly disruptive or difficult prisoner), and an additional route for lifers (whereby the department responsible for lifer prisoners may ask the TC to assess particular inmates) (Genders and Player 1995). As previously mentioned, actual acceptance into the community is controlled by staff following an assessment period on the assessment and induction wing (eight weeks at Grendon (ibid.) and at least three weeks at Dovegate (Smartt 2001)). The inmate needs to be deemed capable of 'with-standing the rigours of the therapeutic process' and 'have an ability to participate and understand what was going on in the therapy' (Genders and Player 1995: 64). Although the referral process at Grendon would appear to be working reasonably well, criticism has been levelled at the Prison Service for their lack of a national referral strategy. Anne Owers, Her Majesty's Chief Inspector of Prisons, following an inspection of Grendon in 2009 commented that 'There is a pressing need for a system-wide strategy to ensure that the role of Grendon . . . is maximised and coherent planning arrangements put in place to ensure the routine identification of suitable candidates and planned progression on graduation' (HMIP 2009: 6). Indeed, at Dovegate there have been criticisms that it was admitting 'for commercial rather than therapeutic reasons' (HMIP 2007b: 5) those who were not suitable for the TC and were thus disrupting its work and the progress of others.[6] This consequentially meant that a large number of inmates housed at Dovegate were not actually undertaking therapy, rather waiting for transfer out. In June 2008, this amounted to approximately 40 per cent of the inmates (HMIP 2008a).

The TC regime

From their study of Grendon between 1987 and 1989, Genders and Player (1995) describe the typical Grendon weekday as follows: 6.30 cells are unlocked with the men given time to wash, have breakfast and carry out chores; 8.00 inmates work as cleaners, in the garden, laundry or kitchen (it is interesting to note that employment is allotted not on the basis of who would do the best job, but who therapeutically would gain the most from it); 10.00 group therapy; 11.30 canteen-style lunch is taken communally on the wing; 1.00 exercise and/or indoor recreation time; 1.40 end of the exercise period; 2.00 work until 4.00; 4.30 tea and then free association on the wing; 8.00 light supper; 8.45 lock up and then lights out at 10.00.

The 90 minutes of formal therapy is divided into small group and wing/community meetings. Each small group is made up of six to eight inmates and one or two prison officers, who act as group facilitators and who often positively contribute to the therapeutic process. Small groups meet three to five times per week for one hour, with frequency dependent on the requirements of each wing (Wilson and McCabe 2002). The therapy combines a mixture of frank talking with behavioural and conditioning elements of therapy, plus social-skills modelling, cognitive behavioural techniques and psychodynamic elements (Morris 1999b). Therapy under Mark Morris, who was the Director of Therapy in 2001, was described as being based on 'permissiveness, democratisation, reality, confrontation and communalism' (Smartt 2001: 20).[7] The remaining 30 minutes comprises of feedback from the small group to the whole wing, where the community is informed about particularly sensitive or traumatic issues (Wilson and McCabe 2002). Men in the small group are expected to actively participate in not only exploring their own individual problems, but also in finding collective solutions for all group members. Inmates are also expected to accept constructive feedback on their behaviour from other inmates and act positively on this. Passive participation is not acceptable and can lead to the group voting an inmate out. If this recommendation is supported by the staff, the inmate is removed from the TC and returned to the main prison estate (Genders and Player 1995).

Twice weekly, inmates will also engage in therapy through wing meetings. All 40 inmates on the wing will attend, plus as many staff as possible. The aim is to facilitate the day-to-day functioning of the community (for example, it considers requests concerning jobs, home leave, changes to the regime or routine (Morris 1999b)), but also acts as a further extension and development of the therapeutic process. Smartt (2001) describes these meetings as direct democracy, where there is often collective decision-making and the challenging of wrongdoers. She also observed how wing meetings concentrated on 'dynamic and non-directive psychotherapy' (27). Extraordinary wing meetings, known as 'Specials' can be called at any time of the night or day if there has been a crisis that needs immediate attention. Outside this formal group therapy, therapy also occurs through education and art projects, psychodrama and dramatherapy, where offenders recreate their lives and offences, with inmates taking it in turns to be their victims. One successful music project is 'Good Vibrations', which has been assessed as having a significant impact on social skills, self-esteem and confidence (see Wilson *et al.* 2009).

In addition to organised treatment, inmates at Grendon enjoy significantly more association time when compared to other main estate prisoners, and so informal therapy takes place during these times as well. This can either be individual sessions between staff and inmates or, more commonly, sessions between inmates. This informal counselling is probably one of the reasons why relations between staff and inmates at Grendon are so good, especially when compared to staff/prisoner relations in traditional prisons. One Grendon inmate, for example, described a psychologist as his 'best friend' (Alexandrovich and Wilson 1999: vi). Grendon works under a no-confidentiality rule and so, interestingly, anything that is discussed out of the group is fed back at the next session.

Through this formal and informal therapy, inmates are expected to achieve a number of things that Genders and Player (1995) have translated into a five-stage career model, shown in Figure 4.1. While inmates will progress at different speeds and not all will reach stage five, either because they are voted out of the community, have made as much progress as they are likely to, or have come to the end of their time on the TC, stage five is obviously the ultimate goal.[8] Active participation and engagement in therapy and constant feedback from others is not easy for inmates, and arguably time within a TC is more punishing and emotionally draining than sitting in a main estate prison cell. As one inmate recounted, 'Doing TC-time is different from doing ordinary bird. It is much tougher' (Smartt 2001: 14). So, while many critics of Grendon and Dovegate view their regimes as being the soft option for offenders, in reality, it is probably harsher and more punitive and, as discussed below, more effective in terms of reducing reoffending rates.

The therapeutic environment at Grendon and Dovegate is thus in stark contrast to the regime that is seen in the main estate. In addition to the emphasis on treatment, other differences between TCs and other prisons include the use of first names, rather than numbers; respect practised between staff and inmates (Wilson and McCabe 2002); the existence of a no-violence rule (with anyone breaking this voted out of the community); less usage of illegal substances; and better motivation to change (Genders and Player 1993). As Wilson explains,

Stage 1	Recognition	Definition of problem
Stage 2	Motivation	Expression of desire to change
Stage 3	Understanding	Recognition of inter-connected and related aspects of life (beginning of therapy)
Stage 4	Insight	Identification of solutions to problems
Stage 5	Testing	Putting into practice new ways of coping (both within the prison and during periods of home leave)

Figure 4.1 Genders and Player's five-stage career model (Genders and Player 1995: 149, bracketed words not in original).

> The greatest difference between Grendon and many other prisons is quite simple: the motivation that inmates have to change their criminal behaviour, and a regime which facilitates as opposed to frustrates that process; and the respect that staff have for the prisoners as individuals. This difference is the 'success' of Grendon.
>
> (1992: 23)

Such differences have resulted in significant changes to the 'inmate culture' (that is, the culture that most inmates would experience in the main estate). In Grendon, for example, there is no pecking order or hierarchy between prisoners. Status and kudos are achieved not by being 'hard' or 'acting up' but by showing a commitment to the therapy and to the community. There is also a high level of integration between Rule 45[9] and 'normal' prisoners, and, completely opposite to standard prison behaviour, inmates are expected to 'grass' on others by informing the officers if there have been breaches of violence or other misdemeanours. Rather than grassing, however, this is seen as 'therapeutic feedback' (Genders and Player 1995:126).

Efficacy

While the TC regime is innovative, it can only be held to be 'the jewel in the crown' of the Prison Service if it delivers in terms of protecting the public and preventing crime. In an attempt to answer this fundamental question, there have been a number of studies that have tried to assess the effect of TCs on reconviction rates. One of the first was carried out by Newton (1971), who compared Grendonites to released 'patients' in Wormwood Scrubs. The control group chosen by Newton was not analogous to the Grendon sample and so it is perhaps unsurprising that he found no significant difference between the two groups. Next was the study undertaken by Gunn *et al.* (1978), which compared Grendonites with a sample from a local prison, again not a fair comparison. Subsequently, a Grendon effect was not found. In fact, Gunn *et al.* found that those who had undertaken treatment at Grendon actually reoffended at a slightly higher rate than the control group. This was then followed up 10 years later, with similar negative results. While the Grendon group was not found to be reoffending at a greater rate than the control sample (both groups were found to have an 80 per cent reoffending rate and to be similar in both frequency and severity of their offending behaviour), there was still no evidence that there was a Grendon effect (Gunn and Robertson 1987).

The 1990s onwards, however, have seen much more positive results, with Cullen (1992), for example, finding correlations between treatment effect and the length and quality of therapy. This was also emphasised by Genders and Player (1995), who noted that the greater benefits of Grendon were experienced by those who had been there the longest. Those who had been at Grendon for between 6 and 12 months reported benefits of increased self-confidence, improvements in social skills and communication, and higher levels of tolerance. Those who had served 12 months and over reported all of this, plus having gained insight into their own problems and understanding and empathy of problems faced by others. Relating back to the authors' five-stage career model (Figure 4.1), they found that, the longer the inmate stayed at Grendon, the further along the model the prisoner would progress, with the optimal time for full completion of the model being 18 months or more.

Genders and Player also conducted a reconviction study based on 214 men released from Grendon between January 1984 and December 1989. The Grendonites showed a slightly lower reconviction rate when compared to a prison control group, with Grendon graduates reoffending at a rate of 33.2 per cent within the first two years, as compared to a rate of 42–47 per cent from the prison control group. Broken down further, those who stayed 18 months or more at Grendon reoffended at a rate of 20 per cent, which was significantly lower than the 40 per cent rate for those whose term at Grendon was less than 18 months. Interestingly, the reconviction rate was only 16 per cent when the inmate had been released directly into the community, rather than returned to the main prison estate, and only 7 per cent where the inmate had achieved stage five on the career model (Genders and Player 1995). This would suggest that optimal results will be achieved by offenders who serve 18 months or more at Grendon, achieve stage five on the career model and are released directly into the community rather than being allowed to revert back to inmate culture within the main prison estate.

Marshall (1997) also carried out a further reconviction study in 1997 based on 700 prisoners who had received therapy at Grendon between 1984 and 1989. The 700 Grendonites (the Admitted Group) were compared with 142 prisoners (the Waiting List Control Group) who had been selected for Grendon within the same time period, but for a number of reasons did not actually go. As this was quite a small group, the Grendonites were also compared to a General Prison Group. These were prisoners who had similar characteristics with regards to sentence length, offence type and age (ibid.). Data was collected to allow a comparison of reconviction rates at the four-year stage. Comparing the Waiting List Control Group with the General Prison Group, Marshall found that the former were significantly more likely to have reoffended and more likely to have received a custodial sentence on reconviction. Marshall (1997) suggests that this implies not only that Grendon inmates are those who display a high risk of reoffending, but consequently that previous reconviction studies that compared Grendonites with prison control groups were underselling the effect of the TC, as they were not comparing like with like. When comparing the Admitted Group with the Waiting List Control Group, again it was the latter group who were more likely to have reoffended, more likely to have been imprisoned and more likely to have committed violent offences. On the basis that there is no selection process between being on the waiting list and actually being admitted into Grendon, Marshall argues that this proves a 'treatment effect' (ibid. 1997: 3).

Other interesting findings related to the length of time that the offender spent at Grendon and whether the inmate was released into the community at the end of his Grendon stay. Not surprisingly, Marshall found that, the longer an inmate stayed at Grendon, the lower his risk of reoffending became, with an 18-month stay resulting in a one-fifth to one-quarter reduction in risk of reoffending.

Regarding sexual and violent offenders, results suggested that the best treatment effect was noticed in older inmates who had two or more previous convictions, with greater reductions found among sexual offenders. Lower reconvictions were also noted for those who were released directly into the community, a point also emphasised by Smartt (2001). Despite this evidence, due to the increased lifer population, the vast majority of present offenders, once they have completed their time in the TC, are transferred back to the main prison estate. Smartt (2001) argues that it would be far better if release could be into the community or, if this is not legally possible, prison transfer should be made to at least a Category D or open prison.

To supplement the above study, Taylor carried out a further reconviction study in 2000, using the same inmates as above but with data at the seven-year stage (Taylor 2000). Results showed that the Waiting List Control Group were again more likely to have reoffended, more likely to have committed a violent offence and more likely to have been given a custodial sentence than the General Prison Group. These findings were also true when comparing the Waiting List Control Group with the Admitted Group. With regards to time spent at Grendon, general reconviction rates were found to be 71 per cent for inmates staying less than 6 months, but 62 per cent for those who stayed for more than 18 months. The seven-year study also showed a greater difference in violent reconviction between the Waiting List Control Group and the Admitted Group, when compared to the four-year reconviction study. In particular, Taylor claims that Grendon has a particular effect on 'repeat sexual offenders and older violent offenders' (ibid.: 3). Taylor was also able to show that of the lifers who had spent time at Grendon, at the 4-year stage, 8 per cent were reconvicted for a further standard list offence. This was lower than the 12 per cent of all lifers released from prison in 1987 and significantly lower than the 24 per cent of lifers who in terms of characteristics most closely matched those who were part of the Admitted Group. At the 7-year stage, reconviction rates for lifer Grendonites was 11 per cent compared to the expected rate of 28 per cent. This had led Taylor to conclude that there is a treatment effect of Grendon 'particularly for those who stayed at least 18 months, life sentence prisoners and repeat sexual offenders' (ibid.: 4).

In addition to effectiveness in terms of reoffending rates, it must also be remembered that Grendon and Dovegate are Category B/C prisons and, as described above, house a number of serious sexual and violent offenders. In addition to working as a TC, they also need to work as custodial institutions. Assessing this question, Wilson and McCabe argue that, in its 40-year history, Grendon has had very few disciplinary problems – only one hostage incident, four escapes and no rooftop protests. This, they claim, is proof 'of change amongst the inmates' (2002: 281) and proof that it can work as well, if not better, than a mainstream prison in terms of public protection. Genders and Player (1995) reiterate this, stating that breaches of security are rare (although three inmates did manage to escape in 2001 (Bennett 2009)) – inmates believe it is a privilege to be there, there are no industrial action problems with staff and staff feel enhanced by being involved in the therapy process. Morris (1999b) too sums up the situation:

'Grendon men maintain "good order and discipline" not because they have to, but because they want to' (2). On the basis that Grendon therefore works not just as a prison, but also in terms of reducing recidivism, Morris concludes:

> The fact that security can be maintained in such a humane environment makes Grendon a model of prison craft good practice, and the empirically demonstrated efficacy of the treatment confirms Grendon's lead in the treatment of severe personality disordered offenders.
>
> (1999b: 2)

This was also emphasised in a 2009 inspection that concluded, 'this inspection reaffirmed Grendon's remarkable achievements with some of the system's most dangerous and difficult prisoners' (HMIP 2009: 6).

Despite such positive results, TCs have been criticised as well. Recent concerns voiced by HMIP, for example, relate to financial efficiency savings that the inspectors claim are having a damaging effect on the TC environment. From an announced inspection at Grendon carried out in March 2009, it was noted that time out of cell, and thus free association time, had been reduced; therapeutic groups had been cancelled and supervision had been restricted. Intended as a dire warning to the Prison Service to avoid disrupting the benefits achieved by Grendon, Anne Owers remarked: 'Therapeutic communities are not cheap, but they are effective. The National Offender Management Service should commission an independent cost-benefit analysis of this unique establishment to ensure that its true value is recognised and, thereafter, properly funded and supported' (HMIP 2009: 6). Such efficiency savings have meant, for example, that there is no therapy at Grendon between Friday afternoon and Monday morning and it is rare that group sessions are now facilitated by the same member of staff (Wilson 2010). Such cuts may have contributed to an incident in August 2010, where one Grendonite was murdered by another inmate. While such an incident is regrettable, and indeed a blot on the establishment's history of good order and discipline, it should not be seen as an excuse to close the institution or used as evidence for the claim that TCs do not work. Concerns have also been raised about the lack of resettlement work that is undertaken within TCs; although, as noted above, due to the fact that many inmates will be transferred back into the main prison estate rather than directly into the community, perhaps it is understandable why such an absence exists. TCs are also often criticised because of their cost, with a Grendon bed costing approximately £10,000 more per annum than a Category B prison bed. Although, when it is taken into account the type of offender that is detained in Grendon, it may be fairer to compare the cost to that spent on beds at high-security hospitals or on DSPD units (see Chapter 9). A place at a high-security hospital costs approximately £250,000 per year and a DSPD place costs £200,000. This makes the figure of £48,000 for a Grendon bed seem almost insignificant (ibid.).

Dovegate has also been criticised for considering financial gain before therapeutic need, with Anne Owers in a recent HMIP inspection stating:

> Population pressures, and a contract focused on filling beds rather than treatment integrity, compounded the problem, but with treatment standards having fallen along with staff morale, urgent action is now required by Serco and the National Offender Management Service to salvage what was previously an innovative unit.
>
> (HMIP 2008a: 6)

When, on the whole, TCs appear to be effective in governing serious sexual and violent offenders, it is imperative that Dovegate is not just turned around and that the small number of TCs in England and Wales remain, but that their number is steadily increased, so that the risk that these serious offenders pose is continually decreased.

Release and recall

As previously mentioned, the vast majority of dangerous offenders imprisoned for serious sexual and violent offences will, at some point, be released into the community. The procedure for this differs depending on whether the offender is categorised as a short-term, medium-term or long-term prisoner, with, for example, short-term prisoners being automatically released at the halfway stage of their sentence. Due to the content of this chapter thus far, this section will concentrate on the parole process for those serving indeterminate life sentences. As outlined above, this includes those serving mandatory life, discretionary life and sentences of IPP (information regarding the parole process for determinate prisoners can be found in HM Prison Service 2005).

For prisoners serving indeterminate sentences, release is dependent on a decision by the Parole Board. The Parole Board is a non-departmental public body that is made up of judges, psychiatrists, those who have the knowledge and experience of supervising discharged prisoners and those who 'have made a study of the causes of delinquency or the treatment of offenders' (CJA 2003: Schedule 19, para. 2(2)). The Board has the power to order release once the minimum notional term has been served. This is the part of the sentence that the prisoner has to serve in custodial conditions for reasons of punishment. A prisoner will only be released prior to this if there are exceptional compassionate circumstances and the Parole Board is satisfied that the risk of harm that the prisoner poses to the public is of an acceptable level (HM Prison Service 2008b). The Parole Board's budget for 2007/08 was £7.6 million, which was increased for 2008/09 to £8.36 million to meet additional casework demands (Parole Board 2010a).

Due to the dramatic increase in indeterminate prisoners, HM Prison Service has recently set out a new Generic Parole Process (GPP) that, since April 2009, is used for all pre-tariff and post-tariff indeterminate-sentenced prisoners. The GPP timescale and process is divided into three stages, with the first stage commencing 26 weeks prior to week 0, which is the first day of the calendar month in which the Parole Board intend to list and hear the case. This, therefore, gives the Prison Service and all other involved agencies approximately six months to collect information on the offender to go into the parole dossier. The dossier will include reports on the lifer's background and main index offence, the trial judge's comments regarding sentencing, the offender's time in prison (including whether he has completed offending behaviour programmes or has spent time in a TC or within the CSC system, whether he has absconded or attempted to escape and what category of prison he is currently in), the lifer's awareness of the impact of his offending, risk-assessment information, medical, psychological and psychiatric reports, reports from probation officers, and plans for release (Directions to the Parole Board under s. 32(6) CJA 1991). The second stage is the calendar month during which the oral hearing should occur, with all decisions regarding lifers now made after an oral hearing. Since April 2005, all indeterminate prisoners have the right to an oral hearing, although in 2007/08, 397 waived this (Padfield 2009), presumably because they knew that release was highly improbable. If the right is waived, then a decision will be made by a paper panel. Finally, the third stage is two weeks after the oral hearing, at which point the Board needs to provide its decision with reasons (HM Prison Service 2009b).

For long-term lifers, the first parole review will usually occur three years before the end of their minimum tariff and is known as the pre-tariff review. Although the Parole Board cannot release the offender until the tariff expires, they can recommend that the offender be transferred to open conditions, with it being usual that the last two years of a lifer's sentence is spent in a Category D prison (Creighton *et al.* 2005). This has been met with approval by the courts (*R. v Secretary of State for the Home Department, ex p Stafford* [1998] 1 WLR 503). If the prisoner is a short-tariff lifer (that is, is serving less than six years), the pre-tariff review will usually take place at the halfway stage (HM Prison Service 2009b). In assessing whether a prisoner should be transferred to open conditions the Board must consider:

- the extent to which the lifer has made sufficient progress during sentence in addressing and reducing risk to a level consistent with protecting the public from harm, in circumstances where the lifer in open conditions would be in the community, unsupervised, under licenced temporary release;
- the extent to which the lifer is likely to comply with the conditions of any such form of temporary release;
- the extent to which the lifer is considered trustworthy enough not to abscond;
- the extent to which the lifer is likely to derive benefit from being able to address areas of concern and to be tested in a more realistic environment, such as to suggest that a transfer to open conditions is worthwhile at that stage.

(ibid.: 26)

The Parole Board can either recommend transfer to open conditions or issue a 'knockback' (Creighton *et al.* 2005: 230). If it is the latter, the prisoner will be given a date for a subsequent review hearing, which will usually take place at tariff expiry. The right to this review process for transfer to open conditions, and also for eventual release, is protected by Article 5(4) ECHR.[10]

The second parole hearing for most prisoners takes place just before tariff expiry where the Board is asked to consider the prisoner's suitability for release. The GPP, as described above, will be followed once more, with 26 weeks given to collect and present the necessary paperwork to the Board. When deciding whether to release a life-sentenced prisoner, the Parole Board must be satisfied that 'it is no longer necessary for the protection of the public that the prisoner should be confined' (s. 28(6) Crime (Sentences) Act 1997). This has been referred to as the 'life and limb' test (that is, 'whether the lifer's level of risk to the life and limb of others is considered to be more than minimal' (Directions to the Parole Board under s. 32(6) CJA 1991: para. 4)). The risk in question relates specifically to serious sexual or violent offending, regardless of the main index offence, and replaces the previous broader test of 'any imprisonable offence'. It is therefore a breach of Article 5(4) of the ECHR to detain a post-tariff prisoner unless it can be justified on grounds of public protection (*Stafford v United Kingdom* [2002] 35 E.H.R.R. 32). In addition to the parole dossier, the Board will also listen to representations made on behalf of the prisoner and on behalf of the Secretary of State. On the basis of both written and oral evidence, the Board can either recommend or deny release. If it is the latter, the Board can consider whether the prisoner can be transferred to open conditions, if he is not already there, and a date for a subsequent review hearing is given. If the Board decides that the prisoner is suitable for release, they will recommend release to the Secretary of State.

If the Secretary of State agrees, the prisoner will be released on licence under a number of conditions that will be set by the Board. There are seven standard licence conditions that stipulate where the offender should live, that he should report to his supervising probation officer, that he should undertake work, not travel outside of the UK and refrain from offending behaviour. The prisoner may also be subject to additional or non-standard conditions, which can include having to see a psychiatrist/psychologist/medical practitioner, not working with children, and exclusion conditions that aim to keep the offender away from the victim/victim's family (*R. (on the application of Craven) v Secretary of State for the Home Department* [2001] EWHC Admin 850; HM Prison Service 2008b). While on licence, the offender will be supervised for a period of time by the probation service. What this length of time will be depends on the type of life sentence that was originally imposed. If the inmate was sentenced to either mandatory or discretionary life, then the licence and supervision will continue for the rest of his life. The offender may be recalled to prison at any time and made to serve the rest of his sentence in a custodial setting, if it is perceived that his risk is no longer manageable within a community environment. This will usually occur either because a licence condition has been breached or the offender has committed another criminal offence. The decision will be made by the Parole Board based on paperwork, but the offender can request an oral hearing and will be granted one if his reasons are thought sufficient (*Smith v Parole Board* [2005] UKHL 1). The prisoner will be reclassified and will return to the lifer system, having to work through all stages of the LSP, as described above, before being eligible for subsequent parole and release review. If the sentence was one of IPP, the offender can apply to the Parole Board for the licence to be cancelled after a period of 10 years, and then yearly thereafter if the application is unsuccessful. The inmate may be recalled to prison at any time during the period of the licence.

Reoffending rates for those released by the Parole Board have always been relatively low – for example, in 2006, the rate of recidivism was only 6.4 per cent (Bennett 2008a). However, despite this impressive statistic, and caused by a combination of populist punitiveness and the current moral panic with dangerous offenders, but also due to a number of high-profile murders committed by those who had been released (for example, the murders of John Monckton and Naomi Bryant), there has been greater cynicism of late in relation to releasing those offenders who are professed to be dangerous. For instance, despite the dramatic increase in the lifer population, the number of those prisoners who have been released on life licence has steadily decreased. In 2003, 223 lifers were released but this has progressively dropped to 205 in 2004, 200 in 2005 and 135 in 2006 (HC Deb, 20 July 2009, c1125W; HC Deb, 20 July 2009, c1125W). In 2007, the number of releases stood at 146 (HC Deb, 2 July 2009, c411W) and in 2008 was only 138 (Ministry of Justice 2009a). In 2007/08, only 15 per cent of all post-tariff prisoners were released, with the figure for IPP prisoners being a staggering 7 per cent (Padfield 2009). This might suggest, therefore, that Parole Board members are perhaps being over cautious in making release decisions, with such a view being confirmed by research based on four- and six-year follow-up rates of released sex offenders who were released from long-term imprisonment. Hood *et al.* found that, in general terms, 'Board members over-estimated, in particular, the risk of reconviction of sex offenders who had committed their crimes wholly within their own family unit as well as the risk of reconviction posed by deniers' (2002: 391).

The supervision of lifers released on licence has also been more rigorous, again due to the high-profile murders mentioned above, with the number of those recalled to prison dramatically increasing. For example, in 1999, only 34 prisoners on life licence were recalled (Ministry of Justice 2009a). This can be compared to 44 recalls in 2003, 111 in 2005 (Solomon 2008), 134 in 2007, 108 in 2008 and 124 in 2009 (Ministry of Justice 2010a). In 2007/08, the Parole Board considered 31,172 recall cases, which was 22 per cent more than the previous year (Padfield 2009). This reluctance to release, and therefore the need for subsequent hearings, plus the increase in the number of recalled lifers, consequently contributes to an ever-expanding workload for the Board. For example, between 2002 and 2007, the Board had a 73 per cent rise in its workload (ibid.). This, in turn, adds to the increasing lifer population, which subsequently clogs up the parole system and contributes to the already-existing delays in pre- and post-tariff review. Argued elsewhere (Harrison 2010a), this has led to a vicious circle of indeterminate sentencing. For example, between September 2006 and May 2007, only 32 per cent of oral hearings were heard on time, with 20 per cent heard 12 months or more later (Padfield 2009). The National Audit Office identified the main reason of delay as being the inability of the Board to put together a three-member panel due to insufficient Board members. The Parole Board does not, therefore, have sufficient operational capacity to meet its current duty. In September 2007, the Board needed to consider 300 cases, some of which dated back to 2006. In January 2008, this had risen to 460 cases, with operational capacity allowing review of only

100 to 120 cases (ibid.). In January 2010, the backlog stood at 700 pre-tariff cases (Parole Board 2010b), and so an announcement in July 2010 of an additional 48 Parole Board members was welcome (Ministry of Justice 2010b), although it still remains to be seen whether this will be sufficient to combat such huge backlogs of work.

Parole and IPP prisoners

Even though IPP prisoners are regarded as lifers, they serve incredibly short tariffs when compared to their mandatory and discretionary life counterparts. As detailed in Chapter 2, the median tariff given to IPP prisoners between April 2005 and March 2006 was just 30 months, with 20 per cent receiving less than 18 months (HM Chief Inspector of Prisons and HM Chief Inspector of Probation 2008) and, although tariffs should now be at least 2 years, they are still much shorter than the 'normal' lifer term. The introduction of IPP prisoners has therefore caused a massive increase in the workload of the Parole Board. Not only has the lifer population more than doubled in the last few years, but release decisions, which the prison service and other relevant agencies used to have years to prepare for, now need to take place in relatively short periods of time if the prisoner is to be reviewed before tariff expiry. Nichol has argued that the current situation has resulted in prisoners who are:

> entitled to be considered for release almost as soon as [they are] received into custody following trial. The practical effect can often be, therefore, that not only has the prison had no time to assess the individual for the purposes of writing reports, but that the [Parole] Board's role in assessing his risk to the public is rendered almost academic by the fact that nothing has changed in the very short period between the sentencing judge deciding he is a significant risk, and the [Parole] Board considering his case. The [Parole] Board must make up its own mind, regardless of what the judge said, but in practice there is very little to go on. Hence an enormous amount of resources are expended on what can sometimes appear to be a futile exercise.
>
> (Nichol 2007, cited by The Howard League for Penal Reform 2007: 14)

This has therefore led to an expansion of post-tariff prisoners. These are predominantly short-tariff prisoners who are being held under sentences of IPP and who, in the short time prior to their post-tariff status, have not been able to prove that their risk has been reduced to levels thought manageable within the community. Reduction in risk is often shown through completion of accredited offending behaviour programmes and the complaint by many post-tariff prisoners is that the prison service is not providing them with sufficient opportunities to complete such programmes before tariff expiry. In December 2008, there were 3,900 post-tariff IPP prisoners in custody (HC Deb, 12 January 2009, c519W), which slightly reduced in January 2010 to 2,468 (HC Deb, 26 January 2010, c731W), but stood at nearly 3,000 in July 2010 (Blunt 2010). On 5 November 2008, only 39 prisoners serving sentences of IPP had been released, with the average period between tariff expiry and actual release being 49 weeks (HC Deb, 10 November 2008, c873W). This delay in release also appears to be getting worse. On 4 March 2010, 95 indeterminate prisoners had been in prison 3 or more years beyond their minimum tariff (HC Deb, 8 March 2010, c94W), with the Parole Board, on average, releasing only 1 IPP prisoner a week (Blunt 2010).

The inability of post-tariff prisoners to show a reduction in risk was brought to a head in *Wells v Parole Board* ([2008] EWCA Civ 30), when the Court of Appeal were asked to consider whether the Secretary of State had acted unlawfully by failing to provide for measures to allow prisoners (Wells and others) serving indeterminate sentences to demonstrate to the Parole Board at tariff expiry that their detention was no longer necessary for reasons of public protection. This followed a Divisional Court declaration that such behaviour was unlawful and thus continued detention of post-tariff prisoners was also unlawful (*Wells v Parole Board* [2007] EWHC 1835). The prisoners were being held at prisons that were said to have limited resources for offending behaviour work, to the extent that they had not been able to progress through the relevant courses needed to show that they were safe for release by the time that their tariffs had expired. The Court of Appeal found that the Secretary of State's conduct was in breach of his public law duty, because the inadequate provision of offending behaviour programmes meant that a proportion of prisoners would be held in prison for longer than necessary, but that continued detention post-tariff was still lawful, unless the release decision was not adequately reviewed or the point was reached where detainment was no longer necessary for public protection. The latter part of the decision was appealed, with the appellants continuing to argue that post-tariff detention was unlawful (*Wells v Parole Board* [2009] UKHL 22). While the Secretary of State admitted that there had been systemic failures in the availability of behaviour programmes, and that this did amount to a breach of his public law duty, the House of Lords agreed with the Court of Appeal on the issue of the lawfulness of the continued detention. This, therefore, means that it is lawful to detain post-tariff prisoners as long as there is an effective review, so as not to breach Article 5(4) ECHR. The court has therefore taken a minimalist approach to the issue of post-tariff prisoners. As long as there is a policy and/or a procedure in place and this is followed, this has been deemed to be acceptable. If, however, the court had set a higher threshold, for example by stating that more programmes needed to be available by a certain date, and if this did not happen, then HM Prison Service were breaching human rights, this would have had huge implications on resources and governmental policy. For this reason, the House of Lords were always unlikely to order this, but it is a shame that it did not issue a stronger and more far-reaching judgment.

There have also been issues regarding the independence of the Parole Board. As stated above, the Board is a non-departmental public body that advises the Secretary of State in matters concerning the release and recall of indeterminate prisoners. While the Board is free to make its own decisions, these are only recommendations that the Secretary of State does not have to follow. Regarding the recommendation to transfer a prisoner from closed to open conditions, not following the Board's decision has been held to be lawful (*R. (on the application of Mitchell) v Secretary of State for the Home Department* [2008] EWHC 1370), although further cases have recently held that, if the decision not to follow the recommendation is irrational or without clear reasoning, the decision will be quashed (*R. (on the application of Guittard) v Secretary of State for Justice* [2009] EWHC 2951).

In addition, the Secretary of State also has the power to manipulate the makeup of the Parole Board by appointing its members and, through the issuing of rules of procedure and directions, influences how the Board approaches its duties. The Board, until recently, was also financially sponsored by the Ministry of Justice, although this was moved to the Access to Justice Group in April 2008 (Ministry of Justice 2009b). Such concerns led to the case of *R. (on application of Brooke) v Parole Board* ([2008] EWCA Civ 29), where the Court of Appeal held that, due to the above factors, the Parole Board was not sufficiently independent of the government. While this did not matter when the Board just advised on pre-tariff cases, when it began to assess the continued detention of post-tariff prisoners, it took on a judicial function (under Article 5(4) ECHR) and thus needed to be independent from the executive. This means that, arguably, the right to a fair hearing for prisoners under Article 6 ECHR is being denied to post-tariff prisoners. To ensure conformity on this and other issues surrounding the Board's function, power, status and financial sponsorship, the Ministry of Justice (2009b) issued a consultation paper, *The Future of the Parole Board*, in July 2009. While responses were scheduled for publication in February 2010, these were still awaited in December 2010.

Conclusion

The use of imprisonment for dangerous offenders over the last few years has been prolific and, although not all sexual and violent offenders are subjected to custodial terms, it is likely that the majority of serious offences will warrant an indeterminate sentence. Due mainly to the introduction of IPPs in 2005, but also to delays caused by and reticence displayed by the Parole Board, the lifer population imprisoned in England and Wales has almost doubled in the last few years. Despite this increase, there does, at last, appear to be a much greater acknowledgement that mental health is linked to violent and sexual behaviour. For long-term prisoners, especially those serving life, the function of the prison system is therefore not just about containment, but also about rehabilitation and reform. Research would suggest that this can best be achieved through individualised care management plans, whether this is through the MCBS, through the work that is undertaken in the CSC system or through TCs. Although there are some offenders who need to be solitarily confined, this only accounts for a critical few, and the prison service appears now to be favouring an approach much more centred on risk reduction and rehabilitation than ever before. Treating offenders like caged animals will only encourage then to act like animals, but by using TCs and, in general, a more therapeutic approach, risk reduction and a safer lifer population should be much more achievable. Not only does this provide a better environment for the prisoners involved, but makes the task of managing them when they are eventually released into the community much easier. Examples of these strategies of risk management are therefore discussed in the next chapter.

5

STRATEGIES OF RISK MANAGEMENT

Introduction

While some serious sexual and violent offenders will spend significant amounts of time in prison (as discussed in Chapter 4), almost all, at some point, will be granted parole and released into the community. For others, imprisonment will not have played a part in their sentence, with the crimes instead held to be commensurate with either a community order or a financial penalty. Regardless of which group an offender falls into, responsible authorities will employ a number of strategies in order to manage the offender's risk and safeguard the public's protection. This is especially important for those offenders who have been released from custody following a determinate sentence, as a reduction in risk is not required to necessitate release. While HM Inspectorate of Probation has noted that 'it is simply not possible to eliminate risk altogether, the public is entitled to expect that authorities will do their job properly, i.e. to take all reasonable steps to keep risk to a minimum' (2006: 4). Current approaches to achieve this aim include the use of registers, Multi-Agency Public Protection Arrangements (MAPPAs), polygraphs, satellite tracking technology and civil orders. How these risk-management strategies are used, including a brief look at their efficacy, is the subject matter of this chapter.

The use of registers

The first Sex Offender Register in England and Wales was introduced by the Sex Offenders Act 1997. Created largely due to calls from the Police Superintendents Association and the Association of Chief Police Officers (Thomas 2008b), it was thought that a register would help the police to identify suspects, prevent sexual crimes and act as a deterrent to further offending (Home Office 1996). At that time, all sexual offenders who had been convicted, cautioned or found not guilty by reason of insanity of a 'listed' sexual offence (Schedule 1 Sex Offenders Act 1997) were obliged to submit their details to the authorities so that they could be entered on to the register. Relevant information, such as the offender's name, date of birth and address, had to be supplied to the police within 14 days of either prison release, or of the court's sentence if it was to be served within the community. A failure to provide the information or a failure to keep the police notified of changes was a criminal offence punishable by either a level-five fine and/or six months imprisonment. The register did not work retrospectively and so did not include the 110,000 already convicted sex offenders (Thomas 2008b). Despite this, numbers on the register steadily grew and, by 31 August 1998, 6,262 offenders had been registered (Plotnikoff and Woolfson 2000). By 2000, this had grown to 8,608 (Thomas 2008b), with compliance rates noted as 94.7 per cent in 1998 (Plotnikoff and Woolfson 2000) and 97 per cent by 2001 (Home Office/Scottish Executive 2001).

When the register[1] was first created, the Home Office was adamant that it was 'a measure aimed at protecting the community from sex offenders not an additional penalty for the offender' (Home Office/Scottish Executive 2001). While this viewpoint has been affirmed by a number of court judgments (for example, *Attorney General's Reference (No 50 of 1997)* [1998] 2 Cr. App. R. (S.) 155; *Adamson v UK* (1999) 28 EHRR CD209 ECHR; *Forbes v Secretary of State for the Home Department* [2006] 1 WLR 3075; for more discussion on these cases see Rainey 2010), academics, and Thomas (2008b, 2010) in particular, have argued that changes made to the register since its creation have made it more punitive in nature. Whether this is so or whether it is just working as a better risk-management tool will be assessed in the remainder of this section.

The first of these changes was introduced by Schedule 5 of the Criminal Justice and Court Services Act 2000, and included a reduction in the timescale in which offenders had to register with the police from 14 to 3 days, foreign travel notification requirements (s. 86(1) Sexual Offences Act (SOA) 2003),[2] and powers allowing the police to photograph and fingerprint offenders at initial registration. Moreover, the punishment for failing to register or failing to notify the police of changed details rose from six months imprisonment to a maximum of five years. Further changes were then introduced under the SOA 2003, which completely overhauled the law regarding sexual offences. In force since 1 May 2004, the register and the notification requirements under it apply to all those who have been convicted, cautioned, found not guilty by reason of insanity or found to have been under a disability and to have committed an offence under Schedule 3.[3] The offender must, within three days of the relevant date, notify the police of his name and any other names used now or in the past, home address and any other address where he resides, date of birth, national insurance number and any other prescribed information (s. 83 SOA 2003). In Scotland, the requisite information also includes passport numbers and the Home Office in 2007 recommended that this should also be given in England and Wales in addition to email addresses, bank account details, particulars of any children living within the household and provision of a DNA sample (Home Office 2007). In the USA, additional information to that already mentioned includes 'previous criminal convictions, description of victim(s), modus operandi, detail and paraphernalia used in the offence, employment history, assessed level of risk, history of weapon use, history of substance abuse, [and] previous criminal justice contacts' (Hebenton and Thomas 1997:10). To date, none of this additional information has been made obligatory, although time will tell as to whether future changes will incorporate any of these suggestions. The offender has an ongoing duty to notify the police of any changes to this information, which has been reduced from eight to three days (s. 84 SOA 2003) and again it is a separate offence to fail to notify the police of changes or to provide false information. It is worth noting that the onus is placed on the offender to notify the police and not the other way around.

Other changes brought in by the SOA 2003 included the introduction of annual verification exercises, where the authorities are now obliged to verify, by personal visit, that the offender does indeed live where he says he does. Many new offences were also created, arguably widening the net of potential offenders who would then need to be added to the register: offenders had to notify the police of changes to their address even if the change was for eight days, the penalties for non-compliance for young offenders were raised (Thomas 2008b) and the obligation to register was widened to include those who had committed sexual offences abroad. Further 'strengthening' (Thomas 2010) was also seen in 2006, when the Home Office announced another six offences that were being added to the list of offences that would lead to registration. While it was accepted that these were not per se sexual (the offences include theft, burglary, harassment, outraging public decency, child abduction and sending prohibited articles by post), the Home Office argued that there could still have been a sexual motive involved (Home Office 2006, as cited in Thomas 2008b).

Another fundamental change came when the Home Office announced the creation of the Violent and Sex Offender Register (ViSOR), a national computer system that, in 2005, contained details of 47,000 dangerous people, 25,000 of whom were sex offenders (BBC News 2005). In 2009, this had reached 77,000 (National Policing Improvement Agency 2009), 32,000 of which were from the sex offender register (White 2010). Introduced following the Bichard Inquiry Report (Bichard 2004), which sought to establish how the Soham murderer Ian Huntley was able to work in a school following allegations of sexual offences, the database allows police, probation and prison services to share information on a national basis and has been designed to support the multi-agency approach (as detailed below). Although the creation of the register was announced in March 2005, the database only began to be rolled out into probation areas in October 2007 and was not nationally available until the spring of 2008 (Hansard 19 Nov 2007: Col 525W). ViSOR is currently managed by the National Policing Improvement Agency of the Home Office and is used by all police forces in England, Wales, Scotland and Northern Ireland, as well as HM Forces and other specialist police units. Other agencies include the Serious Crime Analysis Section, the Child Exploitation and Online Protection (CEOP) Centre and the Joint Border Operations Centre (National Policing Improvement Agency 2010).

ViSOR has been controversial in many respects. One of the most contentious is the fact that it includes details of both convicted and unconvicted people. For example, in July 2009, Greater Manchester Police confirmed that 16 people had been registered on ViSOR and categorised as potentially dangerous, even though they had not been convicted of a relevant offence. What is worse, of these 16, 4 had completely clean criminal records (Information Governance Unit 2009). People are therefore being labelled as potentially dangerous despite the fact that they have never committed a criminal offence. When the original register required a 'listed' sexual offence, this is a massive net widening of potential registrants. When the consequences of being on the register can be serious, such as community notification, it is questionable whether the decision to allow such labelling and inclusion is correct. Furthermore, it has been estimated that, between 2005 and 2015, ViSOR will cost the Home Office approximately £37.18 million (Hansard 19 Nov 2007: Col 526W). Despite these concerns, anecdotal evidence would suggest that ViSOR is a welcome addition. Terry Grange, Chief Constable of Dyfed-Powys Police, stated in 2007 that:

> We have been using the Violent and Sex Offenders database for a couple of years and this has ensured better risk assessments, linked-up intelligence and quicker information sharing between forces. I welcome the work that the National Offender Management Service is doing to roll out ViSOR to the Probation and Prison Services as this will further improve public protection arrangements.
>
> (Ministry of Justice 2007)

Roger Hill, Director of the probation service has confirmed this view: 'There are no easy solutions with offenders having such complex histories and multiple needs but here we see detailed sentence planning, careful monitoring and swift intervention before behaviour escalates to serious re-offending' (Ministry of Justice 2007). Perhaps due to this perceived success, there have been further suggestions that the European Parliament may be ready to implement an EU-wide register (BBC News 2007). Whether this will occur is presently unknown, but can be taken as evidence to suggest that the existence of registers is widely favoured. Whether there is any sound evidence that having such registers actually meets public protection aims will be assessed below.

Notification periods

The length of time that an offender will be on the register will depend on the original offence. This is known as the notification period and is outlined in Table 5.1. One aspect of this that has recently been considered by the courts is in relation to life notification. As noted in Table 5.1, if an offender is sentenced to 30 months or more, then he is subject to registration for an indefinite period of time. This life registration is without review and the recent case of *R (on the application of F) and Thompson v Secretary of State for the Home Department* has questioned whether registration for life without the possibility of review is lawful, both within the UK and under the ECHR. The case was first heard in the Divisional Court ([2008] EWHC 3170) in December 2008, where the applicants claimed that section 82 of the SOA 2003 was incompatible with Article 8 of the ECHR in that it subjected certain sex offenders to notification requirements indefinitely without the opportunity for review. This was felt to be worse in the case of F, who was only 11 at the time of his offence. The Divisional Court held that the absence of a review, especially in the case of a young offender, was incompatible with Article 8(3). Even in the case of an adult, lifetime registration without review was also found to be unjustifiable, with the court arguing that a person should be given the opportunity to question whether the notification requirement still served a legitimate aim. The Secretary of State appealed to the Court of Appeal ([2009] EWCA Civ 792), arguing that the interference with the rights of offenders was only slight, amounting to mere inconvenience and nothing more. Dismissing this claim, the Court of Appeal confirmed that life registration without review was incompatible with Article 8, especially in the case of young offenders, and on principle an offender was entitled to have the legitimacy of the notification requirements determined by a review process. While the Secretary of State argued that initiating a review process would be too burdensome on resources, the Court conversely argued that it may actually help the police, so that their work was not hindered by a register that contained large numbers of offenders who were no longer

Table 5.1 Notification periods under s. 82 Sexual Offences Act 2003

Description of relevant offender	*Notification period*
A person who, in respect of the offence, is or has been sentenced to imprisonment for life, to imprisonment for public protection under section 225 of the Criminal Justice Act 2003 or to imprisonment for a term of 30 months or more	An indefinite period beginning with the relevant date
A person who, in respect of the offence or finding, is or has been admitted to a hospital subject to a restriction order	An indefinite period beginning with that date
A person who, in respect of the offence, is or has been sentenced to imprisonment for a term of more than 6 months but less than 30 months	10 years beginning with that date
A person who, in respect of the offence, is or has been sentenced to imprisonment for a term of 6 months or less	7 years beginning with that date
A person who, in respect of the offence or finding, is or has been admitted to a hospital without being subject to a restriction order	7 years beginning with that date
A person within section 80(1)(d), i.e. someone who has been cautioned for a sexual offence	2 years beginning with that date

at risk of committing sexual offences. The Secretary of State appealed once more, with judgment delivered by the Supreme Court in April 2010 ([2010] UKSC 17). In a unanimous decision, the Supreme Court Justices upheld the decisions of the both the Divisional Court and the Court of Appeal, stating

> The indefinite notification requirements in section 82(1) of the Sexual Offences Act 2003 are incompatible with article 8 of the European Convention on Human Rights because they do not contain any mechanism for the review of the justification for continuing the requirements in individual cases.
>
> (*R. (on the application of F) and Thompson v Secretary of State for the Home Department* [2010] UKSC 17: para. 59)

What the Ministry of Justice will now do in response to this decision is currently unclear, although it is undisputed that some kind of review process will have to be developed and implemented. While the case will not result in the automatic ending of notification requirements, it will at least give offenders the chance of showing that their risk has reduced and that they no longer need to be kept on the register. How offenders will do this and whether the burden of proof will be on them to show this reduction is currently unknown.

Community notification

When the Sex Offender Register was first introduced, the Home Office refused to include a public right of access, believing that it could result in vigilante behaviour (Thomas 2003), and indeed this was what happened in some instances when the *News of the World*, through its 'Name and Shame' campaign, published photographs of known sex offenders on its front page in 2000 (see Thomas 2001; Silverman and Wilson 2002). Information was therefore only passed to individuals and agencies on a need-to-know basis in a 'controlled' fashion. This included agencies such as probation, social services, housing, schools and, in some instances, victims of offenders (Thomas 2003).

Over the last few years, however, access to the register has slowly been extended, with the first extension seen in November 2006 with the CEOP Centre creating a 'most wanted' internet site. The site displays details of convicted sex offenders who have gone missing and thus failed to comply with their notification requirements under the SOA 2003. A typical profile contains a photograph or photographs of the offender at differing ages, name, date of incident (if known), gender, age range, height, build, hair colour, hair length, ethnic appearance, distinguishing marks or features, and location (CEOP 2010a). Offenders are selected by the police, with their details uploaded once they have gone underground. When the site was first set up, five offenders were placed on it, and this would appear to be an average number of participants, with it only being used for the most prolific of missing offenders. For example, in April 2010, it was reported by the police that the whereabouts of 316 sex offenders were unknown (Davis 2010) while, on the same date, only five offenders were on the CEOP site. Since 2006, CEOP claims it has located 75 per cent of the offenders posted on the site (CEOP 2010b), with the first handing himself into police within days of it going live.

Due to the small numbers involved, the CEOP site is not akin to Megan's Law in the USA, where in all 50 states the public have a right of access to their own state's sex offender register (Thomas 2003). Forms of community notification in the USA include internet sites, where the public can input a zip code (postcode) and find out where offenders live in that area (for example, see www.meganslaw.ca.gov); informational leaflets being dropped into letterboxes; community notification meetings where the community meets the offender and listens to what he has done; use of the media to publish information, including having adverts placed in local newspapers; the marking of car documentation; advertising signs in front gardens or windows; and an obligation on registered offenders to go door to door introducing themselves to the community (for more information on all of these methods, see Thomas 2003). All of these forms of notification are disintegrative (Braithwaite 1989; McAlinden 2007), which means that they place stigma on the offender and therefore work to isolate him from the community that he is attempting to settle in. It can be argued, therefore, that such techniques only work to encourage offenders to go underground where they cannot be monitored by the authorities, and also encourage the setting up of what are perceived to be supportive sex offender networks. The closest that the CEOP site gets to such disintegrative practices is the 'most wanted' alerts, whereby the public can sign up to be notified when new offenders are entered on to the list (see www.ceop.gov.uk/wanted/newsletter.asp), but even this is not equivalent to Megan's Law.

Further extensions to community notification have also recently been seen through the 'presumption to disclosure'. This was first suggested by the Home Office in Action 4 of its *Review of the Protection of Children from Sex Offenders* (hereafter known as the Review) in 2007. Referred to in this and the subsequent chapter, the Review sought to explore how child protection could be improved and how greater reassurance to the public on the management of sex offenders could be provided. In addition to several other proposals, the Review suggested that information from the register should be provided to anyone who was in a personal relationship with a known sex offender and who was thus being given regular unsupervised access to children in a private context (Home Office 2007). A new legal duty was therefore created under the CJIA 2008, which states that responsible authorities have to consider whether information concerning an offender's previous convictions should be disclosed. Under section 140 of the Act (which inserts s. 327A of the CJA 2003), a presumption of disclosure exists where the responsible authority for the area has reasonable cause to believe that:

(a) a child sex offender managed by it poses a risk in that or any other area of causing serious harm to any particular child or children or to children of any particular description, and

(b) the disclosure of information about the relevant previous convictions of the offender to the particular member of the public is necessary for the purpose of protecting the particular child or children, or the children of that description, from serious harm caused by the offender.

(s. 327A(3) CJA 2003)

Interestingly, the presumption to disclose exists whether or not 'the person to whom the information is disclosed requests the disclosure' (s. 327A(4) CJA 2003). This, therefore, means that the responsible authority, in most cases the police, can decide to warn a parent even if that parent has not actively contacted them. Such practice is not new, with 'discretionary disclosure' seen in the cases of *R v Devon County Council ex parte L* ([1991] 2 FLR 541) and *R v North Wales Police ex parte AB and CD* ((1997), *The Times*, 14 July), where authorities warned parents and neighbours about the actual and/or suspected sexual offences of individuals. Despite the existence of such cases, the court in the latter case did make a point of noting that access should never be made on a blanket basis and should only be made where there was a specific risk of reoffending, and therefore risk to children (Thomas 2003; for information on the extent of discretionary disclosure prior to the disclosure pilots, see Cann 2007).

Following the new legal duty to disclose, disclosure pilots began in September 2008 in Hampshire (Southampton), Cleveland (Stockton District), Cambridgeshire (Northern Division, including Peterborough and surrounding villages) and Warwickshire (force-wide) (Directgov 2008). At the 6-month stage, in March 2009, positive results led to the decision to extend the pilot force-wide in Cleveland, Cambridgeshire and Hampshire (including the Isle of Wight) (Home Office 2009a). The Home Office claimed that at least 10 children had been protected from potential abuse following 153 enquiries and 79 applications for information. Six months on from this, the results of the research study were released (Kemshall and Wood 2010). Over the first 12-month period, the police areas involved received 585 enquiries, of which 315 were proceeded with as applications and 21 sexual offending disclosures made. A further 11 general disclosures (including violence) were also given, while another 43 cases led to a range of other child safeguarding actions, including referral to Children's Social Care (ibid.). The Home Office claimed that this had protected approximately 60 children (Home Office 2010). The police forces involved noted how they were not overrun with enquiries and importantly, as stated by Chief Constable Paul West, 'there has been no evidence to suggest that any registered sex offenders in the pilot areas have gone missing and driven underground' (White 2010). The research undertaken by Kemshall and Wood (2010) also noted that there was no evidence to suggest serious breaches of confidentiality and how most applicants were satisfied with the process of applying for information, although they felt on their own if they received distressing news.

Following such positive results, the Home Office announced a further extension to the scheme on 3 March 2010. This will include 18 additional police force areas from August 2010, with a national roll-out to all remaining forces by the end of

March 2011 (Home Office 2010). The scheme therefore gives parents, carers and guardians a statutory right to register an interest in a person whom they have suspicions or concerns about if they have access to their children and, interestingly, in the pilots, the largest number of queries were said to come from fathers who were worried about the men that their children were living with (White 2010). If the named person is considered to be a risk, the police will disclose information on that person. Anyone providing false information, in an attempt to find out whether a neighbour is on the register, will be subject to police action, as too will those who pass on information.

Efficacy

As has been documented above, since initial creation, the Sex Offender Register has arguably gone from strength to strength, both in terms of the numbers who are currently on it but also in terms of its power over dangerous offenders and their lives. One question that must be asked, however, is whether the existence of registers actually contributes to public protection and, bearing in mind the attention that the registers have been given, both by the public and politicians, it is perhaps somewhat surprising that evidence of actual efficacy is negligible. One of the first studies that looked at this question was undertaken by Hebenton and Thomas (1997), which, among other issues, looked at whether the existence of registers in the USA helped in the investigation and prevention of further sexual offending. While there was anecdotal evidence from the police, who argued that it did help, the overall finding was that there was simply not enough evidence to answer the question either way. Logan has concluded that the register in the USA is an 'untested article of faith' (Logan 2003, cited by Thomas 2010: 76) and Long asserts that there is simply no evidence to suggest that community notification is effective in terms of general public protection (2009). Subsequent evaluations in the UK have been similarly inconclusive in their findings (Plotnikoff and Woolfson 2000), with the fact remaining that we simply do not know whether the register is an effective risk-management strategy. The only information that has been provided is that of compliance rates, which, as already mentioned, are incredibly high, but even compliance rates do not tell us whether the register aids in terms of risk management. Controversially, the fact that Roy Whiting was on the register did not prevent him from kidnapping and murdering Sarah Payne – arguably the case that has been used as justification for many of the recent changes documented here.

Bearing all of this in mind, the obvious question is, therefore, why we continue to have a register and why, over the last decade, the government has proceeded to tighten, strengthen and spend huge amounts of money on it. While the answer to this could be a chapter in its own right, suffice to say here, it is because of populist punitiveness, a desire for the government to be seen as tough on law and order and even worse a desire to respond to media agendas (for more on this, see Garland 2001; Tonry 2004; Thomas 2010). As Thomas concludes, 'The sex offender register is arguably a prime example of criminal justice policy made at political level in response to perceived populist demands and with no real supporting experience or research to support it' (2008b: 93).

Multi-Agency Public Protection Arrangements

In addition to the register, the main way in which offenders are managed in the community is through Multi-Agency Public Protection Arrangements (MAPPAs). These were first introduced into England and Wales through the Criminal Justice and Court Services Act 2000, which created a statutory duty on both the police and the probation service (known as the responsible authority) to establish arrangements for assessing and managing the risks posed by community-based offenders. MAPPA is now governed by sections 325–327 CJA 2003, which adds the prison service to the responsible authority and imposes a duty on a number of agencies to cooperate with it. These 'Duty to Cooperate Agencies' are listed in the Act and include: Youth Offending Teams; Ministers of the Crown exercising functions in relation to social security, child support, war pensions, employment and training; Primary Care Trusts, NHS Trusts, Strategic Health Authorities and Local Health Boards; registered social landlords who accommodate MAPPA offenders; Local Housing Authorities; Local Education Authorities; and relevant electronic monitoring providers (s. 325(6) CJA 2003).

MAPPA panels are therefore made up of representatives from the police, probation, prison, social services, health and housing, although it is also good practice, where appropriate, to additionally include forensic psychiatrists and psychologists (Maguire *et al.* 2001). The CJA 2003 also introduced the appointment of two lay advisors to the Strategic Management Board (which the responsible authority is accountable to) who act as independent informed observers and are able to ask questions of the professionals that they themselves may not have thought of. The idea behind their introduction is that they bring an understanding of the local community to MAPPA. The purpose of MAPPA is therefore to help in reducing the risk that sexual and violent offenders pose to the public. This is achieved by identifying MAPPA offenders, sharing information safely and securely, assessing risk and managing offenders through the most suitable risk-management plans (National Offender Management Service (NOMS) 2009). In addition to this, as noted above, the responsible authority is also under a duty to decide whether it should disclose information regarding the previous convictions of those who it supervises, with this duty operational irrespective of whether information is actually requested. Due to the 'professional' nature of MAPPA, Kemshall and Wood explain how it fits in with the 'community protection model' (Connelly and Williamson 2000):

> This model is embedded in the criminal justice system and is characterized by the use of restriction, surveillance, monitoring and control, compulsory treatment and the prioritization of victim/community rights over those of

> offenders. Special measures such as license conditions, tagging, exclusions, registers and selective incapacitation are all extensively used. Risk management plans are devised and delivered by statutory agencies in partnership with police and probation as key drivers . . . Risk decisions are seen as the preserve of the experts, with the public largely excluded and characterized as both irrational and as a potential site of risk.
>
> (Kemshall and Wood 2007a: 207)

The community-protection model views offenders as rational choice agents and thus takes the view that they are responsible for their own actions (that is, they can decide whether or not to reoffend) (Kemshall and Wood 2007a).

To qualify for MAPPA, the offender must be one of three categories of offenders. Category 1 offenders are registered sex offenders, Category 2 are violent and other sex offenders, and Category 3 are all other offenders who the responsible authority consider are likely to cause serious harm to the public. For the purposes of Category 1, a sex offender is defined as anyone who is subject to the notification requirements in the SOA 2003, as outlined above. To qualify as a violent offender, the person must have been convicted either of murder or of one of 65 specified violent offences listed in Schedule 15 of the CJA 2003 *and* have been sentenced to at least 12 months imprisonment or made subject to either a Hospital or Guardianship Order under the Mental Health Act (MHA) 1983. Other sexual offenders in Category 2 are either those who are not required to abide by notification requirements or those whose offence is not listed in Schedule 15 CJA 2003 (such as those subject to disqualification orders),[4] or where the sentence imposed is less than 12 months (NOMS 2009). Category 3 offenders are all those who do not qualify under either Category 1 or 2, yet it is still thought that inter-agency management is necessary. For a responsible authority to register an individual as a Category 3 offender, it must

> Establish that the person has committed an offence which indicates that they are capable of causing serious harm to the public; and reasonably consider that the offender may cause serious harm to the public which requires a multi-agency approach at level 2 or 3 to manage the risks.
>
> (ibid.: 56)

A potential Category 3 offender must have either been convicted of or cautioned for a criminal offence, although this does not need to be listed in Schedule 15 nor committed within the UK (NOMS 2009). Potentially dangerous persons may also come under the umbrella of MAPPA if they have been placed on ViSOR (ibid.).

The MAPPA panel will work together by sharing information and assessing risk to ensure that each offender within its remit has an individualised risk-management plan. On the basis that risk management is the primary aim, offenders will initially be placed into a MAPPA level, of which there are three. Level 1 deals with low- and medium-risk offenders who either do not have any factors that suggest a real risk of harm, or, while they do have some identified risk factors and thus the potential to cause harm, they are thought unlikely to do so, unless some factor changes such as alcohol or drug misuse (Craig *et al.* 2008). Risk management will therefore only involve one agency, usually police or probation, who will manage the offender without the active or significant involvement of the other agencies. In 2008/09, 75.59 per cent of all MAPPA offenders were managed at this level (Ministry of Justice 2010c), with this type of intervention known as normal agency management. Referral of an offender to Level 2 is made where the active involvement of more than one agency is needed in order to effectively address risk. This will usually involve both police and probation, supported by information provided by other relevant agencies. Level 2 offenders are seen as high risk in that they are viewed as having identifiable risk factors, with the chance of them reoffending regarded as fairly high (Craig *et al.* 2008). In 2008/09, 22.34 per cent of MAPPA offenders were managed in this way (Ministry of Justice 2010c), with Level 2 working known as local inter-risk agency management. Finally, Level 3 is reserved for the critical few (that is, those very high-risk offenders who pose the highest risks of causing serious harm and whose management is so problematic that not only is multi-agency cooperation needed at a senior level, but it is likely that the commission of exceptional resources will be required). Management at this level is known as Multi-Agency Public Protection Panels, or MAPPPs. In 2008/09, the critical few made up 2.06 per cent of all MAPPA offenders (ibid.). All Level 2 and 3 offenders will be placed on ViSOR, with the record being archived when they are no longer under the management of MAPPA, but not removed until the offender's 100th birthday (NOMS 2009), although in light of *R (on the application of F) and Thompson v Secretary of State for the Home Department* (see above) this may now have to be reviewed.

The time period that an offender will remain eligible for MAPPA largely depends on which category of offender the person is classified as being. For example, Category 1 offenders will remain eligible until their period of registration expires, which, for some, will mean life. Category 2 offenders will remain eligible until either their licence expires or they are discharged from either a Hospital or Guardianship Order. Finally, a Category 3 offender will remain eligible until the responsible authority decides that their risk of harm has sufficiently reduced so that MAPPA intervention is no longer needed (NOMS 2009).

Efficacy and use

The numbers of offenders managed through MAPPA can be seen in Tables 5.2 and 5.3. As with all risk-management techniques, efficacy is highly important, with MAPPA being one of the few strategies that has been systematically researched and assessed regarding its use. In fact, one of the most influential studies (Maguire *et al.* 2001) looked at the work of public protection panels before MAPPA was even introduced. While the study found that, in general, risk-management practice was 'sound' (ibid.: 2), considerable variance was noted in practice, procedure, values

Table 5.2 Total number of MAPPA offenders in the community

Category	*2004/05*	*2005/06*	*2006/07*	*2007/08*	*2008/09*
1. Registered Sexual Offender (RSO)	28,994 17.99%	29,983 3.41%	30,416 1.44%	31,392 3.21%	32,336 3.0%
2. Violent offenders and other sexual offenders	12,662 –0.72%	14,292 12.87%	14,895 4.22%	16,249 9.09%	11,527 –29.1%
3. Other dangerous offenders	2,936 35.55%	3,313 12.84%	3,132 –5.46%	2,569 –17.98%	898 –65%
Totals	44,592 12.91%	47,588 6.71%	48,443 1.8%	50,210 3.65%	44,761

Source: Ministry of Justice 2010c

Table 5.3 MAPPA-eligible offenders on 31 March 2010

	Category 1	*Category 2*	*Category 3*	*Total*
Management levels	*Registered Sexual Offenders*	*Violent Offenders*	*Other Dangerous Offenders*	
Level 1	32,965	11,522	–	44,487
Level 2	1,856	1,183	576	3,615
Level 3	118	61	57	236
Total	34,939	12,766	633	48,338

Note: Category 3 offenders are only managed at Level 2 and Level 3.

Source: Ministry of Justice 2010d

and ideologies. Inadequate resourcing, preciousness over agency services, a lack of coordination and a lack of a multi-disciplinary approach were also cited as problems (Wood and Kemshall 2010). In an attempt to rectify this, the researchers recommended the use of a two-tier system; encouraged the involvement of agencies such as Health, Housing and Psychiatry; suggested a checklist of points that should be discussed at MAPPA meetings; and noted the need for a management committee. Most, if not all, of these recommendations have been brought into effect.

The next study, undertaken between 2003 and 2004 (Kemshall *et al.* 2005), was in effect an update to the research carried out by Maguire *et al.* (2001). On the whole, it was noted that there was greater effectiveness and consistency than before, areas were meeting the specifications of MAPPA as outlined in the guidance notes and, on the whole, 'MAPPA made a significant contribution to the effective management of high-risk offenders' (Kemshall and Wood 2009: 538). Despite this, a number of recommendations were still made, including a call for further Home Office guidance, the introduction of National Standards in relation to the critical few, that appropriate administrative support should be allocated and prioritised, and that protocols regarding disclosure and information sharing should be devised for 'Duty to Cooperate Agencies' (Kemshall *et al.* 2005). An additional review was subsequently carried out in 2006 (Kemshall and Wood 2007b), which again found that inter-agency cooperation and arrangements were well developed, there were minimal difficulties highlighted by the practitioners and, overall, MAPPA was thought to positively contribute to the supervision of offenders within the community. In particular, factors that were thought to be key to the effective supervision and management of MAPPA offenders were identified as 'timely and focused pre-release work', 'MAPPP attendance of victim liaison workers', 'early identification of need and referral to relevant treatment/group work programmes', 'offence-focused individual work', 'appropriate external controls', 'home visits to check and be lifestyle vigilant', 'police surveillance' and 'swift and appropriate information exchange' (ibid.: 3). More recently, Kemshall and Wood (2009) have added the correct identification and assessment of high-risk offenders, the encouragement of self (offender) risk management, swift enforcement and the use of supervised accommodation.

While the aforementioned studies have provided valuable advice on process and procedure, less is known on actual effectiveness (that is, does MAPPA manage, or even reduce, risk?). In some respects, this is difficult to assess. Some high-risk offenders will never reduce in risk even though the correct interventions have been employed and, conversely, lack of high-profile failure is not evidence of success (Kemshall and Wood 2009). What is needed, therefore, is research concentrating on serious further offending, which is now published in annual MAPPA reports, although only for Level 2 and 3 offenders. Between 2008/09, MAPPA statistics state that there were 48 SFOs carried out by Level 2 and 3 offenders. This is a significant reduction from the 79 committed in 2007/08 and the 82 carried out in 2006/07 (Ministry of Justice 2010c). For the period of 2008/09, this equated to only 0.44 per cent of all MAPPA offenders, suggesting that MAPPA is making a real contribution to risk management. However, what these figures do not show is the number of SFOs committed by the remaining 75 per cent of Level 1 offenders. From a freedom of information request, the BBC Panorama programme obtained information relating to SFOs committed by Level 1 offenders from 51 out of 84 police and probation services. For the period of 2008/09, 47 SFOs were reported to have been committed by Level 1 offenders (BBC 2009). Bearing in mind that only 61 per cent of those services contacted actually replied, the true figure is likely to be higher than this, although this still equates to a very low percentage rate of offenders who commit SFOs, especially when taking into account the thousands of offenders that MAPPA supervise. In fact, as noted by Wood and Kemshall (2010), the real threat to the effectiveness of MAPPA is often not the offenders themselves but the lack of adequate resources to allow the responsible authorities to do their job, and impossible expectations placed on it by politicians and the public alike.

Polygraph testing

In addition to structured ways of working, there are also a number of specific conditions/requirements that have been specifically created with violent and sexual offenders in mind. One such requirement for sex offenders is the polygraph condition. A polygraph is an instrument that measures physiological activity associated with the autonomic nervous system. Convoluted tubes are positioned on the offender's chest and abdominal area to record respiratory activity, two small metal plates are attached to his fingers to measure sweat gland activity and a blood pressure cuff is applied around the arm to record cardiovascular activity (Wilcox *et al.* 1999). During the test, physiological responses to a carefully structured set of questions are measured and recorded. These measures are then used to determine whether or not the subject has been telling the truth on the belief that the polygraph can detect any arousal associated with deception (Madsen *et al.* 2004). The use of polygraphs based on this theory is therefore fairly controversial, mainly because of questions regarding whether a polygraph really can determine whether someone is or is not telling the truth.

Polygraphs, for use with sex offenders, were first introduced into England and Wales in 1999, when trials were undertaken in West Midlands Probation Service. As with all of the pilots discussed in this section, the trial involved post-conviction testing and involved five offenders participating in a sex offender group-work programme (Wilcox *et al.* 1999). On the whole, results were positive, with probation officers finding out offence-specific and offence-related information that they otherwise would not have known about, even though four out of five offenders were found to have actually failed the tests (Wilcox and Sosnowski 2005). A further pilot study, involving 10 probation areas in England and Wales began in May 2003 and ran until June 2006 (Grubin 2006). In that time, 347 offenders were polygraphed, with 483 examinations carried out in total and a voluntary take-up rate of 43 per cent. In the first test, 79 per cent revealed previously undisclosed information and, in the second, 78 per cent revealed further previously undisclosed material; this was so regardless of whether the test result was 'passed', 'failed' or 'inconclusive' (ibid.: iv). Of these disclosures, 15 per cent were assessed as being medium in terms of seriousness and 19 per cent were thought to be high. Grubin concluded that

> Evidence arising from the pilot indicates that polygraphy has the potential to make an important contribution to the treatment and supervision of sex offenders on probation, contributing to public safety by enabling probation officers to better monitor risk and to bring about more effective and timely interventions.
>
> (ibid.: viii–ix)

However, it was also noted that the findings were 'indicative rather than definitive' (Grubin 2006: 57). Advocates of polygraphy therefore argue that it can be used with post-conviction sex offenders to 'obtain more reliable sexual histories and more accurate offence behaviour descriptions, both of which assist in overcoming denial and can improve the assessment of treatment need and risk of reoffending' (Grubin *et al.* 2004: 210).

Further research on polygraphs has been carried out by Madsen *et al.* (2004). Findings were founded on 50 community-based male sex offenders who had agreed to participate in the research, although it is worth noting that 116 offenders were initially approached, and so 57 per cent refused to be involved. At the first polygraph test, 64 per cent of the men were polygraphed, with 30 per cent refusing to participate at this stage. Of those who underwent the testing, 97 per cent revealed relevant 'risky' behaviours, 94 per cent of which had not been disclosed to their probation officers. The one subject who did not disclose any information failed the test. Three months later, a second test was undertaken, with 47 per cent agreeing to participate. On this occasion, 71 per cent disclosed relevant behaviours, although there was a significant decrease in levels of seriousness when compared to the first test. Madsen *et al.* therefore concluded that, while polygraphy had its merits, the most risky behaviour was disclosed at the first-test stage and was not maintained at the second testing phase. They also noted how the high refusal rate suggested that several offenders had behaviours that they obviously did not want to share.

Such findings have also been reiterated by Wilcox and Sosnowski (2005), who looked at how polygraphs could help probation officers in establishing the sexual history of offenders. Testing of offenders who had volunteered to be involved took place 3 to 6 months after a treatment programme had commenced, and involved 14 men. On average, the research found that the offenders were reporting 3.9 times more victims per offender than they had previously disclosed. There were 4.5 times more incidents of sexual offending reported and subjects admitted to more paraphilic interests; for some the difference was as great as 5.9 times than previously admitted. In addition, subjects admitted earlier sexual offending, with the average age difference between when they actually committed their first sexual offence as compared to when they were identified as sex offenders being 14 years. For one subject, he disclosed that he had committed his first offence at 13, rather than when he was identified at 28.

Results would therefore appear to be positive, although it must be noted that all of these aforementioned studies only included those who had *volunteered* to be a part of the project. Those offenders who were choosing not to participate were presumably doing so because they did not want to disclose further information, did not want to be found to be lying and thus may be considered to be the more risky in terms of reoffending. Despite this caveat, the government has appeared supportive of using polygraphy as a risk-management tool. In 2005, the Labour Party Manifesto contained a commitment that the government would test the use of mandatory polygraph tests for sex offenders supervised within the community (Explanatory Memorandum to the Polygraph Rules 2009) and, furthermore, in 2007, the Review included the use of polygraphs in its suggestions on how to improve public protection. Perhaps due to the caveat mentioned above, however, Action 19 of the Review was to 'pilot the use of *compulsory* polygraph (lie detector) tests as a risk management tool' (Home Office 2007: 23, emphasis added). In an attempt to gain advice concerning how the tests should be carried out and to identify what issues needed to be considered, a public consultation was undertaken between

September and November 2008 (Ministry of Justice 2008a). Although the consultation period was only 9 weeks (it is usually 12), 7 responses were received, most of which were supportive of the scheme and its draft proposals (Ministry of Justice 2009c). This then led to the publication of the Polygraph Rules 2009, which came into force on 8 April 2009. The Rules detail matters such as what qualifications polygraph operators need, the requirements of polygraph sessions and how information should be recorded and reported.[5]

In addition to having procedural rules, the government also had to legislate for a polygraph condition. This now exists in section 28 of the Offender Management Act (OMA) 2007, which allows the Secretary of State to include a polygraph condition in an offender's licence. The offender must be 18 or over, have been convicted of a relevant sexual offence (defined in Schedule 15 CJA 2003) and have received at least a 12-month term of imprisonment. Furthermore, the polygraph condition has been held not to breach Article 8 of the ECHR (*R. (on the application of C) v Ministry of Justice* [2009] EWHC 2671 (Admin)). Under the Act, the purpose of polygraphy is to 'monitor whether offenders are complying with their licence conditions or to improve the management of the offender during his release in the community on licence' (Explanatory Notes, OMA 2007: 13), with these statutory purposes seen in section 29 OMA 2007. Operators are therefore looking to see whether the offender is engaging in 'risky' behaviour or in any other behaviour that puts him in breach of his licence conditions. Information disclosed under polygraphy or evidence of physiological reactions to questions cannot be used in criminal prosecutions against the offender and therefore should only be used as general risk-assessment information. Sections 28–30 of the OMA 2007 came into force on 19 January 2009, but so far are only in force for those police areas that are piloting the project and will cease to be in force on 31 March 2012 (OMA 2007 (Commencement No. 3) Order 2009).

With the OMA 2007 and the Polygraph Rules 2009 in place, mandatory testing pilots began on 8 April 2009 in nine police areas in the East and West Midlands. The purpose of the pilot is 'to determine whether polygraph testing is a useful risk management tool for offender managers supervising sex offenders in the community' (Explanatory Memorandum to the Polygraph Rules 2009: para. 4.4) and for this purpose will run for just over three years.

Efficacy

As already highlighted, the use of polygraphy, even at a post-conviction stage, is controversial, mainly because of disputes concerning its accuracy, application and interpretation of results (Madsen *et al.* 2004). While there have been a number of studies that have shown the merits of using polygraphy with sex offenders, much of this research has concentrated on offenders who have voluntarily chosen to take the tests and, even where there have been licence conditions in place, Madsen *et al.* (2004) caution that much of this literature is either methodologically flawed or involved such small sample sizes that its results are not significant. Wilcox *et al.* additionally warn that, while accuracy has been found to be as high as 98 per cent, 'it is not infallible' (1999: 235) and errors, especially human errors, can occur, such as failing to prepare the subject correctly or misinterpreting the results (further debate on the pros and cons of polygraphy can be seen in Grubin 2008c; Ben-Shakhar 2008).

Deacon (1999) further advises that not only has there been too little consideration given to the ethical implications of using polygraph tests, but that there may also be reasons, apart from deception, as to why offenders fail the tests, including differing perceptions of what is classed as 'risky' behaviour. Simply put, she argues that it is not always possible to 'polarise interactions into truth and lies' and that 'denial per se is not in itself an indicator of future risk' (242). Moreover, she cautions how mandatory polygraphy may jeopardise the relationship between an offender and his supervising officer and may, in this sense, be counter-productive to risk-management aims. In a similar vein, if an offender knows that he is to be polygraphed and is afraid that he will fail, there is a possibility that he will create 'risky' behaviours to satisfy what he thinks the operator wants to hear. Of more concern would be the situation where risk of failure results in an offender 'going underground'. Deacon therefore concludes with the view that 'careful consideration should be given to the question of whether their [polygraphs] use enhances or undermines engagement in the supervision process' (Deacon 1999: 244) and, indeed, this would seem a sensible approach for the Ministry of Justice to adopt.

One final thought in this section is the relevance of polygraphy to violent offenders. If the pilot projects confirm that it does have merits with sex offenders and does contribute to their risk management, should it then also be extended to all those who are considered by the authorities to be dangerous? While violent offenders may not be in denial in respect of previous offences and victims in the same way as some sex offenders, polygraphy may still be a useful risk management tool to ensure that violent offenders also abide by their licence conditions.

Satellite tracking technology

Another risk-management technique is the tracking of offenders, which, in the form of electronic monitoring, has existed in England and Wales since government pilots in 1989 (Nee 1999). Electronic monitoring works on the basis that an offender wears a tag that is linked to a control centre via a box and telephone line situated at the offender's residence. While it can monitor whether the offender is at home at any given time, if he is not, it cannot alert the authorities to where he is. Satellite tracking technology is therefore an expansion to the original idea of electronic monitoring and was originally suggested by the Correctional Services Review in 2003. As Carter stated, 'it would help control the movement of offenders', 'would help to ensure offenders attend work or rehabilitation programmes' and 'provide the police with information on the behaviour of persistent offenders' (2003: 29). The technology therefore allows for 'incessant oversight' (Nellis 2007: 11), with the aim being to deter offenders from reoffending, in addition to providing authorities with intelligence about an offender's whereabouts so that, if necessary, swift interventions can be employed to prevent crime.

The Home Office were supportive of the suggestions made by Carter and, in 2004, announced the introduction of 'satellite tracking for high risk offenders' (Home Office 2004: Foreword). Pilots ran from September 2004 until June 2006 in Manchester, the West Midlands and Hampshire. Interestingly, this was the first time that a European country had used satellites to monitor offenders (BBC News 2004), even though it has been used in the USA since 1996 (Nellis 2007). Through a combination of Global Positioning System (GPS) satellites for outdoor monitoring and mobile telephone devices for indoor monitoring, responsible authorities can check whether offenders are complying with requirements of their community orders or conditions of their licence and, more generally, for those on licence, where offenders are spending their time. During the pilots, the use of the technology was prioritised for use with sex offenders, domestic violence perpetrators and prolific offenders (National Probation Service 2004).

The technology used in the pilots involved a two-piece tracking device. The offender wore a tag, known as a personal identification device, attached to the ankle and a personal tracking device (PTD), approximately the size of a mobile phone, near the waist (Shute 2007). The tracking device communicates with a control centre run by the electronic monitoring contractors through GPS satellites. Some of the tracking devices were also fitted with Global System Mobile (GSM) communication, which enables the contractors to identify which mobile cell the offender is in. This can be used as an extra backup where GPS positioning is lost due to either high-rise buildings or tree-lined streets, although this is not as accurate as GPS (ibid.). To ensure that the technology works and that the two devices are always together (they must generally be no further than five metres apart), the tag will alert the contractor if the two pieces of technology are separated. Alerts will also be sounded if the tag is removed or damaged. Location data provided by the technology is thought to be accurate within two metres when there are at least three satellites visible (National Probation Service (NPS) 2004).

Current technology allows for three types of tracking. The first, known as passive tracking, provides information on the offender's whereabouts once the tracking device is connected to a landline telephone. This would usually occur at the end of the day, although could be up to four times a day if the PTD includes GSM technology (NPS 2004). Information is then transmitted down the phone line to the control centre, which will retrospectively tell the contractors where the offender has been that day. Alternatively, hybrid tracking is the option used when the aim of the technology is to monitor whether the offender is abiding by exclusion requirements/conditions. The system is similar to passive tracking in that information is uploaded at the end of the day, so in that sense is retrospective, but if the offender enters into the exclusion zone during the day, the control centre will be alerted in real time. This, therefore, requires that there are personnel in the control centre ready and waiting to respond to these alerts and, for this reason, is more expensive than passive tracking (Shute 2007). A text message can be sent to the PTD warning the offender to leave the zone as soon as possible and, if he does not, the police are then informed (Mercer *et al.* 2000). Knowledge concerning the exact whereabouts of an offender in real time is important if the offender is a known paedophile and the exclusion zone is a school or a park often frequented by children. The technology therefore allows the police to know within two metres exactly where the offender is at a time when, presumably, the risk of reoffending becomes increased. Interestingly, since May 2005, it is a separate offence for an excluded person found within his exclusion zone to knowingly contravene a direction by a police officer to leave that area (Shute 2007). The third type of tracking is known as active tracking, which allows information to be transmitted in real time, usually at intervals of one minute (NPS 2004). While this is obviously the best in the sense that it really does provide a 'big brother' experience, it is the most costly of the three types and, for this reason, was not used in the initial pilots.

The first research on the pilots was carried out by Shute (2007). During the time period of the research, September 2004–December 2005, 336 offenders had been ordered to be satellite tracked. Of these offenders, 94 per cent had been released from prison on licence, while the remaining 6 per cent were subject to a community order. 80 per cent of the offenders were adults and 20 per cent were young offenders, with the total age range spanning from 13 to 70 years. Of interest for this book, 96 per cent were described as high-risk offenders, with 36 per cent regarded as sufficiently risky to warrant MAPPA supervision. The average daily cost of the passive tracking technology per offender was found to be £42. On the basis that offenders spent an average of 72 days being passively tracked, this equated to an average spend of £3,024 per offender, although this does not include the costs of supervision from other involved agencies. During the time of the pilots, 58 per cent of the offenders were recalled to prison, either because of breach of licence conditions or because they had had their community order revoked. Twenty-six per cent of these offenders were recalled solely on the basis of the information gathered through the technology (ibid.). Overall, the research concluded that, 'satellite tracking may offer further protection for the public from those released from custody and known to be high risk' (ibid.:15).

Efficacy and use

Research evidence from the pilots in England and Wales was therefore largely supportive of the technology. The only limitations that Shute identified were the problems of cloudy skies, high-rise buildings and tree-lined streets (although this can be overcome to an extent with the added provision of GSM communication) and the fact that, if an offender was intent on reoffending he could remove the tag or leave the PTD behind, although this would be picked up by the control centre (2007). Satellite tracking technology also seemed to gain further governmental support in 2007, when the Home Office included it as an Action in their Review. Action 20 was therefore to 'review the potential to expand the use of satellite tracking to monitor high-risk offenders' (Home Office 2007: 24). Despite this positive research and strong intention, all has gone remarkably quiet. There has been no national roll-out of the scheme and no announcement that this is even an intention. Indeed, the last public mention of it was in the 2007 Review. This would seem odd, especially when, as Nellis notes, 'the pilots were not to ascertain *whether* satellite tracking was a wise or sensible thing to do – the decision to pursue it has already been taken' (2005a: 128, emphasis in original). Indeed, in their Strategic Plan of 2004, the Home Office stated, 'once the technology has been tested we will make tracking much more widely available' (Home Office 2004: 78). Why there has therefore been a loss in this impetus is unclear and arguably irrational.

Civil orders

In addition to using registers, licence conditions and structured ways of working, public protection in England and Wales is also contributed to through the use of civil orders. The preference for civil orders has grown over the last few years (for more on this and a consideration on how this effects human rights, see Ashworth 2004b), partly because the government has to be seen to be tackling the moral panic of the day but also because it was initially thought that, by using civil rather than criminal orders, the standard of proof needed would be less, hearsay evidence would be admissible and so it would be easier to prove that the order was necessary, even though criminal sanctions could be initiated on breach. This, however, has been clarified by the House of Lords, which stated that civil orders that have criminal consequences require the criminal standard of proof (*R. (McCann and Others) v Crown Court at Manchester* [2003] 1 AC 787). This civil/criminal law crossover was first seen with the introduction of antisocial behaviour orders under the Crime and Disorder Act (CDA) 1998, with other examples designed to manage all manner of 'dangerous offenders', including terrorists and suspected terrorists (Control Order), drug and human traffickers (Serious Crime Prevention Order), young people (Dispersal Orders) and bad parents (Parenting Order). This section, however, will only deal with those that have been specifically designed to deal with sexual and violent offenders, including the Notification Order (NO), the Sexual Offences Prevention Order (SOPO), the Foreign Travel Order (FTO), the Risk of Sexual Harm Order (RSHO) and, more recently, the Violent Offender Order (VOO).

Notification Order

In addition to the notification requirements for convicted or cautioned sex offenders, the SOA 2003 also introduced Notification Orders (NOs), which are primarily designed for sex offenders who have been convicted of sexual offences outside of the UK and either intend to return or are being deported on release from custody. If a Chief of Police believes that either such a person is in his area, or is about to come into his area, he can apply to the Magistrates' Court for an NO if three conditions are met. These are that the person has been convicted, cautioned, found not guilty by reason of insanity or found to be acting under a disability or the equivalent of a sexual offence in another country; the conviction or finding was on or after 1 September 1997; and, if the offence had been committed in the UK, the offender would still be subject to notification requirements under the SOA 2003 (s. 97 SOA 2003). The offender is subject to these notification requirements for the period of time that he would have been had he been convicted of his offence in the UK, and so the date of the original offence is important. Interim orders pending an application for a full order can also be made. The NO has received very little criticism. This is because all it does is to ensure that all who are resident in the UK, but have been convicted of a sexual offence abroad, are treated exactly the same as those whose offence was committed within the UK and, in many respects, closes a loophole that existed prior to the introduction of the SOA 2003.

Sexual Offences Prevention Order

Previously known as restraining orders (s. 5A Sex Offenders Act 1997) and sex offender orders (s. 2 CDA 1998), the Sexual Offences Prevention Order (SOPO) is now governed by section 104 of the SOA 2003. It applies to all offenders who have been convicted or cautioned for a qualifying offence, found not guilty of such an offence due to reasons of insanity, or committed such an offence but were acting under a disability at the time. Qualifying offences are listed in Schedule 3, which includes more than 50 sexual offences, and Schedule 5, which contains 72 violent offences. While the Schedule 5 offences are not sexual in nature, they are included on the basis that they may, nevertheless, indicate risk of sexual harm, and indeed this risk of sexual harm needs to be proven for an SOPO to be granted. With over 120 qualifying offences, however, this considerably widens the net of potentially qualifying offenders.

An SOPO can be made either on conviction for a qualifying offence or following an application by the Chief of Police to a Magistrate because it is believed that such an order is 'necessary . . . for the purpose of protecting the public or any particular members of the public from serious sexual harm from the defendant' (s. 104(1)(a) SOA 2003). This 'test' is thought to be lower than that in the dangerousness legislation (see Gillespie 2006) and could mean that an order is made without proof of actual criminal activity. For example, the Explanatory Notes to the Act state that an application for a SOPO by the police may be suitable when

> An offender has a conviction for sexual activity with a child and has been released after his term of imprisonment. Following his release he behaves in a way that suggests he is likely to offend again, for example by loitering around schools or inviting children back to his house.
>
> (Explanatory Notes, SOA 2003: para. 211)

The order prohibits the offender from doing anything that is outlined in the order and must last for 'not less than 5 years' (s. 107(1)(b) SOA 2003), arguably making the chance of breach incredibly high. The prohibitions have to relate to measures that are designed to protect the public from serious sexual harm and can include prohibitive activities such as associating with other known sex offenders and being in areas/places at certain times such as schools and fast-food restaurants. Doing anything that is prohibited in the SOPO is a separate criminal offence. Another effect of the order is that it will extend the offender's registration notification period for the length of the SOPO, even if otherwise he would no longer be subject to notification requirements (s. 107(3) SOA 2003). More controversially, if the person in question was not a relevant offender prior to the SOPO, and thus not on the register, the SOPO will place him on the register (s. 107(4) SOA 2003). This will also subject the offender to MAPPA (Shute 2004).

The order can be varied, renewed and/or discharged, but such applications can only be made by the defendant or the relevant Chief of Police (that is, they cannot be made by families or victims/victim's families). An interim order can also be applied for, to cover a fixed period, while information is being gathered on the offender in preparation of an application for a full order (s. 109 SOA 2003). The order is not a criminal conviction, nor should it be recorded in this way, although details of it will be placed on the Police National Computer.

Foreign Travel Order

The Foreign Travel Order (FTO), governed by section 114 of the SOA 2003, is designed to impose travel restrictions on those convicted or cautioned of sexual offences against children under 16, either in the UK or overseas. Relevant offences are found in section 116 of the Act and can include taking, making, distributing or importing indecent photographs, and trespass with an intent to commit a sexual offence, where the victim is 15 or younger. The aim of the order is thus to protect children outside of the UK from serious sexual harm from offenders based in the UK. Unlike the SOPO, the order cannot be made on conviction and so can only be ordered where the Chief of Police believes that the order is 'necessary . . . for the purpose of protecting children generally or any child from serious sexual harm from the defendant outside the United Kingdom' (s. 114(3)(b) SOA 2003). Prohibitions in the order can include travel to a named country or countries, a ban on travelling anywhere apart from a named country or countries, or, the most draconian, a universal ban. Since 1 April 2010, if the FTO includes a universal ban on travel, there will also be a requirement for the offender to surrender his passport (s. 117A SOA 2003, as amended by s. 25(2) Policing and Crime Act 2009). The FTO will also subject the offender to the notification requirements of foreign travel as outlined in section 86(1) of the Act (discussed above). The maximum duration of the order is for six months and can be renewed, varied and discharged. Breach of any of the prohibitions is a separate criminal offence, punishable by up to five years imprisonment.

Risk of Sexual Harm Order

The Risk of Sexual Harm Order (RSHO), unlike the SOPO and the FTO, can only be used for offenders who are 18 or over, but can be used irrespective of whether the 'offender' has been previously convicted or cautioned for a sexual offence and, for this reason, is the most controversial. In fact, the defendant does not have to have committed any kind of offence, sexual or otherwise, meaning that, while it is justified on a purely preventative basis, it has also been described as 'legislative overkill' (Shute 2004: 431). Justice has stated that it is 'very dangerous . . . to allow a plethora of orders to come onto the scene in terms of acts which are not actually prosecuted against' (ibid.) and Shute (2004) reminds us of the stigma that an order with the prefix of risk of sexual harm is bound to have.

Introduced by section 123 of the SOA 2003, an RSHO can be applied for by a Chief of Police when it is thought that the defendant has, on at least two occasions, engaged in 'acts' and the order is necessary to protect children from *harm*. This is far less stringent than both the SOPO and the FTO where the test is whether the order is necessary to protect children from *serious sexual harm*. The acts referred to in the Act are defined as including:

- engaging in sexual activity involving a child or in the presence of a child;
- causing or inciting a child to watch a person engaging in sexual activity or to look at a moving or still image that is sexual;
- giving a child anything that relates to sexual activity or contains a reference to such activity;
- communicating with a child, where any part of the communication is sexual.

(s. 123(3) SOA 2003)

Interestingly, all except the latter of these acts are illegal and so Craven *et al.* (2007) argue that the RSHO is therefore designed for those instances where the criminal standard of proof cannot be met, although, as mentioned above, the case of *McCann* suggests that such a standard is still required in an RSHO application. For the latter act, the Explanatory Notes to the Act state that an RSHO may be suitable where the activity is giving a child a condom or sex toy or describing sexual acts that the person would like to carry out on the child (Explanatory Notes, SOA 2003: para. 253). Whether the activity or communication is 'sexual' is measured using a reasonable man test (Shute 2004).

The order must last for at least two years and can prohibit the 'offender' from doing anything that is contained in the order, on the proviso that such prohibitions are necessary to protect a child or children from harm. The order, as with those mentioned above, can be varied, renewed, discharged and ordered on an interim basis. A person under an RSHO will not be subject to the notification requirements as outlined above, although breach of any of the prohibitions is a criminal offence, punishable by up to five years imprisonment, which will then entail compliance with notification requirements (s. 129 SOA 2003). Breach will also bring the offender under the umbrella of MAPPA (Shute 2004).

Violent Offender Order

Finally, there is the Violent Offender Order (VOO), which was first announced in April 2006 in response to the murder of John Monckton (who was killed by two men who were being supervised by the probation service), but was not introduced into law until the CJIA 2008, and did not come into force until 3 August 2009. Part 7 of the Act (sections 98–117) outlines the order, which, in many respects, is similar to those already mentioned above, in that it is applied for by a Chief of Police on the basis that it is necessary to protect the public, although is, of course, designed for violent rather than sexual offenders. Qualifying offences are listed in section 98(3) CJIA 2008, which perhaps surprisingly is rather short in length, only including manslaughter, soliciting murder, wounding with intent to cause GBH, malicious wounding, attempting or conspiring to commit murder and relevant service offences. It is worth noting that a VOO is not available for murder. This is because the offender will mandatorily either be in prison or on licence for life. A VOO is, therefore, only available for those who have previous convictions for serious violent offences, unlike the SOPO, which is available for all manner of offences, even those that are not sexual in nature. Also unlike the SOPO and the FTO, the offender must be 18 or over, have served at least 12 months in prison, or been subject to a Hospital or Supervision Order. In many respects, the VOO is therefore harder to apply for than the SOPO, which arguably is its sexual counterpart. Why this disparity exists is unclear. One answer, however, may be that we fear sexual offenders more and thus we are more punitive towards those who have committed sexual crimes or who are suspected of having committed such offences. This can also be seen in the extended sentence (see Chapter 2), where the extended supervision period for sexual offenders is 8 years, but for violent offenders is only 5.

A person is also considered to be a qualifying offender if he has committed a serious violent offence outside of England and Wales and served an equivalent custodial term. Eligibility for all qualifying offenders will remain until death (Home Office 2009b), meaning that the order can be applied for at any time as long as there was once a qualifying offence. For those offenders whose qualifying offence warranted less than two and a half years imprisonment, this arguably goes against the principle that convictions can be spent and will no longer be of any legal value once a rehabilitation period has been served (see Rehabilitation of Offenders Act 1974).

As with the civil orders for sexual offenders, the VOO is designed to protect the public from the risk of serious violent harm posed by the offender and, to enable this, will contain any prohibitions, conditions or restrictions that the court deems are necessary for this purpose. These can prevent the offender from going to a specified place (for example, a public house or football stadium), from attending a specified event or having contact with a specified individual (s. 102(1) CJIA 2008). The order can last for between two and five years, but can, in that time, be renewed, varied or discharged, with the offender's risk of serious violent harm being reviewed every six months (Home Office 2009b). This review of risk is not mentioned for the civil orders designed for sex offenders. Like all other civil orders, it can also be made on an interim basis. When making the order, the Magistrates must consider what other risk-management strategies are in place and cannot make an order when the offender is either in prison or has been paroled on licence. This, therefore, means that the VOO should only be used for determinate prisoners, as those who are subject to an IPP would only have their licence conditions terminated by the Parole Board if it was thought that their level of risk no longer justified such conditions, and presumably, if this was the case, then a VOO would not be necessary. Circumstances where a VOO may be appropriate are essentially where an IPP sentence has not been given because either they were not assessed as sufficiently dangerous on conviction, the offence was not a specified one, their level of risk has since increased, or the previous conviction was before IPPs were introduced. Liberty argue that the order will be used overwhelmingly for those offenders eligible under the last category, which they believe may breach Article 7 of the Human Rights Act 1998. This prevents the imposition of a heavier penalty than the one that was applicable at the time the offence was committed (Liberty 2007). Breach of any of the conditions, restrictions or prohibitions is a criminal offence, punishable by up to five years imprisonment.

Any offender subject to a VOO (full or interim) will be required, within three days, to register his details with the police and be entered on to ViSOR (see above). Relevant information includes the offender's date of birth, national insurance number, name and previously used names, home address and previous addresses, and any other prescribed information. Such information may then be subject to disclosure. There is also an ongoing duty to notify the police of any changes to this information, inform them of any travel plans outside of the UK and, on an annual basis, confirm that information held is valid. A failure in any of these obligations or providing the authorities with false information is again a separate criminal offence with a five-year maximum penalty.

Efficacy and use

Use of civil orders can be seen in Table 5.4. This, therefore, shows that, while the SOPO is being used (although statistics do not reveal whether the orders were made on conviction or by application to the Magistrates' Court), the others do not share the same momentum, with nothing published on how many RSHOs were granted. Despite this usage, there is no real evidence base to suggest that the orders are working to effectively risk manage dangerous offenders, with Shute (2004) arguing that, in all likelihood, those who intend to reoffend will do so irrelevant of whether they are subject to a civil order.

Another concern is the fact that many of these orders require risk-assessment judgements for them to be initiated. The problems of using risk-assessment tools and subsequently relying on their findings has been discussed in Chapter 3, which means that, in some cases, a false diagnosis as to necessity for these orders will be

Table 5.4 Usage of civil orders (Ministry of Justice 2010c)

Sexual Offences Act Orders	*No. of orders (2005/06)*	*No. of orders (2006/07)*	*No. of orders (2007/08)*	*No. of orders (2008/09)*
Sexual Offences Prevention Orders (SOPOs) granted	937	1114	1440	1512
Notification Orders (NOs) granted	37	62	70	72
Foreign Travel Orders (FTOs) granted	1	3	1	12
Total number of orders	975	1179	1511	1596

made. This obviously has human rights implications for those who are wrongly subjected to restrictions, conditions and prohibitions, especially when, in some cases, the people subjected to them have not committed a criminal offence, or have already been punished for those that they have. Bearing such factors in mind, care needs to be taken to ensure that the need to protect the public is carefully balanced with the actual risk that these 'offenders' actually pose, and indeed this same care needs to be employed when using all of the risk-management strategies discussed thus far.

Conclusion

Once an offender has been assessed as dangerous, this opens him up to a wide variety of criminal and civil risk-management strategies, including registers, structured ways of working and specific conditions and requirements. The efficacy of each of these methods is mixed with better evidence bases, surprisingly existing for those techniques that appear to have less governmental support. For example, regarding the use of satellite tracking technology, the government appears to have a strategy that, on a small scale, has been proven to aid in risk management, but currently appears reticent to use it. Rather, it is spending millions of pounds on strategies such as ViSOR, which, in all probability, do not provide the same levels of effectiveness. Despite the intrusive nature of this type of 'big brother' surveillance, satellite tracking technology and its predecessor, electronic monitoring, is a relatively unemotive issue, not really picked up by either the media or the public (Nellis 2005b). Perhaps this disinterest is partly why it has been considered to 'not entirely embody all the characteristics of the new punitiveness – and, significantly, it has been dismissed in some quarters as not punitive enough' (ibid.: 178). The reason why the government has concentrated its resources on sex offender registers and not on this technology may therefore have nothing to do with evidence-based policy but rather because it is the registers that feed media agendas, win public votes, nourish populist punitiveness and consequently help to dissipate public anxiety. Surely, however, this should not be the basis on which government decides which risk-management strategies should and should not be employed.

Other techniques such as MAPPA, polygraphy and civil orders require more research to establish whether or not they are contributing to the ultimate goal of public protection. Not only is this important in terms of cost effectiveness, but also in terms of human rights, bearing in mind the restrictions and prohibitions that are being placed on those offenders who are brought within the net of such risk-management techniques. While 'big brother' surveillance, community notification and the use of civil orders for non-offenders may be controversial, they are even less acceptable if they cannot be proven to serve a legitimate aim. Proving this is therefore imperative for England and Wales to stay within its obligations under the ECHR.

6

STRATEGIES OF RISK REDUCTION

Introduction

However effective risk-management strategies may be, they are not designed to actually lower risk, and so, in addition to managing serious sexual and violent offenders, responsible authorities are also committed to interventions which set out to reduce risk. It is thought that risk reduction can be achieved through a variety of means, both in prison and within the community, and indeed one of the main aims of the 'What Works' policy (Home Office 1998) was to provide seamless sentencing so that programmes of work could commence in a prison setting and then continue when the offender was released into the community. While there are no guarantees that risk will be reduced, there are a number of strategies that are currently employed to try to achieve this goal, with the three main methods of treatment arguably being psychotherapy, surgical interventions and pharmacotherapy, although practices involving restorative justice techniques are also gaining support. What these methods are, the strategies that they use and whether they work in terms of public protection are the subjects of this chapter.

Psychotherapy

Psychotherapy is where the offender is 'taught' how to behave differently. This can be achieved in a variety of ways including offending behaviour programmes, covert and assisted covert sensitisation (where either a horrible smell or a feeling of pain is linked to deviant imagery) and aversive behavioural rehearsal (where the offender is videotaped abusing a mannequin in the hope that he will be shocked by his actions). The main use of psychotherapy in England and Wales, however, and thus the method assessed here, is the use of accredited offending behaviour programmes based on cognitive-behavioural theory. In line with the main purpose of psychotherapy, these programmes educate and teach self-control mechanisms and re-evaluation of attitudes. This is achieved by focusing on a number of key areas that have been shown to help in the reduction of risk, including enhancing self-esteem (Thornton *et al.* 2004); challenging cognitive distortions, (for example, the victim wants and enjoys the sexual contact); denial and minimisation (Marshall *et al.* 1999); victim empathy (Marshall *et al.* 1996); the development of social functioning skills such as intimacy defects, assertiveness difficulties and stress management (Marshall *et al.* 1995); and relapse prevention. It is hoped that working on all of these aspects will change how an offender thinks and acts, and ultimately will prevent reoffending.

While this type of intervention is often referred to as 'treatment', Brown warns how this can be misleading, especially if it is compared to medical treatment. Rather, she explains how cognitive-behavioural programmes:

> require offenders to engage in them actively, learn skills, and assimilate ideas/messages, etc., that they are then expected to employ in order to live non-offending lives in the community. Although medical treatment usually requires some kind of engagement/participation, it is more passive in nature . . . The same can never be said for cognitive-behavioural treatment, which requires the client to be alert, to be motivated to some extent to learn and absorb the messages, thoughts, skills and behaviours in their lives.
>
> (2010: 82–3)

This also links in with the idea of responsibilisation, where we expect the offender, to some extent, to take responsibility for his own behaviour and risk reduction, rather than expecting the authorities to do everything. As explained by Maguire and Kemshall, 'individuals – theoretically in return for greater individual freedom and reduced regulation – are expected to a large extent to "manage their own risks" by both refraining from criminal behaviour and protecting themselves against crime' (Maguire and Kemshall 2003: 107). The prison and probation services have an array of general offending behaviour programmes including Thinking Skills, Think First, Reasoning and Rehabilitation and the Priestley 1:1 programme, although, due to the nature of this book, this section will concentrate on sex offender treatment programmes and those specifically designed for anger management and domestic violence.

Sex offender treatment programmes

In England and Wales, there is currently one HM Prison Service sex offender treatment programme (SOTP) package. This is made up of six accredited programmes, with programme dose and type dependent on the specific risks and needs of the offender. The six available programmes are the Rolling Programme, the Core Programme, the Adapted Core Programme, the Extended Programme, the Healthy Sexual Functioning Programme and the Better Lives Booster Programme (Mann and Attrill 2006). Although each sex offender programme differs slightly in design and content, all are based on cognitive-behavioural theory and therefore have the common goal of teaching individuals to understand and control behaviour, feelings and thinking. All of the programmes are delivered on a group-work basis and involve methods such as role play, group discussion and skills practice (NPS 2002). Between 2007 and 2008, 1,037 SOTPs were completed in prison, which narrowly exceeded the target of 1,035 (HM Prison Service 2008c).

In addition to the programmes in prison, there are also three accredited community SOTPs.[1] These are the West Midlands Community Sex Offender Treatment Programme (C-SOTP), which is used in 15 probation areas; the Thames Valley Sex Offender Treatment Programme (TV-SOTP), used in 12 probation areas; and the Northumbria Sex Offender Treatment Programme (N-SOTP), used in 16 probation areas (Christodoulou 2010). For reasons of space, only the C-SOTP will be discussed in detail.

The C-SOTP is suitable for male offenders over the age of 21, who have been convicted of a contact or non-contact sexual offence against adults or children, and either do not have alcohol or drug problems or such issues are deemed to be at a manageable level. The offender must have stable mental health, speak and write English at a satisfactory level and have the personality and thinking ability to meaningfully take part (Derbyshire Probation Trust 2010). Once an offender has been assessed as suitable for the programme, he will first undertake a 50-hour induction module. This is designed to decrease any denial or minimisation of the index offence and will usually take place every day for 5 days, and then either 10 half-day sessions or 5 full-day sessions delivered on a weekly basis. The induction programme therefore tries to ensure that, before the programme formally begins, the offender has reached the stage where he is not only willing to accept the severity of his offending, but also, importantly, ready to take responsibility for his own behaviour. Through induction, the offender may also have begun to identify patterns in his offending behaviour (NPS 2002). This is then followed by psychometric testing and other clinical assessments, where the offender is categorised regarding risk of reoffending and levels of deviance (see Chapter 3). If he is classified as being at a low risk of reoffending and is also low in terms of deviance, he will complete a further 50-hour programme that focuses mainly on relapse prevention strategies. The programme is designed for those offenders whose behaviour is 'less entrenched or who can build on treatment gains made elsewhere' (ibid.: 15). The modules worked through include challenging distortions, relapse prevention, victim empathy and lifestyle change (NPS 2002).

If the offender is seen as being medium or high in risk and/or deviance he will complete the full programme, which takes approximately 190 hours. This 'long term therapy' (NPS 2010) targets a number of offending-related factors broken down into the six modules of 'cycles of offending and cognitive distortions (thinking errors); relationships and attachment styles; self management and interpersonal skills; the role of fantasy in offending; victim empathy; relapse prevention and lifestyle change' (ibid.). An offender can join the group at the beginning of any module apart from victim empathy (NPS 2002). The full programme can take up to two years to complete, although those offenders who have already undertaken the SOTP in prison, and have a licence condition to participate in a community programme, will not normally need to undertake the initial induction module. Presumably, if the work in prison has achieved its aim of reducing risk and deviance, he will also only need the additional 50-hour module on relapse prevention rather than the full 190-hour programme. For risk-management and risk-reduction purposes, the offender will be assessed for his individual progress three times: before induction (to ensure suitability), after induction (as described above) and on completion. A decrease, or indeed an increase, in risk will not only alert programme tutors as to how effectively the programme is working, but will also be used to inform other risk-reduction and risk-management decisions.

Available since May 2006, developments in sex offender treatment include the Internet Sex Offender Treatment Programme (i-SOTP), which has been designed for those offenders convicted of internet-related sexual offences and is available in all probation areas (Christodoulou 2010). Examples of suitable offences include taking or making indecent photographs of children, possessing indecent photographs of children, and arranging or facilitating child pornography (NPS 2006). I-SOTP is suitable for all male internet sex offenders, aged over 21 years, who have been assessed as low in deviance and low, medium or high in risk (NPS 2005a) and are within the normal IQ range. Those offenders who are classified as either very high in risk or high in terms of deviance will undertake the general SOTPs as detailed above. The i-SOTP is much shorter than the other programmes and is available in both a group-work and a one-to-one format. The group programme is made up of 35 2-hour sessions, while the one-to-one format is a minimum of 20 and a maximum of 30 90-minute sessions (ibid.). The programme will therefore last for between four and nine months depending on which format is used and how well the offender responds to treatment. The modules look at risk factors relevant to internet offenders and are broken down into the six modules of: emotional dysregulation, intimacy deficits, lack of victim empathy, skills practice, compulsive behaviour aspects and relapse prevention (Middleton *et al.* 2009). It is thought that approximately 70 to 80 per cent of all internet offenders are suitable for the i-SOTP (NPS 2006) and, as with the general SOTPs, offenders will be risk assessed pre- and post-programme.

Violent offender treatment programmes

There are also a number of treatment programmes designed specifically for violent offenders, including the Cognitive Self-Change Programme (CSCP); Controlling Anger and Learning to Manage It (CALM); Healthy Relationships Programme; Aggression Replacement Training; Integrated Domestic Abuse Programme(IDAP); and Chromis. Chromis is designed for violent offenders who display severe and/or multi-aspect psychopathic disorders and so will be looked at in more detail in Chapter 9. Due to space, three of these programmes will be considered: one designed for high-risk violent offenders, one for domestic violent perpetrators and one for general violent behaviour.

The CSCP, adapted from a North American programme (see Bush 1995), is designed for high-risk male offenders, aged 24 years or over, with a normal IQ, who have been convicted of serious violent offences and are serving sentences of either life imprisonment or IPP (Brady and Crighton 2003). It takes places predominantly in prison settings, although Block Six (see below) is designed to be completed in the community following prison release (NPS 2005b). It is a high-intensity cognitive-behavioural programme that aims to reduce violent behaviour and reoffending by changing individual patterns of antisocial thinking and distorted thinking processes that can lead to violence. Due to the nature of the offending in question, the programme consists of between 136 and 257 group-work sessions, lasting 8–17 months, and, on average, 26 one-to-one sessions (ibid.). This is then followed by monthly sessions until the offender is either released or transferred to another prison. CSCP is designed as a rolling programme, which means that offenders can join and leave it as and when necessary, with more experienced veterans expected to support and facilitate the progress of new members (Jordan and O'Hare 2007). Before commencing CSCP, prisoners should have completed a general offending behaviour programme, such as Reasoning and Rehabilitation, or have been assessed as not requiring it (Christodoulou 2010).

Different from other cognitive-behavioural programmes, CSCP does not presuppose that the offender has any motivation to change his behaviour, and so the fundamental aim of the programme is the teaching of four skills or steps to self-change (Jordan and O'Hare 2007). These are summarised as:

- Learning how to pay attention to thoughts, feelings and attitudes.
- Learning how to see when thoughts, feelings and attitudes are leading towards doing something potentially hurtful, violent and/or criminal.
- Being able to generate new thinking that will lead away from the old, offending-related thinking, yet allow participants to feel good about themselves.
- Practice using this new thinking in real life situations.

(2007: 127–8)

This is achieved through six blocks of the programme, with the final one taking place in the community once the offender has been released from custody.

- Block One: Foundation sessions that develop skills for the objective observation of thoughts, feelings, attitudes and beliefs.
- Block Two: Identifying and understanding the connections; how thoughts, feelings, attitudes and beliefs lead each individual to violence.
- Block Three: Identifying new thoughts and intervention strategies, boosting cognitive skills and developing skills for managing individual violence risk factors.

- Block Four: Creating a relapse prevention plan and consolidating interventions.
- Block Five: Practice in the prison setting.
- Block Six: Practice in the community and consolidation of the relapse prevention plan.

(NPS 2005b: 2)

In 2005, CSCP was available in six male prisons (NPS 2005b). However, despite 61 per cent of offenders in the high-security estate requiring an intervention such as CSCP, it is now only available at one high-security prison, HMP Long Lartin, and then only to a very limited capacity (Christodoulou 2010). When arguably one of the aims of imprisonment is reducing risk so that public protection is enhanced once offenders are released into the community, this provision is wholly inadequate.

Designed specifically for domestic violence perpetrators, IDAP (based on the Duluth Domestic Violence pathfinder, see Bilby and Hatcher 2004; Gadd 2004) is a community-based programme that aims to reduce the risk of violent and abusive behaviour towards women in relationships by helping offenders to change their attitudes and behaviour. It is suitable for heterosexual male offenders, aged over 17, who have committed at least one violent act against an intimate partner, have been assessed as medium or high in risk, have a normal IQ, basic literacy comprehension and language skills, and have signed a consent form that allows the authorities to share information with the spouse or partner (NPS – South West 2010). It was awarded full accreditation in 2004 (McGuire 2007) and is currently used in 34 probation areas (Christodoulou 2010). The programme involves 4 initial pre-programme sessions, which are carried out on an individual basis, and are then followed by 27 2-hour group-work sessions. The final part of the programme consists of four sessions of relapse prevention (NPS – South West 2010). IDAP also promotes multi-agency working, with probation officers often working with women's safety groups, child protection teams and the police (Liebmann and Wootton 2008).

During his time on the programme, the offender will work through nine modules covering: non-violence, non-threatening behaviour, respect, support and trust, accountability and honesty, sexual respect, partnership, responsible parenting, and negotiation and fairness (West Mercia Probation 2010a). Each module follows a three-session process that includes defining the theme and identifying beliefs and intents, examining individual abusive behaviour and identifying and challenging beliefs and behaviour, and exploring and practising non-abusive and non-controlling behaviour (ibid.). Progress is monitored through six individual meetings with the case manager that take place every three weeks (Liebmann and Wootton 2008). Offenders are expected to talk openly about their violent behaviour in the groups and listen to the experiences of others, with sessions on the programme addressing both physical and psychological violence. Victims (if willing) will also play a part in the treatment (see Madoc-Jones and Roscoe 2010 for how the programme affects women victims), with other methods of treatment including role play, video clips, written exercises and group discussions (West Mercia Probation 2010b). It is hoped that exercises such as these will allow the offender to not only recognise the impact of his behaviour, but to also take responsibility for the harm he has previously caused (West Yorkshire Probation Trust 2010). In 2008, the programme cost between £8,000 and £10,000 per offender (Doward 2008).

CALM is a cognitive-behavioural programme designed for those high- and medium-risk offenders who have shown difficulty in controlling their emotions, which then often leads to offending behaviour. It is based on a Canadian programme (Anger and Other Emotions Management) and is accredited for use in both prison and probation settings. The aim of CALM is to reduce the frequency, duration and intensity of the offender's anger in an attempt to prevent reoffending, and can be undertaken in conjunction with other violent and SOTPs, with offenders often completing Think First or Reasoning and Rehabilitation first (Christodoulou 2010). It is suitable for males, over the age of 18, who have a pattern of violent and aggressive behaviour where there is evidence of anger and a loss of emotional control. It is not suitable for domestic violence perpetrators or those who use violence to achieve a desired outcome (for example, robbery) (Northamptonshire Probation Trust 2010) and is most effective with those who have committed violent offences against either property or persons. CALM is broken down into 6 core modules that are covered in 24 2-hour sessions, which can be run at a rate of 2–3 sessions per week (Prison Service News 2006). These include: introduction and motivational enhancement, managing arousal, thinking patterns, assertiveness and communication, other emotions, and relapse prevention (Orbis Partners 2009). The programme is currently available in 31 prison establishments and 16 probation areas (Christodoulou 2010).

Efficacy

Problems with measuring efficacy

While it is imperative to measure the efficacy of risk-reduction programmes, especially considering the vast resources spent on them and the desired need to reduce and manage the risk of dangerous offenders, there are, however, a number of issues with this. Such problems centre on concerns regarding the methodology of the numerous research studies that exist, coupled with other practical and ethical difficulties (Brown 2010). For example, while it is acknowledged that randomised control trials are probably the most robust way of testing efficacy, it is questionable whether it is ethically correct to deny an offender treatment just so that the 'perfect' research methodology can be achieved. Although, as Brown (2010) notes, this argument presupposes that the intervention does in fact work to reduce risk, with it perhaps being more ethically important to establish whether this is in fact true.

Practical difficulties can include problems in achieving equal randomised samples and the fact that most offenders need to complete a treatment programme, either because it is court ordered, or, if they do not, then progress through the prison system for release purposes will be inhibited (see Chapter 4). Such factors, therefore, rule out using randomised control methods in the vast majority of cases. Another debate has existed over what the most appropriate follow-up period is, especially considering that, in Hedderman and Sugg's (1996) original study on SOTPs, only 20 per cent of the high-risk group had reoffended after two years; but after 6 years, this had increased to 40 per cent (Beech *et al.* 2001).

Sex offender programmes

Despite these caveats, it is still worthwhile looking at the effectiveness studies that have been published regarding cognitive-behavioural programmes. Starting with those designed specifically for sex offenders, research has suggested that some success can be achieved, with Hedderman and Sugg concluding that offenders who were referred to a programme were less likely to be reconvicted for a sexual offence (4.5 per cent) when compared with a sample placed on probation alone (8.9 per cent) (Hedderman and Sugg 1996). Moreover, Hanson *et al.* (2002) conducted a meta-analytic review examining the effectiveness of psychological treatment for sex offenders by summarising data collected from 43 studies and involving 5,078 treated sex offenders and 4,376 untreated offenders. Averaged across all of the studies, the sexual offence recidivism rate was found to be lower for the treatment groups (12.3 per cent) than the comparison groups (16.8 per cent), although the difference was so marginal that it is difficult to identify if it was attributable to a treatment effect. A further meta-analysis conducted by Losel and Schmucker looked at 80 independent comparisons between treated and untreated sex offenders, finding that, on the whole, 'treated offenders showed 6 percentage points or 37% less sexual recidivism than controls' (Losel and Schmucker 2005: 117), although they also acknowledged that surgical and pharmacological interventions were more effective[2] (see page 117).

Other research has shown that, while treatment programmes can have an effect on the reoffending rates of low-deviancy and low-denial offenders, they do not have the same effect for those who are high in deviancy and/or high in denial (Beech *et al.* 1998; Beech *et al.* 2001). Indeed, Beech *et al.* found that 'more than half [of the high deviance group] showed no treatment change at all' (1998: 4). Beech *et al.* thus argue that programmes of at least 160 hours are needed for high deviancy men, although even then they acknowledge that this may still only produce a 'reasonable treatment change' (2001: 4). Furthermore, Friendship *et al.* found that, while the prison SOTP had 'a significant impact on sexual and violent reconviction for medium risk offenders' (2003: 4) with reconviction rates for treated medium-low offenders being only 2.7 per cent, compared to 12.7 per cent for the untreated sample, the same could not be said for high-risk offenders. Indeed, treated offenders were reconvicted at a rate of 26 per cent, compared to 28.1 per cent for the untreated group. In conclusion, they argued that 'additional treatment should be provided to high risk sexual offenders' (ibid.).

The only treatment programme that seems to have consistently produced positive results with dangerous offenders is the one-year intensive programme that used to be available at the Wolvercote Clinic (see Ford and Beech 2003). Despite the encouraging results found by Ford and Beech (2003), largely thought to be due to the intensive and long-term nature of the programme (on average, each offender was subjected to 869 hours of treatment), the clinic closed in July 2002 due to the existing site becoming unavailable and a new site not being readily identified. There would appear to be no plans to reintroduce the clinic in its original form or to re-use its intensive behavioural programme. Despite such positive findings, Marshall (2008) nevertheless warns that you can have people in treatment for too long and that, if you over-treat some offenders, this can actually have a negative effect on what has been previously taught. For this reason, he argues that the correct dosage of intervention, even with high-risk offenders, is two to three sessions per week, for four months. Based on research conducted on the Rockwood Psychological Services Program with 100 sex offenders over a time period of 7.4 years, it was found that, using this treatment dosage, only 3.2 per cent of the treated offenders committed further sex offences compared to 16.8 per cent of the untreated sample. This, he claims, proves that long-term therapy is not necessary (ibid.).

The only alternative for high-risk offenders deemed not suitable for the accredited sex offender programmes is a consultancy service provided by the Lucy Faithfull Foundation, which has been available since 2003 (NPS 2003). The partnership was first set up in recognition of the closure of the Wolvercote Clinic and the acknowledgement that it was essential to maintain the expert support and advice of the Foundation's staff, and initially included outreach work to former Wolvercote residents (ibid.). Advice is now provided on a case-by-case basis but can include advice on risk management, child protection, interventions with partners, and support with the assessment and development of risk-management and intervention plans (NOMS 2007a). Despite such expert support existing, however, it arguably only helps to manage rather than reduce risk, meaning that, while the low- and medium-risk offenders are treated, the high-risk and arguably dangerous offenders are not.

Research has also taken place regarding the efficacy of i-SOTP, with Middleton *et al.* (2009) basing their findings on 264 convicted internet sex offenders who completed the programme between 2006 and 2008. Risk-assessment information was available for 161 of the sample, with 51 per cent classified as low risk, 39 per cent as medium risk, 9 per cent as high risk and 1 per cent as very high risk. Deviancy information was known for 148 of the sample, with 70 per cent assessed as low deviance and 30 per cent as high deviance. Of interest, 10 per cent had already completed previous SOTPs. Results showed that 'offenders were assessed to have changed post-treatment in the desired direction' (Middleton *et al.* 2009: 13), with increases seen in levels of self-esteem and acceptance of responsibility. Impulsive behaviour was being controlled better, there were large changes witnessed in the offender's responses to victim empathy questions and the prevalence of cognitive distortions supportive of child sexual abuse was reduced. Although further research is still required, including comparisons with a control group and based on long-term reconviction studies, such findings are nevertheless 'sufficiently encouraging to justify the continuation of the wide-scale delivery of the treatment programme' (ibid.: 17).

Violent offender programmes

Despite the plethora of studies concerning SOTPs, research concerning the efficacy of violent offending and domestic violence programmes has been minimal, with Polaschek claiming that there has only been one true meta-analysis concerning programmes for domestic violence perpetrators (see Babcock *et al.* 2004). Even taking into account other research studies, he argues that 'the most optimistic conclusion that can be reached is that the best programmes may help a little' (Polasckek 2006: 127). Concerning IDAP, for example, there appears to be no conclusive research evidence, although there has been some positive anecdotal verification (Home Affairs Committee 2008). In one systematic review of 31 studies of behavioural interventions for domestic violence perpetrators, of which 22 were based on the principles found in IDAP, treatment effects were found to be in the 'small range' (Liebmann and Wotton 2008: 13). Hollis, summarising the available evidence in the UK, similarly reported 'inconclusive but encouraging finding of reduced violence and reduced frequency of violence according to partner's self reports' (2007: 28; see also Gadd 2004). A more recent report (Bullock *et al.* 2010) looks at the implementation and delivery of IDAP in prison and probation in England and Wales, but comments hardly at all on actual effectiveness, although comments from group members include:

> In general just the way I come across and deal with situations, you know, I didn't understand, I don't think I really realised that I was coming across in my voice and my body language quite aggressive towards my partner always. I've controlled that a lot more, so it's, you know, I'm conscious of it, which means that you do tend to control it. You know, as soon as it starts happening, you can nip it in the bud, because you're now conscious of it, you know you're doing it.
>
> (16)

The government has also been criticised for failing in its pledge to tackle domestic abuse, on the basis that fewer than half (1,800 out of more than 4,000) of the men ordered to carry out domestic violence treatment programmes in 2007 had done so (Doward 2008). The main reason for this was not attrition rates, as perhaps might be expected, but was due to a backlog of people waiting to join the programmes. For example, probation officers in West Midlands claimed that their backlog was so serious that they were only able to place high-risk abusers on IDAP; in Avon and Somerset, waiting lists were between 8 and 12 months; and, in Yorkshire, some offenders had been waiting for as long as 2 years (ibid.). This desperate shortage of places was also acknowledged by the House of Commons (Home Affairs Committee 2008). An immediate increase in programme provision is therefore urgently required.

Research in England and Wales concerning CSCP and CALM has also been negligible, with most research taking place either in North America (Henning and Frueh 1996), Canada (Dowden *et al.* 1999), or Northern Ireland (Jordan and O'Hare 2007). To test the effectiveness of CSCP, Henning and Frueh (1996) used a sample of 124 men who had been incarcerated in a prison in Vermont and had been released into the community. 28 of the sample had voluntarily completed the programme while in prison. Looking at reconviction data over a period of 2 years from release, 50 per cent of the CSCP group were charged with a new crime, which, while high, was less than the 70.8 per cent charged from the comparison group. Regarding CALM, the main efficacy study was carried out by Dowden *et al.*, who compared 110 male offenders who had completed the Canadian equivalent of the programme, with an untreated sample who were similar in age, index offence and risk group. While completion of the programme did not seem to reduce violent recidivism in low-risk cases, there was a marked difference for those offenders classified as high risk, translating into an 86 per cent reduction. Interestingly, the programme was also found to reduce general recidivism for high-risk offenders, translating into a 69 per cent reduction. In conclusion, the findings were held to be 'encouraging' (1999: 21). This was later followed up by Dowden and Serin (2001), who included dropout and institutional incident data into their findings. Perhaps surprisingly, they found no difference in the frequency of institutional incidents between the two groups, and worryingly that those who started treatment but later dropped out reoffended at a higher rate than those who had never commenced treatment. This would therefore suggest that attrition can have a drastic impact on the programmes' effectiveness and perhaps weakens the 'encouraging' results noted above.

Another consideration to bear in mind is that the most crucial feature in any treatment programme is the therapist and not the actual content or procedure. Marshall (2008) argues that, if the programme tutor is critical, devaluing or confrontational, the offender is unlikely to respond, whatever the nature of the intervention. Indeed, he believes that the tutor can contribute to 20–25 per cent of any treatment change, with the largest influence being seen with sex offenders who, in most cases, are highly motivated to change. Vast resources spent on designing treatment programmes may, therefore, be counterproductive unless money is also spent in ensuring that they are effectively and positively delivered.

With so many problems with not just the way in which efficacy is assessed in cognitive-behavioural programmes, but also due to the fact efficacy data is inconclusive, it is unsurprising that England and Wales has sought other means of risk reduction for its dangerous offenders. The remainder of this chapter will therefore look at these options, including a very brief look at surgical interventions, but will concentrate more on pharmacotherapy and techniques based on restorative justice.

Surgical interventions

Neurosurgery

The use of neurosurgery, also known as stereotaxic hypothalamotomy, involves the removal of parts of the hypothalamus in the brain. The operation causes a disruption in the production of male hormonal agents, including testosterone, which causes a reduction in sexual arousal, deviant sexual behaviour (Grossman *et al.* 1999) aggressiveness and violent behaviour (Sano and Mayanagi 1988). It was first used on sex offenders in Germany in 1962, where two thirds of the ventromedial nucleus of an offender's hypothalamus was removed (Rieber and Sigusch 1979), which worked to eliminate erotic fantasies and deviant urges (Icenogle 1994). Research has also been carried out regarding its use with violent offenders, with Bufkin and Luttrell (2005) claiming that it is possible to localise the areas of the brain that are associated with aggressive and/or violent behaviour. Indeed, Japan has been known to treat its violent offenders by making small stereotactic lesions in the ergotropic portion of the posterior hypothalamus, with good results found in follow-ups of between 10 and 25 years (Sano and Mayanagi 1988). Despite the practice being used, and with some success, the complex interactions between the brain and sexual/violent behaviour are not sufficiently understood for the practice to be considered safe. It is therefore seen as an imprecise procedure that can cause unpredictable behavioural results (Lockhart *et al.* 1989), often contributing to the offender committing suicide or further violent crime.

Surgical castration

Another surgical option is the use of surgical castration or bilateral orchiectomy, which is the removal of a man's testes. The operation eliminates the primary supply of testosterone, as approximately 95 per cent of testosterone is produced in the testes (Prentky 1997). This has the effect of reducing sexual desire and urges and, in some cases, aggression, although it is only used for sex offenders. Surgical castration as a means of treating sex offenders has been used by several European countries, with Switzerland, in 1892, being the first to use it (Carpenter 1998). In the Netherlands, between 1930 and 1969, 400 sex offenders were surgically castrated (Frenken *et al.* 1999); in Denmark, between 1929 and 1959, the figure stood at 738 (Ortmann 1980); while, in Germany, during the period of 1955 and 1977, the number was 800 (Prentky 1997). Surgical castration has also been used in the USA, Norway, Sweden, Finland, Estonia, Iceland and Latvia, and is currently still used in the Czech Republic.

Evaluation studies on the whole have been positive, with Ohm (1960, cited by Wille and Beier 1989), who evaluated 224 castrated sex offenders in Germany, noting that only 8 (3.5 per cent) had reoffended. Likewise, in Switzerland, Cornu's study (1973, cited by Wille and Beier 1989) of 121 offenders found the recidivism rate to be 4.1 per cent. Even more encouraging is the study carried out by Sturup (1968, cited by Wille and Beier 1989) in Denmark, which found a 0 per cent recidivism rate. More recently, Wille and Beier (1989) compared 99 castrated offenders with 35 non-castrated offenders. Using a follow-up time of 11 years, the research discovered that, of the castrated group, only 3 per cent had been involved in another sexual crime, while 46 per cent of the non-castrated group had reoffended. Most of the castrated offenders were also found to have experienced a reduction in sexual desire, sexual ability, erotic fantasies and erectile function.

Despite such positive results, the use of surgical castration, while still legal in many European countries and some states in the USA, is now only practised on a very small scale. Many regard the practice as 'barbaric' (*Weems v United States*, 217 US 349, 377 (1910)) and in contravention of Article 3 of the ECHR, and/or Amendment 8 of the USA Constitution (*State v Brown*, 326 S.E.2d 410 (S.C. 1985)). Arguably, on matters of family life, it also contravenes Articles 8 and 12 ECHR. It is also worth noting that the operation can produce the negative side effects of hot flushes, softening of the skin, lethargy, decrease in muscle mass (Russell 1997) and osteoporosis (Aschwanden and Ermer 2008). While the operation is irreversible, effects of surgery can be modified by testosterone injections, which can be acquired illegally on the black market. Constant monitoring through MAPPAs of even surgically castrated sex offenders is thus required.

Pharmacotherapy

In contrast to surgical interventions is the option of pharmacotherapy. Usually, and wrongly, referred to under its more emotive title of chemical castration (as the aim is to reduce sexual drive rather than to achieve impotency (Miller 1998)), pharmacotherapy is the use of drugs to achieve the *effect* of surgical castration but through less invasive and irreversible means. While it is often thought that pharmacotherapy is a relatively new risk-reduction intervention, this is not the case, with the use of oestrogen on sex offenders being recorded in the 1940s (Dunn 1940; Foote 1944). Initial reports concerning its efficacy were largely positive, although trials were ended due to the existence of negative side effects, including gynaecomastia (enlargement of the breasts), thrombosis, nausea, severe headaches and impairment of vision (Bowden 1991). Largely due to such side effects, oestrogen was succeeded in the 1960s by drugs known as anti-libidinals. Examples include medroxyprogesterone acetate (MPA), which is used in the USA, and cyproterone acetate (CPA), utilised in Europe, Canada, England and Wales. More recently, Luteinizing Hormone-Releasing Hormone (LHRH) inhibitors have also been used, as too have Selective Serotonin Reuptake Inhibitors (SSRIs). These are more commonly employed in the treatment of depression, bulimia nervosa and obsessive compulsive disorder, and come under the grouping of psychotropic medication.[3]

The effect of anti-libidinal drugs is to reduce levels of testosterone in the offender's body. This, in turn, will reduce sexual drive, decrease erotic and deviant fantasies (Hicks 1993), and lessen potency, sperm production, sexual frustration and the frequency and pleasure of masturbation (Craissati 2004). SSRIs, on the other hand, enhance levels of the hormone serotonin. This consequently reduces sexual functioning, sexual desire and associated sexual performance behaviours (Kafka 1997). The drugs have also been found to reduce an offender's frustration and anger levels, making him more relaxed and thus able to concentrate on other forms of treatment such as psychotherapy (Weiss 1999). Thus, it is argued that, in order to achieve the most effective results, pharmacotherapy should always be used alongside and in conjunction with psychotherapy and other treatment methods (Craissati 2004; Harrison 2007b).

Use in England and Wales

Previous use

Data on the use of pharmacotherapy with sex offenders is limited, so it is unclear what practices and which drugs have previously been used in England and Wales. It is apparent, however, that Benperidol, an antipsychotic drug often used to treat schizophrenia, was available in prisons between 1971 and 1973 for the treatment of deviant behaviour, despite the fact that its product licence was not granted until July 1973 (Sim 1990). In 1971, Field conducted a study on its use at Wormwood Scrubs. Of the 28 men involved, all noticed a reduction in sexual desire, although for two this was not accompanied by additional decreases in erotic fantasies (*The Times*, 10 September 1973: 3). CPA was also available between 1970 and 1974, with trials ending due to the effects of gynaecomastia (Sim 1990). Figures for November 1975 to November 1978 suggest that 138 sex offenders in British prisons were involved in one or more types of drug treatment for deviant sexual behaviour (ibid.), with this number reducing to 18 in 1987 (Bowden 1991).

Current use

While it is apparent that some sex offenders are being prescribed CPA by psychiatrists and other health professionals, there is no data in England and Wales to show exactly how many offenders are involved in such practices (Grubin 2008d). Since June 2007, however, the role of referral for sex offender medication has been given to the Ministry of Justice (Home Office 2007). Medication is offered on a voluntary basis, in conjunction with other treatment programmes, and is available only to convicted offenders through referrals by prison or probation personnel (NOMS 2007b). Offenders are deemed to be appropriate for referral where either: 'specific mental health issues are identified that relate directly to assessment or treatment (for instance, where mental illness is thought to contribute to the risk of reoffending . . .)', or where there is evidence of hyper-arousal, intrusive sexual fantasies or urges, sexual urges which are difficult to control and/or sexual sadism (ibid.: 3). Depending on the needs of the offender, SSRIs, CPA or LHRH inhibitors are used.

Treatment has been available in England and Wales since 1 December 2007, with a contract issued to Northumberland Tyne and Wear NHS Trust to run the pilot scheme for an initial period of three years. In addition to treatment provision, the Sexual Behaviour Unit in Newcastle also provides a national advisory service and arranges for psychiatric assessments to establish whether a mental health problem has contributed to sexual offending (NOMS 2007b). Data on treatment take-up has not yet been published, although, in November 2008, it was acknowledged that 11 offenders had been referred for initial assessment, although information as to whether they had been accepted on to the programme was unavailable due to medical confidentiality (HC Deb, 26 November 2008, c1692W).

Efficacy

In contrast to violent offender behaviour programmes, there have been a multitude of efficacy studies regarding the use of pharmacotherapy with sex offenders.[4] On the basis that England and Wales is currently using CPA, LHRH inhibitors and SSRIs, it will be these drugs that will be assessed regarding their effectiveness.

CPA

The first reported efficacy study regarding the use of CPA with sex offenders was in 1966. Findings showed how the drug produced reductions in sexual drive, erections and the ability to orgasm (Laschet and Laschet 1971, cited in Bradford and Pawlak 1993). Cooper *et al.* (1972) reported its use with one man where testosterone was reduced by 50 per cent, morning erections disappeared and the patient was unable to masturbate to orgasm. Based on these results, a larger investigation was undertaken involving nine men. The results showed a 'significant action for cyproterone acetate . . . in reducing sexual interest and concomitant physiological arousal' (Cooper 1981: 461), with a parallel 30 per cent reduction in testosterone levels.

Additional studies on the use of CPA with sex offenders suggest that an offender's libido is usually decreased within two weeks of treatment beginning (Ott and Hoffet 1968, cited by Bradford and Pawlak 1993) and that it can have a tranquilising effect, making patients less irritable, more relaxed and thus amenable to treatment (Bradford and Pawlak 1993). Both psychological and physiological effects are reversed within four weeks of withdrawal (Cooper 1981), although its positive effects in controlling deviant behaviour may last much longer (Craissati 2004). However, similar to Oestrogen, CPA can produce negative side effects including fatigue, hypersomnia (sleepiness), lethargy, depression, a decrease in body hair, an increase in scalp hair and weight gain (Bradford and Pawlak 1993). Other effects include liver damage, bone mineral loss, nausea, indigestion, skin rashes, galactorrhoea (abnormal production of breast milk), shortness of breath, and decreased production of oil from sebaceous glands in the skin (Harrison 2010b). Of interest, however, is the claim that CPA does not cause gynaecomastia (Davis 1974).

LHRH inhibitors

Saleh *et al.* (2004) evaluated the effectiveness of the LHRH inhibitor leuprolide acetate, looking at six patients, all of whom had at least one paraphilia and had been involved in previous unsuccessful treatment efforts. When the subjects were given 7.5 mg per month, all of them reported a reduction in their sexually deviant symptoms. There was a marked reduction in the frequency of masturbation to deviant sexual thoughts and imagery, and also in the frequency of inappropriate behaviour, although most reported a reduction in their behaviour and thoughts rather than complete eradication. Briken *et al.* (2001) also looked at LHRH inhibitors, testing the effect of Trenantone on 11 men with severe paraphilias over a period of 12 months. Sexually aggressive behaviour was eradicated and patients reported a reduction in penile erection, ejaculation, masturbation and sexually deviant impulses and fantasies, with no sexual offending recorded during the treatment period. Testosterone levels were significantly reduced after three months, with six men who had previously used CPA or SSRIs feeling that Trenantone was better at reducing deviant fantasies.

Despite such positive findings, negative side effects of LHRH inhibitors include weight gain, depression, pain at the injection site (Briken *et al.* 2001), mild to moderate bone demineralisation, nausea, depression and mild gynaecomastia (Krueger and Kaplan 2001). Aschwanden and Ermer (2008) also record instances of allergic reactions to the drugs that can cause redness and swelling at the injection site, but, more importantly, can affect effectiveness. These authors also warn how long-term use may result in cognitive problems. Grasswick and Bradford (2002, cited by Briken *et al.* 2003) additionally report concerns of osteoporosis.

SSRIs

To assess the effectiveness of SSRIs, Adi *et al.* (2002) conducted a review concentrating on 9 USA studies, involving 225 subjects. Using psychometric tests to analyse and record change, most offenders showed a level of improvement, which was held to be statistically significant in six of the studies. Bradford *et al.* (1995, cited by Greenberg *et al.* 1996) looked at the use of Sertraline in the treatment of 21 paedophiles, with results showing a decrease in paedophilic fantasies, urges and arousal. Interestingly, conventional relations with adults were maintained. When some psychotherapy programmes work to encourage sex offenders, particularly child sex offenders, to have age-appropriate relationships, medication that allows this must be seen in a better light than medication that does not. Furthermore, Greenberg and Bradford (1997) looked at a group of 95 paraphilics treated with SSRIs, comparing them to 104 patients receiving psychosocial interventions. Results showed that, following a twelve-week period, those patients who were part of the SSRI group had significantly more reductions in fantasies and urges than the control group.

While the possible side effects with SSRIs are considered to be less severe than those associated with CPA, they can still include gastrointestinal problems, increased appetite and weight gain, rashes, anxiety, headaches, sweating, convulsions, and hallucinations. SSRIs should therefore not be used if the patient is hypersensitive to the drug or enters into a manic phase, is receiving electroconvulsive therapy, or has a history of epilepsy, cardiac disease, diabetes, renal and hepatic impairment or bleeding disorders (Adi *et al.* 2002). While positive results have been reported, Adi *et al.* (2002) note that many studies are vulnerable to bias; comparative control groups are rarely used and there are little or no follow-up periods. Similarly, Beech and Mitchell (2005) argue that, while there are several examples of SSRIs' use, many are single case studies, meaning that more research, including large-scale double-blind randomised controlled trials, are required, a thought also shared by Maletzky and Field (2003). A double-blind controlled trial of SSRIs in imprisoned sex offenders was commissioned to take place in England and Wales by the National Programme on Forensic Mental Health but, to the author's knowledge, this has not yet taken place.

Efficacy studies on CPA, LHRH inhibitors and SSRIs would thus appear to be positive, giving hope that the pilot projects currently underway in England and Wales will be successful, although similar caveats concerning methodology, as those seen with cognitive-behavioural programmes, are also evident here. Furthermore, pharmacotherapy will probably only work with those offenders who are classed as paedophiles and, to be more specific, it is probably only useful for those who are preferential paedophiles (that is, those who have sexual relationships with children and never adults). It is therefore not effective for rapists (with rape often being more about power than sex), violent sex offenders, those who offend due to alcohol, drugs or pressure, or those who deny their offending. It would also appear that, to achieve maximum effectiveness, the drugs need to be used in combination with psychotherapy or some other form of counselling to address areas such as distorted perceptions, denial or minimisation of the offending, attitudes towards children, and pro-criminal attitudes (Harrison 2007b). It may, therefore, mean that success is ultimately only achieved with those offenders who want to control their offending behaviour and are thus motivated to change. Efficacy data is only relevant, however, if there is an adequate take-up of pharmacotherapy, and so it will be interesting to see whether, in practical terms, it really will add to risk-reduction interventions.[5]

Restorative justice techniques

In addition to the more conventional interventions, practices involving restorative justice techniques have also begun to gain ground in the last few years, although arguably they still largely exist on the fringes of the criminal justice system, despite having deep historical roots (see Johnstone 2002). While there has been some debate regarding whether it is a set of principles or an actual practice (see Daly 2009), restorative justice can be defined as 'a process whereby all the parties with a stake in a particular offence come together to resolve collectively how to deal with the aftermath of the offence and its implications for the future' (Marshall 1999: 238). Key values that underpin all restorative approaches include:

- Inclusivity – where the interests of the victim and others are brought more fully into the process of dealing with the offender.
- A balancing of interests – where an appropriate balance between all stake holders in the process is sought.
- Consensual non-coercive participation and decision making.
- Problem-solving orientation – where the focus is on reintegrating the offender back into the community with the focus placed on forward looking and the prevention of reoffending.

(McAlinden 2007: 39)[6]

The main difference between restorative and more conventional criminal justice approaches is the former's emphasis on reintegration, restitution, reparation (Kemshall 2008), reconciliation and community partnership, which consequently allows for earned redemption (McAlinden 2007). Sherman, furthermore, notes how it is also different to traditional psychological interventions, as there is no set model on how reintegration is to be achieved, with 'offenders becom[ing] law-abiding through acts and relationships rather than through a personality change or "treatment"' (2000: 269). The emphasis of interventions based on restorative principles is therefore on reintegrative shaming rather than on disintegrative shaming. Traditional models of criminal justice work by shaming the offence and the offender, which often results in the offender being marginalised by his community and which can often lead to further offending. Restorative justice, however, shames the offence, but not the offender, instead working to reintegrate him back into his community so that future offending is prevented (see Braithwaite 1989; McAlinden 2007).

While the use of restorative techniques has increased, they have traditionally been associated with low-level crime or used when dealing with young offenders. Arguments against using restorative justice with the more sensitive crimes of domestic violence and sexual offences centre on the risk of re-victimisation, the possibility that the seriousness of the offence could be trivialised and the power imbalance that could be further re-enforced. Cossins (2008) also argues that there is insufficient evidence to justify using it in sexual assault crimes. Despite this, it has been argued that restorative interventions can be useful with high-risk offenders (see Morris and Gelsthorpe 2000; McAlinden 2007; Daly 2008), including those who have committed serious sexual and violent offences. Proponents argue that it is important to give the victim the choice of restorative justice and that the technique can be used to redress the power imbalance caused by the offence. Although restorative justice is usually used instead of the court process, and so in this sense is a diversionary technique, considering the nature of the discussion here (that is, serious sexual and violent offenders), it is suggested that restorative interventions should be used after and in addition to normal criminal justice programmes rather than instead of them. This would allow for punishment and deterrence, but also reparation, reconciliation and rehabilitation. Interventions that are based on the values of restorative justice, designed with sexual and violent offenders in mind, include Circles of Support and Accountability (COSAs), victim/offender mediations and family group conferencing. These methods and the programmes that employ them will be assessed below.

Restorative interventions for sex offenders

The main programme designed for use with sex offenders, based on restorative principles is Circles of Support and Accountability (COSA), although instead of the offender meeting with the victim, the offender meets with volunteers from the community and is held accountable by them, arguably on behalf of the victim. The development of COSA can be traced back to the restorative work carried out by the Canadian Mennonite Church in 1994 in response to sex offenders being released from prison into their communities (Wilson *et al.* 2008). Based on the two pillars of safety and support, COSA offer public protection and reintegration, with the key idea being that it is the community who accepts responsibility for its own members and for addressing the sex offender's problem (McAlinden 2007). The aim is therefore to 'control wrongdoers within a communitarian society and informally sanction deviance by reintegration into cohesive networks, rather than by formal restraint', with the community becoming an important 'resource in the risk management process' (McAlinden 2007: 171).

Circles have existed in England and Wales since 2002, when three pilot projects were funded by the Home Office. These were Hampshire, managed by The Hampton Trust; Thames Valley, managed by The Religious Society of Friends (Quakers); and the Lucy Faithfull Foundation, which, as described above, was initially established to support ex-residents of the Wolvercote Clinic (Saunders 2004). Different to their Canadian forefathers, COSA in England and Wales have developed in a more systemic way and have been formed within a greater framework of governmental supervision (Wilson *et al.* 2008). Arguably, in Canada, COSA were community driven and professionally supported, while, in England and Wales, they are professionally driven and community supported. They are now managed by Circles UK, who work in partnership with police, probation and local

MAPPA professionals, and are funded by the Ministry of Justice, statutory agencies and a number of charitable trusts and foundations.[7]

Circles in England and Wales consist of four to six people who act as a support network to an offender, who is referred to as the core member. All are collectively known as the inner circle. An outer circle also exists, which is made up of MAPPA professionals who have expert knowledge in risk and who will offer support to the inner circle (Wilson *et al.* 2008). The size of the circle is said to be extremely important (that is, it is small enough to facilitate communication and trust, but large enough to share responsibility for the needs of the offender). All volunteers are asked to sign a covenant that will specify the individual's area of assistance, with the offender also signing the covenant to signify his agreement to the conditions. The core member must accept responsibility for his behaviour and, for this reason, it is preferable that he has already completed either the SOTP or a community-based alternative. He must also be motivated not to reoffend and be willing to engage with the circle (Saunders 2004). Work is focused upon three key principles (see Figure 6.1) and will often focus on accommodation, employment, developing social skills, finding appropriate hobbies and achieving acceptance by the community; although support is individualised depending on the offender's needs (Circles UK 2010a). This is coupled with appropriate amounts of disapproval and challenge concerning inappropriate behaviour, thoughts and feelings. It is thought that support at this level can help the core member grow in self-esteem, develop healthy adult relationships and maximise his chances of successful reintegration (Circles UK 2010a). The circle will initially meet weekly, with accompanying mid-week telephone calls. Future contact depends on the

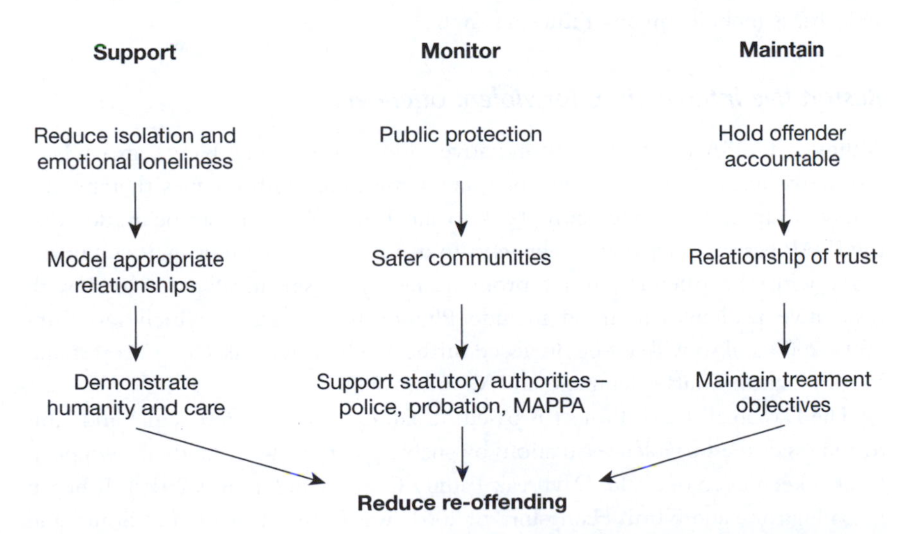

Figure 6.1 The three key principles of COSA working (Saunders and Wilson 2002, cited by Yorkshire and Humberside Circles of Support and Accountability 2010).

individual needs of the offender, with most circles lasting 12 months, although this can be extended if deemed necessary and worthwhile.

Circles now operate in Hampshire and Thames Valley, North Wales, Cumbria, the East of England (covering Hertfordshire, Bedfordshire, Essex, Cambridgeshire, Norfolk and Suffolk), Greater Manchester, Leicestershire and Rutland, Yorkshire and Humberside, Devon and Cornwall, Dorset, Avon and Somerset, and Northumbria. The Lucy Faithfull Foundation (although no longer funded by the Ministry of Justice) is able to cover all other remaining areas (Circles UK 2010b). Initial data on the effectiveness of circles has been extremely encouraging, with the first evaluation of COSA in England and Wales appearing in 2007 (Bates *et al.* 2007). This involved the follow-up of 16 members of the original Thames Valley COSA from 2002–6, with no reconvictions recorded during this time, although 4 were recalled to prison for breaching licence conditions, showing evidence of the accountability aspect (ibid.). In conclusion, it has been held that 'the Circle process provides unique insights into the details of Core Members' behaviours and lifestyles well beyond statutory supervision by agencies such as the police, probation and treatment services' (Wilson *et al.* 2008: 34).

More general research from Canada has also been positive, with studies conducted using matched controls. In one study, those involved in COSA reoffended 70 per cent less for sexual reoffending, 35 per cent less for general reoffending and 57 per cent less for violent reoffending when compared to the matched control. This was also confirmed in a second study, where recidivism rates were 2 per cent versus 13 per cent for sexual reoffending, 9 per cent versus 32 per cent for violent reoffending and 11 per cent versus 38 per cent for general recidivism (Wilson *et al.* 2008). Such promising results perhaps also open up the possibility of using circles with violent offenders and, indeed, this should be an area that is included in any future research.

Restorative interventions for violent offenders

Although COSA is a fairly new initiative, domestic violence is one area where restorative justice has been used for quite some time, with couples therapy and family group conferencing dating back to the 1980s. While it can be argued that the IDAP has some restorative elements to it, in that the victim is included in the work with the offender, other programmes more specifically designed with restorative principles in mind include Plymouth Mediation (which ran from 1994–2000 and so will not be discussed further), The Daybreak Dove Project and Victim Liaison Units (Liebmann and Wootton 2008).

The Daybreak Dove Project is based on family group conferencing[8] and aims to address domestic violence situations by enabling families to make their own plans to help keep everyone safe (Daybreak Family Group Conferences 2010). It began in Basingstoke and North Hampshire in 2001, was further extended to South and Central Hampshire in 2006 (Taylor 2008) and now additionally runs in Portsmouth, Bournemouth and Poole (Daybreak Family Group Conferences 2010). It has been described as 'a way to bring together the extended family to make decisions and to come up with a plan that will create a way forward' and 'as a practical tool for building partnerships among the family and community to keep family members safe and to promote their well being' (Taylor 2008). Such work is supported by the means of a coordinator who works to encourage the making of plans, but importantly also ensures that participants are protected (Cox 2007). The programme is managed by Daybreak Family Group Conferences and is funded on a multi-agency basis, including the Children's Fund, the Department for Education and Skills, local police, health and social services departments (ibid.). Referrals include those families who have experienced 'domestic abuse in its widest interpretation of physical, emotional, psychological, financial or sexual' (Daybreak Family Group Conferences 2010) abuse, and who have at least one child. Those who refer to the programme include statutory or voluntary agencies, family members and community groups. Since its inception, the project has had contact with over 300 families (ibid.), with Liebmann and Wootton (2008) noting a 73 per cent success rate in Hampshire, with 11 out of 15 families involved in the project not coming to the police's attention again.

More traditional offender/victim mediation is carried out by Victim Liaison Units, which form a part of NOMS and are initiated when a perpetrator has received a custodial term of 12 months or more, for either a violent or a sexual offence. The unit may be used to solely keep the victim informed of the sentencing outcome, although trained mediators can also help parties to communicate and, in some instances, meet, so that pertinent issues can be resolved prior to the offender's release, with agreed outcomes often forming part of the offender's licence conditions (Liebmann and Wotton 2008).

Efficacy

In light of the fact that the criminal justice system is often described as too lenient on those who commit serious offences, it is perhaps to be expected that the public would be opposed to restorative programmes with serious sexual and violent offenders. This is not, however, true, with some preferring restorative interventions over more punitive options, (Roberts and Hough 2005) and some showing support towards restorative elements if they are used in addition, rather than instead of, imprisonment or probation supervision. Braithwaite and Daly (1995) also contend that, in cases of domestic violence, a community conference can be more effective than a more traditional response because it

> makes men more accountable for violence against women (including rape) because women may be less likely to drop the case; exposes the fact that men may have been violent many times, not just once [and] is less likely to re-victimise the victim than the court process.
>
> (Liebmann and Wootton 2008: 15)

Research carried out by the Australian Institute of Criminology also notes how victims and offenders of violent crimes who participated in restorative interventions showed higher levels of satisfaction when compared to those whose cases had gone through more traditional criminal justice channels. Offenders were more likely to come out of restorative justice conferences more satisfied, yet more ashamed, than if they had followed the normal court route, with victims reporting a much greater sense of closure and reduced levels of fear (Sherman 2000).

The main research in England and Wales concerning restorative interventions has been carried out by the University of Sheffield, with results published in four reports between 2004 and 2008.[9] The first report concentrated on how restorative interventions should be set up, with recommendations including a clear statutory footing to encourage agencies to refer to the schemes, basing the projects within criminal justice agencies and raising awareness of the benefits of restorative interventions so as to build confidence in the eyes of sentencers and professionals working within criminal justice (Shapland *et al.* 2004). The second looked at victim participation, with up to 77 per cent of victims agreeing to participate in mediation, although in the majority of cases victims preferred the option of indirect mediation rather than direct, face-to-face conferencing (Shapland *et al.* 2006). The third report looked at the impact of the interventions on victims, with 85 per cent very or quite satisfied with their experiences and, in 98 per cent of the cases, conferences ending with an agreed outcome (Shapland *et al.* 2007). Finally, the fourth report looked at recidivism and value for money. Regarding recidivism, while it was found that the projects did not eradicate reoffending, offenders were reoffending at a lesser level, with a statistically significant fall in the frequency of reconviction noted. The research showed that 27 per cent fewer crimes were committed by those who had been involved in a restorative intervention, when compared with those who had not (Shapland *et al.* 2008). Restorative justice was also found to be cost effective, with the taxpayer found to be saving £8 (which would have been spent on reoffending) for every £1 spent. The case for restorative justice from this research is therefore patently clear, with McAlinden arguing that it is 'a viable alternative in a justice system that has yet to come up with a better answer to an extremely difficult societal problem' (2007: 223). While more research is needed, so that an evidence base can be formed, the case for using restorative techniques in addition to normal criminal justice options is encouraging. It will therefore be interesting to see whether the Ministry of Justice now begins to include more restorative interventions in its strategy for dangerous offenders and, if it does, whether sentencing judges and MAPPA personnel will support and ultimately use them.

Conclusion

As has been detailed throughout this chapter, there are a number of risk-reduction strategies currently available in England and Wales for serious sexual and violent offenders. While surgical interventions are not widely practised and pharmacotherapy is only currently used on a very minimal basis, there is evidence of high usage of psychotherapy and, increasingly, methods based on restorative justice. Evidence of efficacy in all of these methods is essential and, while there are problems with how this is measured, there have been a number of studies that suggest risk can be reduced even in the most dangerous of offenders. Serious sexual and violent offenders are often complicated individuals and so it is imperative that a full package of risk-reduction strategies is designed for these people. MAPPA personnel therefore need to ensure that they are using all available options rather than restricting themselves to the more traditional alternatives, especially when evidence suggests that psychotherapy on its own does not work for high-risk and/or high-denial offenders. When public protection is at stake, anything that can be used to help secure this should be tried, tested and an evidence-base built up. Only then can the Ministry of Justice claim that it is 'protecting the public and reducing reoffending' (Ministry of Justice 2010e).

7
WOMEN OFFENDERS

Introduction

Thus far, this book has principally dealt with male adult offenders and, in consequence of this, considered risk-assessment tools, intervention programmes and risk-management strategies that have been designed almost exclusively with adult males in mind. Serious sexual and violent offenders are not, however, limited to men, with them also encompassing women, children and young people. This and the subsequent chapter will therefore look at these distinct groups. With regards to women offenders, this chapter will evaluate whether there is a need for different risk-assessment tools, consider prison regimes for women and assess whether they are different to those experienced by men, and measure the availability, and more importantly, the suitability of risk-reduction interventions. For introduction purposes, it will first look at the prevalence of women who have committed serious sexual and violent offences and also consider how female offenders are viewed by both professional practitioners and the public.

The prevalence of dangerous women offenders

While it is true that the majority of serious sexual and violent offenders are male, there are still a number of offenders who are women, with notorious examples including Rosemary West, Beverley Allitt, Myra Hindley and, more recently, Vanessa George. In fact, in terms of sexual offending, it is thought that women make up 4–5 per cent of all convicted offenders (Cortoni and Hanson 2005) and account for 1 per cent of the prison population (see Table 7.1 below). Despite this low figure, the NSPCC estimate that women in all likelihood commit up to 5 per cent of all female abuse and 44 per cent of male abuse (NSPCC 2007, cited by Cortoni 2010). Reports of child sexual abuse by women are also thought to have a lower reporting rate than those committed by men, so in reality abuse rates are probably far higher. This disparity in reporting may be for a number of reasons; for instance, some victims may feel that they are less likely to be believed when the offender is a female as compared to when it is a man, with Elliott (2004) finding that 86 per cent of victims who had tried to tell someone about abuse committed by a woman not being initially believed. Victims may be too young to articulate a complaint or may not have access to a telephone or, where the child is being abused by a single-parent mother, there may not be a significant other for the child to confide in (Faller 1987). Moreover, male victims may not report the behaviour because they may not feel that they are being abused, thinking rather that it is enjoyable or that they are lucky to be selected by an older woman. For example, 8 per cent of the male victims in Elliott's study found the sexual relationships with their mothers or other female members of their family 'wholly beneficial and natural' (2004: 5), with some of the relationships continuing into adulthood. Even if males do come forward and report the abuse, they may be congratulated rather than assisted. Alternatively, males may not report the abuse, thinking that it will make them look less of a man.

Between 2005 and 2006, 447 homicides were committed by men and 31 (6.94 per cent) by women (Hunter *et al.* 2009), suggesting that, on the whole, men are more violent. Between 2008 and 2009, women were involved in 19 per cent of all violent crime: 14 per cent offended on their own and 5 per cent co-offended with men. Women were involved in 16 per cent of all wounding offences, 12 per cent of all robberies and 13 per cent of all street muggings (Roe *et al.* 2009). This reduced between 2009 and 2010 to 16 per cent of all violent crime, with 9 per cent offending on their own and 7 per cent co-offending with men. They were involved in 13 per cent of all woundings, 6 per cent of robberies and 7 per cent of street muggings (Hall and Innes 2010).

In 2007, of the 1,117,300 men sentenced in the criminal courts, 87,400 (7.8 per cent) received an immediate custodial sentence. This can be compared to the 289,500 women sentenced overall, with 7,800 (2.7 per cent) receiving immediate imprisonment. In terms of actual offences, of those convicted for sexual offences, 56 per cent of men but only 31 per cent of women were sentenced to immediate custody. This lack of correspondence is also visible regarding violent offences, with 32 per cent of men sentenced to immediate custody but only

Table 7.1 Breakdown of prison population in 2007 by sex and offence type

Offence type	*Number of male offenders*	*% of male offenders*	*Number of female offenders*	*% of female offenders*
Violence	16,929	27%	687	21%
Sexual offences	7,287	12%	48	1%
Robbery	8,437	14%	311	9%
Burglary	7,723	12%	197	6%

Source: Hunter *et al.* 2009

16 per cent of women receiving the same sentence (Hunter *et al.* 2009). The available statistics do not detail actual offences, so it is unclear as to what the levels of seriousness involved were, but this could suggest that, on the whole, men commit more serious offences. An overview of the prison population in 2007, with regards to sex and offence type (see Table 7.1), shows women to be nearly as violent as men (although levels of seriousness are again unknown) but to sexually abuse on a much lower level. So, while female offending is in the minority, serious sexual and violent offences are being committed by women and, importantly, would appear to be prevalent enough to justify separate strategies and policies to combat and deter such offending. Whether such strategies and policies actually exist in England and Wales is the question of exploration for the remainder of this chapter.

Views and perceptions

Despite the fact that serious offending is committed by men and women, the public's attitude to serious female offenders would appear to be more judgemental. While it is unlikely that a male sex or violent offender would gain much public support, women who commit such offences, especially against children, are viewed more negatively than men. This is not only because they are committing a crime but because they are also going against the stereotype of women and feminism and thus committing the ultimate taboo. As Lloyd (1995) explains, they are 'doubly deviant' and 'doubly damned'. It was once thought that women only abused children if they were being controlled and coerced by men, but this view has now been disproved, with it currently accepted that women can be solo offenders, co-offenders (with other males and females) and even in control of males (Ford 2006). An example of the latter would be Rosemary West, who was thought to be the controlling force behind the offences committed by herself and her husband Fred.

Professionals only began to accept the thought that women could sexually abuse children from the mid 1990s (Ford 2006). It is unclear why it has taken longer to accept women as child sex offenders, although it may be due to the fact that some consider female sexual abuse to be more threatening to us as a society, because it undermines how we feel a woman should act (that is, as a nurturing and caring mother) (Nichols and Stewart 2008). Saradjian argues it is

> because the social construction of women has been such that this behaviour remains 'unthinkable', that knowledge is dismissed. Consequently, each time it is 'discovered', it is again greeted with surprise followed by collective cognitive distortions relating to that knowledge, ensuring that the secret is kept.
>
> (2010: 9)

Furthermore, women are often socialised to be the sufferers of sexual abuse rather than the perpetrators (Allen 1990, cited by Ford 2006), with many people thinking that sexual abuse is caused through male power and aggression. Others find it difficult to understand how a woman could abuse a child, thinking that they cannot be capable of such behaviour (Nichols and Stewart 2008), while a few still believe that you need a penis in order to abuse (Ford 2006). Offences by female offenders are also thought to be more harmful and to have a greater impact upon the victim, not only because the abuse may start at an earlier age, but also because there is a double betrayal, as the offender is the one who is meant to nurture and take care of the victim. Furthermore, as it is the female who is meant to protect the child, the victim may feel that they have done something wrong and, as a result, deserve the abuse.

An alternative view is that abuse by female perpetrators is not harmful. Rather than the acts being labelled as abuse, some may perceive it to be a 'confused form of love' (Saradjian 2010: 13). This response is also sometimes reflected in responses from criminal justice and mental health professionals (see Bunting 2005). Similarly, we appear to have a different view where the offender is a teacher/lover (Matthews *et al.* 1989) and the victim is a teenage boy. As mentioned above, when this is the situation, the victim may feel that he is fortunate to have been selected by an older and more experienced woman and therefore not view the behaviour as being abusive. Indeed, the media have almost encouraged this view, with one example being the portrayal of a sexual relationship between a female teacher in her thirties and a boy of 15 in *Dawson's Creek*, a US teen drama (Sony Pictures Television 1998). In Season One, the relationship was depicted as enviable and almost a part of a normal rites of passage. Mendel (1995, cited by Ford 2006) confirms this representation, stating that, while portrayals of sexual abuse are often filmed with sensitivity, those between adult women and boys are often represented in neutral, positive or even humorous ways. The literature also suggests how the sexual abuse of men by women is likewise rarely classified as such, rather seen as foreplay or harmless flirtation (Ford 2006). If the sexes were reversed however, this same acceptance would not be witnessed. It is therefore interesting that women who abuse young children are seen as demonic (for example, Myra Hindley and Vanessa George), while those who sexually abuse teenagers or men are somehow not considered to be as bad or as potentially dangerous (see Ford 2009).

The public's view of women violent offenders would not appear to be as complicated, with the same contempt felt for both men and women. As with female sex offenders, however, there has traditionally been the view that women who commit serious crime do so due to psychiatric problems rather than their offending being through rational free choice. This allows us to rationalise those cases where a woman goes against her female stereotype and paternalistically sees female serious offending explained through biological or medical conditions, with women needing care rather than punishment (Viki *et al.* 2005). This medicalisation of women offending has also been seen in the criminal justice system; for example, in the 1970s HMP Holloway (the largest women's prison) was redeveloped into an entirely therapeutic environment with the regime centred on the provision of comprehensive psychiatric services, medical and general hospital facilities and legally prescribed drugs (Medlicott 2007). The regime, however, was highly unsuccessful, with consecutive inspection reports noting dehumanising conditions and one inspector in 1995 suspending a visit due to the high levels of overcrowding, filth, self-harm, time spent in cells, racial discrimination and physical and verbal bullying (ibid.). Another problem with medicalising the problem was that several women were entering prison as shoplifters and leaving as drug addicts (Carlen and Worrall 2004). Despite this emerging acceptance of women as dangerous offenders, a study looking at magistrates' attitudes towards women offenders in the mid-1990s found that most viewed them as 'troubled' rather than as 'troublesome' (see Hedderman and Gelsthorpe 1997).

Risk assessment

Synonymous with male offenders, all females who have committed serious sexual and violent offences will be assessed regarding their risk of reoffending. This will take place prior to sentencing and is to assist with risk-management and risk-reduction plans. As discussed in Chapter 3, this is achieved through the use of risk-assessment tools, which are commonly developed using the known risk factors of the offender group for which the tool is designed. For example, for violent offending, these can include a history of previous violent offending and aggression, coming from a lower social class and living in poverty, being unemployed, parental criminality and family violence, drug and alcohol misuse, mental disorders, levels of environmental stress, and a history of impulsive behaviour (Powis 2002). While Hollin and Palmer (2006) argue that the best predictors of recidivism for women are similar to those identified for men, importantly they contend that the significance and weight of each aspect may be different. For example, concerning female sex offenders, Craissati (2004) states that, while both male and female sex offenders tend to be young, from low socioeconomic backgrounds, have poor education, are likely to be unemployed, deny and/or minimise their behaviour and have substance abuse issues, women are more likely to show remorse, victimise female children known to them and are less likely to use force.

Strickland (2008, cited by Nichols and Stewart 2008) moreover identifies the importance of focusing on not just known risk factors, but also individual needs, such as the woman's experience of emotional, physical and sexual abuse, particularly as this is likely to be more prevalent among women. Steen (2010) argues that female sex offenders are more likely to have co-morbid mental disorders than men and come from lower socio-economic backgrounds and have few social supports. Moreover, Ford (2009) notes the paucity of research concerning the variables associated with reoffending in female sex offenders and how these might overlap or differ with those associated with their male counterparts. Likewise, Cortoni (2010) explains how male sex offenders are more likely to be reconvicted, although there is less of a difference when looking at rates of general recidivism. Consequently, risk factors for women are therefore likely to be different to those that exist for men. If this is the case, risk-assessment tools designed with male needs in mind will not accurately reflect female needs, which, accordingly, will affect predictive validity. Blanchette and Brown (2006) therefore explain how tools designed for men will often overclassify risk, making females appear as if they are more violent than they actually are, with this having devastating effects regarding imprisonment, sentence length and supervisory/licence conditions. Furthermore, female sex offenders may be more complicated than their male counterparts due to the fact that they are more likely to abuse with male co-perpetrators. Indeed, Matravers (2008) notes how lone offenders often abuse because of individual factors, partner offenders commit offences due to relational factors and group offenders abuse due to socio-cultural and situational issues.

All of this would suggest that what is needed are risk-assessment tools designed specifically for women offenders and, more particularly, for female sex offenders, female violent offenders and female domestic violence perpetrators; in fact, the tools need to reflect the diversity of those that currently exist for male offenders (see Chapter 3). When, as previously discussed, risk-assessment classification can determine sentence, prison release and the extent and duration of risk-management and risk-reduction strategies, it is imperative that risk information is as accurate as possible. Despite the necessity for information concerning the risk factors of women who commit serious sexual and violent offences, most of the work regarding female offenders has largely focused on identifying different typologies. For example, with female sex offenders they can be divided into (1) teacher/lover, (2) predisposed molester, (3) male-coerced molester, (4) experimenter/exploiter, and (5) psychologically disturbed (Vandiver and Kercher 2004; see also Sandler and Freeman 2007). While such typologies confirm that, like men, women are a heterogeneous group, they offer little in terms of how risk should be assessed and which factors need to be concentrated on for risk-management and risk-reduction purposes.

The paucity of such research is partly due to the small number of serious female offenders (Ford 2009) and partly due to the fact that their recidivism rates are generally very low (Cortoni 2010). However, even taking these stipulations into account, there is an emerging evidence base of both static and dynamic risk factors that *may* be associated with female sex offending. Looking at static risk factors first, it is thought that previous offending, including prior arrests for violence and drugs, prior imprisonment and being a solo offender, may indicate a higher risk of sexual, violent and general reoffending (ibid.). Regarding dynamic factors, relevant issues are thought to include relationship problems, prior victimisation, emotional dysregulation problems, a desire for intimacy, revenge or a goal of humiliation, pro-offending cognitions, and sexual gratification (ibid.; see also Blanchette and Brown 2006: ch. 5). As already noted, however, risk factors will differ depending on whether the female is a lone offender or co-offender, and, where she is a co-offender, whether she is a willing or coerced participant. This again suggests that, in terms of determining risk, female offenders are potentially more complicated than their male counterparts.

Currently, in England and Wales, there are no specifically designed risk-assessment tools for women, let alone separate tools designed for different offending groups, with most practitioners using the OASys for both men and women (Onyejeli 2010). The Offender Group Reconviction Scale (OGRS) 3 (a static general offending risk assessment tool) does calculate the effect of age differently for female and male offenders, making results a little more focused for the female market, but this is only used when the offender does not meet the targeting criteria for OASys (ibid.). This lack of specialised tools has left MAPPA and prison personnel with the choice of relying solely on clinical judgement or with using those tools designed for men. While it may be thought that something may be better than just the clinical interview (see Chapter 3 for the problems in using this type of assessment), Bunting (2005) found that using male risk-assessment tools not only sometimes resulted in risk classification being downgraded but consequently also impacted negatively on MAPPA risk-management plans. Through research with MAPPA professionals working with female offenders, she found that, while two out of five offenders were assessed as being either medium or high in risk, another two had had no risk assessment at all. She therefore recommended the introduction of national guidance to ensure at least uniformity of practice.

This is currently being developed by NOMS, which has recently started writing a manual to guide practitioners in both prison and community settings on how they should go about assessing and working with female sex offenders. The new Female Sex Offender Assessment and Management Framework will therefore enable a more consistent and service-wide approach to managing and treating female sex offenders, which, it is hoped, will become embedded in the offender management process for all women offenders (Onyejeli 2010). The framework is being developed from advice given by the Correctional Services Accreditation Panel, findings of an assessment pilot and by looking at the wider research literature relating to female sex offenders, and 'is intended to provide a greater understanding of the factors that escalate risk and assist in the identification of high risk women, and those in need of more intensive interventions' (ibid.).

The manual for the framework is not yet readily available and therefore there is very little detail, but guidelines on how women should be risk assessed will include:

- Pre-sentence checklists focusing on dynamic and static risk factors.
- Post sentence assessment measures including:
  - Life Graph (long term antecedent information).
  - The Social Re-adjustment Rating Scale.
  - Supplementary Questions (information feeding into OASys).
  - Short term Antecedents Interview.
  - Functional Analysis of the offence behaviour.
  - Female Risk and Need Checklist.
  - The Forcefield Analysis.
  - The Informal Risk Assessment.

(Onyejeli 2010)

Assessment procedures will be divided into two stages, with the first comprising of a primary contextual assessment that will collect information relating to static or historical information. The secondary assessment is offence-focused and aims to collect information about the female's offence-related thinking and consequent behaviour. Once both phases are completed, the practitioner will then, based on the information, create a treatment plan that will be prioritised according to the woman's individual risk and needs (Onyejeli 2010).

Another option that the Ministry of Justice could consider is the Level of Service/Case Management Inventory (LS/CMI), which has been designed by Andrews *et al.* (2004). Andrews and Bonta were the original designers of Level of Service Inventory-Revised (LSI-R), a general offending risk-assessment tool that was used throughout England and Wales in prisons and by probation until the early 2000s (see Andrews and Bonta 1995). While the tool is not specifically for serious sexual or violent offenders, it has been validated for use with women offenders – one aspect that makes it an obvious choice over tools currently used. The tool has been based on data collected from over 20,000 women (Andrews *et al.* 2008) and consists of 11 sections, addressing:

1 General risk/need factors;
2 Specific risk/need factors;
3 Prison experience – institutional factors;
4 Other client issues (social, health, mental health);
5 Special responsivity considerations (including gender-specific issues);
6 Risk/need summary and override;
7 Risk/need profile;
8 Programme/placement decision;
9 Case management plan;
10 Progress record; and
11 Discharge summary.

(Blanchette and Brown 2006: 74)

To date, two studies have been carried out regarding the predictive accuracy of the tool (see Blanchette and Brown 2006; Andrews *et al.* 2008), with both confirming that LS/CMI is 'among the strongest predictors of female re-offending in the entire offender risk assessment literature' (Andrews *et al.* 2008: 3), with average correlations between the risk score and reoffending being 0.41 and 0.35. Although more research is needed in order to confirm these claims, this would appear to be at least a step in the right direction. While it is accepted that England and Wales have now moved away from using LSI-R, favouring OASys instead, there would appear to be no reason why a version designed specifically for women could not be implemented, in much the same way as there is now a version designed specifically for violent offenders (OVP; see Chapter 3). While it is accepted that the development of the Female Sex Offender Assessment and Management Framework is positive progress, surely a risk-assessment tool tested on and validated for use with women would be even better. As Blanchette and Brown conclude, 'the ultimate solution is the development of actuarial measures that are informed by gender and built *from the ground up* for application to women' (Blanchette and Brown 2006: 82, emphasis in original). What the framework will look like and how it will work still remains to be seen, although what is clear is that reliance on tools designed specifically for men is no longer acceptable and that, to enhance public protection, women need to be assessed with gender differences taken fully into account.

Imprisonment

Notwithstanding the common, often traditional, belief that women are less likely than men to be sentenced to custody, and hence more likely to receive community or financial penalties, the landscape of sentencing practice for women has changed in the last 15–20 years (see Matthews 2009). For example, the proportion of women aged 21 and over who were sentenced to immediate imprisonment at the Crown Court rose from 30 per cent in 1994 to an estimated 44 per cent in 2002. This has resulted in significantly more women going to prison and, consequently, between 1993 and 2001, the average population of women in prison rose by 140 per cent – rising from 1,560 to 3,740 (Ash 2003). Likewise, between 1992 and 2002, the number of women on remand increased by 196 per cent (Medlicott 2007). In 1992, women made up 3.5 per cent of the overall prison population in England and Wales, which rose to just over 5 per cent in 2010, and while, at the end of the 1990s, the average female daily prison population stood at 3,000, this had risen to 4,500 by 2009 (Matthews 2009). While it is possible that some of this increase is due to levels of serious crime increasing, with arrest rates for women suspected of committing violence against the person more than doubling between 1997 and 2007 (ibid.), this is unlikely to account for all of this alteration. In fact, Medlicott (2007) denies that the nature and seriousness of women's offending has changed at all, with many academics believing instead that the fundamental cause of increased prison use is attributable to changing attitudes and reactions to women offending. Rather than being seen as predominantly weak and victims of crime, it is now accepted that women are culpable, responsible and thus more deserving of punishment (Matthews 2009).

When a female offender is sentenced to imprisonment, her time in prison can be somewhat different to that experienced by her male counterpart. For example, while there are 103 prison establishments for adult males in England and Wales, there are only 14 women's prisons in England and none in Wales. Many women are therefore held vast distances from their homes, putting immense strain on family links and relationships with children, with women more frequently being the main carer of children than men. Approximately 55 per cent of all women in prison have a child under 16 and 33 per cent have a child under 5 (HM Prison Service 2010a). It is thought that 17,700 children are separated from their mothers each year due to the mother being imprisoned, with only 5 per cent of these being able to stay in their own homes (Epstein and Russo 2010). The scarcity of women's prisons also means that individual prisons have to accommodate a wider range of offenders, both in terms of age and offence, which can limit the availability of work placements, training, education and offending behaviour programmes (Matthews 2009). The recent Corston Report has called for 'a distinct, radically different, visibly-led, strategic, proportionate, holistic, woman-centred, integrated approach' (Corston 2007:79) to women's prisons and, while the government has implemented 40 of the 43 recommendations held within the report, whether this is enough will be considered below.

Prison regime

The regime and day-to-day life that a female prisoner will follow is largely similar to that experienced by men, with Prison Rules applying to both category of offender. The only rule that is specifically for women is Prison Rule 9, which states that 'women prisoners should be kept entirely separate from male prisoners'. Unlike men, women are not assigned to the security categories of B, C, or D, but instead are classified on the basis of whether they need open or closed conditions, and currently there are 2 open and 12 closed prisons within the female prison estate (HM Prison Service 2010a). Like men, however, women can be given Category A status if it is thought that escape would be highly dangerous for the public (see Chapter 4 for more details on categorisation), although women are far less likely to escape than men and, if they do so, it is more often because of childcare issues (Carlen and Worrall 2004). Moreover, Carlen and Worrall (2004) argue that it is unnecessary to categorise women as highly dangerous and that, in the majority of instances, holding women in maximum-security conditions is superfluous. This is because the majority of women who have been convicted of homicide carried out their offences in domestic settings and therefore do not pose the same security risks as those men who have committed similar offences. Holding such women under maximum-security conditions (see Chapter 4 for details on this) is therefore not only unfair for those women involved, but is also an unnecessary expense.

Women, like men, will follow a structured timetable described by one inmate as:

> Rising at 6.30am, muster [roll call] at 7.00 am, breakfast, 8.30 am pill parade and, if you're fortunate, off to work or class, sandwich lunch and muster, work till 3pm, back to the wing, 3.30 pm pill parade, cook or collect meals from the kitchen, eat, muster, lock-in wing at 4 pm and in cell at 6 pm and the same again tomorrow.
>
> (Hampton 1993: 45, cited by Carlen and Worrall 2004: 48)

What is striking from the quote and perhaps different from men is the twice daily 'pill parade' and the suggestion that you are fortunate if you have the opportunity to work. Indeed, it has been argued that there is less emphasis regarding work and training for women, believing that it is men who make up the workforce in the community and that women only need to be able to cook, clean and sew (Carlen and Worrall 2004). While placements are not abundant in male prisons, there is generally an assumption that women can 'make do with poorer prison provision' (ibid.: 67).

While the Prison Rules apply to both men and women, there are separate standards for women's prisons, which attempt to provide a more woman-centred approach as recommended by Baroness Corston. These were developed in April 2008 due to a Gender Equality Duty (see Epstein and Russo 2010) that was imposed on NOMS in April 2007 and implemented in April 2009. The standards are divided into 19 sections covering guidance on areas such as pre-custody, reception and first-night procedures, health, supporting women at risk of self-harm, day-to-day living, resettlement, women prisoners with disabilities, women foreign nationals, and women from black and minority ethnic groups. Each section lists a number of possible situations, with gender-specific guidance provided for each possible scenario. For example, under reception and first night, the given situation is '40–50% of women in local prisons have never been in custody before' (HM Prison Service 2008d: 9), with the gender-specific guidance being:

> At least one 5 minute free phone call should be offered on reception to enable women to resolve urgent family and childcare issues. Women should be allowed to split the call where necessary to sort out complicated childcare arrangements. Women should be told when they will be able to have a visit and how they will be able to ring their families when moved to a wing.
>
> (ibid.)

Furthermore, it is recognised that women need a lower carbohydrate diet than men and that this should be reflected in the menus provided, that women may need a much broader range of toiletries such as makeup and hair brushes, and, because women tend to be more concerned about cleanliness, they should ideally have a shower in their room or at least access to daily showers and baths (HM Prison Service 2008d).

Although these standards are an improvement on the pre-existing situation, it is questionable whether they go far enough in realising the vision set out by the Corston Report. In fact, it has been argued that 'there is little evidence of the effect of the Gender Equality Duty on women prisoners in practice' (Epstein and Russo 2010: 332). While it is acknowledged that they attempt to create a more woman-centred approach, they do not necessarily change the prison environment, the locality or the overall experience of prison for women. Rather, what Baroness Corston had in mind was the introduction of geographically dispersed, small, multi-functional custodial centres, and that these should be phased in over a period of 10 years (Corston 2007). In particular, she was basing her recommendations on the Asha Centre, which is a community based one-stop shop that helps women to overcome disadvantages and problems (see www.ashawomen.org.uk/index.html). While this would appear to be a sensible suggestion, unfortunately this is one of the four recommendations that were not endorsed by the government.

Similar projects have been set up in Canada and Ireland, with the Dochas Centre in Dublin being a collection of a number of small buildings that house women offenders. The Centre is said to offer a more constructive regime, with more visits and activities and greater interaction with outside agencies. An Irish Prisons Inspectorate report in 2003 noted how mutual respect had improved and disciplinary measures had decreased, and there are now plans to increase the model throughout Ireland (Matthews 2009).

While it is unclear whether such units will be introduced into England and Wales, the Ministry of Justice (2009d) has recently pledged £9 million to support third-sector providers to deliver a number of Women's Community Projects (WCPs). A WCP is described as 'a central hub, which could be a building or a key-worker, where women at any point in the criminal justice system can access support to meet a whole range of needs' (ibid.: 6). Current WCPs include Anawim, a charity supporting women in Birmingham; The Women's Turnaround Project in Cardiff; and the Together Women Programme, which works across Yorkshire and Humberside. One criticism, however, is that they are only available to women on community orders or at risk of offending, so again they do not quite live up to the hopes of Baroness Corston in terms of having small custodial centres for women.

Another perhaps more controversial suggestion is to have mixed prisons. Not only would this allow women to be incarcerated much nearer to their homes, it would also allow them to have access to a much broader range of offending behaviour programmes and other facilities. Suggestions have been made to have separate wings or units for women in male prisons and, following Prison Rule 9, ensure that the two never meet. There would, however, appear to be no reason why men and women should be separated. If the punishment aspect of prison is the deprivation of liberty, there is no reason why men and women cannot be mixed in custodial settings. Indeed, Matthews (2009) argues that mixed prisons would be more normalising and could additionally aid in rehabilitation methods, although he does also warn how they may not be suitable for women, particularly those who have been victims of physical, mental and sexual abuse. He also contends that, as men will always be in the majority, women and their needs could become even more marginalised, which could result in them being worse off than they already are. As Carlen and Worrall explain, they could very easily become 'second-class citizens' (2004: 55). All in all, therefore, small, women-centred units would appear to be the better option.

Life-sentenced prisoners

In 2008, there were over 300 women serving life or indeterminate sentences of IPP, with women lifers managed by a separate Women and Young People's Group at Prison Service Headquarters. Due to the relatively small number of prisons for women, most of them have to operate on a multifunctional basis, with all local female prisons having facilities to take newly sentenced lifers. Women will follow the same three stages as men, (see Chapter 4), with HMP Holloway, HMP Low

Newton, HMP Peterborough and HMP New Hall designated as first-stage prisons (HM Prison Service 2008b). At stage one of the process, the woman will be supported through any appeals and helped to come to terms with her sentence. Importantly, a life and indeterminate sentence plan (LISP) will be developed, which will involve a number of assessments and will identify which offending behaviour programmes are thought to be appropriate for completion. As for men, time on stage one is dependent on individual risk and progression (ibid.).

Prisoners can then 'graduate' to HMP Foston Hall, HMP Send or HMP Styal, which are classified as second-stage lifer prisons. While interventions such as offending behaviour programmes will continue, the main purpose of these establishments is to prepare the woman for her Parole Board review. HMP Drake Hall also accepts women who are in the latter part of stage two and who have completed offence-focused work to reduce their identified risk. Finally, prisons identified for stage three (that is, open conditions) include HMP Askham Grange and HMP East Sutton Park, with a female lifer being able to be transferred to open conditions following a recommendation by the Parole Board. Here, the purpose is to test the prisoner in more challenging conditions and to support resettlement through supervised outside activities such as work placements and temporary release (HM Prison Service 2008b).

The specific standards set out for women, as mentioned above, also cover indeterminate-sentenced prisoners. Therefore, in addition to following the principles set out for lifers (see Chapter 4), the needs of women lifers are also regularly assessed by talking to them as a group. Officers need to be trained in not only how a life sentence can affect an individual, but importantly how it impacts differently on women prisoners, with distance from home often further exacerbated because of the few establishments within the female prison estate equipped for life-sentenced prisoners. Issues associated with women lifers, in particular, are maintaining good relationships with children (with the children of lifers more likely to be cared for by local authorities and freed up for adoption (Walker and Worrall 2000)), the provision of clothes (especially if they have no financial support in the outside world) and the desire to be located with other lifers, rather than living on mixed wings (HM Prison Service 2008d). Walker and Worrall (2000) further note issues surrounding a woman's biological clock, with a life sentence for some women meaning that they are prevented from having children. When recent case law (*Dickson v UK* (2007) 44 EHRR 21) has allowed men to donate sperm so that their partners in the community may become pregnant through *in vitro* fertilisation, this has clearly become a gender-specific pain of life imprisonment. However, whether it would be proper to allow women to become pregnant in prison is debatable, especially considering the fact that the child would, in all likelihood, be separated from the mother and may then be subject to local authority care (see the following).

While the above outlines a theoretical LISP with release at the end of it, as with men serving life sentences, there are many women who are past their minimum tariff due to the inadequate provision of offending behaviour programmes and Parole Board delays (see Chapter 4). Indeed, Creighton (2007), in written evidence to the House of Commons, submitted how women lifers, due to insufficient resources, spend on average two more years in custody than their male counterparts, despite having a much lower recidivism rate. He further argued that, because HM Prison Service has not been in a position to invest in the specialist support, treatment and assessment needed for female lifers, women who receive indeterminate sentences, especially those with short minimum tariffs, 'are the group least likely to be released on tariff expiry' (3). Other problems identified with women lifers, especially those serving sentences of IPP, include the fact that many women are uncertain about the LISP process and at what stage they are at; they are unclear about what the LISP contains (that is, what programmes they are expected to complete); and they do not understand what targets they need to achieve in order to progress to the next lifer stage (HM Chief Inspector of Prisons and HM Chief Inspector of Probation 2008). While the IPP process needs to be amended for both men and women, it appears that extra consideration needs to be given to women serving indeterminate sentences. The gender-specific standards are indeed a start to such progress, but arguably they do not go far enough. While allowing pregnancy in prisons is not necessarily advocated, more could be done to maintain links with children and to explain the lifer process. If these two issues are achieved, then this could very well help the inmate feel more settled and less stressed, and could ultimately aid in rehabilitation and progress through the lifer system.

Mother and Baby Units

Another gender-specific difference between men and women is the fact that approximately 120 women give birth in custody each year (HM Prison Service 2008d). While some babies will stay with their fathers or extended families in the community, reflecting society's normal assumption that the best place for a young child is with its mother, there are seven Mother and Baby Units (MBUs) within the female prison estate. The legislative basis for MBUs is provided under Rule 12(2) Prison Service Rules 1999, which states that 'The Secretary of State may, subject to any conditions he thinks fit, permit a woman prisoner to have her baby with her in prison, and everything necessary for the baby's maintenance and care may be provided there'. MBUs in England and Wales currently provide housing for 75 mothers and 82 children (HM Prison Service 2008e). Two units at New Hall and Holloway allow the mother to keep her baby for 9 months, while the other five (HMP Bronzefield, Styal, HMP Eastwood Park, Askham Grange and Peterborough) allow the child to stay for up to 18 months (HM Prison Service 2010a). A child is not normally allowed to be kept in prison for any longer than 18 months due to the belief that he/she may become institutionalised (HM Prison Service 2008e).

For a woman to be accepted on to a unit, she must apply, with each application being judged on its own individual merits and with the best interests of the child being the primary factor for consideration (HM Prison Service 2008e). Other factors taken into account will be the woman's risk and offending behaviour profile, her behaviour while she has been imprisoned, family circumstances and release plans. When making an application, the woman may have to consider the fact that going to an MBU could take her further away from her family and already existing children, with geographical preference rarely being taken into account (ibid.). The decision is made by an Admission Board that is made up of an MBU manager, an independent chair, the mother, and a representative from either social services or probation. It can also include psychologists, mental health professionals, health visitors and drug workers (ibid.). Length of sentence will be taken into account by the Board, which can negatively affect those serving life and IPP sentences. This is because the desirable scenario is one where the mother and child will leave prison together (that is, within 18 months). Where the sentence is more than this, and for some serious sexual and violent offenders it will be significantly more than this, the Board may decide that, due to the fact that the child will have to be separated from the mother, in any event, it would be in the best interests of the child to avoid the negative consequences of separation at a later date and separate him/her at birth. Also, regarding sex offenders, and depending on the woman's index offence, it will be additionally considered whether it is appropriate for the mother to keep her child.

While in the MBU, the mother will maintain parental responsibility for the child and therefore has full responsibility for his/her care, although there are crèche facilities available so that she can take advantage of opportunities relating to education, training, employment and intervention programmes. Due to the fact that the child is not a prisoner, the mother will not be locked in a cell, although must remain in her room for certain periods of the day/night. Also, because of the child, the regime in an MBU is much more child-focused, with the adverse affects of imprisonment alleviated wherever possible (HM Prison Service 2008e).

As explained above, residence in an MBU is temporary, with the longest stay usually restricted to 18 months. This limit has been tested in the courts (see *R. v Secretary of State for the Home Department Ex p. Q* [2001] EWCA Civ 1151), with the Court of Appeal ruling that, while in the majority of circumstances it is preferable to separate the mother and child before the latter is 18 months, the limit should be applied flexibly depending on individual circumstances, such as the mother's length of time left to serve, alternative placement arrangements for the child and whether the harm caused by the separation is likely to outweigh other considerations. In the case of serious sexual and violent offenders serving life sentences, it is likely that they will be separated from their children due to the length of time they have left to serve. It becomes more complicated, however, with those serving sentences of IPP because of the indeterminate nature of the sentence. As discussed in Chapters 2 and 4, these sentences provide a minimum tariff at which time the prisoner is eligible for release if approved by the Parole Board. However, due to the lack of accredited offending behaviour programmes and a massive backlog, many IPP prisoners are spending months, if not years, in prison past their minimum tariffs. While in some cases this is correct, in that risk has not reduced and therefore they are not safe to be released into the community, for others detainment is due to administrative bureaucracy rather than for reasons of public protection. When this involves a mother placed on an MBU, it will therefore be incredibly difficult to ascertain her exact release date when the Separation Board is asked to consider whether she and her child should be separated. If a mother and child are therefore broken up due to administrative delay, rather than for any other reason, this is wholly unacceptable. If a mother is separated from her child, HM Prison Service should make every possible arrangement to ensure that contact is maintained between the two parties, which, bearing in mind the scarcity of women prisons, can be difficult to achieve. One way around this problem, and also to help with maintaining relationships with other family members, is, as discussed above, to introduce more local prisons that are designed and run with women's needs in mind.

Therapeutic communities

As mentioned in Chapter 4, in addition to the therapeutic community (TC) units available for male offenders, there is also a TC unit for women at Send, which provides capacity for 40 females (HM Prison Service 2010a). A TC has existed in the female prison estate since 2003, when it was originally located at HMP West Hill, which was a small prison on the side of HMP Winchester (a local male prison) and had a capacity for 80 women (Stewart and Parker 2006). The unit was moved to Send when West Hill was re-rolled as a male prison in March 2004 and initially there was a crisis situation due to many of the women being unsettled by the move and the change in TC staff. This resulted in half of the women on the unit withdrawing from the scheme, which, at one stage, left only two (HMIP 2006b). There were also problems with recruiting staff that were not fully resolved until the summer of 2005. Numbers have steadily increased since then, although they have never reached the full capacity of 40. For example, in November 2005, there were 18 women on the unit (Stewart and Parker 2006), which dropped in February 2006 to only 10 (HMIP 2006b). This increased in March 2007 to 17 (Independent Monitoring Board (IMB) 2007) and again to 24 in March 2009 (IMB 2009a).

Unlike the TC at HMP Grendon, women are not kept separate from the main prison population, with women at Send involved in TC work in the mornings but then integrating with the rest of the prison population for education, work and chaplaincy activities. While this could be viewed negatively in that the same TC environment (that is, intensive round-the-clock therapy) that exists at Grendon (as described in Chapter 4) is unlikely to exist at Send, this has been viewed by others as a positive aspect, with some prisoners liking the ability to have a break from the therapy involved (HMIP 2006b). Julia Fraser, a therapist on the unit in 2005, explained that this integration was due to the unit running under capacity. This, she described, was 'a compromise we have to make until the unit is full which can be challenging because of the confidentiality aspect, but is by no means impossible' (Savidge 2005a).

The therapy is similar to that found on male TC units, although is developed and tailored with female needs in mind. For example, Michael Parker, the Director of Therapy, in 2006, stated how:

> Women are more likely to be the primary child carer and are often far from home. Being separated often long distances from their children can be particularly distressing. Self harm is also an issue that tends to be more prevalent amongst female prisoners and they can often be more emotionally volatile. So while we are based on the existing TC model, we are developing and tailoring it to be more female orientated.
>
> (Savidge 2005a)

In 2008, it was noted how women offenders valued the TC unit, finding it a positive experience, but that there were also a number of problems, including the fact that women on the unit shared their wing with others not involved on the programme and that there was insufficient room to cook or eat communally (HMIP 2008b). Another problem has concerned staff shortages. This, coupled with problems of recruitment, was noted by HMIP in 2008 (ibid.), with such issues being identified by the IMB in 2009 as the main reason why the unit had not reached capacity. In conclusion, they argue that 'if the TC is an effective programme that reduces reoffending, the programme should be adequately resourced so that the unit can reach its full capacity' (IMB 2009a: 11). In essence, then, it would appear that, while some women have been able to experience therapy on the TC unit at Send, it could be described as a half-hearted attempt to create a therapeutic environment, with insufficient staffing to provide the full therapeutic experience. While there is little available research, it has to be questioned whether such factors will affect the efficacy of the unit. When the research evidence from Grendon and HMP Dovegate suggests that TC units can provide serious sexual and violent offenders with the opportunity to substantially reduce their risk, it would appear a great shame that Send has not yet been as successful as perhaps it could be. It therefore needs continued support and development by HM Prison Service, so that, like Grendon for men, it too can be the jewel in the crown of the female prison estate.

Risk-reduction strategies

Bearing in mind the discussion regarding risk assessment, it is perhaps unsurprising that the vast majority of interventions currently used with women offenders were not originally designed with females in mind. While there has been some evidence that programmes can work with both male and female offenders (Ford 2006), the overwhelming viewpoint is that women have different criminogenic needs, such as low self-esteem, self-injury/attempted suicide and personal victimisation (Blanchette 2004), and different responsivity styles. Bouffard and Taxman (2000) explain how most programmes designed for men contain confrontational strategies that are used to combat resistance to change, and challenge beliefs and attitudes thought to contribute to their offending behaviour. For women, however, especially those who have experienced abuse and victimisation, they question how relevant this model is, with Marshall and Serran (2000) noting that methods that challenge women need to be more supportive in nature. Moreover, Carlen and Worrall (2004) note how women need to be able to relate to the examples used in behaviour programmes, which may be difficult if they are all focused on the needs and behaviour often exhibited by men. Further criticisms include the fact that programmes designed with men in mind do not contextualise 'women's offending within their often long-term victimisation, and insist that they have more rational choice in their lives than they do' (Carlen and Worrall 2004: 69). Women, therefore, undoubtedly need different offending behaviour programmes.

Gannon *et al.* therefore argue, on the basis that clinical practice is informed by the 'scientist practitioner model, which asserts that clinical practice should be informed by empirical theory and research' (2008: 353), this places those who are working with serious women offenders in an unenviable position. Another problem is the fact that the number of serious sexual and violent offenders who are women is relatively small, with them often dispersed throughout the prison estate or across the country if supervised within the community. This makes running group programmes almost impossible, not just because of the sparsity of offenders but also due to the fact that there is unlikely to be the professionals who have the necessary skills and competencies in working with women offenders (Nichols and Stewart 2008). This has resulted in most practitioners working with serious female offenders in a one-to-one setting and, in some instances, using ad hoc measures. Some evidence-based interventions designed solely for women offenders are, however, beginning to emerge, and the remainder of this chapter will evaluate what these are and also how effective they are in reducing and managing risk.

General interventions for women

Within the 14 female prisons, there are currently 8 accredited programmes, although these are not available in all penal institutions, with the greatest provision provided for drug addiction. For example, all 14 prisons have CARATs workers (Counselling, Assessment, Referral, Advice and ThroughCare), the short-duration drug programme is available in 6 prisons, the 12-step drug programme is available in one other prison and Prison-Addressing Substance Related Offending (P-ASRO), a further drugs programme, is currently utilised in another 2 prisons. General offending behaviour programmes include Thinking Skills (available in four establishments), Enhanced Thinking Skills (available in three prisons) and Cognitive Skills booster (available in one prison), and three establishments run the Focusing on Resettlement programme (Christodoulou 2010). Of these programmes, however, only one, P-ASRO, is designed exclusively for women. Another programme designed exclusively for women who have been convicted of acquisitive crime does exist, but this is not available in prison and currently is only used in five probation areas (Christodoulou 2010).

Interventions for women sex offenders

Even though there are three community and one prison SOTPs, all of these are designed for and used exclusively with men. This therefore means that all intervention work with female sex offenders in England and Wales is carried out on an individual basis, with the Lucy Faithfull Foundation offering consultancy, assessment and limited forms of interventions with female sex offenders (NOMS 2007a).[1] The service is available for those females who are over 18, who are currently subject to probation supervision and who have been convicted of sexual offences against children or vulnerable adults. The facility provides risk/needs assessment, including the use of psychometric tests; advice regarding what programme of work should be undertaken with the offender; and the appropriateness of risk-management strategies (ibid.).

The programme focuses on issues such as sexual arousal, self-management, belief systems and relationships (Gannon and Rose 2008), and is divided into three intervention blocks. Module one focuses on motivational work and looks at which obstacles have to be overcome in order for change to occur, as well as looking at offending behaviour and patterns. Module two then moves on to concentrate on sexual and non-sexual relationships, and additionally looks at victim empathy. Finally, module three draws together all previous work in order that a New Life Plan can be developed. This is a self-help manual that is designed to support the woman at programme completion (Blanchette and Taylor 2010). At the end of the programme, assessment and psychometric tests will be repeated (Ford 2006). In addition to the Lucy Faithfull Foundation, COSA (see Chapter 6) are also being used with female sex offenders, with the Hampshire and Thames Valley area having had three women through their programme (BBC News 2009).

While it is acknowledged that women make up a tiny proportion of all sex offenders, it is still somewhat surprising that the availability of accredited risk-reduction interventions is not greater than it is. It would appear that there is very little provision available in custodial settings, and not significantly more available in the community. When, as discussed above, sexual abuse by women occurs at a much greater rate than is currently being reported, more resources need to be prioritised to 'treat' female sex offenders so that public protection can be enhanced and future victims saved. One suggestion put forward by Gannon *et al.* (2008) is the Descriptive Model of Female Sexual Offending, which documents the contributory roles of affective, behavioural, contextual and cognitive factors pertinent to women who sexually offend, and is able to verify commonalities between female sex offenders while being sensitive enough to account for heterogeneity (see Gannon *et al.* 2008). While the Model is not an intervention per se, it does help in intervention planning by identifying the needs of the offender in question, and could be a valuable contribution to what is currently available.

Interventions for women violent offenders

Analogous to sex offender programmes, those violent offender programmes previously mentioned in Chapter 6 (that is, the CSCP, the IDAP and CALM) are also only used with men. The only violent offending behaviour programme that is available for both men and women is Aggression Replacement Training, which is currently used in 16 probation areas, although the statistics do not show whether these areas use it for women as well as men (Christodoulou 2010). It is also worth noting that Aggression Replacement Training was designed predominantly with men in mind and therefore suffers from the same criticisms as listed above.

Different to the situation with female sex offenders, however, NOMS has recently designed an accredited programme called Choices, Actions, Relationships and Emotions (CARE), which is specifically targeted at women who have a history of violence and who additionally have complex needs. The programme was initially piloted in HMP Cookham Wood but, following accreditation, is now also available in HMP Downview, with Foston and Send also interested (Halford 2010). CARE is divided into the five key treatment areas of: motivation and engagement; awareness; emotion management; coping skills; and social inclusion and resettlement (Onyejeli 2010). It is designed for women who have been classified as being at either a medium or high risk of violent recidivism and who also have two or more of the following needs:

- History of substance misuse problems.
- History of self-harming or suicidal behaviours.
- Mental health difficulties.
- Personality disorder diagnosis.
- Past difficulties in accessing or benefitting from help or treatment.

The programme comprises of 30 group-work sessions and 10 individual sessions (Onyejeli 2010) based around narrative therapy. This is where the women look at the actual story of their offending and their lives, but after counselling, they will start to engage with writing a preferred story (that is, how their lives could be). Attached to the programme are advocates/mentors who work with the women inside and outside of prison for at least two years, concentrating on through-the-gate services. The mentors are from the voluntary sector, with one organisation involved being Women in Prison. Statistics obtained from Women in Prison suggest that the programme has been highly successful. Of the 28 women who they have worked with, so far, 2 have been recalled for breach of licence, but there has been no reoffending (Halford 2010).

Efficacy

While there are problems with measuring the efficacy of any programme (see Chapter 6 for details), these are multiplied when it comes to measuring what works with female offenders. This is due to the sparsity of serious women offenders held within the criminal justice system, the lack of accredited offending behaviour programmes that are used with them and the low reconviction rates that are currently present. Due to all of this, the vast majority of evaluations that do exist within the literature are small-scale, often single case study reports. For example, the work carried out by the Lucy Faithfull Foundation has been found to demonstrate improvements in its key target areas, but little is known as to whether this will actually work to reduce reoffending (Ford 2006). Also, other interventions such as CARE are too recent for full-scale evaluation work to have commenced (although some success has been noted above) so, in reality, it would appear that we just do not know what works with women who commit serious sexual and violent offences. Much more research and focus on women offenders is therefore needed, with particular emphasis placed on those who commit serious and potentially dangerous offences.

Conclusion

The situation with women offenders is therefore rather poor. While it is acknowledged that women have different criminogenic needs and responsivity styles, and thus need different risk-assessment tools, intervention programmes and conditions in prison, there is little evidence of these in any practical form in England and Wales. Work is developing in this much-needed area, with the Ministry of Justice and NOMS working towards new interventions and specific standards and frameworks that have a more woman-centred approach, but much more is needed. Baroness Corston and the Corston Report have undoubtedly helped with this progress and it is important that developmental work continues at the pace it is currently pursuing, if not actually increasing in tempo. While it is true that women only make up a small percentage of the overall offender population, they do still commit serious sexual and violent offences and thus it is imperative that separate strategies and policies are further developed so that their different needs can be taken into account and their risk of reoffending reduced. Without this extra developmental work, there could be a gaping hole in public protection provision in both our criminal justice and penal systems.

8

CHILDREN AND YOUNG PEOPLE

Introduction

Following on from the previous chapter, this chapter looks at another distinct group of people who commit serious sexual and violent offences, namely children and young people. In particular, it will consider how many 'dangerous' young offenders there are, how they are dealt with by the criminal justice and penal systems in England and Wales and whether the decisions taken regarding such young offenders should be based on the principles of welfare or punishment. The chapter will also look at the juvenile secure estate and establish whether there are any specific risk-assessment, risk-management and risk-reduction strategies that have been designed specifically with this special group of offenders in mind.

Prevalence

Although as a society we are perhaps reticent to believe that serious sexual and violent offences are committed by children and young people, this is unfortunately not the case. For example, juvenile sexual offences resulting in a disposal have risen in England and Wales from 1,664 in 2002/03 to 1,988 in 2005/06 and, in May 2010, Youth Justice Board (YJB) figures stated that, over the last 5 years, 346 youngsters had been dealt with for serious sexual offences (Schladale 2010). In terms of violent crime, 8 per cent of all violence in 2008/09 was perpetrated by those under the age of 16 (Walker *et al.* 2009), which rose to 12 per cent in 2009/10 (Flatley *et al.* 2010). Examples of well-known incidents of serious offending involving children include the murder of James Bulger by two 10-year-old boys in 1993; the case in Edlington, South Yorkshire, in 2009 where brothers of 10 and 11 violently attacked, strangled, stripped and forced two boys aged 9 and 11 to sexually abuse each other (BBC News 2010); and a copycat attack in Bristol later on in the same year where three boys of 11, 12 and 12 forced four boys, all aged 10, to drink urine, strip and perform sex acts on each other (This is Bristol 2009). As with all forms of serious crime, especially sexual offences, actual incidence rates are probably far higher.

Welfare versus punishment

When it is borne in mind that children and young people can commit such horrific crimes, it is important that they are dealt with by both the criminal justice and penal systems in an appropriate way. What this appropriate way is has always been controversial. Historically, children and young people were treated the same as adults in terms of sentencing and punishment, with the aims of sentencing being focused on retribution and deterrence rather than reform and rehabilitation. Welfare as a sentencing philosophy was therefore not introduced into the management of young offenders until the latter part of the nineteenth century, when the principle of acting in the best interests of the child was introduced (Arthur 2010). This is now enshrined in section 1 of the Children Act 1989, which provides that 'when a court determines any question with respect to the upbringing of a child the child's welfare shall be the court's paramount consideration', although the guidance only applies to proceedings under the 1989 Act and therefore does not directly apply to young offenders or the criminal courts.

Despite this, the welfare principle is provided for in a number of international instruments, with perhaps the most important being the United Nations (UN) Convention on the Rights of the Child 1989. This was adopted by the General Assembly of the UN on 20 November 1989 and ratified by the UK in 1990. Under international law, the UK therefore has an obligation to abide by its articles, although, because it has not been incorporated into domestic law, remedies are not necessarily available in the domestic courts. Rather, the UK must periodically report on its progress in fulfilling its obligations under the standards to the UN Committee on the Rights of the Child (Arthur 2010). The Convention recognises that children and young people under the age of 18 may need special protection not just because of their age, but also due to their emotional development and provides that, in all decisions affecting children, 'the best interests of the child shall be a primary consideration' (Article 3). This therefore means that the aims of rehabilitation and the objectives of restorative justice must always give way to the more punitive agendas of incapacitation, deterrence and retribution. In furtherance of this, Article 40 of the Convention requires states to develop measures for dealing with young people who offend through non-judicial measures. The Convention also prohibits the use of the death penalty and life imprisonment, and states that imprisonment should only be used as a measure of last resort, and, if it is used, it should only be for the shortest appropriate period (Article 37).

Moreover, the UN Standard Minimum Rules for the Administration of Juvenile Justice 1985 (the Beijing Rules), declares that member states must 'further the well-being of the juvenile and her or his family' (Article 1.1) and that any action taken against a child must be proportionate not just to the seriousness of the offence, but also to the 'circumstances and the needs of the juvenile' (Article 17.1a). Furthermore, the Riyadh guidelines (the UN Guidelines for the Prevention of Juvenile Delinquency 1990) emphasise that policies should avoid criminalising children, and requires governments to legislate to promote the well-being of children and young people.[1] Key international standards are therefore heavily based on the principles of welfarism and, as Arthur comments, are underpinned by three core principles: 'recognition that children's status is different from adults, emphasis on children's welfare and participation of children in all decisions affecting them' (Arthur 2010: 38). Despite this, he also argues that:

> These instruments of international law are too vague on detention as a last resort, too weak on the age of criminal responsibility and are incomplete on the trial process, sentencing and serious crime committed by children. This weakness has allowed youth justice law and policy in England and Wales to focus primarily on retaliatory responses to youth crime. Young offenders have been conceptualised as violent predators warranting retribution, rather than as wayward children in need of a guiding hand.
>
> (ibid.: 39)

Whether this is the situation for those children and young people in England and Wales who have been assessed as dangerous and then managed as such will be evaluated below.

Charging policy

As with all suspected criminal offences, it is the role of the Crown Prosecution Service (CPS) to determine whether or not children and young people who are thought to have committed serious sexual and violent offences are charged and processed through the criminal justice system. In recognition that such decisions involve children, the welfare principle does appear to be taken into account. For example, during the passage of the SOA 2003, and in relation to sexual acts between minors where consent was present in fact, if not in law, it was made very clear that the primary concern was to protect children and that it was not Parliament's intention to punish unnecessarily. For example, Lord Falconer stated:

> In those cases where sexual activity between minors is truly mutually agreed and there is nothing to suggest that the activity is in any way exploitative, we would not expect and would not want the full weight of the criminal law to be used against them. Our overriding concern is to protect children, not to punish them unnecessarily. Where sexual relationships between minors are not abusive, prosecuting either or both children is highly unlikely to be in the public interest; nor would it be in the best interests of the

> children involved. In such cases, protection will normally best be achieved by educating the children and providing them and their families with counselling services.
>
> (HL Deb, 1 April 2003, c1176)

Even where the sexual acts may have involved some form of exploitation, it was still felt that the CPS 'may consider that it was not in the public interest to prosecute someone under 16 if other courses of action were likely to be more effective' (HL Deb, 1 April 2003, c1176). Therefore, in any case where there is sufficient evidence of a sexual or violent offence committed by a child or young person to justify instituting criminal proceedings, Crown Prosecutors must carefully consider whether the public interest requires a prosecution to be commenced (Bushell 2009). In deciding whether or not to prosecute, prosecutors must have careful regard to a number of factors, with the weight to be attached to these factors depending on the circumstances of each case. The factors include:

- The age and understanding of the offender. This may include whether the offender has been subjected to any exploitation, coercion, threat, deception, grooming or manipulation by another which has lead him or her to commit the offence;
- The relevant ages of the parties, i.e. the same or no significant disparity in age;
- Whether the complainant entered into sexual activity willingly, i.e. did the complainant understand the nature of his or her actions and that (s)he was able to communicate his or her willingness freely;
- Parity between the parties in regard to sexual, physical, emotional and educational development;
- The relationship between the parties, its nature and duration and whether this represents a genuine transitory phase of adolescent development;
- Whether there is any element of exploitation, coercion, threat, deception, grooming or manipulation in the relationship;
- The nature of the activity e.g. penetrative or non-penetrative activity;
- What is in the best interests and welfare of the complainant; and
- What is in the best interests and welfare of the defendant.

(ibid.)

It is also important to gain the views of the victim and essential that, before any decision is made, the prosecutor has as much information as possible from sources such as the police, Youth Offending Teams (YOTs) and any other professionals assisting those agencies about the defendant's home circumstances and the circumstances surrounding the alleged offence. Failure to do so may lead to a judicial review of the decision (see *R v Chief Constable of Kent ex parte L*; *R v DPP ex parte B* (1991) 93 Cr. App. R. 416).

Sentencing policy

In line with general sentencing principles, offence seriousness, rather than welfare, is the starting point when sentencing all children and young people (for criticism on this, see von Hirsch 2001), with this being especially important when the crime in question relates to a serious sexual and/or violent offence. However, in addition to this and in recognition that the offender is under 18, under section 44(1) of the Children and Young Person Act 1933:

> Every court in dealing with a child or young person who is brought before it, either as an offender or otherwise, shall have *regard to the welfare of the child or young person* and shall in a proper case take steps for removing him from undesirable surroundings, and for securing that proper provision is made for his education and training.
>
> (emphasis added)

However, it is worth noting that this only requires the court to have *regard* to the welfare of the child, not for it to be the primary or paramount consideration as stipulated in family and international law. Therefore, as long as consideration has been given to the best interests of the child or young person, it is perfectly lawful to sentence giving precedence to more punitive aims.

Factors that need to be taken into account when sentencing children and young people have recently been affirmed by the Sentencing Council. Their guidance states that the court *must* have regard to:

> (a) The principal aim of the youth justice system (to prevent offending by children and young persons); and
> (b) The welfare of the offender.
>
> (Sentencing Guidelines Council 2009: 3)

While this may appear laudable, the 'must' part of the provision does not apply to either mandatory life sentences or detention for life under dangerousness legislation. For those children and young people who have been labelled as dangerous, crime prevention and welfare will only therefore be taken into account when the court is minded to impose an extended sentence. This arguably puts crime prevention and public protection before the welfare needs of the offender and therefore breaches international standards, which state that the best interests of the child should always be paramount. Despite this concern being raised by the Joint Committee on Human Rights (Anderson 2009), these sentencing principles have received statutory status through section 142A CJA 2003, which was inserted by section 9 of the CJIA 2008 and which amends section 44 of the Children and Young Persons Act 1933.[2] In fact, section 142A goes one step further by including the need to take into account the general adult aims of sentencing as mentioned in section 142 CJA 2003. Factors that Arthur (2010) argues should have been included (that is, 'the individual's age and vulnerability; evidence of the effectiveness of the proposed sentence; and what particular interventions have been tried if the person has been sentenced before and what would be appropriate now' (ibid.: 56)) are nowhere to be seen.

Of more concern is the fact that the YJB does not advocate welfare as the primary consideration in sentencing young people either. In its latest Corporate Plan (2008–11), the Foreword talks about bringing the 'welfare and the justice agendas closer together' and, five lines later, explains how the Plan reflects the task of 'balancing children's welfare, criminal justice and the community safety agenda . . .' (YJB 2008a: 1). The word welfare is not, however, mentioned again. Rather, the strategic objectives are to:

- prevent offending and reoffending by children and young people under the age of 18
- increase victim and public confidence [and]
- ensure safe and effective use of custody.

(ibid.: 2)

The fact that welfare is not the primary consideration in the sentencing of children and young offenders has been criticised by the UN Committee on the Rights of the Child (2008). In 2008, it recommended that the UK should

> take all appropriate measures to ensure that the principle of the best interests of the child, in accordance with article 3 of the Convention, is adequately integrated in all legislation and policies which have an impact on children, including in the area of criminal justice and immigration.
>
> (UN Committee on the Rights of the Child 2008: 7)

To the author's knowledge, this has not been taken on board by the government, and there would appear to be no plans to do so either.

On 6 Feb 2008, the House of Lords did debate an amendment to the Criminal Justice and Immigration Bill that would have put the welfare of the child above all other sentencing considerations by allowing the court to take into consideration the 'age of the offender and the intellectual and emotional maturity of the offender' (HL Deb, 6 February 2008, c1076). As Baroness Butler-Sloss explained:

> Of course, the community must be protected. Of course, we must be certain that the press, which is powerful and militant in seeing children as wicked, rather than having needs as well as being offenders, will dislike anything that is not seen to be robust. But it is not lacking in robustness for the court to be reminded, as it should be, of the age and mental capacity of the offender. It will in no way reduce the protection of the public.
>
> (HL Deb, 6 February 2008, c1080)

Despite this and many other supporting views, the amendment did not make the final Act, with the agreed-upon amendments outlined above. It is therefore questionable who is governing England and Wales – the tabloid press or the Houses of Parliament. While principles of welfare would thus appear to be a consideration in sentencing children and young people, it is not a primary consideration and, in reality, and especially for dangerous young people, the aims of punishment and just deserts would appear to be more apparent.

The age of criminal responsibility

Following on from the welfare versus punishment debate, another important issue to consider when dealing with children and young people is the age at which they are held to be criminally responsible. To be held legally responsible for a criminal offence in England and Wales, a person must be 10 years old (s. 50 Children and Young Persons Act 1933, as amended by s. 16(1) Children and Young Persons Act 1963). This contrasts with Belgium, Switzerland and Luxembourg where the age of criminal responsibility is 18 and Spain, Argentina, Poland and Portugal, where it is 16 (Urbas 2000). The age of criminal responsibility in England and Wales is therefore misaligned with the age limit set by other European countries, although until 1998 a child aged 10 to 13 would have been presumed to have been *doli incapax*, meaning that it was presumed that they were incapable of committing a crime. This presumption could be rebutted by the prosecution, by it establishing beyond a reasonable doubt that the defendant committed both the *actus reus* and the *mens rea* and that he realised that what he was doing was seriously wrong rather than just naughty, but it did offer a level of protection for some young children charged with criminal offences, and did place England and Wales more in line with other EU States. Section 34 of the CDA 1998 has, however, overruled this presumption and, while at first it was thought that it was only the presumption that had been overruled (see *DPP v P* [2007] EWHC 946), thus allowing a child to still raise the defence of *doli incapax*, the House of Lords has quashed this belief, stating that both the presumption and the defence have been abolished for children aged 10 years and over (*R v T* [2009] UKHL 20). This therefore means that all children and young people aged 10 and over are deemed to be capable of committing criminal offences. Not only does this apply to young people with impaired mental capacity but again puts England and Wales out of kilter with its European counterparts.

The CDA 1998 was the first major piece of legislation introduced into England and Wales by New Labour, a government that was trying to prove to its voters that they were the party of law and order and that they were the ones who were going to be 'tough on crime' and 'tough on the causes of crime' (Labour Party 1997). Youth crime was seen as one of its priorities, and it was against this backdrop that it was thought that the presumption of *doli incapax* needed modernising so that youth crime would be prevented, deterred and punished (Bandalli 1998). Furthermore, Justice Laws argued that a belief that a child between the ages of 10 and 14 did not understand the moral obliquity of his actions was 'unreal and contrary to common sense' (*C (A Minor) v DPP* [1994] 3 WLR 888, although this was later overturned by the House of Lords (*C (A Minor) v DPP* [1995] 1 AC 1)). In the preceding White Paper, *No More Excuses*, the government argued that it was time to 'stop making excuses for children who offend' (Home Office 1997: para. 4.1) and stated that

> Punishment is necessary to signal society's disapproval when any person including a young person breaks the law and as a deterrent . . . Young people . . . should be in no doubt about the tough penalties they will face – including custody if that is necessary to protect the public.
>
> (ibid.: para. 5.1)

The CDA 1998 can therefore be said to have replaced a welfare emphasis on youth crime with a more punitive approach, even though its actual reasons for abolishing the *doli incapax* presumption appear to be based on the 'practical difficulties which the presumption presents for the prosecution' (para. 4.4) rather than any actual evidence that children aged between 10 and 13 understood the difference between what was just naughty and what was seriously or gravely wrong (see *R v Gorrie* (1918) 83 JP 186). Interestingly, the relevant section of the White Paper was entitled 'Are children incapable of evil?' (para. 4.3). Considering that the traditional meaning of *doli incapax* was always 'incapable of wrong', this overstatement of evil not only exaggerated the current position of youth crime but also highlights the punitive element towards young people that New Labour appeared, at that time, to be displaying.

In terms of serious sexual and violent offences, the abolition of *doli incapax* is extremely important. While a child between 10 and 13 may know that it is naughty to take a sweet from a shop or mischievous to hit their brother or sister, it is submitted that many may not know that it is 'seriously wrong' to partake in sexual activity with a child of a similar age. Even though it is accepted that, according to the law, children of this age cannot legally consent to sexual activity, if two children are playing 'doctors and nurses' and there is factual consent present then should those involved be seen as sexual offenders? It is also interesting that the government feels that a child must reach the age of 16 in order to have the maturity and capacity to consent to sexual activities, but has the maturity and capacity at 10 to understand that such behaviour is seriously wrong. Likewise, with violent crimes, do children as young as 10 understand the consequences that violent acts may cause, do they comprehend that life is not like a Tom and Jerry cartoon, where Tom always survives whatever Jerry does to him or, as in a Nintendo DS game, life is not restored once the next level is achieved?

As von Hirsch (2001) points out, children and young people do not have the cognitive capacity to fully grasp the harmful consequences of their actions, arguably making their crimes less serious than if they had been committed by an adult. One example that he uses is domestic burglary. While a young person may appreciate that he is stealing property from another person's home, he may not understand how his entry into a person's private space can cause feelings of fear, insecurity and vulnerability, and so arguably he should not be judged on the basis that such comprehension does indeed exist. Effectively what the abolition of *doli incapax* has done, therefore, is to measure every defendant on the same standard (that is, that of the reasonable *adult* man). The House of Lords has recognised in *R v G* ([2003] UKHL 50) that this is not appropriate and that age should be taken into account when assessing liability, but there does not appear to be any willingness to further extend this appreciation to the age of criminal responsibility. As Bandalli therefore explains, the erosion of the defence reflects the steady erosion of treating children as children and is 'symbolic of the state's limited vision in understanding children, the nature of childhood or the true meaning of an appropriate criminal law response' (Bandalli 2000: 94).

Youth court

All offenders aged 10–17 years who have been prosecuted for a criminal offence will normally be tried in the youth court, which is a Magistrates' Court for the young. Youth court magistrates are drawn from a special panel who have experience in dealing with children or young people or who have an interest in this area. When a case involving a violent or sexual offence comes before a youth court, the magistrates must decide whether or not to send the matter to the Crown Court. This must be done if the court is of the opinion that the child is a dangerous offender (that is, where the court is of the opinion that there is a significant risk of the offender causing future serious harm; see Chapter 2). Examples of relevant violent offences include ABH, GBH or wounding and robbery, while relevant sexual offences include sexual assault, possession of indecent photographs of children and rape (Judicial Studies Board 2010). The committal decision can be made at a number of different stages of the proceedings, including at mode of trial, pre- or post-pleas or post-conviction, although should only be used where the court believes that, if found guilty, the young person would receive a determinate sentence of more than four years.

Different to adult legislation, there has never been a presumption of dangerousness regarding children (although this no longer exists for adults either; see Chapter 2) and, since amendments made by the CJIA 2008, if the child is found to be dangerous the court has the power, rather than a duty, to impose dangerousness provisions. The court may additionally decide to hear the case but transfer the matter to the Crown Court for sentencing purposes. In determining whether or not a child is dangerous, the Sentencing Council's guideline on *Overarching Principles – Sentencing Youths* (Sentencing Guidelines Council 2009) requires sentencers to take into account the child's level of maturity, the likelihood that change will occur in a much shorter time than if the offender were an adult and the wider circumstances of the young person. This also reflects the decision in *R v Lang & Ors* ([2006] 1 W.L.R. 2509), where the Court of Appeal stated:

> It is still necessary, when sentencing young offenders, to bear in mind that, within a shorter time than adults, they may change and develop. This and

their level of maturity may be highly pertinent when assessing what their future conduct may be and whether it may give rise to significant risk of serious harm.

(at 2521)

Guidance in the Youth Court Bench Book states that the power to commit to the Crown Court should only be used 'rarely' (Judicial Studies Board 2010: 36). If the matter is committed to the Crown Court, the Court can impose the sentences as detailed below. A flowchart to illustrate this decision process can be seen in Figure 8.1.

Regarding assessing young people as dangerous, the government, when the dangerousness provisions were being debated in the House of Commons, stipulated that the legislation would only be appropriate for a 'very small minority of juveniles' and thus would be used 'infrequently'. It was therefore estimated that around 30 would receive detention for life, one or two would be sentenced to detention for public protection (DPP) and approximately 10 would receive the extended sentence (HC Debates, Hansard, 18 March 2003: Column 705W). As detailed below, actual numbers have been much higher than this.

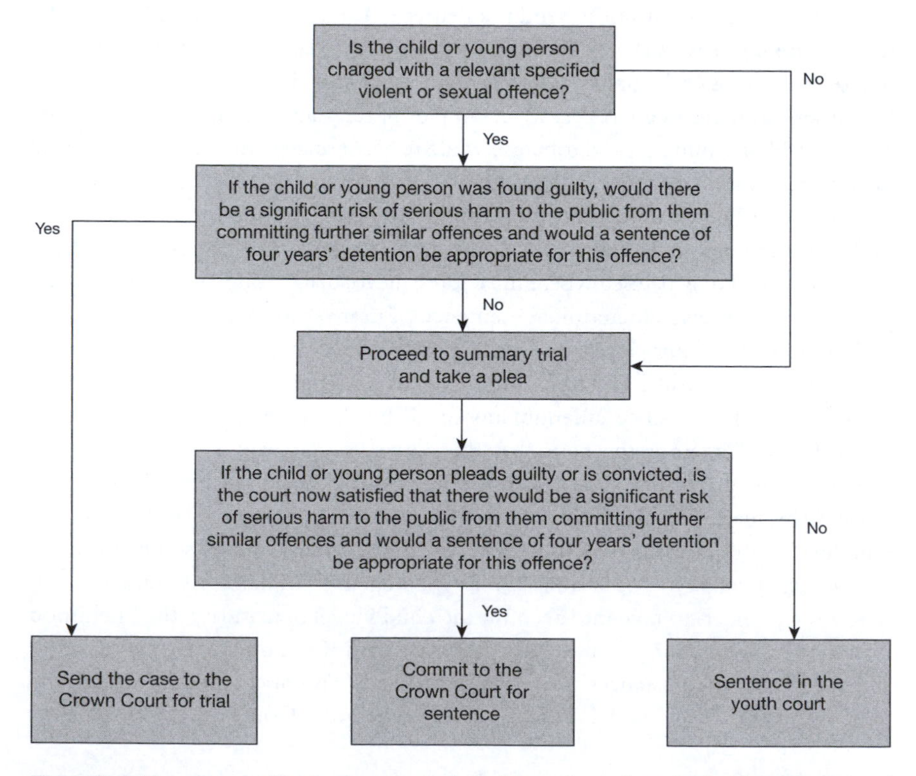

Figure 8.1 Dangerous offenders' committal decisions flow chart (Judicial Studies Board 2010: 38).

Despite the prevalence of young people committing serious sexual and violent offences, there is not a separate youth Crown Court. Historically, the reason for this would have been the belief that such a court was not needed due to the inadequate number of indictable cases involving young people, but such a justification would no longer appear to ring true. Children and young people who have committed serious sexual and violent offences are therefore tried in adult Crown Courts, subject to the committal process as outlined above. The Consolidated Criminal Practice Direction 2007 outlines some special measures that must be taken into account when a child is committed to the Crown Court, including the fact that regard should be given to section 44 of the Children and Young Persons Act 1933 and that the process should not expose children to 'avoidable intimidation, humiliation or distress' (Arthur 2010: 124). The court must take into account the young person's age, maturity and ability to understand the procedure, and should allow the child to sit with members of his family and permit easy communication with his legal representatives. Lawyers should not wear wigs and gowns, there should not be a recognisable police presence and all participants should be sat on an equal or similar level (Arthur 2010).

The fact that England and Wales does not have a youth Crown Court has been looked at by the European Court of Human Rights (ECtHR) in *T and V v United Kingdom* ((2000) 30 EHRR 121), which concerned the use of an adult Court in the trial of Thompson and Venables, two 11 year olds who were convicted for the murder of a 2-year-old boy. The argument put forward by the applicants was that, due to their immaturity, youth and state of emotional disturbance, a public trial in an adult Crown Court was in breach of both Article 3 (inhuman and degrading treatment) and Article 6 (right to a fair trial, including the ability to participate effectively) of the ECHR. While the Court held by 12 votes to 5 that there had been no violation of Article 3, it was held by 16 votes to 1 that Article 6(1) had been breached. The Court held that, while trying a child on criminal charges was not in violation of Article 6 per se, it was incumbent on the Member State to ensure that the child was 'dealt with in a manner which takes full account of his age, level of maturity and intellectual and emotional capacities, and that steps are taken to promote his ability to understand and participate in the proceedings' (at 125). While it was accepted that some steps had been taken to promote the applicant's understanding much of this, including holding the trial in public, further exacerbated the applicant's sense of discomfort. Medical evidence, furthermore, stated that, in view of V's maturity, it was 'very doubtful that he understood the situation' (at 126) and thus it was highly unlikely that he was able to fully participate in the proceedings. The findings in the case led to a Practice Note (trial of children and young people) (cited by Easton and Piper 2008), which led to a number of practical changes, although as Fortin explains, 'children are still required to sit in a dock, [be] stared at by a jury, and cross-examined by barristers' (Fortin 2003, cited by Easton and Piper 2008: 445).

The treatment of Thompson and Venables can be contrasted with a similar case that occurred in Norway in 1994. Here, three six-year-old boys attacked a five-year-old girl by stoning her and leaving her to die in the snow. The boys' names were never revealed in the media and they were treated like victims rather than killers. The boys were given counselling for four years, but were not prosecuted and, in fact, returned to school the week following the incident. In stark contrast to England and Wales, rather than demonising the children, Norway expressed compassion and understanding for all of the children and families involved (BBC World Service 2000).[3]

Available sentences

Where the Crown Court deems that a person between the ages of 10 and 17 is dangerous, it has a number of options open to it with regards to disposal. In essence, these are very similar to those that are available for adult offenders, although are named differently. For example, if the offence in question would have had a penalty of 14 years or more if the offender was aged 21 or over, the court, under section 91 of the Powers of Criminal Courts (Sentencing) Act 2000, may sentence the offender to be detained for such a period, not exceeding the maximum term of imprisonment with which the offence would have been punishable in the case of an adult offender. This is known as Detention at Her Majesty's Pleasure (as the maximum penalty may be life) and includes not just those offences whereby the maximum term is 14 years, but also a number of additional sexual and firearms offences. Under section 90 of the same Act, Detention at Her Majesty's Pleasure also applies to those aged 17 or under who have been convicted of murder.[4] While these two sentences still exist in their own right, they have been brought within dangerousness legislation under section 226(2) of the CJA 2003 and are known as detention for life. If a young offender is labelled as dangerous and the seriousness of the offence justifies such a sentence, detention for life *must* be used. Where the specified offence carries a sentence of 10 or more years (known as a serious specified offence), and the seriousness of the offence does not justify detention for life as outlined above, under section 226(3) CJA 2003 a young offender can be sentenced to DPP. If the offence is not a serious specified offence, but is nevertheless specified, under section 228 CJA 2003 a young offender *may* be sentenced to an extended sentence, which, like the adult equivalent, is made up of a determinate custodial term and an extended period of supervision within the community (see Chapter 2 for details on the equivalent adult sentences).

In determining which public protection sentence is the most appropriate, the court can chose between a sentence of DPP and an extended sentence, even where the offence in question is a serious specified one, with the age of the offender often being used as a determining factor. This is on the basis of the decision in *R v D* ((2006) 1 Cr. App. R. (S.) 104), where the Court of Appeal held that, in relation to a particularly young offender, an indeterminate sentence may be inappropriate even where a serious offence has been committed and there is a significant risk of serious harm from further offences. Furthermore, guidance for Crown Prosecutors states that CPS officers, when determining whether a young person is dangerous, should take into account

> [t]he need, in relation to those under 18, to be particularly rigorous before concluding that there is a significant risk of serious harm by the commission of further offences: such a conclusion is unlikely to be appropriate in the absence of a pre-sentence report following assessment by a young offender team.
>
> (Easton and Piper 2008: 433)

If one of the above options is used, on the basis that the custodial period of the extended sentence of detention must be for a minimum of 12 months and the offender is eligible for release at the halfway stage, the legislation ensures that all dangerous offenders are detained in custodial establishments for at least 6 months, even if they are regarded as being particularly young. The different available sentences are illustrated in Figure 8.2.

As with adult indeterminate sentences, the dangerous young offender will be given a minimum term that he has to serve in custody, for reasons of just deserts, retribution and deterrence, before he becomes eligible to be released by the Parole Board. Obviously, release is not guaranteed and it is at this stage that the offender

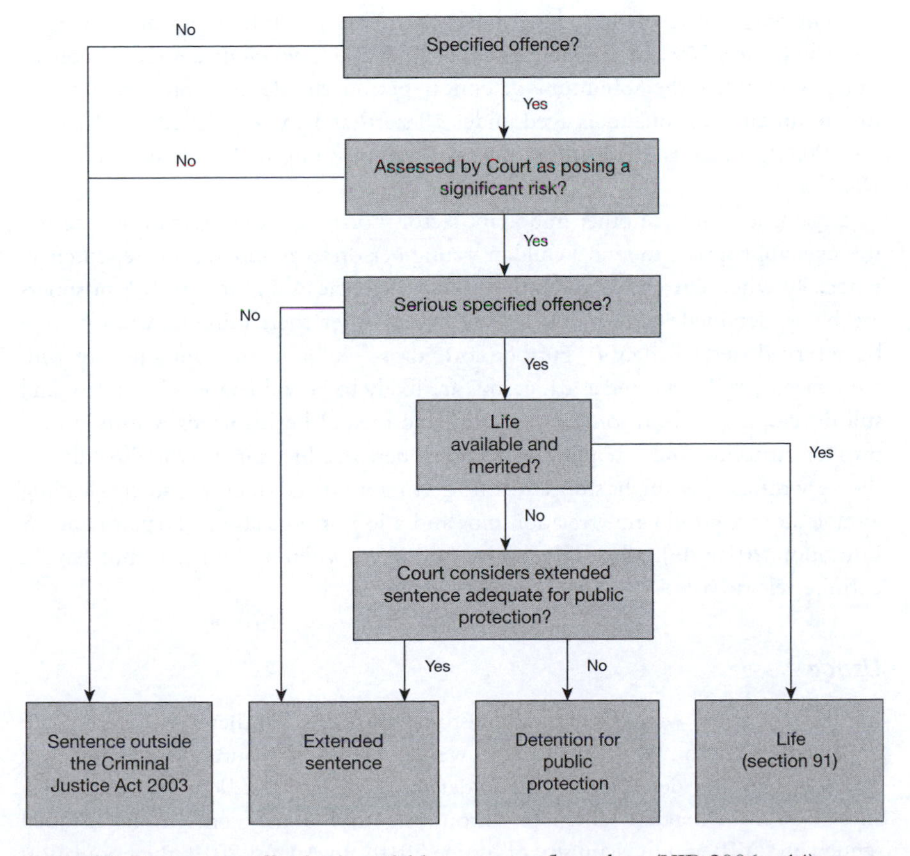

Figure 8.2 Dangerous offenders' available sentences flow chart (YJB 2006a: 14).

will then be detained under public protection rationales. The minimum term for those offenders held under Her Majesty's Pleasure used to be set by the Home Secretary, but, as with adults, this was held to breach Article 5(4) of the ECHR by the ECtHR in *T and V v United Kingdom* ((2000) 30 EHRR 121). In this case, the trial judge initially recommended a minimum tariff of eight years. The Lord Chief Justice argued that this should be raised to 10 years and recommended this to the Home Secretary, although following a public outcry on the basis that this was still too lenient, the Home Secretary set the minimum tariff at 15 years. The ECtHR held that, in order to comply with Article 5(4), those detained under Her Majesty's Pleasure must be able to have their tariffs reviewed by an impartial judicial body that had the power to order release where it was appropriate to do so. If the tariff was set solely by the Home Secretary, a breach of the Convention had occurred. Following this decision, The Lord Chief Justice issued a Practice Statement ((CA (Crim Div): Juveniles: Murder Tariff) [2000] 1 W.L.R. 1655) confirming that the judiciary, rather than Ministers, would set minimum tariffs. This has subsequently been updated by *R. (on the application of Dudson) v Secretary of State for the Home Department* [2005] UKHL 52), which sets out the procedure that must be undertaken in setting the minimum detention period, taking into account the welfare of the young defendant. This was further updated in April 2010 by section 269 and Schedule 21 of the CJA 2003, which makes recommendations as to what the minimum detention period should be. Interestingly, the minimum tariff for offenders aged under 18 starts at 12 years (Schedule 21 para 7 CJA 2003), which is 4 years more than the sentence imposed in *T and V v United Kingdom*.

Legal issues aside, another important factor worthy of consideration is whether it is ever appropriate to send a child or young person to an indeterminate sentence, especially when current delays in the adult system mean that several IPP prisoners are being detained many months, if not years, after their minimum tariffs have been served (see Chapter 4). Furthermore, those children and young people who are expected to be assessed as dangerous are likely to be vulnerable, dependant and still developing and, in some cases, will have mental health needs. Custody may provide structure and discipline in a young person's life, but it will also 'disrupt the very things that might stop someone getting involved in crime, such as having a stable home, good family relationships and a job or education' (Department for Education 2010: 49), all of which are multiplied when a child does not have a definite release date.

Usage

In 2008/09, there were 6,720 youth custodial disposals. Of these, 462 were made under either section 90 or 91 of the Powers of Criminal Courts (Sentencing) Act 2000; 24 were for detention for life under section 226 CJA 2003; 45 were DPPs; and 47 were extended sentences, amounting to 8.6 per cent of all custodial sentencing (YJB and the Ministry of Justice 2010). In August 2010, the population of the juvenile secure estate, excluding those aged 18, was 2,156. This can be broken down into 162 held in secure children's homes, 266 held in secure training centres (STCs) and 1,728 held in young offender institutions (YOIs). Thirty-six were held under section 226 of the CJA 2003, 30 under section 228 of the same Act, 22 under section 90 of the Powers of Criminal Courts (Sentencing) Act 2000 and, perhaps surprisingly, 313 under section 91 (YJB 2010a). Of those children and young people held under DPP sentences, most have convictions for robbery, violence and sexual offences, with more than half having previous convictions for similar offences and one in five having at least three such previous convictions. The average length of tariff for DPP prisoners convicted by the end of 2007 was 36 months, only 2 months shorter than the average for IPP prisoners for the same period of time (HM Chief Inspector of Prisons and HM Chief Inspector of Probation 2008). The fact that the courts are being as punitive with children and young people as they are with adults is perhaps surprising, especially when welfare and other children-centred principles are supposed to be taken into account. Such similarity in sentencing would therefore suggest that welfare is not viewed by sentencers as the primary consideration when sentencing young people, nor indeed does it suggest that it is being taken into account at all. This is particularly worrying when YJB data suggests that many children sentenced to DPPs have complex psychological needs and over 60 per cent have some sort of vulnerability (ibid.).

Risk assessment

While the assessment of dangerousness and of risk in general is difficult for adult offenders (see Chapter 3), there are particular complications involved when assessing children and young offenders, specifically when the focus is in relation to sexual or violent offences (NACRO 2005). Myers (2001), for example, argues that, while previous serious offending may be a good predictor of future offending for adults, this is not always the case for young people. In fact, Schladale (2010) argues that youth who have caused sexual harm, for example, are at a significantly greater risk of committing non-sexual criminal offences than of reoffending sexually. Adult risk-assessment tools are therefore unsuitable for use with children and young people, and any tool that is used must be developed with these differences in mind.

Asset

The main risk-assessment tool that is currently used with children and young people in England and Wales is Asset. This is made up of three sections: Asset – Core Profile, What do YOU think? form and Asset – Risk of Serious Harm. While all parts of the tool need to be completed, the section perhaps most relevant in terms of assessing dangerousness is the risk of serious harm assessment, even though it is worth noting that it was not specifically designed for the purposes of determining dangerousness under the CJA 2003 (NACRO 2005). The assessment is divided into four sections: current or previous harm-related behaviour, current risk indicators, future harmful behaviour and a conclusion. The risk of serious harm section should be completed where:

> 1 A young person has been convicted of a serious specified offence;
> 2 A young person is being sentenced in the Crown Court for a specified offence; or
> 3 A youth court specifically requests that the risk assessment in a PSR should contribute to its assessment of dangerousness in order to determine whether to remit the case to the Crown Court for sentencing.
>
> (YJB 2006a: 9)

On the basis of the Asset result, a young person will be allocated into one of the four serious harm categories, namely low, medium, high and very high. A child should only usually be classified as dangerous if he/she is assessed as being in the very-high risk of serious harm category, although young people regarded as high risk may be regarded by the courts as dangerous as well (YJB 2006a). While YJB guidance acknowledges that Asset findings do not necessarily correlate with findings of dangerousness, and that it is for the court to make the finding of dangerousness, it is perhaps worrying that children as young as 10 who are assessed by YOTS as being in the high-risk group are then at risk of being classified as dangerous by the courts.

A further worry is that, in 2004, YOTs were criticised for their poor identification of risk of harm as a common feature and that this was a matter that needed urgent attention. Pressure placed on YOTs to get it right may therefore result in even more children and young people being assessed as representing a risk and therefore being suitable for dangerousness legislation (NACRO 2005). Annison argues that this has led to a culture of blame, 'leading to a consequent tendency among professionals to over-predict risk and for risk procedures to become over-bureaucratic' (2005: 121). In order to counteract such tendencies, Kemshall (2009) therefore suggests that practitioners should ensure that assessment decisions should be holistic and defensible.

Other assessment tools

Although Asset is able to produce a risk score, it should not be used in isolation. For example, if the young person has displayed sexually harmful behaviour, practitioners can use the common-assessment model of AIM (Assessment, Intervention, Moving-on), which has now been revised and is known as AIM2 (YJB 2008b). The model considers offence-specific and developmental static and dynamic factors that are thought to contribute to the risks posed by young people. It is divided into 10 steps to assist and encourage practitioners in gathering and analysing risk information, and is linked to Asset and the Department of Health's Core Assessment Framework. The tool produces a score based on high, medium and low concern factors and high, medium and low strengths, with results used to inform appropriate penal sanctions and treatment interventions. The overall aim of the tool is therefore to properly assess and manage young sex offenders and protect their victims (Grimshaw 2008). Initial data on the use of the tool has been largely positive (Griffin and Beech 2004), with it aiding in a multi-agency approach in dealing with those children and young people who commit serious sexual offences.

Other tools that are being developed specifically for young sex offenders include J-SOAP (Juvenile Sex Offender Assessment Protocol) (see Prentky *et al.* 2000) and ERASOR (Estimate of Risk of Adolescent Sexual Offense Recidivism) (see Worling and Curwen 2001), although there is currently no clear evidence that they are able to make effective risk predictions (Grimshaw 2008). Furthermore, the Structured Assessment of Violence Risk in Youth (SAVRY) tool can be used with young people who have committed violent offences, although it is not a regular part of a young offender's assessment and is used fairly rarely across England and Wales (Finnigan 2010). In recognition of this dearth of assessment tools for young people who sexually and violently offend, the YJB is currently embarking on a project to consult on the future needs of the youth justice system's assessment and intervention framework. It is therefore hoped that, by 2011/12, there will be some revisions and improvements to Asset that will be relevant to this group of offenders (ibid.).

The juvenile secure estate

If an offender is assessed as dangerous, it is likely that he/she will receive a custodial sentence and be detained within the juvenile secure estate. The juvenile secure estate is the collective name for all youth custodial and secure facilities for those under the age of 18 and is made up of secure children's homes, STCs and YOIs. Under international law, children and young people held in custody should be held separately from adults, and this is one convention that is abided by in England and Wales. It used to be the case that not all female children and young people were separated from adult women due to the small numbers involved, but this has now been rectified by the building of three specialist units for young women within HM Prison Service. Interestingly, there is also a young women's MBU at Rainsbrook STC and provision at Hassockfield STC if it is required (YJB 2010b). Young people can be contained in secure units from the age of 10, although if the person is under 17, rather than being sent to a YOI, they may well be contained in local authority accommodation. While it is the court that sentences a child or young person to a custodial sentence, as the commissioner and purchaser of custodial places for young people the YJB will determine which type of unit is most appropriate for an individual offender. In 2010, approximately 84 per cent of young offenders were placed in YOIs, 10 per cent were sent to STCs and 7 per cent were accommodated in secure children's homes (Department for Education 2010).

Secure children's homes are run by local authority social services departments and focus on 'attending to the physical, emotional and behavioural needs of the young people they accommodate' (YJB 2010c). In order to achieve these aims, the units tend to be small (ranging from 6–36 beds) and have a high ratio of staff to young people. In general, they are used for young offenders aged between 10 and 14, girls up to 16 and boys up to 15 or 16 if they have been assessed as vulnerable (YJB 2010d). There are currently 19 secure children's homes across England and Wales, although only 10 of them have beds suitable for young people who have committed criminal offences. The remaining centres are used for those children who have been detained for welfare reasons under section 25 Children Act 1989 (see www.secureaccommodation.org.uk/unitdirectory.htm). The homes are all purpose built and provide intensive regimes of education and offending behaviour programmes centred on a therapeutic environment. An average place costs £215,000 per year (Department for Education 2010) and, on 1 January 2010, there were 148 children detained in this form of secure accommodation (HC Deb, 1 February 2010, c124W).

STCs are aimed at young offenders up to the age of 17 who have been sentenced to custody or who have been remanded to secure accommodation. There are currently four STCs in England – Oakhill in Milton Keynes, Hassockfield in County Durham, Rainsbrook in Rugby and Medway in Kent, all of which are operated under private contracts (YJB 2010d). The units range in size between 58 and 87 beds and again have a high staff to young person ratio, although this will not be as high as that seen in the secure homes. This relatively high staff/young person ratio allows the centres to focus on education and individuals' needs, something that the YOIs are unable to achieve. For example, trainees are provided with formal education for up to 30 hours a week, 52 weeks of the year (Department for Education 2010). The centres are designed to accommodate young people aged between 12 and 14, girls up to the age of 16 and boys of 15 and 16 where, again, they have been assessed as vulnerable. An average annual place costs £160,000 (ibid.) and, in January 2010, they accommodated 234 children and young people (HC Deb, 1 February 2010, c124W).

The final option is YOIs, which are run by HM Prison Service and, in some cases, by private operators. YOIs detain young people between the ages of 15 and 21, although those aged 18 and over (young adults) will be accommodated in separate units. Girls of 17 will be detained within YOIs, as will boys aged between 15 and 17 (Department for Education 2010). The establishments are much larger than the other secure alternatives, with units ranging between 28 and 360 beds, and staff/young person ratios being much lower (YJB 2010e). This consequently means that there is a lot less emphasis on the individual, with more concern placed on detention and security. There are 13 YOIs in England and Wales (YJB 2010f), although there are only 5 institutions that hold those under the age of 18. These are YOI Ashfield, YOI Cookham Wood, YOI Warren Hill, YOI Wetherby and YOI Werrington (HM Prison Service 2010b). An average annual cost per place is £60,000 (Department for Education 2010).

Considering the punitive attitude towards children and young people who commit crime, it is perhaps to be expected that England and Wales detains more children in prison than any other Western European country (Anderson 2009).

For example, while in 2006 there were 2,400 children in custody in England and Wales, there were only 646 in France, 244 in Germany, 10 in Norway and none in Spain (ibid.). In the last 15 years, child incarceration in England and Wales has increased by:

- 90% for 15–17-year-old prisoners,
- 142% with regards to child remand prisoners,
- 400% for girl prisoners, and
- 800% for 12–14-year-old prisoners.

(Goldson 2010)

In December 2009, there were 2,203 under 18 year olds held in secure accommodation in England and Wales. Of these young people, 77 per cent were either 16 or 17, 94 per cent were male and 6 per cent were female (Department for Education 2010).

Prison regime

For children and young people serving sentences of DPP, it is worrying to note that, unlike the adult IPP, there is no documentation of the 'lifer' process that should be followed. *The Indeterminate Sentence Manual* (HM Prison Service 2008b) provides a process for young adult offenders (that is, those aged between 18 and 21) but is silent on those aged under 18. This has meant that children have either followed the procedure as laid out for IPP prisoners, with no appreciation of the fact that young people's needs are different, or officers have used the normal determinate detention and training order process, with it being manifestly clear that neither are appropriate (HM Chief Inspector of Prisons and HM Chief Inspector of Probation 2008). In fact, in a 2008 inspection on the use of IPPs and DPPs, the situation was described as 'troubling' (ibid.: 3). The report made 30 separate recommendations, 13 of which were specifically for the YJB, including the need to 'develop a strategy to accommodate and manage young people sentenced to DPP within a wider strategy for young people serving long-term sentences' and creating 'a sufficient number of specialist units to accommodate young men serving DPP and other long sentences, resourced to meet their *welfare*, offending behaviour and learning needs' (ibid.: 9, emphasis added). A second thematic inspection took place in 2010, although this focused more on the IPP than the DPP (HM Chief Inspector of Prisons and HM Chief Inspector of Probation 2010) and so it is unclear whether any of these recommendations have been brought into practice.

Managing disruptive behaviour

On the basis that this chapter is dealing with those children and young people who have committed serious sexual and violent offences, it is unsurprising that some of these will behave in a disruptive manner when being held in custodial institutions.

For example, on 28 March 2008, 40 per cent of all offenders held in secure children's homes had been convicted of violent offences. Violent offenders made up 52 per cent of the total population in STCs and 46 per cent of the population in YOIs (Smallbridge and Williamson 2008). While some of the strategies for managing the behaviour of 'troubled and troublesome' (YJB 2010g) children are controversial, especially those that involve physical intervention, they are, in some cases, a part of maintaining not only good order and discipline, but also a safe and secure environment for all within the institution. In all cases, the YJB state that physical interventions with children are used 'only ever as a last resort, when behaviour is so challenging it presents an assessed risk to others, [are only used] for the shortest possible duration [and] never as a punishment or to secure compliance with staff instructions' (YJB 2010g). While it is therefore acknowledged that restraining children and young people is sometimes necessary, the fact that these offenders are typically the most vulnerable in society also needs to be taken into consideration, especially when it is borne in mind that a large proportion of children and young people in custodial institutions have physical or mental health problems, and that there is a significant overlap between children in custody and children previously held in care (Smallbridge and Williamson 2008).

In secure children's homes, a child can only be restrained 'to prevent a child harming himself or others or from damaging property. Force should not be used for any other purpose, nor simply to secure compliance with staff instructions' (Smallbridge and Williamson 2008: 73). In STCs, it can be used for the purpose of ensuring good order and discipline or for the purpose of preventing the offender from:

> (a) escaping from custody;
> (b) injuring themselves or others;
> (c) damaging property; or
> (d) inciting another trainee to do anything specified in paragraph (b) or (c) above.
>
> (Rule 38 of the Secure Training Centre Rules 1998)

In YOIs, restraint and the use of force can be used where it is deemed to be reasonable, necessary and proportionate to the seriousness of the circumstances (HM Prison Service 2010c).

Methods of control and restraint with children and young people can include single separation, where the child is removed from association with his or her peers and is kept in solitary confinement. Although there are no time limits imposed on this in secure children's homes, single separation can only be used for up to 3 hours in STCs and cannot exceed 72 hours in YOIs if the reason for the separation is to maintain good order and discipline (Smallbridge and Williamson 2008). It is worth noting that, if a young person is held in solitary conditions, the institution still has a duty to offer him education, training and physical education in addition to providing minimum regime activities (*R. (on the application of BP) v Secretary of*

State for the Home Department [2003] EWHC 1963 (Admin)). Other methods include prone restraint, where a child is held face down on the ground; supine restraint, where he is held face up on the ground; seated holds; basket holds, where a young person's arms are held across his chest in an x shape; and the use of batons and ratchet handcuffs. All of these methods have been found to inflict pain and, in some cases, injury (ibid.).

Between April and November 2007, there were, on average, 24 restraints occurring every day across the juvenile secure estate, with a peak in July 2007 when there were a total of 891 restraint incidents, amounting to, on average, 29 per day (Smallbridge and Williamson 2008). Restraint techniques were found to be used most commonly in YOIs, which is not surprising considering they detain the highest proportion of young offenders, but were also found to be considerably high in STC. Further reports have noted an over-reliance on emergency measures and, in particular, the 'staggering levels of use of force by staff' (HMCIP 2008: 4), with force at an STC at Oakhill being used in 757 instances over a 9-month period. Even more worryingly, of these occasions, the highest level of restraint was used over 70 per cent of the time (that is, restraint involving three members of staff with one staff member holding the young person's head) (HMCIP 2008). Likewise, at HMYOI Castington, an inspection in 2009 found 'an unacceptably high number of serious injuries had been suffered by young people in the deployment of use of force by staff' (HMCIP 2009a: 5), resulting in seven confirmed fractures and two suspected fractures in a two-year period.

The controversy surrounding the use of control and restraints with young people in secure settings has therefore focused more on the privately operated STCs than on any other custodial institution, with this reaching its height in 2004 following the deaths of Gareth Myatt, aged 15, and Adam Rickwood, aged 14. Both boys were being held in STCs, with Gareth dying while being restrained, using a technique called the seated double embrace (this technique has now been suspended) and Adam taking his own life after being restrained. The restraint used on Adam involved a technique known as nose distraction, which has been described as a karate-like chop to the nose and caused a nosebleed. Following the inquests into these deaths, the Minister for Youth Justice and the Minister for Children, Young People and Families commissioned an independent review into the use of restraints in secure settings (see Smallbridge and Williamson 2008). In all, the review made 58 recommendations, including better staff training, the introduction of institutional restraint reduction strategies and the permanent removal of nose distraction and the double basket techniques of restraint. Furthermore, the review recommended that restraint should only be used 'for preventing the risk of harm . . . [it] should not be used simply to secure compliance with an instruction [and] should be subject to risk assessment and debriefing with young people and staff (ibid.: 72).

In response to the review, the government promised that 'significant changes' would be made, although weakened this somewhat by stating that some of these changes would 'require further commitment and time to become full working practices' (Ministry of Justice 2008b: 5). There is also a YJB code of practice for managing the behaviour of children and young people in the secure estate (YJB 2006b) but this was developed prior to the review carried out by Smallbridge and Williamson, and therefore does not take any of their recommendations into account. Notwithstanding this, since December 2009, the YJB has started to develop and implement restraint minimisation strategies in all secure settings (see YJB 2009) and, since July 2010, there is also a Physical Control in Care Training Manual. This stipulates that any force used must be reasonable, necessary and proportionate to the circumstances. The manual is an interim measure, pending the introduction of a new holistic behaviour-management system to be known as Conflict Resolution Training (Ministry of Justice 2010g).

Specialist units

The Keppel Unit

In relation to adult offenders, perhaps the most effective form of intervention with offenders who commit serious sexual and violent offences is through the use of TCs and, in an attempt to try to counter some of the criticisms of the juvenile secure estate, the YJB commissioned and set up a vulnerable young offender unit at YOI Wetherby. The Keppel Unit has been running since 6 October 2008 and holds up to 48 boys aged between 15 and 17 who have been identified as being vulnerable and thus unable to cope in the mainstream under-18 estate (Ahmed 2009). Many of those on the Keppel Unit have mental health problems and have been socially excluded from a young age, and therefore need individualised care and support rather than a regime based on discipline and control. To aid with this, Keppel is divided up into 4 sections, with 12 single occupancy beds per section, and has the highest staff to offender ratio in the juvenile secure estate, often with more staff on the unit than boys. Due to this intensive staff presence, an annual place at Keppel costs approximately £90,000 per year (Pemberton 2009), which, while cheaper than a place in an STC or a secure children's home, is £30,000 more expensive than a normal YOI place.

The unit is said to feel and look like a secure children's home, with walls full of artwork, soft lighting, a fishing lake and a garden. Cells have en-suite bathrooms and in-cell televisions (Pemberton 2009). While the regime at Keppel is not strictly a TC, it is similar to one, as it fosters a culture of enhanced and individualised support where young people can access an enhanced range of programmes and services including education, substance misuse work, counselling, sex offender treatment, anger management and development courses. Each child has an individualised care plan that will not only identify priorities for intervention, but will also make plans for release. In addition to these formal interventions, the offenders are also expected to engage in other unit activities such as gym sessions, visits to the library and shared mealtimes (Department for Education 2010). Due to this difference in regime from normal YOIs, staff are expected to undertake an eight-week training programme before they are allowed to work on the unit. This includes training on mental health awareness, child protection training, pro-social modelling, sex offender training, behaviour management, and suicide, self-harm and resilience training (ibid.).

There are currently 70 staff working on the unit, 36 of whom are HM prison officers. The average bed occupancy is 40–42, with it being expected that 25 per cent of trainees will complete the whole of their sentence on the unit, with the remainder being returned either to the main YOI Wetherby site or to their original establishments when the time is thought to be appropriate. Many of the offenders on the unit are sex offenders and, in recognition of this, counsellors from the Lucy Faithfull Foundation also provide intervention sessions (IMB 2009b). Despite its relative newness, the unit has been inspected by HMCIP, who, in a post-opening inspection, noted that it was 'an impressive facility, achieving a great deal with some very damaged young people with a range of complex problems' (HMCIP 2009b: 5). The unit was thought to be a fundamentally safe place, with little self-harming, little bullying and excellent staff/offender relations. In conclusion, it was stated:

> The Keppel Unit is among the most impressive custodial facilities to have opened in recent years. In a very short time, a committed group of staff have established a safe, supportive and purposeful unit in which the risks and needs posed by some very damaged and complex young people are effectively addressed. However, after only a few months in existence, the unit is already a victim of its own success, with referrals coming from across the country rather than merely from its original northern catchment area. This strategic drift is unhelpful and inhibits resettlement and family ties. The Youth Justice Board and the Prison Service need to clarify the unit's role and, perhaps, replicate it in the south of the country, to help meet the evident need and to ensure that this much needed resource can fulfil its immense potential.
>
> (ibid.)

While the extension of the service is essential, with the opening of another unit in the south of the country, it is suggested that units such as these need to be even more widespread. On the basis that the Keppel Unit offers a regime akin to a TC, and one where individualised needs of children and young people are taken into account, it is submitted that all vulnerable children and young people should be treated within a similar regime, even if they have not been officially classified as such.

The Anson Unit

This extension of provision has been seen, to some extent, with the opening of the Anson Unit, which is another specialist unit at HMYOI Wetherby. Anson is a 48-bed residential unit that is dedicated to the management of young people, aged 15–17, who are serving life sentences. This can either include those sentenced under sections 90 or 91 of the Powers of Criminal Courts (Sentencing) Act 2000, or under the dangerousness legislation in the CJA 2003. Following on from the success of HMP Grendon (see Chapter 4), the unit is run on a therapeutic basis and focuses on work that aims to reduce reoffending and achieve parole. As with the Keppel Unit, staff at Anson are also specially trained, with each young person given a dedicated case worker. The case worker will work on a one-to-one basis with the offender, but will also liaise with YOTs and families in the community (YJB 2010h).

To be accepted on to the unit, the offender must be a 'lifer' and must have at least nine months left to serve on his sentence, or have nine months before he reaches his 18th birthday. Referral can come either from within the YOI estate, from an STC, a secure children's home or from the community (YJB 2010i). While there is no catchment area as such, if the removal of a young person to YOI Wetherby would involve taking him far away from his home and family, the referral may be rejected due to the needs of resettlement. While this is perfectly understandable, it highlights the need to have more specialist units such as Anson geographically dispersed throughout England and Wales. A referral may also be rejected if the young person has a history of disruptive behaviour.

While there is no current evidence concerning the efficacy of the unit, on the basis that it is modelled on the regime at Grendon (see Chapter 4), it is hoped that it will be effective. It is therefore argued that all children and young people who have been assessed as dangerous should be held within specialist units, especially considering the fact that there is no separate 'lifer' process for young offenders. Not only will this take into account the welfare of the individual child, but will be more effective in the YJBs' and government's desire to stop reoffending.

Prison conditions

Even though the welfare principle is not the primary consideration when determining a sentence for a child or young person convicted of a serious sexual or violent offence, there are a number of minimum standards that must be met by those authorities who detain young people. It was originally thought that the duties under the Children Act 1989 and Article 3 of the UN Convention did not apply to HM Prison Service and subsequently to young people held within YOIs, although the High Court has dispelled this belief, explaining that, while the legislation does not apply to HM Prison Service and YOIs per se, the duties under the Children Act cannot be suspended just because a person is being detained within a YOI (*R. (on the application of the Howard League for Penal Reform) v The Secretary of State for the Home Department* [2002] EWHC 2497 (Admin)). This has been legislated for in section 11 of the Children Act 2004, which states that arrangements must be made to ensure that 'functions are discharged having regard to the need to *safeguard* and *promote* the *welfare* of children' (emphasis added).

Despite section 11,[5] recent years have seen a crisis in the juvenile secure estate based on alarming levels of sexual assault, violence, intimidation, bullying, drug taking and extortion (Goldson 2002). Inspection reports have been equally damming, including one that expressed concern relating to harassment and bullying:

> Children are made worse by the experience of imprisonment [and] the bullying and harassment that they inflict on each other . . . The emphasis on Child Protection procedures should be not so much on children being molested by staff, although this must, of course, be guarded against, but on protecting them from bullying and intimidation by their peers when staff are not present. The worst examples of this are reflected in establishments where verbal intimidation is practiced by shouting from cells and physical bullying takes place in unsupervised places such as showers and recesses on landings. It is essential that all parts of establishments holding children and young adults are made safe, so that the ravages of bullying and intimidation cannot be wrought.
>
> (HMCIP 2001: 9)

In addition to high levels of violence, incidents of self-harm and suicide have also increased over the last few years. Recorded numbers of self-inflicted deaths of young offenders can be seen in Table 8.1, while recorded numbers of young offenders who have self-harmed is presented in Table 8.2. As acknowledged by Lord Low of Dalston in July 2010, 'There is a high incidence of bullying and self-harm, and there are too many suicides – often by young people. It would be easy to conclude that the system was broken beyond repair . . .' (HL Deb, 15 July 2010, c785). Goldson also reiterates this view, claiming that child imprisonment 'systematically harms and damages children: physically, emotionally and psychologically' (Goldson 2005: 83).

On 6 February 2008, the Lords debated Amendment 71 to the Criminal Justice and Immigration Bill, put forward by Baroness Linklater of Butterstone.[6] This involved restrictions on custodial sentences for offenders aged under 18, and stated:

1 A court shall only pass a sentence of custody on a person under 18 as a measure of last resort and where –
   a) The offence committed caused or could reasonably have been expected to cause serious physical or psychological harm to another or others and;
   b) A custodial sentence is necessary to protect the public from a demonstrable and imminent risk of serious physical or psychological harm.
2 The court shall state in open session its reasons for passing any sentence of custody under this section.

As with the amendment concerning welfare, this did not make the Act either. It is therefore perhaps unexpected that it is the traditional and conservative members of the House of Lords who favour welfare-orientated policies and the House of Commons who decide not to approve them; although, as it is the Commons members who need to appease the voting public, perhaps this is not as surprising as first thought.

Table 8.1 Recorded numbers of self-inflicted deaths of young offenders

	2004	*2005*	*2006*	*2007*	*2008*	*2009*	*2010*
Young people aged 14 to 17 years	2	2	0	1	0	0	0
Young people aged 18 to 21 years	6	13	3	10	8	11	2
Total	8	15	3	11	8	11	2

Source: Inquest 2010

Table 8.2 Recorded numbers of young offenders who have self-harmed

	2004	*2005*	*2006*	*2007*	*2008*
Young people aged 15 to 17 years	317	434	381	344	430
Young people aged 18 to 21 years	970	1,053	1,124	1,140	1,194
Total	1,287	1,487	1,505	1,484	1,624

Source: HC Deb, 3 November 2009, c907W

Risk-management strategies

Youth Offending Teams

All children and young people who receive either detention for life, DPP or an extended sentence are likely to be referred to MAPPAs on their release. To be MAPPA-eligible, the child or young person must have committed a serious sexual or violent offence under Schedule 15 of the CJA 2003 (s. 325 CJA 2003). Supervision of 'MAPPA-eligible' young people is largely carried out by YOTS, who, with the police, probation and prison services, have a statutory duty to make arrangements for ensuring that 'their functions are discharged having regard to the need to safeguard and promote the welfare of children' (s. 11(2) Children Act 2004). YOTs were established by the CDA 1998 and, in recognition of the service users being children and young people, they *must* include representatives from both criminal justice and welfare agencies. Organisations involved in YOTs, as stipulated by section 39(5) of the CDA 1998, therefore include social services, police, probation, education and health.

In recognition of the fact that children and young people are different to adults and that their welfare needs to be taken into account when supervising and making risk-management arrangements, separate MAPPA Guidance exists that states that 'children must *not* be treated . . . as a mini-adult, and should *not* be managed using the same risk assessment tools or management processes' (NOMS 2009: 140, emphasis added). Following on from an assessment of risk using Asset, offenders are allocated as either Category 1 or Category 2 cases, with the YOT making an initial decision concerning the level of MAPPA management that is needed and, as with adults, there are three levels of management available (see Chapter 5). The eventual risk-management plan and the arrangements put in place to effectively manage the young person will be very similar to those described in Chapter 5 for adults, but again there is the added requirement that all MAPPA personnel must ensure that the correct balance is achieved between public protection and the rights and needs of the child (NOMS 2009).

Registration and notification requirements

In addition to being supervised by YOTs, children and young people who have committed a sexual offence under Schedule 3 of the SOA 2003 are also placed on the ViSOR. The information that must be provided to the police is exactly the same as with adults (see Chapter 5), with the only allowance for the age and immaturity of the offender being that the time periods for the length of the registration are halved (s. 82(2) SOA 2003), although this does not apply if the notification period would have been for an indefinite period if the offender was an adult. In these cases, the notification requirement is also for life. While a number of organisations and charities such as the Howard League for Penal Reform, Save the Children, Liberty and the National Organisation for the Treatment of Abusers have all argued that there should be different registration policies for children and young people (see Thomas 2009), the most controversial issue has been that of lifetime registration, particularly because of the lack of review.

As detailed in Chapter 5, in December 2008, a 16-year-old boy (F) made a successful application to the High Court that his indefinite registration on ViSOR without review was incompatible with Article 8 of the ECHR (*R. (on the application of F and T) v Secretary of State for Justice* [2008] EWHC 3170(Admin)). The argument before the court was not that registration and the notification requirements were unlawful per se, but that the indefinite time period without the opportunity to show that the young person had changed in such a way that the rationale for the notification no longer applied, was unlawfaul. The court agreed, stating that the absence of a review in the case of young offenders amounted to a breach of Article 8. On appeal, the Court of Appeal (*R. (on the application of F) v Secretary of State for Justice* ([2010] 1 W.L.R. 76) held that an offender was entitled to have the question of whether the notification requirements continued to serve a legitimate purpose determined by periodic review, with the argument that section 82 of the SOA 2003 breached Article 8 ECHR, being even stronger in the case of young offenders. This was also affirmed by the Supreme Court in April 2010 ([2010] UKSC 17).

Risk-reduction strategies

In addition to managing risk, it is also imperative that suitable interventions are employed in order to reduce risk of reoffending. If it is accepted that, for risk-assessment purposes, children and young people are different from adults and therefore need separate risk-assessment tools, it must also be accepted that their different criminogenic needs demand different treatment programmes and approaches. Wood, for example, argues that the most important aspect to bear in mind when deciding how to 'treat' those children and young people who commit serious sexual and violent offences is 'the recognition that treatment interventions should have the specific needs of young people as their foundation and the flexibility to adapt interventions to accommodate these needs' (Wood 2007: 149). While some of the adult programmes are available in YOIs (although it is not clear from the data whether they are being used with those aged under 18), there do not appear to be any accredited programmes specifically designed with young people in mind. In a survey carried out by Hackett *et al.*, it was found that interventions with children and young people who had sexually offended differed across the country and that there was a 'range of assessment and intervention packages', with only 17 per cent of services offering a community-based group-work programme and just 14 per cent a residentially based intervention (2005: 103). A lack of specialist services for children and young people who had caused sexual harm was repeatedly noted by the authors, with one of their main recommendations being the development of best practice guidance for this specialist group. Other recommendations included an identifiable assessment service, identifiable intervention provision, accredited training, good quality supervisions and consultation, and supporting the families of children who had sexually offended (Hackett *et al.* 2005).

A further review in 2008 looked at the provision for services for children and young people who had sexually abused and the effectiveness of a number of treatment interventions (Grimshaw 2008). It was noted that interventions still differed across the country but, more worryingly, that 'it is premature to conclude that programmes have a clearly established effect' (ibid.: 28). In fact, the authors found no clear evidence of a treatment effect with young people, largely because of the low base rates of recidivism and the small groups that were being worked with. While the research acknowledged that some approaches were beneficial, such as TCs and programmes that concentrated on emotional competence skills, general developmental assessment, family work, pro-social, emotional, cognitive and behavioural skills, no set intervention pathway was established. Such a gap is perhaps astounding, especially when we take into account the number of children and young people who are being labelled as dangerous and need to show a reduction in their risk before they are able to be considered for release into the community.

Lucy Faithfull Foundation

Perhaps in recognition of this treatment gap, but only in relation to those young people who have committed serious sexual offences, the Lucy Faithfull Foundation has been contracted by the YJB since 2009 to provide an assessment and intervention service for young people in four male YOIs. The service is geographically distributed throughout England and Wales and is available at YOI Wetherby (18 spaces), YOI Warren Hill (9 spaces), YOI Hindley (6 spaces) and YOI Ashfield (6 spaces). For an offender to be referred, he must be 15–17 years old, have been sentenced to custody for a sexual offence, be detained within a YOI and have at least 12 months left to serve on his sentence. In practice, however, the offender may need to be much younger. This is due to the need to be under 18; the fact that the programme takes 12 months to complete; the low turnover of beds, again due to the length of the programme; and the existence of waiting lists, all suggesting that more units are required. The treatment involves comprehensive assessments and interventions that are focused on meeting the offender's individual criminogenic needs and, where appropriate, will involve working closely with families and YOT workers so that release, resettlement and future life planning can be enhanced (YJB 2010j). Unfortunately, there is no similar service for young female offenders, although there may be the option to 'spot purchase' (YJB 2010k: 3), no equivalent service for children below the age of 15, and no service for those children and young people serving sentences for violent crime.

Conclusion

When compared to adult offenders and all juvenile offenders, those children and young people who commit serious sexual and violent offences are rare, especially when we exclude those who have been charged with sexual offences where consent existed in fact, if not in law. Despite this rarity, this does not mean that there should not be special policies, risk-assessment tools and interventions in place to manage and treat these children. The debate as to whether young people who commit crime are troubled or troublesome will always exist, especially in relation to those who commit serious sexual and violent offences, but arguably it is these children who actually need more help and understanding from the authorities, rather than traditional censure. International law emphasises the need to put the welfare of the child as the primary consideration in all matters, but, as described above, the courts and agencies working with young offenders in England and Wales at best only have regard to what is in their best interests. To help the young offender but to also ensure greater public protection, it is suggested that the youth justice system becomes more focused on welfare and less focused on justice. There is some glimmer that this is occurring through the creation of specialist units such as the Keppel and Anson Units but, due to their size and locality, much more still needs to be done. There should also be a greater emphasis on community penalties with those young people and children who have been assessed as dangerous. Space has precluded an evaluation of the many impressive community options that exist for young people, including the youth rehabilitation order, intensive supervision and surveillance, and restorative justice approaches. When such programmes do exist, and when we know that many children and young people who display such worrying behaviour have been harmed themselves in some way, it appears counterproductive to send them to custodial institutions and, in many respects, treat them as 'mini-adults'.

9

MENTALLY DISORDERED OFFENDERS

Introduction

In addition to women and young offenders, another special and oft-considered separate group are those offenders who suffer from mental disorders.[1] While the mentally ill have, for centuries, been perceived to be dangerous (see Chapter 1), 'most mentally disordered offenders are neither seriously ill nor dangerous' (Burney and Pearson 1995: 292), despite the fact they are often perceived to be 'an unquantifiable danger' (Peay 2007: 497). It is therefore difficult to ascertain whether such offenders should be contained within the penal system or within a more welfare-orientated mental health system, even though current policy regarding mental health and crime is largely dominated by notions of risk rather than by humanitarian concerns (Peay 2007). The presence of mental and personality disorders in those who commit serious sexual and violent offences is not a recent discovery, although, interestingly, depression is thought to be associated with higher rates of violence than actual schizophrenia (Easton and Piper 2008). Despite this knowledge, a number of high-profile crimes committed by mentally disordered offenders (MDOs) have brought them to the forefront of the political agenda, and so it is perhaps to be expected that separate policies and risk-management strategies exist to deal with this collection of offenders. Whether this is the case and whether such policies and strategies work is the subject matter of this chapter. In particular, it looks at the prevalence of MDOs, how they are dealt with by the courts, what assessment tools are used to determine their levels of risk, how and where they are detained, and what is in place in terms of risk-management and risk-reduction strategies.

Definition, prevalence and public perceptions

Definition

Before looking at the prevalence of MDOs, it may first be worthwhile to briefly define what is meant by these offenders. Definitions of mental disorder have usually been found in mental health legislation, with, until recently, a mental disorder being classified as 'mental illness, arrested or incomplete development of mind, psychopathic disorder and any other disorder or disability of mind' (s. 1(2) MHA 1983). The MHA 2007 amends and broadens this definition, stating it is 'any disorder or disability of the mind' (s. 1(2)), with examples including schizophrenia, bipolar disorder, anxiety or depression, personality disorders, eating disorders, autistic spectrum disorders and learning disabilities, although the latter will only qualify if the disability is associated with 'abnormally aggressive or seriously irresponsible conduct' (s. 2 MHA 1983). The amendment therefore makes it far easier to classify someone as mentally disordered and thus widens the net of those who are deemed to be potentially dangerous and in need of detainment.

Interestingly, a person did not previously suffer from a mental disorder by reason of immoral conduct, promiscuity, dependence on alcohol or drugs or sexual deviancy. While dependence on alcohol or drugs (s. 1(3) MHA 1983), promiscuity or sexual orientation are still not within the realms of mental disorder, sexual deviancy now is (Bowen 2007). Indeed, it was argued in the House of Commons that 'the amendment [in the new Act] makes it clear that paedophilia is not within the scope of the exclusion' (Hansard 19 Jun 2007: col. 1326). While it remains the case that a person cannot be detained under mental health legislation solely due to his/her sexually deviant behaviour, as other tests involving appropriateness also need to be met, it does, in theory, offer a means by which sexual deviants can be forcibly detained and treated (Harrison *et al.* 2010).

Prevalence

The commonness of MDOs is difficult to measure, especially considering that the new definition, as explained above, covers such a broad range of disorders and disabilities. Taken in its broadest sense, it is likely that the vast majority of offenders who have committed serious sexual and violent offences are suffering from some kind of disorder or disability of the mind, especially when such matters can be transient and momentary. Looking at it more narrowly, however, the number of MDOs is probably far lower than the average man would think, especially when only counting those who commit serious sexual and violent offences, with more offenders found in local facilities supported by social services, housing and health than in psychiatric wards (Peay 2007).

In 2009, in England and Wales, 4,300 restricted patients were detained in hospital, an increase of 8 per cent from 2008. 3,700 (87 per cent) were men and 550 (13 per cent) were women, with the proportion of restricted female patients standing at more than twice than that in the general female prison population (5 per cent). 2009 saw 1,500 hospital admissions, an increase of 3 per cent from the previous year, with 96 per cent of all admissions to high-secure hospitals being men. The number of MDOs transferred from prison to hospital also rose, from 930 in 2008 to 940 in 2009. This made up 61 per cent of the total 2009 admissions, with 520 MDOs being transferred after sentence and 420 while either unsentenced or on remand. Interestingly, a slight increase was also noted regarding discharges/disposals of restricted patients in 2009, with the figure of 1,300 being a 2 per cent rise from 2008. Of these, 540 (40 per cent) were released into the community (Ministry of Justice 2010e).

Of interest is also the number of MDOs detained within prison, with a far greater proportion of prisoners suffering from one or more mental disorders when compared to the general population. In 1991, 37 per cent of the prison population had a diagnosable mental disorder. In 1996, in the remand population, this stood at 63 per cent. In 1997, out of 3,000 prisoners studied, 10 per cent of those on remand and 7 per cent of sentenced men were found to be suffering from functional psychotic disorders (Peay 2007). Furthermore, in one Office of National Statistics survey, it was discovered that 39 per cent of sentenced males and 62 per cent of sentenced women had significant neurotic problems, such as depression, anxiety and phobias. Those on remand, however, had still higher rates, with 58 per cent of men and 75 per cent of women experiencing neurotic disorders (Mind 2010a). Moreover, over 75 per cent of men on remand, nearly 66 per cent of sentenced men and 50 per cent of sentenced women were suffering from a personality disorder. These included antisocial personality disorder, paranoid personality disorder and borderline personality disorder (ibid.). The Sainsbury Centre for Mental Health (2008) go further in stating that up to 90 per cent of prisoners have at least one mental health problem. Undoubtedly linked to this is the high rate of self-harm among prisoners, with 50 per cent of all self-harm cases in prison involving women, particularly worrying when they make up only 5 per cent of the overall prison population. Between 2004 and 2008, self-harm incidents increased by 25 per cent overall, but by 42 per cent in women's prisons. In 2008, the total number of self-harm cases was 12,560 for women and 10,466 for men (Mind 2010a).

A number of prisoners therefore receive medication for mental health issues, with over 50 per cent of all women in prison receiving drugs and one sixth being prescribed hypnotic or anxiolytic medication. When only 17 per cent of these women were taking medication prior to imprisonment, this arguably proves that the conditions of imprisonment can exacerbate or even cause mental health problems (Knight and Stephens 2009). This was further emphasised by HMCIP who found that 90–95 per cent of women in HMP Holloway were on psychotropic medication such as benzodiazepines (HMCIP 2002, cited in Knight and Stephens 2009), although it is unclear here whether the prevalence of MDOs is really as high as the study suggests or whether medical staff were prescribing antidepressants as a method of control.

Public perceptions

The public perception of people who suffer from mental illness is often that they are dangerous, in all manner of forms, including being violent and committing lewd and sexually depraved acts. As Rubin notes,

> Certain mental disorders [are] characterized by some kind of confused, bizarre, agitated, threatening, frightened, panicked, paranoid or impulsive behaviour. That and the view that impulse (i.e. ideation) and action are interchangeable support the belief that all mental disorder must of necessity lead to inappropriate, anti-social or dangerous actions.
>
> (1972: 398)

This perception of MDOs can be linked to the discussion of dangerousness in Chapter 1 and the idea that often dangerousness is linked to what we fear most rather than what is actually dangerous. This is emphasised by Gunn, who argues that dangerousness is made up of 'destructiveness, prediction and fear'. Interestingly, Gunn also states how 'the latter, fear, makes it at least partially subjective, therefore it can never be entirely objective' (Gunn 1982: 7), with it being commonplace to believe that MDOs are dangerous. Often, however, this is because they are a group of individuals who we do not understand and arguably it is this discomfort of not understanding that generates the fear, rather than anything more substantial. Another commonly held belief is that community care policies have failed and that there are more people with mental health problems on our streets due to a deinstitutionalisation programme in the 1980s under the rule of Thatcher. Again, this perpetuates the belief that, because of such people, we are at risk of being harmed.

The media has also played a significant role in making us believe that MDOs are more dangerous than they actually are. High-profile cases are often reported at the time of the incident, when the court case is taking place and also during the public inquiry, often exaggerating the number of cases in the public's mind (Mind 2010b). Furthermore, as with other high-profile cases, newspapers are saturated with information, again making it appear as if all MDOs are dangerous and are rightly to be feared. In one research study, homicide and crime were the most frequent reports covered in relation to mental health, with people who have experience of mental health problems rarely interviewed or quoted. Shockingly, as one journalist explained, 'there is no sexiness in mental health unless someone has committed a terrible crime' (ibid.). It is therefore of little wonder that the public have a skewed opinion of MDOs.

Despite such negative perceptions, the reality concerning MDOs is far different to that displayed above. Mentally ill people commit far fewer homicides than mentally ordered offenders, they are more likely to kill themselves than other people, and their rates of reoffending are no higher than other mainstream prisoners (Peay 2007). Evidence from the USA suggests that only 3 per cent of all violent crime is committed by those who have major mental disorders, with alcohol, drugs and poverty being much more likely contributors (ibid.). This has also been seen in England and Wales, although the rate is slightly higher here. Between April 1996 and April 1999, of the 1,564 people convicted of a form of homicide, 164 (10 per cent) were found to have mental health problems at the time of the offence. This same proportion was also found in a later study that looked at 5,189 homicides committed between January 1997 and December 2005. Here, 510 (10 per cent) were found to have mental health issues (Mind 2010b). When this information is put into the context of mental disorder prevalence in the population – one in six of the adult population will have a significant mental health problem, amounting to more than 7 million people – the 50–70 cases of homicide per year clearly suggests that the vast majority of those who have mental health problems are not dangerous and do not present significant risks to the community (Mind 2010a). Furthermore, evidence, again from the USA, suggests that those people who suffer from psychosis are 14 times more likely to be the victims of unprovoked serious attacks rather than to be the perpetrators of them (Mind 2010b).

Moreover, those who have been released from hospital following a restriction order are actually less likely to reoffend when compared to those offenders who were held in prison (Peay 2007). Between 1999 and 2006, 1,500 patients were discharged from hospital detention in England and Wales. Of these offenders, 1,331 were located on the Police National Computer, with it being established that only 7 per cent had reoffended within 2 years of discharge. 2 per cent committed violent and/or sexual offences and 1 per cent were reconvicted of grave offences (Ministry of Justice 2010e). Furthermore, the prevalence of violence among those who have been discharged from a psychiatric hospital, and who do not have substance abuse problems, is approximately the same as those people living in the community who have not spent time in a psychiatric hospital and do not have substance abuse issues (Mind 2010b).

Criminal justice issues

Traditional practice with MDOs has always been to divert them away from the criminal justice system, using medical and therapeutic responses rather than punitive alternatives (see Home Office 1990). Classification of an offender as an MDO will first take place at the police station, where a number of special protectionist policies will come into action, such as having an appropriate adult present during the interviewing process. The CPS will also consider whether it is in the public interest to prosecute the offender or whether it would be better for him to be diverted away from the criminal justice system (see CPS 2010). If an MDO is criminally prosecuted, one of the first things that the trial court will need to establish is whether the defendant is fit to plead (that is, whether he has the mental capacity to understand the charge, its meaning, and the nature and consequences of pleading guilty). Following this exercise, the court must then establish whether he is fit to stand trial. Again, this is judged on mental capacity, with the question being whether the person understands the nature and process of the court trial and can instruct counsel (Ashworth 2005). If an MDO is found either not fit to plead or to stand trial, the court can make a number of orders found in mental health legislation (see below).

If the offender is fit to plead and stand trial, the offender can still rely on the defence of insanity, if he can show that

> at the time of committing the act, the party accused was labouring under such defect of reason, from disease of the mind, as not to know the nature and quality of the act he was doing, or, if he did, that he did not know what he was doing was wrong.
>
> (see *McNaughten's case* [1843] 10 Cl. & F. 200 at 210)

It is worth noting, however, that, despite the existence of the McNaughten Rules, some offenders would rather avoid the insanity label, preferring 'to be criminalized and maintain one's free will than to be psychiatrized and lose it' (Peay 2007: 502). The vast majority of MDOs therefore tend not to use the insanity defence, but instead seek a therapeutic disposal at the sentencing stage (Ashworth 2005).

In addition to the above provisions, there has also been a mental health court pilot that ran from January 2009 to January 2010 in Brighton and Stratford (East London) Magistrates' Courts. The aim of the pilot was to 'provide timely access to health services, offering tailored sentences and ultimately reducing reoffending' (Ministry of Justice 2009f). The courts were established in the wake of the Bradley Report, which recommended 'a nationally guided approach' (Bradley 2009: 1) to dealing with people with mental health problems or learning disabilities in the criminal justice system. At that time, it was thought that approximately 350 mental health cases were going through the court system each year and thus a need for such provision was identified. The courts work by screening offenders for mental health problems and then ensuring that there is closer working between agencies and support services for the good of the MDO. Different to normal courts, the mental health court has been seen as a problem-solving environment and, to aid in this endeavour, always has a psychiatric nurse present (Ministry of Justice 2009f). The aim of the court is therefore to:

> - identify defendants with mental health and/or learning disability issues through screening and assessments conducted by a dedicated practitioner;
> - provide the court with information on a defendant's mental health needs to enable the court to effectively case manage the proceedings;
> - offer sentencers credible alternatives to custody to ensure offenders with mental health/learning disability are supported, be it with a community order with a supervision requirement or mental health treatment;
> - offer enhanced psychiatric services at court;
> - implement regular reviews of orders; and
> - direct those individuals not suitable for the mental health court community order to mental health and other services that can appropriately address their needs.
>
> (ibid.)

To date, there has been a feasibility study looking at whether it is possible to evaluate the impact of the pilots (Pakes *et al.* 2010), a process evaluation (Winstone and Pakes 2010) and emerging findings that the courts can lead to stronger cooperation between criminal justice and health agencies. While the pilots have now ended, mental health courts remain in both pilot areas and are now part of the court's usual business (Ministry of Justice 2010f). Whether the courts will be rolled out on a national basis is presently unclear, although, if they have worked as well as the Ministry of Justice has claimed, it would perhaps be negligent if such national expansion was not made.

Sentencing policy

Although previous policy regarding MDOs largely focused on treatment-based approaches, therapeutic considerations and, as mentioned above, diversion away from the criminal justice system, contemporary sentencing policies have focused much more on risk penology and public protection (Peay 2007). This is so even though our knowledge concerning mental behaviour and why individuals act in a particular way is, at best, rudimentary. For example, with any given MDO, it is difficult to be sure whether that person has offended due to his mental disorder and thus needs 'special care' or whether the mental disorder is a factor that contributes to dangerousness, thus justifying 'special control' (ibid.: 500), with this dichotomy typifying the sentencer's difficult decision between a prison or hospital disposal.

Acknowledging the fact that the presence of mental and personality disorders should be taken into account when sentencing occurs, section 166(5) CJA 2003 states that the court does not have to impose a custodial sentence on someone who is considered to be mentally disordered. This therefore allows the sentencer to decide between penal, welfare and hybrid solutions. Prior to the changes in the CJA 2003 and the introduction of IPP (see Chapter 2), the Judge could have chosen between a determinate prison sentence and an indeterminate hospital disposal, often favouring the latter because of the needs of public protection. Due to the fact that indeterminacy can now be achieved through an IPP, the number of hospital orders has consequently fallen, with there being a resulting increase in the number of prisoners housed within the main prison estate suffering from mental and personality disorders (Bickle 2009). The decision between a prison or hospital disposal can therefore be difficult for any sentencing judge, although *R. v Beulah Birch* ((1989) 11 Cr. App. R. (S.) 202) does provide some guidance on which is the most appropriate. For example, where the offence and the mental disorder are not connected, or where there was a level of culpability that merits punishment, a custodial sentence is deemed to be correct. However, for those considered to be 'dangerous and disordered', Mustill LJ considered that, in those situations, hospital was always the accurate choice (*R. v Beulah Birch* (1989) 11 Cr. App. R. (S.) 204). Even if the court does favour a hospital disposal, there may still be circumstances, such as a lack of hospital beds, where the judge will be forced to send the offender to the main prison estate, even though it is acknowledged that a therapeutic disposal would be the more appropriate option.

A final, somewhat hybrid alternative is for the court to impose an IPP but to simultaneously direct that the prisoner should be sent to hospital for treatment.

This option is available under section 45A MHA 1983 and is known as a hospital direction. The offender's sentence will be calculated in accordance with normal sentencing and dangerousness principles in mind (see Chapter 2), but will include a proviso that the prisoner be transferred to a hospital within 28 days. If treatment is completed, or thought at a later date to be inappropriate, the offender will be transferred to prison to serve the remainder of the tariff. It is also worth noting that the Sentencing Council has identified 'mental illness or disability' as a factor that should lower culpability and, consequently, the seriousness of an offence. In this sense, therefore, a mental disorder or disability can be legitimately used to mitigate an offender's sentence (see s. 166 CJA 2003). This could result in the judge deeming an absolute or conditional discharge to be the most suitable response, although for serious sexual and violent offenders the use of such disposals will be relatively rare.

Orders under mental health legislation

If the court finds that the MDO is unfit to plead or stand trial, or he is found not guilty by reason of insanity, or a hospital disposal is thought to be the most appropriate sentencing disposal, the person will be dealt with under mental health legislation. Controversially, this also permits the detention of people who have not been convicted of criminal offences. Accordingly, under section 1 MHA 1983 (as amended by the MHA 2007), those who have been categorised as 'mentally disordered' and who meet the necessary criteria can be provided with various therapeutic disposals. To ensure such treatment, the Act allows for the detention of mentally disordered people, including those who have committed criminal offences, if an appropriateness test is passed. The test thus considers whether medical treatment exists that is appropriate in the case of the MDO, taking into account the nature and degree of the medical disorder and all other circumstances. This appropriate treatment test was introduced by the MHA 2007, replacing a treatability test, and therefore now allows those with severe mental and personality disorders to be detained and given treatment even where there is no specific medical benefit. This potentially widens the scope of the Act and has been criticised as demonstrating a shift from providing therapeutic benefit through detention and treatment to a method of social control (Harrison and Rainey 2009).

In relation to dangerous offenders, it may be unlikely that the change in the law will have a great impact for those who have already offended and whose behaviour reaches the nature and degree necessary for compulsory treatment. However, the wider definition of mental disorder, coupled with a less restrictive appropriate treatment test, could, in theory, mean a rise in the number of paedophiles, for example, being detained and treated under the Act. There is also the possibility of compulsory treatment for those who have not actually committed criminal offences, for example those who may have expressed sexual fantasies about children but have not yet acted upon them (Harrison and Rainey 2009). It would therefore seem apparent that, by extending the definition of mental disorder and by removing the treatability test, the government has made it far easier to detain, in a hospital setting, those who have been classified as suffering from a mental disorder and are *perceived* to be dangerous. While this net-widening is concerning, some would argue that it is better than the indeterminate DSPD order that was proposed, but not enacted, in 2000 (see McAlinden 2001).

Of the orders that exist, one of the most common is the hospital order. This is available to the court where the person has been convicted of an imprisonable offence and, the court is satisfied that the offender is suffering from 'mental illness, psychopathic disorder, severe mental impairment or mental impairment' (s. 37(2)(a) MHA 1983); that treatment will 'alleviate or prevent a deterioration of his condition' (s. 37(2)(a)(i) MHA 1983), making detainment in a hospital appropriate; and the court is of the opinion that a hospital order is the 'most suitable method of disposing of the case' (s. 37(2)(b) MHA 1983). The court will rely on two registered medical practitioners to provide this information and, if it makes a hospital order, cannot then pass additional sentences of imprisonment, or impose a financial or community penalty (s. 37(8)(a) MHA 1983). The effect of a hospital order is that the offender will be compulsorily detained in a psychiatric institution or unit in a general hospital. Each treatment site is categorised in terms of its level of security, in much the same way as male adult prisons, with the existence of high-secure hospitals, regional secure units, NHS psychiatric in-patient acute units and independent hospitals (Easton and Piper 2008).

The court, under section 41 MHA 1983, also has the power to make a restriction order when a hospital order has been made. This similarly authorises detainment but also states that the person should not be released until a Tribunal deems it safe to do so, and so is meant to be protectionist rather than punitive. Section 41 can only be used if the court believes 'that it is necessary for the protection of the public from serious harm' (s. 41(1) MHA 1983), having regard to the offender's index offence, previous convictions and risk of reoffending. In this sense, the test is very similar to the dangerousness test seen in the CJA 2003 for IPPs. An additional effect of a restriction order is that decisions regarding leaves of absence or transfer to another hospital cannot be made without the consent of the Secretary of State. Offenders who are subject to restriction orders are examined at least annually to decide whether the restriction order needs to remain, with reports being sent to the Secretary of State. It is then his decision as to whether the restriction order remains or can be lifted (s. 42 MHA 1983). At the end of 2006, there were 3,601 offenders held under a restriction order, of which 650 men and 56 women were held in high-secure hospitals (Easton and Piper 2008).

Other orders under the MHA 1983 include the ability to remand offenders to hospital for the purposes of reports (s. 35 MHA 1983) and treatment (s. 36 MHA 1983), and under section 38 an interim hospital order can also be made. Moreover, under section 47, if it is deemed that a person held in the main prison estate should be detained in a hospital (with the test being similar to that seen in s. 37), the Secretary of State can order a transfer direction, which effectively is a retrospective hospital order. This will last for 14 days and authorises the transfer of the prisoner to a hospital setting. A transfer direction also applies to those held on remand or in asylum centres (s. 48 MHA 1983) and, if appropriate, can be a restriction direction, which additionally includes the restrictions under section 41 (s. 49 MHA 1983). In 2004, 63 per cent of all admissions of restricted patients into hospitals were those who had been transferred directly from prison (Peay 2007).

For those offenders who have been sentenced to an IPP but simultaneously have had hospital treatment recommended under section 45A MHA 1983, a limitation direction, which has the same effect as a restriction direction, should also be attached. Both restriction and limitation directions ensure that an MDO is not released into the community earlier than he would have been had he served his sentence in prison under IPP conditions. If the order is just for transfer, then the offender will be released at the end of his sentence. However, if the order is one of restriction or limitation, this will last until either the MDO would have been released from prison or the Parole Board directs release on life or IPP licence. When the restriction direction lapses, the Secretary of State will cease to have responsibility for the offender under mental health legislation. Instead, arrangements under indeterminate criminal justice legislation will apply in the normal way (see Chapter 4).

In reverse to the above, section 50 allows for the transfer of offenders from hospitals to prisons. This will occur either when it is deemed that the person no longer requires treatment or, more commonly, where it is thought that the mental disorder will not benefit from further treatment. The latter is obviously of more concern due to the fact that the disorder has not been dealt with and the prison system is arguably in a much worse position than the hospital to deal with such matters. It is therefore unsurprising that violent prisoners with unresolved mental disorders are often those who are found in CSCs or held in segregation units due to their antisocial, disruptive and violent behaviour.

Risk assessment

As with general dangerousness legislation, for an MDO to be compulsorily detained with restrictions, the court must establish that such restrictions are 'necessary for the protection of the public from serious harm' (s. 41(1) MHA 1983). This finding is often achieved through the use of risk-assessment tools. In addition to OASys (the main general offending risk-assessment tool) and the HCR-20 risk-assessment scheme, version 2 (see Chapter 3), the principal tool used to assess MDOs in England and Wales is the Hare Psychopathy Checklist-Revised (PCL-R) (Hare 1991), although this arguably measures levels of psychopathy rather than actual risk. Psychopathy for this purpose is therefore defined as 'a constellation of affective interpersonal and behavioural traits associated with a marked absence of compassion and a lack of personal integrity' (Blanchette and Brown 2006: 59). To measure this, the PCL-R is a 20-item checklist, covering areas such as lifestyle, criminal behaviour, need for stimulation, pathological lying, behavioural controls, impulsivity, lack of remorse and callousness, and can predict not just risk of reoffending, but also, importantly, the probability of rehabilitation working. This latter part is important considering the existence of the appropriate treatment test in current mental health legislation. Each item is scored using a value of 0 if it does not apply, 1 if it applies somewhat and 2 if it fully applies, with final scores ranging between 0 and 40 (Hare 1991). The final score is based on a semi-structured interview with the offender, but is also gained through a review of the subject's records and history. Scores at the higher end of the scale signify higher levels of psychopathy, with a prototypical psychopath scoring 40. A score of 25 or more however is considered to signify a significant level of psychopathy, with 30 or more resulting in a diagnosis of psychopathy (Taylor 2003). People with no criminal backgrounds are expected to score in the region of 5, while many non-psychopathic offenders may score as high as 22 (Encyclopaedia of Mental Disorders 2010). The tool has been validated for use with male, female and adolescent forensic populations (that is, those in prison or psychiatric hospitals), although, interestingly, average PCL-R scores tend to be lower with female populations when compared to their male counterparts (Blanchette and Brown 2006).

In terms of efficacy, PCL-R has been described as 'state of the art . . . both clinically and in research use' (Fulero 1995: 454) and is widely accepted to be the best single predictor of violent behaviour currently available in the Western world (Blanchette and Brown 2006). Studies concerning the predictive validity of the tool have largely been based in Northern America, although one study, involving 728 adult male offenders, examined the use of the tool in HM Prison Service in England and Wales. As a predictor for violent behaviour, it correctly predicted reoffending in 92 per cent of cases and increased predictor validity from 78 per cent to 81 per cent when added to other risk-assessment tools such as LSI-R and OGRS (see Chapters 3 and 8). Interestingly the research also noted how those offenders who had been classified as showing high levels of psychopathy, as measured by the PCL-R, showed little to no treatment effect with short-term anger management and social skills training programmes (Hare *et al.* 2000), suggesting that individualised programmes designed specifically with psychopathy in mind are required.

High-secure hospitals

If an MDO is sentenced using a therapeutic order under mental health legislation, he will then be transferred to a hospital setting. Forensic services in England and Wales include evaluation and care in open, low-secure, medium-secure and high-secure hospitals and, in 2009, there were 4,500 medium- and high-secure hospital beds in England, amounting to a cost of £1 billion (Duggan 2010). On the basis that this book is concerned with serious sexual and violent MDOs, it will only be the high-secure institutions that will be examined. There are presently three high-secure psychiatric hospitals in England and Wales: Ashworth, Broadmoor and Rampton. All cater for violent and/or dangerous MDOs and are overseen by the High Security Psychiatric Services Commissioning Board within the NHS

Executive, although each hospital is an Authority in its own right (Mersey Care NHS Trust 2010a).

Broadmoor, situated in Berkshire, is probably the most well known and houses approximately 260 patients, all of whom, since September 2007, are men (West London Mental Health NHS Trust 2010). Notorious patients have included Ronald Kray, Charles Bronson, Peter Sutcliffe and Daniel McNaughten (who the McNaughten Rules on insanity were named after). Although Broadmoor is not a prison, it has security conditions reminiscent of a Category B establishment, with higher levels of security present for certain units, depending on who is detained there. Despite this security element, the design and day-to-day routine of the hospital is set up for therapeutic reasons and to emphasise this it is run by West London Mental Health NHS Trust rather than by HM Prison Service. Patients are allowed their own rooms, but are routinely searched and have to remain within the hospital grounds, although as this amounts to 55 acres, a fair amount of liberty can be granted to an MDO if deemed appropriate. The average stay in 2002 was thought to be eight years, although this included patients not involved and detained as part of the criminal justice system. The site is divided into sections providing facilities for education, gardening and therapeutic interventions (Judd and Goodchild 2002).

Rampton Hospital in Nottinghamshire houses approximately 400 patients, three quarters of whom are detained through the criminal justice system, and has a staff of over 1,900 (Nottinghamshire Healthcare NHS Trust 2010a). Similar to Broadmoor, patients are able to have their own rooms, but are also routinely searched in order to maintain its high security status. The care provided at Rampton is split into five areas focusing on mental health, women's services, learning disability, personality disorders and DSPD (Nottinghamshire Healthcare NHS Trust 2010a). The mental health directorate, for example, consists of nine wards, including two admission wards, two continuing care/treatment wards, one intensive care unit, one high dependency villa, one dual function villa for those with physical disabilities and the National High Secure Deaf Service (Nottinghamshire Healthcare NHS Trust 2010b). The National High Secure Healthcare Service for Women at Rampton is the sole provider of high-secure services in England and Wales for women and is located in a 2-storey 50-bed female only unit. As detailed by Nottingham Healthcare NHS Trust, it aims 'to provide a safe, gender-sensitive, therapeutic service for women with mental health needs who cannot be managed in a less secure setting, so that they can receive the appropriate assessment, care and treatment, to enable their progression along an identified care pathway' (Nottinghamshire Healthcare NHS Trust 2010c). The women's unit has four wards encompassing a learning disability service, an enhanced needs unit, a mental illness service and a personality disorder service (ibid.). Rampton is set in expansive grounds of 57 hectares and is currently managed by Nottinghamshire Healthcare NHS Trust. Notorious offenders have included Beverley Allitt and Ian Huntley.

Finally, Ashworth hospital is located in Merseyside and houses approximately 275 male patients. The original building, Moss Side, became a special hospital in 1933, with Ashworth being an amalgamation of this and a second hospital, Park

Lane, with the merger taking place in 1989 (Mersey Care NHS Trust 2010a). Perhaps best known for its brutalising regime uncovered by the Fallon Report (Fallon *et al.* 1999), treatment is now separated into two clinical services: the admission and high-dependency service and the specialist service. There are also two care services, namely the primary healthcare service and the rehabilitation service (Mersey Care NHS Trust 2010b). The rehabilitation service, for example, provides interventions that are focused on activities designed to meet the care plan of the individuals involved and can include expressive arts, joinery and metal work, pottery, cookery classes, occupational therapy, sport, and horticulture (Mersey Care NHS Trust 2010c).

Release

The First-Tier Tribunal (Mental Health)

As with those prisoners held within the main prison estate, there is also a review process for testing the legitimacy of holding indeterminate patients under the MHA 1983, which arguably came about due to the case of *X v UK* ((1981) 4 EHRR 181). Previously known as Mental Health Review Tribunals, the First-Tier Tribunal (Mental Health) has existed since 3 November 2008 and sits within a Health, Education and Social Care Chamber. The change was brought about by the Tribunals, Courts and Enforcement Act 2007, which not only introduced this First-Tier Tribunal, but also created an Upper Tribunal that is used to review and decide appeals. The Tribunal, in many respects, acts in a similar way to the Parole Board in that its role is to decide when it is safe for an offender, detained under the MHA 1983, to be released. The Tribunal is therefore an independent judicial body, with Tribunal Judges appointed by the Lord Chancellor and non-legal members appointed by the Secretary of State for Health or the Secretary of State for Wales, depending where the offender is based. Each Tribunal Panel is made up of one judge and two other members, one of whom must be a medical specialist (Tribunals Service Mental Health 2010a). The Judge on the panel is there to not just chair the hearing, but also to ensure that the legal requirements of the MHA are adhered to and that the proceedings are conducted fairly. The medical specialist would have examined the patient prior to the hearing and is there to provide a medical opinion on whether or not it is still necessary to detain the offender. Finally, the third Tribunal member is typically a representative from the community, although will often have some experience in health and welfare (Tribunals Service Mental Health 2010b). The Panel will usually meet in the hospital where the offender is being detained (Padfield 2008).

The overriding question for the tribunal is to determine whether detention is still justified. This is assessed by considering a number of factors, including whether the offender is suffering from a mental disorder that makes it appropriate to keep him incarcerated for treatment; whether it is necessary for the public's safety and the offender's own health and safety that he should receive such treatment; and whether such treatment is available (s. 72(1) MHA 1983). Interestingly, the section is worded so that the Tribunal shall direct release unless a mental disorder can be proven. This puts the onus of proof on to the Tribunal and is in direct contrast to previous legislation, where the burden of proof rested on the MDO to show that he no longer suffered from a mental disorder. Such legislation was found to be incompatible with the Human Rights Act 1998 (*R. (on the application of H) v Mental Health Review Tribunal for North and East London Region* [2001] 2 WLR 512) and thus the new section was part of the amendments made by the MHA 2007. This therefore makes it easier for an MDO to be released, especially in the situation where it cannot be proven that he is still suffering from a mental disorder; although it is acknowledged that the wider interpretation of mental disorder does work somewhat to counteract this ease. The Tribunal's principle powers therefore include the ability to:

- Discharge a detained patient from hospital immediately or after a short further period of detention;
- Recommend a leave of absence;
- Recommend Supervised Community Treatment; and/or
- Recommend transfer to another hospital.

(Tribunals Service Mental Health 2010a)

Where the patient was previously an indeterminate-sentenced prisoner who was transferred into a hospital setting, the Tribunal may decide that treatment is either no longer required or is no longer effective. If this is the case, the MDO will be transferred back into the prison system, unless to do so would be detrimental to his health (HM Prison Service 2008b). In transfer cases, the prisoner will return to the initial sending unit, while, for those subject to section 45A orders, an appropriate prison will be identified by the Mental Health Casework Section in the Public Protection and Mental Health Group of NOMS. For all prisoners transferred from psychiatric institutions, a Care Programme Approach care plan must accompany the MDO, which will outline whether or not ongoing mental health services are required (ibid.). Once the prisoner leaves the hospital setting, release decisions will then be transferred to the Parole Board.

The justification test also exists under section 73 MHA 1983 for those MDOs subject to restriction orders. For restricted patients, however, the Tribunal may decide to direct conditional, rather than absolute discharge, which means that the offender can be recalled for treatment at any time. It is also worth noting that, in some circumstances, the Tribunal only has the power to make recommendations to the Secretary of State, with it being the executive that makes the final decision. For example, in the case of discharging transfer or hospital directions, the Tribunal needs the prior agreement of the Secretary of State. If any recommendations made to the Secretary of State are not complied with, the Tribunal can reconvene and rehear the case (Tribunals Service Mental Health 2010a), but this still does not offer true independence from government and arguably is something that should still be reviewed.

The Parole Board

Not all MDOs are contained within mental health settings, however, either because of insufficient beds or because the offender has been transferred back to the main prison estate. If, at the time of possible release, the offender is being held within a criminal justice establishment, release will be determined by the Parole Board as detailed in Chapter 4. As identified in that chapter, prisoners under this system are responsible for proving that their risk of reoffending has reduced. For the majority of indeterminate prisoners, this is achieved through satisfactory completion of accredited offending behaviour programmes, which has been proven to be difficult because of insufficient provision. While it is therefore difficult for 'normal' IPP prisoners to gain release, those suffering with mental health issues have an even steeper mountain to climb. Not only do MDOs find it harder to complete offending behaviour programmes because the programmes have not been designed with their needs in mind, HM Prison Service has placed a greater focus on treating MDOs with medication rather than with therapeutic alternatives. Cluley (2009) notes how several MDOs are refusing medication and mental health services to enhance their chances of being selected for offending behaviour programmes, but if the medication is being prescribed in order to control their behaviour, this would seem to be counterproductive to the aim of risk management. While more programmes are needed nationwide, this situation does reiterate the point that it is not just general offending programmes that are needed, but those that are adapted to suit all different types of offenders, including those who suffer from mental and personality disorders.

Risk-management strategies

Similar to all serious sexual and violent offenders, those who have been additionally diagnosed as suffering from a mental disorder will be supervised using MAPPAs if/when they are released into the community (see Chapter 5). While MAPPA personnel are conversant in matters pertaining to risk and factors that may indicate acute increases in risk, it is arguable whether the average offender manager would have the expertise to comment on mental and personality disorders. To enhance and aid with public protection, a number of regional projects have recently developed that involve psychologists and psychiatrists so that the best information is always readily available to MAPPA panels. Such projects work in addition to the Care Programme Approach, which is a Department of Health initiative that ensures the coordination and continuity of care for people in the community with mental health problems (Bradley 2009). While what is emerging is briefly detailed below, it is concerning that there would appear to be no national strategy for offender management and that the development of these strategies and initiatives appears to be occurring on a piecemeal and regional basis. National planning, development and evaluation are therefore urgently required.

Forensic Personality Disorder Assessment and Liaison Teams

One such addition to MAPPA is multi-disciplinary Forensic Personality Disorder Assessment and Liaison Teams, with three existing in the Northwest of England (Greenall 2009). The teams are made up of experienced psychiatrists, psychiatric nurses and psychologists, and assess men serving sentences of IPP who either require transfer from prison or a high-security prison to a medium-secure unit or are due to be released into MAPPA supervision. The teams exist to provide the most accurate information possible so that adequate strategies to manage risk can be put in place and public protection decisions can be made. To ensure this, psychopathy is measured using the PCL-R, risk is assessed using HCR-20 and the existence of a personality disorder is classified using internationally recognised standards and guidelines (Greenall 2009). Currently, information is used by local MAPPPs, the Parole Board and the First-Tier Tribunal (Mental Health), with the Greater Manchester team receiving over 60 referrals in its first year of existence (ibid.).

Resettle

Another community project that provides aid to local MAPPPs is Resettle, which is a service for personality disordered offenders in Merseyside who have been released from prison. The project has been running since 2007 and is a four-year pilot study funded by the Department of Health and Health and Offender Partnerships (DSPD Programme 2010a). For an offender to be accepted on to the scheme, he must have lived in Merseyside prior to imprisonment and intend to return there on release, have an offender manager in the Merseyside area, be supervised at MAPPA level 2 or 3, and have a personality disorder (DSPD Programme 2010a). Referrals will take place while the MDO is still in prison and, if accepted on to the project, in-reach work will start while he is still inside. Services that Resettle are able to provide include a 24/7 telephone helpline service, long-term support based on social therapy, housing support, help with employment/education/training, appropriate psychological/psychiatric interventions, and, if appropriate, COSA (see Chapter 6). The aim of the scheme is to establish whether coordinated community psychosocial provision for personality disorder offenders is effective in reducing reoffending and managing risk in the community, with the first evaluation results expected in 2011.

Risk-reduction strategies

In addition to containment and control, it is also necessary to focus on strategies designed to reduce risk with those offenders diagnosed as suffering from a mental and/or personality disorder. Intervention strategies with MDOs have arguably had a chequered history, with methods based on psychology, psychiatry and psychotherapy considered to be experimental even in the early twentieth century

(Knight and Stephens 2009). Even when such techniques were better understood, and a care and treatment regime was devised for MDOs, some commentators still argued that such interventions were premised on security and control rather than on rehabilitation (Sim 1990). This was further emphasised after the Mountbatten Report in 1966, which followed a number of high-security escapes and led to a number of interventions being restricted, including activities on the therapeutic units at Grendon (see Chapter 4). There is also the problem that an MDO is often both a patient and an offender and, as identified by Knight and Stephens, there is a 'dichotomy between the Prison Service ideology of security and control, and the health service ideology of welfare and care' (Knight and Stephens 2009: 3). Which should be the prevailing philosophy is a widespread dilemma, especially if the offender is held within the prison estate rather than in a hospital setting, although wherever the MDO is held, this should not fundamentally change the need for some form of positive intervention.[2] The work on therapeutic units has previously been discussed in Chapters 4 and 7, with the remainder of this chapter considering other risk reduction interventions currently available within hospitals and prisons in England and Wales.

The Dangerous and Severe Personality Disorder Programme

The DSPD Programme has been running in England and Wales since 2000 and brings together the Ministry of Justice, HM Prison Service, the Department of Health and the National Health Service. It was originally designed to treat serious sexual and violent offenders who were not diagnosed with a treatable mental illness and therefore could not be detained under previous mental health legislation (Kettle 2008), although of course this loophole has now been closed by the MHA 2007. Such a programme was thought to be necessary in the wake of a number of high-profile murders by offenders suffering from mental disorders, including the 1996 killings of Dr Lin Russell and her daughter Megan by Michael Stone. It is therefore interesting that the programme's development has been driven by political considerations of populist punitiveness rather than by concerns for individual MDOs[3] and in this sense fits in nicely with other dangerousness policy and legislation. Nash (2006), for example, questions whether the DSPD Programme was truly needed, suggesting that its introduction just further perpetuates the myth of a connection between mental illness and dangerousness. The programme was also developed following a highly critical report on the personality disorder treatment unit at Ashworth that found evidence of trading in pornographic material, sexual grooming of children, misuse of drugs and alcohol, and lapses of security (see Fallon *et al.* 1999). The programme's overall objective is thus 'to provide authority for the detention of dangerous severely personality disordered people on the basis of the risk they present, and if necessary, for detention to be indefinite' (Rutherford 2006: 55), including, controversially, those without criminal convictions but thought to present a risk of serious offending.

There are currently four pilot DSPD units: the Fens Unit at HMP Whitemoor; the Peaks Unit at Rampton, which opened in 2004; the Paddock Centre at Broadmoor, which opened in December 2005; and one at HMP Frankland. In addition to these units, which cater exclusively for men, is the Primrose Project, which is designed for women offenders. This is a collaborative pilot project developed between the Ministry of Justice, the Department of Health, HM Prison Service and Tees, Esk and Wear Valleys NHS Trust and is based at HMP/YOI Low Newton (DSPD Programme 2010b). While the aim of the Primrose Project is similar to the male DSPD Programme, it is run with the needs of women in mind. Also different is the fact that women on the DSPD Programme are housed with mainstream prisoners and not segregated on a DSPD unit. Whether this will affect the efficacy of the programme will remain to be seen, although see Chapter 7 for comments regarding the efficacy of the therapeutic unit at HMP Send, which is run on a similar basis.

The aim of all of the units is threefold, to:

1 Ensure high quality detailed risk assessment to protect the public from some of the most dangerous people in society.
2 Provide high quality services for the individuals themselves to improve their health outcomes.
3 Reduce the risk that they pose and enable them to work towards successful integration into the community or to be able to be detained at the lowest level of security without harm to others.

(Saradjian *et al.* 2010)

Funding for the programme was initially set at £126 million, which was designed to cover 300 participants over a time period of 3 years. This was split into £70 million allocated to HM Prison Service (Whitemoor and Frankland) and £56 million for the NHS (Broadmoor and Rampton) (Gosling 2009).

For a patient/offender to be accepted on to the programme, he must pass three criteria. The first is that he is dangerous. This is where the MDO is or represents a grave and immediate danger to the general public and where the risk of the individual committing serious harm to others, from which the victim is unlikely to recover, is more likely than not (DSPD Programme 2010c). The second criterion is that the offender suffers from a 'severe personality disorder', that is, he:

1 has a PCL-R score of 30 or greater;
2 has a PCL-R score of 25-29 and one or more personality disorders (other than antisocial personality disorder);
3 has two or more personality disorders.

(NPS 2005c: 7)

Finally, it must be shown that the offending and the personality disorder are linked.

Interestingly, it has been found that approximately 15 per cent of those offenders in prison serving sentences of two years or more (excluding life) for sexual or violent offences meet the criteria for entry on to the DSPD Programme (Sheldon and Krishnan 2009), although at present there are only 286 places: 86 at Frankland, 70 at Whitemoor, 48 at Broadmoor, 70 at Rampton and 12 at Low Newton (DSPD Programme 2010b, 2010c). Typical men found on the DSPD units are those who have been violent in prison, who have caused significant operational management issues, suffer from considerable emotional distress and have spent time both in segregation and CSCs (see Chapter 4). Due to the presence of personality disorders, these high-risk men are also often excluded from prison treatment programmes and so, without the DSPD Programme, would remain untreated (Saradjian *et al.* 2010).

If an offender is thought to be suitable for the programme, he will be transferred on to a DSPD unit and will undergo a full DSPD assessment, involving risk assessment, clinical interviews and behaviour observations to identify whether he meets the entrance criteria as described above (Sheldon and Krishnan 2009). Such assessment can take three to four months to complete (Bennett 2008a). It is also worth noting that referral, transfer and assessment can be completed even if the offender does not consent (Creighton *et al.* 2005). Due to the fact that there is currently no clear evidence base as to the dynamic risk factors of MDOs, each unit has developed its own treatment model, with methods of intervention including cognitive-behavioural approaches, manualised programmes and other holistic methods that focus on past experiences and emotional factors (Kettle 2008). The intervention programme can therefore last for a number of years depending on the needs of the individual MDO, with detention indefinite or until the MDO is no longer judged to be dangerous or further treatment is no longer appropriate. Unit personnel, therefore, differ depending on the types of interventions used, with a DSPD prison unit place often costing three times as much as a normal prison bed. Despite this extra cost, however, such a place is still cheaper than a hospital DSPD unit bed or a place in a CSC, and offers considerable savings when taking into account the costs of moving Category A prisoners through the dispersal system and the cost of damage done to staff and property that such offenders often cause (Saradjian *et al.* 2010).

Treatment at HMP Whitemoor, for example, is based on a cognitive interpersonal treatment model, where 'the aim is to develop boundaried relationships with prisoners through which they can experience reparative interventions that will affect all aspects of their functioning' (Saradjian *et al.* 2010: 48). The programme has eight components: individual therapy and group-work sessions focusing on cognitive interpersonal skills, affect regulation, personality disorder awareness, schema-focused therapy, offending behaviour, addictive behaviour and healthy sexual relationships. For most offenders, treatment will take three years to complete, with individual relapse prevention plans also devised by unit personnel (for more details on each element, see Saradjian *et al.* 2010).

Following discharge, the offender will return to the sending unit (Beck 2010), but can be given a lower security categorisation or even released into the community under MAPPA supervision (DSPD Programme 2010d). The DSPD Programme also has a separate progression service, with its aim being to integrate those men who have completed the programme into the TC at Grendon. To be accepted into the TC, the men must meet the standard referral criteria discussed in Chapter 4. Once accepted, the MDOs will be treated the same as all other offenders on the unit (DSPD Programme 2010e). There is also the provision of medium secure and hostel beds for men who have completed the DSPD Programme. These are also currently run on a pilot basis but presently include St. Nicholas' Hospital (Northumberland, Tyne and Wear NHS Trust), Bethlem Royal Hospital (South London and Maudsley NHS Foundation Trust) and the John Howard Centre (East London and City Mental Health NHS Trust) (Joseph 2010). As stated in the planning and delivery guide, 'the underpinning philosophy of the DSPD Programme is that public protection will best be served by addressing the mental health needs of a previously neglected group' (Ministry of Justice, Department of Health 2008: 6).

While long-term treatment evaluation has not yet been completed, initial data concerning the effectiveness of the programme has been encouraging, with the first evaluation looking at 55 male prisoners who had volunteered to be a part of the initial pilot assessment programme at Whitemoor between September 2000 and September 2002 (Taylor 2003). All of the men involved were serving sentences for serious sexual and violent offences, with the purpose of the study being to measure them against actual and expected numbers of violent adjudications while within the unit. Before entering the programme, 33 of the 55 men had 97 adjudications for violence noted against them, which equated to an expected 36.5 adjudications on the unit. However, despite this rather high number, only 10 incidents were recorded, suggesting that the programme had reduced violence in the offender group (ibid.). Furthermore, Sheldon *et al.* (2010) found that non-completion levels of the DSPD Programme at the Peaks Unit at Rampton Hospital were relatively low, with reasons for non-completion including affective arousal, and volitional and other cognitive readiness factors.

A more recent study by Saradjian *et al.* (2010) has looked at the first cohort of prisoners who have completed treatment at the Fens Unit at HMP Whitemoor, although key outcome data is not yet available. However, despite this, the authors noted an attendance rate of 95 per cent in all interventions and a dramatic reduction in the number of reported incidents and adjudications. Importantly, 88 per cent of the men also showed a reduction in risk when assessed throughout treatment using HCR-20. Of the 18 men who started in the unit, 6 have been moved to Category B establishments, with another 5 waiting for places at the same level; 2 have joined the hospital system; 2 were returned to the dispersal system; 2 have been placed on medical hold but are expected to be decategorised; and 1 has been released into the community. Again, this suggests that the DSPD Programme can work to reduce risk.

Other published research largely concentrates on the types of offenders that have been referred and accepted on to the DSPD units, with Hogue (2009) explaining in detail the programme at Rampton Hospital. For example, of the first 46 individuals accepted at Rampton, 51 per cent had a sexually motivated index offence, 92 per cent had previous convictions for violence and 32 per cent had previous convictions for sexual offences. Regarding PCL-R scores, 78 per cent were classified at 25 or over and 24 per cent at 30 or more, all suggesting that the majority of participants were dangerous offenders. While Hogue argues that this dangerousness element was to be expected, in terms of mental disorders there was an array of different clinical and criminogenic needs noted, with many rejecting or failing previous treatment interventions. Such diversity in needs consequently makes treatment difficult, with it being necessary that it is delivered on a highly individualised basis, making the standard HM Prison Service group-work structure problematic. Offenders at Rampton are therefore dealt with using a four-phase strategy that concentrates on assessment, personality, offending and transition. This is claimed to be fairly successful (see Hogue 2009).

Despite some promising results, the DSPD Programme has not been without its critics. Even at the initial developmental stages, many psychiatrists were concerned over the lack of clarity in the term DSPD, even though the government did acknowledge that DPSD was not a clinical or medical term and was not intended to describe a psychiatric condition (Rutherford 2006). In fact, Professor Hare, the author of the PCL-R assessment tool argued that the term DSPD was 'an amalgam of clinical disorders that makes no sense as a diagnostic category' (Gosling 2009: 635). Moreover, practitioners were uncomfortable with the concepts of severity, dangerousness and the ability to predict reoffending, believing that the intended programme emphasised the role of psychiatrists too readily over the contribution that could be made by other agencies. Furthermore, there have been ethical concerns, including whether the control ethos of the programme breaches the General Medical Council guidelines, which state that the *care* of the patient is the first consideration for any doctor and that treatment should not be recommended if it is not in their best interests (Haddock *et al.* 2001). Nash explains how the situation for doctors could change from one 'where doctors treat the sick to one where they become agents of social control' (Nash 2006: 73). As Peay summarises:

> This is not to be an evidence-based programme. And how, anyway could it be? If there is no agreed definition, no clear diagnosis, no agreed treatment, no means of assessing when the predicted risk may have been reduced, and no obvious link between the alleged underlying condition and the behaviour, how could outcome measures be agreed upon and then evaluated? Finally, the pilot programme recruits volunteers (and how could it be any other way, given the 'treatments' involved?); yet, if legislation were to be enacted to support the programme, offenders could be sent on a compulsory basis. Thus any 'results' emerging from these pilots are likely to be fundamentally inapplicable to the target groups. Yet, the programme and all its associated

> publicity have the potential to further demonize this group; the possibility of discrimination against them thereafter is self evident.
>
> (Peay 2007: 518–19)

There has also been some opposing research data, notably the studies carried out by Tyrer *et al.* (2010) and Ullrich *et al.* (2010). Tyrer *et al.*, for example, note concerns regarding risk assessment and allocation into the programme, with them estimating that between six and eight people are unnecessarily detained under the programme in order to correctly contain one. Furthermore, they argue that there is no evidence base for the treatments used, that the main motive behind the initiative is one of public protection and not treatment, and that its main purpose appears to be that of 'warehousing', especially those who are coming to the end of their sentence tariff. In terms of cost effectiveness, it has been estimated that the DSPD Programme has cost over £400 million to date. Prisoners in DSPD units cost on average £3,500 more over six months when compared to those held in control prisons. When 'these substantially higher costs were accompanied by an observed deterioration in functioning, quality of life and aggression', the benefit of the DSPD programme, it is argued, is 'unclear and needs further exploration' (Tyrer *et al.* 2010: 98).

In the second study, Ullrich *et al.* (2010), through interviewing 1,396 DSPD offenders, found a very high rate of false positives in terms of actual reoffending, concluding that 26 DSPD offenders would need to be detained and treated in order for one violent act to be prevented. This re-emphasises the view that the DSPD categorisation and criteria, as laid out by the now Ministry of Justice, is incorrect. Also of note was their finding that the vast majority of offenders who had committed sexual offences had not been classified as suffering from DSPD and all sexual offences committed during the follow-up period were by non-DSPD offenders. In conclusion, the authors felt that TCs such as those in Grendon offered the most promising evidence for treating MDOs.

Chromis

Chromis is another programme currently being run within HM Prison Service for the treatment of psychopathy. It is currently available at the purpose-built Westgate Unit at HMP Frankland, HMP Low Newton (a woman's prison) and is also used at the Peaks Unit at Rampton. Interestingly, this is the first time that a prison programme has been custom built and used in both prison and health settings from inception. The programme is based on cognitive-behavioural theory and is specifically designed to target the risk factors associated with psychopathic offenders and, through this, reduce violent behaviour. This is achieved by focusing on the identification, reduction and external management of a range of dynamic risk factors that are thought to lead to an offender's inability to engage in treatment and sustained socio-behavioural change (Ministry of Justice 2009e). Chromis consists of five core modules that focus on motivation and engagement, problem-solving, creative thinking, handling conflict and cognitive self change. A progression and resettlement strategy will also be devised towards the end of the programme (Liell 2007). The modules are delivered through a series of one-to-one and group-work sessions by a multi-disciplinary team of nurses, psychologists and prison officers. Additional complementary activities also take place outside of the more formal treatment sessions. The clinical lead at the Westgate Unit explains how:

> the early part of treatment tries to work out what each participant really cares about in their life – for example, it might be really important that they have a sense of control or autonomy, or that they feel they have a meaning in their life. By developing new ways of viewing the work and skills such as problem solving and conflict resolution they can still achieve these things but in a way that's not too harmful to others.
>
> (Savidge 2005b)

In 2006–7, 20 offenders started the Chromis programme at HMP Frankland (HC Deb, 21 January 2008, c1660W). This increased to 57 in 2008–9 (HC Deb, 9 December 2009, c440W).

The programme was accredited for use in custodial settings in 2005 and, on review in 2009, commended by the Correctional Services Accreditation Panel (Ministry of Justice 2009e). Staff involved in the programme are said to be extremely positive, both about the programme and the effects it is having on the MDOs involved (Savidge 2005b). Bennett comments how it is 'a world-leading programme, accredited as being effective in reducing re-offending among this group previously thought to be untreatable' (Bennett 2008a: 13) and Aldhous notes how 'no other project has a better chance of challenging the notion that violent psychopaths are beyond help' (Aldhous 2007: 9). While such anecdotal evidence is encouraging, a complete evaluation study is urgently needed, either to ascertain that the programme does not work, or, if it does, to be used as evidence to justify a national roll-out across both prison and hospital establishments.

Supervised Community Treatment

In addition to risk-reduction interventions for prison and hospital settings, there are also some interventions designed for those MDOs supervised within the community. One such initiative is Supervised Community Treatment, a relatively new concept introduced into England and Wales in November 2008 as a result of amendments to the MHA 1983. Sections 17A–17G, inserted into the legislation by the MHA 2007, provide for a community treatment order (CTO) that is to be imposed if a number of criteria are met. These are contained in section 17A(5) and are that:

- the patient is suffering from a mental disorder of a nature or degree which makes it appropriate for him to receive medical treatment;

- it is necessary for his health or safety or the protection of other persons that he should receive such treatment;
- subject to their being liable to be recalled, such treatment can be provided without his continuing to be detained in a hospital;
- it is necessary that the responsible clinician should be able to exercise the power to recall the patient to hospital; and
- appropriate medical treatment is available for him.

Any MDO who is issued with a CTO is known as a 'community patient' (section 17A(7) MHA 1983), with eligible patients being those who are held under unrestricted hospital orders, hospital directions or transfer directions. Offenders held under restriction orders are not eligible. The order is designed for those MDOs who have a history of non-compliance, relapse and re-admission, and is an attempt to break the 'revolving door' of detention.

An application for a CTO is made to the hospital managers by the MDO's responsible clinician, with the risk of deterioration in the patient's mental health being a key factor as to whether the order is granted (Mind 2010c). The responsible clinician also needs to consider the patient's history of mental disorder and any other factors that will contribute to deterioration in the MDO's mental health (s. 17A(6) MHA 1983). If the CTO is granted, under section 17B(3), it must contain conditions specifying that the MDO has to make himself available for future examinations for purposes of review and can contain other conditions such as avoiding illegal drugs or alcohol. If the MDO has committed a violent or sexual offence, under the Domestic Violence, Crime and Victims Act 2004, the victim has the right to make representations concerning the content of these conditions. Although the MDO becomes a community patient, he can be recalled at any time by the responsible clinician if it is thought that treatment is required and without it there 'would be a risk of harm to the health or safety of the patient or to other persons if the patient were not recalled to hospital' (s. 17E(1)(b) MHA 1983). Recall can also occur if the MDO breaches any of the conditions attached to the CTO and, in such circumstances, the order may be revoked, reinstating the MDO to his previous hospital patient status.

While the use of the CTO is still in its infancy, there has already been criticism and concerns regarding its use. Mental health campaigners, for example, argue that it could be overused, with clinicians defensively issuing them to cover their own backs, rather than choosing to trust the patient involved. The use of chemical treatments in the community is also likely to increase, with Mind arguing that 'CTOs will focus on drugs since this is the only treatment which can be enforced effectively and which is available readily and provides an easy option for over-stretched workers' (Mind 2010c). Compulsive community treatment may also affect the MDO's therapeutic relationship with mental health workers, with them being turned into 'Mental Health Act police officers' (ibid.). Other criticisms focus on the lack of evidence concerning efficacy, with one research study based in Australia finding that 85 people would need to be made subject to a CTO so as to prevent

1 readmission to hospital, and 238 CTOs made to prevent 1 arrest (Kisely *et al.* 2005). How they will work in England and Wales, therefore, needs to be closely monitored and evaluated, especially regarding whether the main purpose of the order is that of care and risk reduction or whether instead it is driven by darker aims of public protection and populist punitiveness.

Community orders with a mental health treatment requirement

Finally, and provided for under section 207 CJA 2003, the sentencing court also has the option of adding a mental health treatment requirement (MHTR) to a community order if a community penalty is deemed to be the most appropriate disposal. The requirement is used for those offenders who have an identified mental health problem, and is issued where the court can:

- ensure that treatment to improve the offender's mental health problem will be provided;
- ensure that any hospital treatment is not given in a secure psychiatric unit;
- be satisfied that the offender's mental health problem requires and may be susceptible to treatment, but is not serious enough to invoke the sections of the MHA 1983;
- be satisfied that the practitioners and services are available to carry out the treatment; and
- ensure that the offender is willing to comply with the requirement.

(Seymour and Rutherford 2008: 13)

The requirement can last for up to three years and, while managed by an offender manager from probation, must be conducted under the direction of a registered medical practitioner or chartered psychologist.

While the name may be relatively new, the MHTR is similar in nature to the previous options of the probation order with psychiatric treatment, and the Community Rehabilitation Order with a requirement for psychiatric treatment. Despite the name change, however, and similar to previous orders, the MHTR is rarely used. For example, in 2006, in England and Wales, only 725 requirements were made, amounting to less than 1 per cent of the total number of requirements (203,323) issued in that 1 year (Seymour and Rutherford 2008). Disappointingly, this has not increased over time, with 652 requirements made in 2007 and only 739 made in 2008. When 120,743 community orders were made in 2008, the prevalence of the MHTR amounted to only 0.6 per cent (HC Deb, 8 February 2010, c770W). Perhaps this is surprising considering the high incidence of mental disorders in offenders, especially when taking the definition at its widest sense. Canton (2008), however, suggests that limited application of the requirement may be due to a lack of confidence in it displayed by both the courts and probation. It may also be indicative of populist punitiveness and the preference of prison and/or hospital disposals over those based within the community. Seymour and Rutherford (2008) further cite legislative obstacles, problems with service delivery, the capability and capacity of practitioners in carrying out mental health assessments and the complex needs that MDOs have as further explanations. For example, while the CJA 2003 requires the offender to have a mental health problem, it cannot be significant enough to warrant treatment under mental health legislation, with further obstacles caused by the need to have the offender's consent, which may be lacking due to the desire not to be stigmatised as an MDO. Furthermore, Seymour and Rutherford share concerns regarding the fact that little is known about the efficacy of the requirement, how it should be delivered and its impact on those suffering from mental disorders. Significantly, more research is thus needed.

Conclusion

Despite the belief that offenders should not be categorised on the basis of changeable mental characteristics (see Peay 2007), the presence of MDOs within prison and hospital establishments is overwhelming, especially when using the term 'mental disorder' in its widest sense. Several initiatives have therefore been devised to deal with this category of offenders, including those that have been designed and amended with the specific needs of women in mind. What is disappointing, however, is that much of what is available is either only at the piloting stage and has not been running long enough to produce any meaningful outcome data, or is only available on a local/regional basis. When the number of MDOs held indefinitely within England and Wales is so high, this is unacceptable. A much more concerted effort is therefore required to evaluate and, if appropriate, validate those programmes and interventions currently running. When mental health legislation can now encapsulate most offenders who commit serious sexual and violent offences, and when treatment can be justified even if it does not have a defined medical benefit, a failure to do so must surely breach human rights. Furthermore, it suggests that only lip service is being paid to welfare-driven policies and desires to reduce risk, with the prevailing aim being that of containment and control driven by public protection and populist punitiveness – a theme prevalent throughout this book.

NOTES

1 Dangerousness and the dangerous offender

1 Although it is accepted that liability for such acts can be complicated, especially if it involves states or other entities.
2 A word used by Scottish Ministers to mean a yob (that is, a non-educated delinquent).
3 Bennett (2008a) contends that the government has, as recently as 2006, been guilty of overemphasising the problem of dangerous offenders in order to get provisions for sentencing them passed.

2 Sentencing policy and dangerousness legislation

1 For more information on the use of cumulative sentencing at this time, see Radzinowicz and Hood (1980).
2 As amended by the Prison Rules (1952, 1956, 1962).
3 These were Parkhurst (maximum security), Nottingham, Eastchurch and Chelmsford. For women, they were housed with long-sentenced prisoners in Holloway.
4 Although the amendments made by the CJIA 2008 only apply to those offences committed after 14 July 2008.
5 These include sexual, violent and, since 12 January 2010 (s. 138 Coroners and Justice Act 2009), 12 terrorism offences.
6 In 2009, Sara Payne, the mother of Sarah Payne, who was killed by convicted sex offender Roy Whiting, was appointed to be the government's victim's champion.
7 For a thorough discussion on this, see Pratt (1996b).

3 From dangerousness to risk and risk assessment

1 'It is unjust to put someone in jail on the basis of a judgement about a class, however accurate, because that denies his claim to equal respect as an individual' (Dworkin 1977: 13).
2 Although, as stated above, you do need to have been convicted of a sexual offence for RM2000/V to be of use.
3 These include: 1) offending information including criminal history; 2) current offence analysis; 3) accommodation; 4) education, training and employability; 5) financial management and income; 6) relationships; 7) lifestyle and associates; 8) drug misuse; 9) alcohol misuse; 10) emotional well-being; 11) thinking and behaviours; and 12) attitudes.

4 More research studies, including those for civil psychiatry, forensic psychiatry and mixed settings, can be found in Douglas *et al.* (2006).

4 The use of imprisonment

1 Although it is acknowledged that imprisonment information is collated in different ways in different countries, and so this statement may be slightly misleading.
2 Although this is probably now 36 considering that, in July 2010, Peter Sutcliffe was told that he would not be eligible for parole.
3 The categorisation system dates back to 1966 and was implemented following a number of high-profile escapes.
4 Prison Rule 46 states:

> where it appears desirable, for the maintenance of good order or discipline or to ensure the safety of officers, prisoners or any other person, that a prisoner should not associate with other prisoners, either generally or for particular purposes, the Secretary of State may direct the prisoner's removal from association accordingly and his placement in a close supervision centre of a prison.

5 There are also four hierarchical TCs for addictions/substance misuse at HMP Channings Wood, HMP Garth, HMP Holme House and HMP Wymott (Turner 2010). These will not be considered further.
6 While there is no space here to discuss the merits of a private prison operating a TC, this has been looked at in detail by Genders (2002, 2003).
7 These are based on the four basic elements of a TC. These are described as:

> a democratic exercise of power over the administrative and therapeutic life of the prison; permissiveness in relation to previous, or ongoing behaviours, thus allowing those behaviours to be acknowledged or worked through; confrontation and presentation of those behaviours so as to reveal how they affect others, within the prison; and communalism, in the establishment of close, interactive relationship.
>
> (Wilson 1992: 20)

8 Examples of how this career model has worked in practice can be found in Wilson and McCabe (2002).
9 Prison Rule 45 states:

> Where it appears desirable, for the maintenance of good order or discipline or in his own interests that a prisoner should not associate with other prisoners, either generally or for particular purposes, the governor may arrange for the prisoner's removal from association accordingly. This is usually to a vulnerable prisoner unit and is used by the majority of sex offenders due to threats/attacks of physical violence and other inmates refusing to live with them.

10 Everyone who is deprived of his liberty by arrest or detention shall be entitled to take proceedings by which the lawfulness of his detention shall be decided speedily by a court and his release ordered if the detention is not lawful.

5 Strategies of risk management

1 Although it is worth noting that there is not an actual physical register, rather information is stored on the Police National Computer.
2 'A notification under this subsection must disclose–

(a) the date on which the offender will leave the United Kingdom;
(b) the country (or, if there is more than one, the first country) to which he will travel and his point of arrival (determined in accordance with the regulations) in that country;

(c) any other information prescribed by the regulations which the offender holds about his departure from or return to the United Kingdom or his movements while outside the United Kingdom'.

3 Schedule 3 includes offences such as rape, sexual intercourse with a child, buggery, sexual assault, causing or encouraging prostitution, incest and taking or possessing indecent photographs of children.
4 A disqualification order is an order that prevents a person who has offended against children from working with children in the future: sections 26–34 The Criminal Justice and Court Services Act 2000.
5 For more information, see www.opsi.gov.uk/si/si2009/uksi_20090619_en_1.

6 Strategies of risk reduction

1 For a history of behavioural and cognitive-behavioural approaches to sex offender treatment, see Laws and Marshall (2003); Marshall and Laws (2003); Brown (2010).
2 For more effectiveness studies, see Mann and Fernandez (2006); Brown (2010).
3 For more information on these drugs and how they work, see Harrison (2010b).
4 For a more detailed analysis, see Harrison (2007b, 2010b).
5 For an analysis of the legal and ethical issues involved in using pharmacotherapy with sex offenders, see Harrison (2010b).
6 For more detail on the principles of restorative justice, see Johnstone (2002); McLaughlin *et al.* (2004); Dignan (2005); McAlinden (2007).
7 For a historical account of the introduction of COSA into England and Wales, see Nellis (2009).
8 For more on the use of this with domestic violence perpetrators, see Braithwaite and Daly (1995).
9 The research looked at three restorative programmes: CONNECT (indirect mediation, direct mediation and conferencing), the Justice Research Consortium (conferencing) and REMEDI (indirect and direct mediation).

7 Women offenders

1 A female sex offender programme was piloted in HM Styal between January 2000 and June 2001, but due to the small numbers involved, it has not been replicated or rolled out on a group-work basis, despite promising results (see Blanchette and Taylor 2010).

8 Children and young people

1 Although it is accepted that these rules are not binding, they do nevertheless represent current international thinking on the minimum requirements on matters of youth justice.
2 It is worth noting, however, that this amendment is not yet in force and, at the time of writing, did not have a commencement date either.
3 For more detail on the two different approaches, see Green (2008).
4 For a review of the sentences use, see McDiarmid (2000).
5 Although it is acknowledged that this has only been in force since 2005.
6 For the debate on this, see Hansard (6 Feb 2008: col. 1135 onwards).

9 Mentally disordered offenders

1 Although the argument that changeable mental characteristics should not be the basis of forming, a distinct cluster is acknowledged (Peay 2007).
2 See Knight and Stephens (2009) for a discussion on how this affects human rights.
3 See Rutherford (2006) for an account of the political background to the DSPD programme.

REFERENCES

Adams, J. (1995) *Risk*. London: UCL Press.

Adams, M. (2004) 'HMP Woodhill's CSC', *Prison Service Journal*, 153: 10–13.

Adi, Y., Ashcroft, D., Browne, K., Beech, A., Fry-Smith, A. and Hyde, C. (2002) *Clinical Effectiveness and Cost-Consequence of Selective Serotonin Reuptake Inhibitors in the Treatment of Sex Offenders*. London: Home Office.

Ahmed, M. (2009) 'YJB Says Keppel Unit Will Offer the Highest Levels of Care', *communitycare.co.uk*, 12 June 2009. Available at: www.communitycare.co.uk/Articles/2009/06/12/111794/New-unit-for-vulnerable-boys-opens-at-Wetherby-YOI.htm (accessed 14 November 2010).

Aldhous, P. (2007) 'Violent, Antisocial, Beyond Redemption', *New Scientist*, 2599: 8–9.

Alexandrovich, A. and Wilson, D. (1999) *The Longest Injustice: The Strange Story of Alex Alexandrovich*. Winchester: Waterside Press.

Anderson, K. (2009) 'Youth Offending: Can the New Sentencing Framework Help Minimise the Use of Custodial Sentences?', *Childright*, April: 27–30.

Andrews, D. A. and Bonta, J. (1995) *Level of Service Inventory – Revised*. Toronto: Multi-Health Systems.

Andrews, D. A. and Bonta, J. (1998) *The Psychology of Criminal Conduct* (3rd edn). Cincinnati: Anderson Publishing Co.

Andrews, D. A. and Bonta, J. (2006) *The Psychology of Criminal Conduct* (4th edn). Cincinnati: Anderson Publishing Co.

Andrews, D. A., Bonta, J. and Hodge, R. D. (1990) 'Classification for Effective Rehabilitation: Rediscovering Psychology', *Criminal Justice and Behavior*, 17(1): 19–52.

Andrews, D., Bonta, J. and Wormith, J. (2004) *The Level of Service/Case Management Inventory*. Toronto: Multi-Health Systems.

Andrews, D., Bonta, J. and Wormith, J. (2008) *The Level of Service/Case Management Inventory. Supplement: A Gender-Informed Risk/Need/Responsivity Assessment*. Toronto: Multi-Health Systems.

Annison, J. (2005) 'Risk and Protection', in T. Bateman and J. Pitts (eds) *The RHP Companion to Youth Justice*. Lyme Regis: Russell House.

Arthur, R. (2010) *Young Offenders and the Law*. Abingdon: Routledge.

Aschwanden, R. and Ermer, A. (2008) 'Leuprorelin Allergy as a Side Effect of Chemical Castration and, as a Consequence, the Discussion about Surgical Castration', *IATSO Conference*, Capetown, August 2008.

Ash, B. (2003) *Working with Women Prisoners* (4th edn). Women's Estate Policy Unit: HM Prison Service.

Ashworth, A. (1989) 'Criminal Justice and Deserved Sentences', *Crim L.R.*, May, 340–55.

Ashworth, A. (2004a) 'Criminal Justice Act 2002: Part 2: Criminal Justice Reform – Principles, Human Rights and Public Protection', *Crim L.R.*, Jul, 516–32.

Ashworth, A. (2004b) 'Social Control and "Anti-Social Behaviour": The Subversion of Human Rights?', *Law Quarterly Review*, 120: 263–91.

Ashworth, A. (2005) *Sentencing and Criminal Justice* (4th edn). Cambridge: CUP.

Association of Therapeutic Communities (2010a) *What is a TC?* Available at: www.therapeuticcommunities.org/index.php?option=com_content&view=article&id=76&Itemid=94 (accessed 8 March 2010).

Association of Therapeutic Communities (2010b) *TC Core Values*. Available at: www.therapeuticcommunities.org/index.php?option=com_content&view=article&id=90&Itemid=124 (accessed 8 March 2010).

Babcock, J., Green, C. and Robie, C. (2004) 'Does Batterers' Treatment Work? A Meta-Analytic Review of Domestic Violence Treatment', *Clinical Psychology Review*, 23: 1023–53.

Bandalli, S. (1998) 'Abolition of the Presumption of *Doli Incapax* and the Criminalisation of Children', *Howard Journal*, 37(2): 114–23.

Bandalli, S. (2000) 'Children Responsibility and the New Youth Justice', in B. Goldson (ed.) *The New Youth Justice*. Lyme Regis: Russell House.

Bates, A., Saunders, R. and Wilson, C. (2007) 'Doing Something About It: A Follow-Up Study of Sex Offenders Participating in Thames Valley Circles of Support and Accountability', *British Journal of Community Justice*, 5(1): 19–42.

BBC (2009) 'Freed to Offend Again', *Panorama*, BBC TV, 26 October 2009. True North Productions.

BBC News (2004) 'Satellite Tracking for Criminals', *BBC News Online*, 2 September 2004. Available at: http://news.bbc.co.uk/1/hi/uk/3620024.stm (accessed 12 May 2010).

BBC News (2005) 'Offenders Database to Cut Crime', *BBC News Online*, 19 August 2005. Available at: http://news.bbc.co.uk/1/hi/uk/4163764.stm (accessed 12 May 2010).

BBC News (2007) 'MEPs Want EU Sex Offender List', *BBC News Online*, 22 August 2007. Available at: http://news.bbc.co.uk/1/hi/uk/6958807.stm (accessed 12 May 2010).

BBC News (2009) 'How Are Female Paedophiles Rehabilitated?', *BBC News Online*, 15 December 2009. Available at http://news.bbc.co.uk/1/hi/magazine/8413119.stm (accessed 28 July 2009).

BBC News (2010) 'Edlington Torture Attack Brothers Detained', *BBC News Online*, 22 January 2010. Available at: http://news.bbc.co.uk/1/hi/england/south_yorkshire/8473978.stm (accessed 4 November 2010).

BBC World Service (2000) 'When Children Kill Children', *BBC World Service*, 9 November 2000. Available at: www.bbc.co.uk/worldservice/people/highlights/001109_child.shtml (accessed 14 November 2010).

Beck, J. (2010) 'Dangerous Severe Personality Disorder: The Controversy Continues', *Behavioral Sciences and the Law*, 28: 277–88.

Beck, U. (1992) *Risk Society: Towards a New Modernity*. London: Sage.

Beech, A., Erikson, M., Friendship, C. and Ditchfield, J. (2001) 'A Six-Year Follow-Up of Men Going through Probation-Based Sex Offender Treatment Programmes', Home Office Findings 144. London: Home Office.

Beech, A., Fisher, D., Beckett, R. and Scott-Fordham, A. (1998) 'An Evaluation of the Prison Sex Offender Treatment Programme', Home Office Research Findings No. 79. London: HORDSD.

Beech, A., Friendship, C., Erikson, M. and Hanson, K. (2002) 'The Relationship between Static and Dynamic Risk Factors and Reconviction in a Sample of U.K. Child Abusers', *Sexual Abuse: A Journal of Research and Treatment*, 14(2) 155–67.

Beech, A. R. and Mitchell, I. J. (2005) 'A Neurobiological Perspective on Attachment Problems in Sexual Offenders and the Role of Selective Serotonin Reuptake Inhibitors in the Treatment of Such Problems', *Clinical Psychology Review*, 25: 153–82.

Belfrage, H., Fransson, R. and Strand, S. (2000) 'Prediction of Violence Using the HCR-20: A Prospective Study in Two Maximum Security Correctional Institutions', *Journal of Forensic Psychiatry*, 11(1): 167–75.

Bennett, J. (2008a) *The Social Costs of Dangerousness: Prison and the Dangerous Classes.* King's College London: Centre for Crime and Justice Studies.

Bennett, J. (2008b) 'Categorization and Allocation', in Y. Jewkes and J. Bennett (eds) *Dictionary of Prisons and Punishment.* Cullompton: Willan Publishing.

Bennett, J. (2008c) 'Category A Prisoners', in Y. Jewkes and J. Bennett (eds) *Dictionary of Prisons and Punishment.* Cullompton: Willan Publishing.

Bennett, P. (2009) 'Reform from Within: The Grendon Example', *Criminal Justice Matters*, 77(1): 14–15.

Ben-Shakhar, G. (2008) 'The Case Against the Use of Polygraph Examinations to Monitor Post-Conviction Sex Offenders', *Legal and Criminological Psychology*, 13: 191–207.

Bichard, M. (2004) 'The Bichard Inquiry Report', HC653. London: The Stationery Office.

Bickle, A. (2009) 'The Interface between Dangerous Offender Sentencing and Psychiatry', *Mental Health Review Journal*, 14(1): 20–3.

Bilby, C. and Hatcher, R. (2004) 'Early Stages in the Development of the Integrated Domestic Abuse Programme (IDAP): Implementing the Duluth Domestic Violence Pathfinder', Home Office Online Report 29/04. London: Home Office.

Blanchette, K. (2004) 'Revisiting Effective Classification Strategies for Women Offenders in Canada', *Feminism and Psychology*, 14(2): 231–6.

Blanchette, K. and Brown, S. L. (2006) *The Assessment and Treatment of Women Offenders.* Chichester: John Wiley & Sons.

Blanchette, K. and Taylor, T. (2010) 'A Review of Treatment Initiatives for Female Sexual Offenders', in T. Gannon and F. Cortoni (eds) *Female Sexual Offenders. Theory, Assessment and Treatment.* Chichester: Wiley-Blackwell.

Blunt, C. (2010) 'Churchill Speech', NACRO, West Norwood Centre, 22 July 2010. Available at: www.justice.gov.uk/news/sp220710a.htm (accessed 26 July 2010).

Bonta, J. (1996) 'Risk Needs Assessment and Treatment', in A. T. Harland (ed.) *Choosing Correctional Actions that Work: Defining the Demand and Evaluating the Supply.* Thousand Oaks CA: Sage.

Bottomley, K. and Hay, W. (eds) (1991) *Special Units for Difficult Prisoners.* Hull: Centre for Criminology and Criminal Justice.

Bottoms, A. E. (1977) 'Reflections on the Renaissance of Dangerousness', *Howard Journal*, 16: 70–96.

Bottoms, A. E. (1995) 'The philosophy and politics of punishment and sentencing', in C. Clarkson and R. Morgan (eds) *The Politics of Sentencing Reform.* Oxford: Clarendon Press.

Bouffard, J. A. and Taxman, F. S. (2000) 'Client Gender and the Implementation of Jail Based Therapeutic Community Programs', *Journal of Drug Issues*, 30(4): 881–900.

Bowden, P. (1991) 'Treatment: Use, Abuse and Consent', *Criminal Behaviour and Mental Health*, 1: 130–41.

Bowen, P. (2007) *Blackstone's Guide to The Mental Health Act 2007*. Oxford: Oxford University Press.

Bradford, J. M. W. and Pawlak, A. (1993) 'Double-Blind Placebo Crossover Study of Cyproterone Acetate in the Treatment of the Paraphilias', *Archives of Sexual Behavior*, 22(5): 383–402.

Bradley, K. (2009) *The Bradley Report. Lord Bradley's Review of People with Mental Health Problems or Learning Disabilities in the Criminal Justice System*. London: Department of Health.

Brady, K. and Crighton, D. (2003) 'Violent Offender Groupwork', in G. Towl (ed.) *Psychology in Prisons*. Chichester: J. Wiley & Sons.

Braithwaite, J. (1989) *Crime, Shame and Reintegration*. Sydney: Cambridge University Press.

Braithwaite, J. and Daly, K. (1995) 'Masculinities, Violence and Communitarian Control', in D. Chappell and S. Egger (eds) *Australian Violence: Contemporary Perspectives II*. Canberra: Australian Institute of Criminology.

Briken, P., Hill, A. and Berner, W. (2003) 'Pharmacotherapy of Paraphilias with Long-Acting Agonists of Luteinizing Hormone-Releasing Hormone: A Systematic Review', *Journal of Clinical Psychiatry*, 64(8): 890–7.

Briken, P., Nika, E. and Berner, W. (2001) 'Treatment of Paraphilia with Luteinising Hormone-Releasing Agonists', *Journal of Sex and Marital Therapy*, 27: 45–55.

Brittles, P. (2009) 'A New National Strategy for Managing Difficult Prisoners in the High Security Estate', *Prison Service Journal*, 181: 37–9.

Brody, S. and Tarling, R. (1980) 'Taking Offenders out of Circulation', Home Office Research Study No. 64. London: Home Office.

Brookes, M. (2010) 'Introduction to the Special Issue on "Fifty Years of HMP Grendon"', *Howard Journal*, 49(5): 425–30.

Brown, A. (2005) 'The War on "Neds": Media Reports as Evidence Base', *Criminal Justice Matters*, 59: 16–17.

Brown, M. and Pratt, J. (2000) 'Introduction', in M. Brown and J. Pratt (eds) *Dangerous Offenders. Punishment and Social Control*. London: Routledge.

Brown, S. (2010) 'An Introduction to Sex Offender Treatment Programmes and their Risk Reduction Efficacy', in K. Harrison (ed.) *Managing High Risk Sex Offenders in the Community: Risk Management, Treatment and Social Responsibility*. Cullompton: Willan Publishing.

Bufkin, J. and Luttrell, V. (2005) 'Neuroimaging Studies of Aggressive and Violent Behavior', *Trauma, Violence & Abuse*, 6(2): 176–91.

Bullock, K., Sarre, S., Tarling, R. and Wilkinson, M. (2010) 'The Delivery of Domestic Abuse Programmes. An Implementation Study of the Delivery of Domestic Abuse Programmes in Probation Areas and Her Majesty's Prison Service', Ministry of Justice Research Series 15/10. London: Ministry of Justice.

Bunting, L. (2005) *Females who Sexually Offend against Children: Responses of the Child Protection and Criminal Justice Systems, Executive Summary*. London: NSPCC. Available at www.nspcc.org.uk/Inform/research/Findings/femaleswhosexuallyoffend_wda48273.html (accessed 13 July 2010).

Burney, E. and Pearson, G. (1995) 'Mentally Disordered Offenders: Finding a Focus for Diversion', *Howard Journal*, 34: 291–313.

Bush, J. (1995) 'Teaching Self-Risk Management to Violent Offenders', in J. McGuire (ed.) *What Works: Reducing Reoffending. Guidelines from Research and Practice*. Chichester: John Wiley & Sons.

Bushell, J. (2009) Personal communication received 22 October 2009.

Campbell, M-A., French, S. and Gendreau, P. (2009) 'The Prediction of Violence in Adult Offenders. A Meta-Analytic Comparison of Instruments and Methods of Assessment', *Criminal Justice and Behavior*, 36: 567–90.

Cann, J. (2007) 'Assessing the Extent of Discretionary Disclosure under the Multi-Agency Public Protection Arrangements', Home Office Findings 286. London: Home Office.

Canton, R. (2008) 'Working with Mentally Disordered Offenders', in S. Green, E. Lancaster and S. Feasey (eds) *Addressing Offending Behaviour. Context, Practice and Values*. Cullompton: Willan Publishing.

Carlen, P. and Worrall, A. (2004) *Analysing Women's Imprisonment*. Cullompton: Willan Publishing.

Carpenter, A. (1998) 'Belgium, Germany, England, Denmark and the United States: The Implementation of Registration and Castration Laws as Protection against Habitual Sex Offenders', *Dickinson Journal of International Law*, 16(2): 435–57.

Carson, D. (1996) 'Risking Legal Repercussions', in H. Kemshall and J. Pritchards (eds) *Good Practice in Risk Assessment and Risk Management*. London: Jessica Kingsley Publishers.

Carter, P. (2003) *Managing Offenders, Reducing Crime. A New Approach*. London: HMSO.

Castel, R. (1991) 'From Dangerousness to Risk', in G. Burchell, C. Gordon and P. Miller (eds) *The Foucault Effect. Studies in Governmentality*. Chicago: The University of Chicago Press.

Cesaroni, C. and Doob, A. N. (2003) 'The Decline in Support for Penal Welfarism. Evidence of Support among the Elite for Punitive Segregation', *British Journal of Criminology*, 43(2): 434–41.

Child Exploitation and Online Protection Centre (2010a) *Most Wanted Profile Reference: CS0612-1316*. Available at: www.ceop.police.uk/wanted/profile-37710.asp (accessed 13 May 2010).

Child Exploitation and Online Protection Centre (2010b) *Tracking the UK's Most Wanted Convicted Offenders*. Available at: www.ceop.police.uk/wanted/ (accessed 13 May 2010).

Christie, N. (2000) 'Dangerous States', in M. Brown and J. Pratt (eds) *Dangerous Offenders: Punishment and Social Order*. London: Routledge.

Christodoulou, E. (2010) Personal communication received 8 June 2010.

Circles UK (2010a) *What is a Circle of Support and Accountability*? Available at: www.circles-uk.org.uk/index.php?option=com_content&view=article&id=6&Itemid=5 (accessed 15 June 2010).

Circles UK (2010b) *Local Projects*. Available at: www.circles-uk.org.uk/index.php?option=com_content&view=article&id=8&Itemid=7 (accessed 15 June 2010).

Clare, E. and Bottomley, K., with Grounds, A., Hammond, C., Liebling A. and Taylor, C. (2001) 'Evaluation of Close Supervision Centres', Home Office Research Study 219. London: HORDSD.

Cluley, E. (2009) 'Imprisonment for Public Protection Prisoners and Mental Health Issues', *Probation Journal*, 56: 73–5.

Cohen, S. (1972) *Folk Devils and Moral Panics*. London: MacGibbon & Kee.

Connelly, C. and Williamson, S. (2000) *A Review of the Research Literature on Serious Violent and Sexual Offenders*. Edinburgh: The Scottish Executive Central Research Unit.

Cooke, D. J., Michie, C. and Ryan, J. (2001) 'Evaluating Risk for Violence: A Preliminary Study of the HCR-20, PCL-R and VRAG in a Scottish Prison Sample', Scottish Prison Service Occasional Papers; No. 5/2001. Edinburgh: Scottish Prison Service.

Cooper, A. J. (1981) 'A Placebo-Controlled Trial of the Anti-Androgen Cyproterone Acetate in Deviant Hypersexuality', *Comprehensive Psychiatry*, 22(5): 458–65.

Cooper, A. J., Ismail, A. A. A., Phanjoo, A. L. and Love, D. L. (1972) 'Antiandrogen (Cyproterone Acetate) Therapy in Deviant Hypersexuality', *The British Journal of Psychiatry*, 120: 59–63.

Copas, J. and Marshall, P. (1998) 'The Offender Group Reconviction Scale: A Statistical Reconviction Score for Use by Probation Officers', *Journal of the Royal Statistical Society*, Series C, 47: 159–71.

Corston, J. (2007) *The Corston Report. A Report by Baroness Jean Corston of a Review of Women with Particular Vulnerabilities in the Criminal Justice System*. London: Home Office.

Cortoni, F. (2010) 'Female Sexual Offenders: A Special Sub-Group', in K. Harrison (ed) *Managing High Risk Sex Offenders in the Community: Risk Management, Treatment and Social Responsibility*. Cullompton: Willan Publishing.

Cortoni, F. and Hanson, R. K. (2005) 'A Review of the Recidivism Rates of Adult Female Sexual Offenders', Research Report R-169. Ottawa, ON: Correctional Service Canada.

Cossins, A. (2008) 'Restorative Justice and Child Sex Offences. The Theory and the Practice', *British Journal of Criminology*, 48: 359–78.

Cox, J. (2007) 'Family Group Conferencing and "Partnership" ', in S. Hunter and P. Ritchie (eds) *Co-Production and Personalisation in Social Care*. London: Jessica Kingsley Publishers.

Craig, L., Beech, A. and Browne, K. (2006) 'Evaluating the Predictive Accuracy of Sex Offender Risk Assessment Measures on UK Samples: A Cross-Validation of the Risk Matrix 2000 Scales', *Sexual Offender Treatment*, 1(1). Available at: www.sexual-offender-treatment.org/19.html (accessed 7 December 2010).

Craig, L., Browne, K. and Beech, A. (2008) *Assessing Risk in Sex Offenders. A Practitioners Guide*. Chichester: John Wiley & Sons.

Craissati, J. (2004) *Managing High Risk Sex Offenders in the Community. A Psychological Approach*. New York: Routledge.

Craissati, J. and Beech, A. R. (2005) 'Risk Prediction and Failure in a Complete Urban Sample of Sex Offenders', *Journal of Forensic Psychiatry and Psychology*, 16: 24–40.

Craven, S., Brown, S. and Gilchrist, E. (2007) 'Current Responses to Sexual Grooming: Implication for Prevention', *Howard Journal*, 46(1): 60–71.

Creighton, S. (2007) *Memorandum Submitted by Simon Creighton*, 6 March 2007. Available at: www.publications.parliament.uk/pa/cm200607/cmselect/cmconst/467/467we06.htm (accessed 29 July 2010).

Creighton, S., King, V. and Arnott, H. (2005) *Prisoners and the Law* (3rd edn). London: Butterworths.

Crown Prosecution Service (2010) *Mentally Disordered Offenders: Legal Guidance*. Available at: www.cps.gov.uk/legal/l_to_o/mentally_disordered_offenders (accessed 15 September 2010).

Cullen, E. (1992) 'The Grendon Reconviction Study Part 1', *Prison Service Journal*, 90: 35–7.

Daly, K. (2008) 'Setting The Record Straight and a Call for Radical Change. A Reply to Anne Cossins on "Restorative Justice and Child Sex Offences" ', *British Journal of Criminology*, 48: 557–66.

Daly, K. (2009) 'The Limits of Restorative Justice', in A. von Hirsch, A. Ashworth and J. Roberts (eds) *Principled Sentencing. Readings on Theory and Policy*. Oxford: Hart Publishing.

Dangerous and Severe Personality Disorder Programme (2010a) *Resettle*. Available at: www.dspdprogramme.gov.uk/progression_service3.html (accessed 18 August 2010).

Dangerous and Severe Personality Disorder Programme (2010b) *Women's Services: The Primrose Project*. Available at: www.dspdprogramme.gov.uk/womens_services.html (accessed 18 August 2010).

Dangerous and Severe Personality Disorder Programme (2010c) *High Secure Sites*. Available at: www.dspdprogramme.gov.uk/high_secure_sites.html (accessed 18 August 2010).

Dangerous and Severe Personality Disorder Programme (2010d) *Progression Service*. Available at: www.dspdprogramme.gov.uk/progression_service1.html (accessed 18 August 2010).

Dangerous and Severe Personality Disorder Programme (2010e) *HMP Grendon*. Available at: www.dspdprogramme.gov.uk/progression_service4.html (accessed 18 August 2010).

Davis, M. (2010) 'Police Defend Sex Offender Monitoring as 300 Remain Missing', *The Independent*, 26 April 2010. Available at: www.independent.co.uk/news/uk/crime/police-defend-sex-offender-monitoring-as-300-remain-missing-1954767.html (accessed 15 May 2010).

Davis, T. S. (1974) 'Cyproterone Acetate for Male Hypersexuality', *Journal of International Medical Research*, 2: 159–63.

Daybreak Family Group Conferences (2010) *Daybreak Family Group Conferences*. Available at: www.daybreakfgc.org.uk (accessed 14 June 2010).

Deacon, J. (1999) 'Some Psychodynamic Reflections on Polygraph Examinations with Sex Offenders', *Probation Journal*, 46: 241–5.

Debidin, M. (ed.) (2009) 'A Compendium of Research and Analysis on the Offender Assessment System (OASys) 2006–2009', Ministry of Justice Research Series 16/09. London: Ministry of Justice.

Debidin, M. and Fairweather, L. (2009) 'Introduction to OASys and research on OASys 2006 to 2009', in M. Debidin (ed.) 'A Compendium of Research and Analysis on the Offender Assessment System (OASys) 2006–2009', Ministry of Justice Research Series 16/09. London: Ministry of Justice.

Department for Education (2010) *Safeguarding the Future. A Review of the Youth Justice Board's Governance and Operating Arrangements*. Available at: http://publications.education.gov.uk/default.aspx?PageFunction=productdetails&PageMode=publications&ProductId=DCSF-00223-2010 (accessed 14 November 2010).

Derbyshire Probation Trust (2010) *Community Sex Offender Groupwork Programme*. Matlock Bath: Derbyshire Probation Trust. Available at: www.dpsonline.org.uk/assets/userfiles/derbyshire/Offender_leaflets/CSOGP_Prisoners_Trust.pdf (accessed 1 June 2010).

Dershowitz, A. (1973) 'Preventive Confinement: A Suggested Framework for Constitutional Analysis', *Texas Law Review*, 51(7): 1277–324.

Dignan, J. (2005) *Understanding Victims and Restorative Justice*. Maidenhead: OUP.

Dingwall, G. (1998) 'Selective Incapacitation after the Criminal Justice Act 1991: A Proportional Response to Protecting the Public?', *Howard Journal*, 37(2): 177–87.

Dingwall, R. (1989) 'Some Problems about Predicting Child Abuse and Neglect', in O. Stevenson (ed.) *Child Abuse Public Policy and Professional Practice*. Hemel Hempstead: Harvester Wheatsheaf.

Dinitz, S. and Conrad, J. P. (1978) 'Thinking about Dangerous Offenders', *Criminal Justice Abstracts*, 10(1): 99–130.

Directgov (2008) *Keeping Children Safe: The Child Sexual Offender Disclosure Pilot*. Available at: www.direct.gov.uk/en/Nl1/Newsroom/DG_171707 (accessed 14 May 2010).

Ditchfield, J. (1990) 'Control in Prisons: A Review of the Literature', Home Office Research Study 118. London: HMSO.

Douglas, K., Guy, L. and Weir, J. (2006) *HCR-20 Violence Risk Assessment Scheme: Overview and Annotated Bibliography*. Available at: www.violence-risk.com/hcr20annotated.pdf (accessed 5 January 2010).

Douglas, K., Ogloff, J., Nicholls, T. and Grant, I. (1999) 'Assessing Risk for Violence among Psychiatric Patients: The HCR-20 Violence Risk Assessment Scheme and the Psychopathy Checklist: Screening Version', *Journal of Consulting and Clinical Psychology* 67(6): 917–30.

Douglas, M. (1992) *Risk and Blame*. London: Routledge.

Doward, J. (2008) 'Pledge to Cut Domestic Violence has Failed', *The Observer*, 17 February 2008.

Dowden, C. and Serin, R. C. (2001) *Anger Management Programming for Offenders: The Impact of Program Performance Measures*. Ottawa, ON: Correctional Service of Canada.

Dowden, C., Blanchette, K., and Serin, R. C. (1999) 'Anger Management Programming for Federal Male Inmates: An Effective Intervention', Research Report R-82. Ottawa, ON: Correctional Service of Canada.

Duggan, S. (2010) 'Diversion', *Criminal Law and Justice Weekly*, 174(24): 68.

Dunn, C. W. (1940) 'Stilboestrol Induced Gynaecomastia in the Male', *Journal of the American Medical Association*, 115: 2263–4.

Dworkin, R. (1977) *Taking Rights Seriously*. London: Duckworth.

Easton, S. and Piper, C. (2008) *Sentencing and Punishment. The Quest for Justice* (2nd edn). Oxford: Oxford University Press.

Elliott, M. (2004) *Female Sexual Abuse of Children: 'The Ultimate Taboo'*. London: Kidscape. Available at: www.kidscape.org.uk/assets/downloads/Femalesexualabuseofchildren.pdf (accessed 12 July 2010).

Encyclopaedia of Mental Disorders (2010) *Hare Psychopathy Checklist*. Available at: www.minddisorders.com/Flu-Inv/Hare-Psychopathy-Checklist.html (accessed 17 August 2010).

Epstein, E. J. and Hing-Yan Wong, S. (1996) 'The Concept of "Dangerousness" in the People's Republic of China and its Impact on the Treatment of Prisoners', *The British Journal of Criminology*, 36(4): 472–96.

Epstein, R. and Russo, D. (2010) 'Women Behind Bars', *Criminal Law and Justice Weekly*, 174: 330–3.

Faller, K. (1987) 'Women Who Sexually Abuse Children', *Violence and Victims*, 2(4): 263–76.

Fallon, P., Bluglass, R., Edwards, B. and Daniels, G. (1999) 'Report of the Committee of Inquiry into the Personality Disorder Unit, Ashworth Special Hospital', Cm. 4191-11. London: The Stationery Office.

Farrington, D., Jolliffe, D. and Johnstone, L. (2008) *Assessing Violence Risk: A Framework for Practice*. Edinburgh: RMA.

Feeley, M. and Simon, J. (1992) 'The New Penology: Notes on the Emerging Strategy of Corrections and its Implications', *Criminology*, 30(4): 449–74.

Finnigan, M. (2010) Personal communication received 26 November 2010.

Flatley, J., Kershaw, C., Smith, K., Chaplin, R. and Moon, D. (2010) 'Crime in England and Wales 2009/10', (2nd edition). Home Office Statistical Bulletin. London: Home Office.

Floud, J. (1982) 'Dangerousness and Criminal Justice', *The British Journal of Criminology*, 22(3): 213–28.

Floud, J. and Young, W. (1981) *Dangerousness and Criminal Justice*. London: Heinemann.

Foote, R. M. (1944) 'Hormonal Treatment of Sex Offenders', *Journal of Nervous and Mental Disorders*, 99: 928–9.

Ford, H. (2006) *Women Who Sexually Abuse Children*. Chichester: J. Wiley & Sons.

Ford, H. (2009) 'Female Sex Offenders: Issues and Considerations in Working with this Population', in A. Beech, L. Craig and K. Browne (eds) *Assessment and Treatment of Sex Offenders. A Handbook*. Chichester: Wiley-Blackwell.

Ford, H. and Beech, A. (2003) *The Effectiveness of The Wolvercote Clinic Residential Treatment Programme In Producing Short-Term Treatment Changes And Reducing Sexual Reconviction*. London: National Probation Service.

Frenken, J., Gijs, L. and van Beek, D. (1999) 'Sexual Offender Research and Treatment in the Netherlands', *Journal of Interpersonal Violence*, 14(4): 347–71.

Friendship, C., Mann, R. and Beech, A. (2003) 'The Prison-Based Sex Offender Treatment Programme – an Evaluation', Home Office Findings 205. London: Home Office.

Fulero, S. M. (1995) 'Review of the Hare Psychopathy Checklist-Revised', in J. C. Conoley and J. C. Impara (eds) *The Twelfth Mental Measurements Yearbook*. Buros Institute, University of Nebraska: University of Nebraska Press.

Gadd, D. (2004) 'Evidence-Led Policy or Policy-Led Evidence? Cognitive Behavioural Programmes for Men who are Violent towards Women', *Criminal Justice*, 4: 173–197.

Gannon, T. and Rose, M. (2008) 'Female Child Sexual Offenders: Towards Integrating Theory and Practice', *Aggression and Violent Behavior*, 13(6): 442–61.

Gannon, T., Rose, M. and Ward, T. (2008) 'A Descriptive Model of the Offense Process for Female Sexual Offenders', *Sexual Abuse: A Journal of Research and Treatment*, 20(3): 352–74.

Garland, D. (2000) 'The Culture of High Crime Societies. Some Preconditions of Recent "Law and Order" Policies', *British Journal of Criminology*, 40(3): 347–75.

Garland, D. (2001) *The Culture of Control: Crime and Social Order in Contemporary Society*. Oxford: Oxford University Press.

Genders, E. (2002) 'Legitimacy, Accountability and Private Prisons', *Punishment and Society*, 4: 285–303.

Genders, E. (2003) 'Privatisation and Innovation – Rhetoric and Reality: The Development of a Therapeutic Community Prison', *The Howard Journal*, 42(2) 137–57.

Genders, E. and Player. E. (1993) 'Rehabilitation in Prisons: A Study of Grendon Underwood', *Current Legal Problems*, 46(2): 235–56.

Genders, E. and Player, E. (1995) *Grendon. A Study of a Therapeutic Prison*. Oxford: Oxford University Press.

Gendreau, P., Goggin, C. and Paparozzi, M. (1996a) 'Principles of Effective Assessment for Community Corrections', *Federal Probation*, 60(3): 64–70.

Gendreau, P., Little, T., and Coggin, C. (1996b) 'Meta-Analysis of Adult Offender Recidivism: What Works!', *Criminology*, 34: 575–607.

Gillespie, A. (2006) 'Dangerousness: Variations on a Theme by Thomas', *Crim L.R.*, Sept: 828–31.

Goldson, B. (2002) *Vulnerable Inside: Children in Secure and Penal Settings*. London: Children's Society.

Goldson, B. (2005) 'Child Imprisonment: A Case for Abolition', *Youth Justice*, 5: 77–90.

Goldson, B. (2010) 'Child Incarceration, State Sanctioned Violence and Cultures of Impunity', paper given at the *Symposium on Controversial Issues in Prison*, 22 September 2010, University of Central Lancashire.

Gosling, M. (2009) 'The DSPD Programme', *Criminal Law and Justice Weekly*, 173: 633–6.

Green, D. (2008) *When Children Kill Children*. Oxford: Oxford University Press.

Greenall, P. (2009) 'Assessing High Risk Offenders with Personality Disorder', *British Journal of Forensic Practice*, 11(3): 14–18.

Greenberg, D. M. and Bradford, J. M. (1997) 'Treatment of the Paraphilic Disorders: A Review of the Role of the Selective Serotonin Reuptake Inhibitors', *Sexual Abuse: A Journal of Research and Treatment*, 9(4): 349–60.

Greenberg, D. M., Bradford, J. M., Curry, S. and O'Rourke, A. (1996) 'A Comparison of Treatment of Paraphilias with Three Serotonin Reuptake Inhibitors: A Retrospective Study', *Bull. Am. Acad. Psychiatry Law*, 24(4): 525–32.

Griffin, H. and Beech, A. (2004) *Evaluation of the AIM Framework for the Assessment of Adolescents who Display Sexually Harmful Behaviour*. London: Youth Justice Board.

Grimshaw, R. (2008) *Young People Who Sexually Abuse, Source Document*. London: Youth Justice Board.

Grossman, L. S., Martis, B. and Fichtner, C. G. (1999) 'Are Sex Offenders Treatable? A Research Overview', *Psychiatric Services*, 50(3): 349–61.

Grubin, D. (1998) 'Sex Offending Against Children: Understanding the Risk', Police Research Series Paper 99. London: Home Office.

Grubin, D. (2006) *Polygraph Pilot Study. Final Report.* London: National Probation Service.

Grubin, D. (2008a) 'Risk Matrix 2000', paper given at the *Royal College of Psychiatrists, London.* Available at: www.fprs.org/London08/dg.pdf (accessed 15 May 2010).

Grubin, D. (2008b) 'Validation of Risk Matrix 2000 for use in Scotland', Report prepared for the Risk Management Authority. Edinburgh: RMA.

Grubin, D. (2008c) The Case for Polygraph Testing of Sex Offenders', *Legal and Criminological Psychology*, 13: 177–89.

Grubin, D. (2008d) 'The Use of Medication in the Treatment of Sex Offenders', *Prison Service Journal*, 178: 37–43.

Grubin, D. and Wingate, S. (1996) 'Sexual Offence Recidivism: Prediction versus Understanding', *Criminal Behaviour and Mental Health*, 6(4): 349–59.

Grubin, D., Madsen, L., Parsons, S., Sosnowski, D. and Warberg, B. (2004) 'A Prospective Study of the Impact of Polygraphy on High-Risk Behaviors in Adult Sex Offenders', *Sexual Abuse: A Journal of Research and Treatment*, 16(3): 209–22.

Gunn, J. (1982) 'Defining the Terms', in J. R. Hamilton, H. Freeman and H. Gaskell (eds) *Dangerousness: Psychiatric Assessment and Management.* London: Gaskell.

Gunn, J. and Robertson, G. (1987) 'A Ten Year Follow Up of Men Discharged from Grendon Prison', *British Journal of Psychiatry*, 151: 674–8.

Gunn, J., Robertson, G., Dell, S. and Way, C. (1978) *Psychiatric Aspects of Imprisonment.* London: Academic Press.

Hackett, S., Masson, H. and Phillips, S. (2005) *Services for Young People Who Sexually Abuse.* London: Youth Justice Board.

Haddock, A., Snowden, P., Dolan, M., Parker, J. and Rees, H. (2001) 'Managing Dangerous People with Severe Personality Disorder: A Survey of Forensic Psychiatrists' Opinions', *Psychiatric Bulletin*, 25: 293–6.

Haist, M. (2009) 'Deterrence in a Sea of "Just Deserts": Are Utilitarian Goals Achievable in a World of "Limiting Retributivism"?', *The Journal of Criminal Law & Criminology*, 99(3): 789–821.

Halford, R. (2010) Interview with Rachel Halford, Director of Women in Prisons, 21 October 2010.

Hall, P. and Innes, J. (2010) 'Violent and Sexual Crime', in J. Flatley, C. Kershaw, K. Smith, R. Chaplin and D. Moon (eds) 'Crime in England and Wales 2009/10', Home Office Statistical Bulletin 12/10. London: Home Office.

Halliday, J., French, C. and Goodwin, C. (2001) *Making Punishments Work. Report of a Review of the Sentencing Framework for England and Wales.* London: Home Office.

Haney, C. (2003) 'Mental Health Issues in Long-Term Solitary and 'Supermax' Confinement', *Crime and Delinquency*, 49: 124–56.

Hanson, R. K. and Bussière, M. T. (1998) 'Predicting Relapse: A Meta-Analysis of Sexual Offender Recidivism Studies', *Journal of Consulting and Clinical Psychology*, 66: 348–62.

Hanson, R. K. and Thornton, D. (2000) 'Improving Risk Assessments for Sex Offenders: A Comparison of Three Actuarial Scales', *Law and Human Behavior*, 24(1): 119–36.

Hanson, R. K., Morton, K. and Harris, A. (2003) 'Sexual Offender Recidivism Risk. What We Know and What We Need to Know', *Ann. N.Y. Acad. Sci.*, 989: 154–66.

Hanson, R. K., Gordon, A., Harris, A., Marques, J., Murphy, W., Quinsey, V. and Seto, M. (2002) 'First Report of the Collaborative Outcome Data Project on the Effectiveness of Psychological Treatment for Sex Offenders', *Sexual Abuse: A Journal of Research and Treatment*, 14(2): 169–94.

Hare, R. D. (1991) *The Hare Psychopathy Checklist – Revised*. Toronto, Canada: Multi-Health Systems.

Hare, R. D., Clark, D., Grann, M. and Thornton, D. (2000) 'Psychopathy and the Predictive Validity of the PCL-R: An International Perspective', *Behavioral Sciences and the Law*, 18: 623–45.

Harrison, D. (2007a) 'What Happens Inside? The Experiences of a Lifer Manager', guest lecture *University of the West of England*, 2008.

Harrison, K. (2007b) 'The High Risk Sex Offender Strategy in England and Wales: Is Chemical Castration an Option?', *Howard Journal*, 46(1): 16–31.

Harrison, K. (2010a) 'Dangerous Offenders, Indeterminate Sentencing, and the Rehabilitation Revolution', *Journal of Social Welfare & Family Law*, 32(4): 423–33.

Harrison, K. (2010b) 'The Use of Pharmacotherapy with High-Risk Sex Offenders' in K. Harrison (ed.) *Managing High Risk Sex Offenders in the Community: Risk Management, Treatment and Social Responsibility*. Cullompton: Willan Publishing.

Harrison, K. and Rainey, B. (2009) 'Suppressing Human Rights? A Rights-Based Approach to the Use of Pharmacotherapy with Sex Offenders', *Legal Studies*, (29)1: 47–74.

Harrison, K., Manning, R. and McCartan, K. (2010) 'Multi-Disciplinary Definitions and Understanding of Paedophilia', *Social & Legal Studies*,19(4): 481–96.

Hayward, K. and Yar, M. (2006) 'The "Chav" Phenomenon: Consumption, Media and the Construction of a New Underclass', *Crime, Media, Culture*, 2(1): 9–28.

Hebenton, B. and Seddon, T. (2009) 'From Dangerousness to Precaution. Managing Sexual and Violent Offenders in an Insecure and Uncertain Age', *The British Journal of Criminology*, 49: 343-62.

Hebenton, B. and Thomas, T. (1997) 'Keeping Track? Observations on Sex Offender Registers in the US', Crime Detection and Prevention Series Paper 83. London: Home Office.

Hedderman, C. and Gelsthorpe, L. (1997) 'Understanding the Sentencing of Women', Home Office Research Study 170. London: Home Office.

Hedderman, C. and Sugg, D. (1996) 'Does Treating Sex Offenders Reduce Reoffending?', Home Office Research Findings No. 45. London: HORSD.

Henning, K., and Frueh, B. (1996) 'Cognitive-Behavioral Treatment of Incarcerated Offenders. An Evaluation of the Vermont Department Corrections' Cognitive Self-Change Program', *Criminal Justice and Behavior*, 23(4): 523–41.

Hicks, P. (1993) 'Castration of Sexual Offenders: Legal and Ethical Issues', *Journal of Legal Medicine*, 14: 641–67.

HM Chief Inspector of Prisons (2000) *Inspection of Close Supervision Centres August–September 1999*. London: HMIP.

HM Chief Inspector of Prisons (2001) *Report of Her Majesty's Chief Inspector of Prisons December 1999–November 2000*. London: HMIP.

HM Chief Inspector of Prisons (2008) *Report on an Announced Inspection of the Management, Care and Control of Young People at Oakhill Secure Training Centre*. London: HMIP.

HM Chief Inspector of Prisons (2009a) *Report on an Announced Inspection of HMYOI Castington, 19–23 January 2009*. London: HMIP.

HM Chief Inspector of Prisons (2009b) *Report on an Announced Inspection of HMYOI Wetherby, The Keppel Unit, 20–24 April 2009*. London: HMIP.

HM Chief Inspector of Prisons and HM Chief Inspector of Probation (2008) *The Indeterminate Sentence for Public Protection – a Thematic Review*. London: HM Inspectorate of Prisons; HM Inspectorate of Probation.

HM Chief Inspector of Prisons and HM Chief Inspector of Probation (2010) *Indeterminate Sentences for Public Protection. A Joint Inspection by HMI Probation and HMI Prisons*. London: HM Inspectorate of Prisons; HM Inspectorate of Probation.

HM Inspectorate of Prisons (2004) *Report on a Full Announced Inspection of HMP Prison Grendon 1–5 March 2004*. London: HMIP.

HM Inspectorate of Prisons (2006a) *Extreme Custody. A Thematic Inspection of Close Supervision Centres and High Security Segregation*. London: HMIP.

HM Inspectorate of Prisons (2006b) *Report on an Announced Inspection of HMP Send 13–17 February 2006*. London: HMIP.

HM Inspectorate of Prisons (2007a) *Report on an Unannounced Short Follow-Up Inspection of HMP Grendon 31 October–2 November 2006*. London: HMIP.

HM Inspectorate of Prisons (2007b) *Report on an Unannounced Short Follow-Up Inspection of HMP Dovegate Therapeutic Community 29–31 August 2006*. London: HMIP.

HM Inspectorate of Prisons (2008a) *Report on an Announced Inspection of HMP Dovegate Therapeutic Community 16–20 June 2008*. London: HMIP.

HM Inspectorate of Prisons (2008b) *Report on an Unannounced Short Follow-Up Inspection of HMP Send 18–22 August 2008*. London: HMIP.

HM Inspectorate of Prisons (2009) *Report on an Announced Inspection of HMP Grendon 2–6 March 2009*. London: HMIP.

HM Inspectorate of Probation (2006) *An Independent Review of a Serious Further Offence Case: Damien Hanson and Eliot White*. London: HMIP.

HM Prison Service (2000) 'Categorisation and Allocation', Prison Service Order 0900. London: HM Prison Service.

HM Prison Service (2004) *Dangerous Offender Stategy for the Prison*. London: Home Office.

HM Prison Service (2005) 'Parole Release and Recall', Prison Service Order 6000. London: HM Prison Service.

HM Prison Service (2007) 'Annual Report and Accounts 2006–2007', HC 717. London: HMSO.

HM Prison Service (2008a) 'Initial Categorisation of Male Indeterminate Sentence Prisoners', Prison Service Instruction 07/2008. London: HM Prison Service.

HM Prison Service (2008b) 'Indeterminate Sentence Manual', Prison Service Order 4700. London: HM Prison Service.

HM Prison Service (2008c) 'Annual Report and Accounts', HC860, London: The Stationery Office.

HM Prison Service (2008d) 'Women Prisoners', Prison Service Order 4800. London: HM Prison Service.

HM Prison Service (2008e) 'The Management of Mother and Baby Units', (4th edn), Prison Service Order 4801. London: HM Prison Service.

HM Prison Service (2009a) 'Close Supervision Centre Referral Manual', Prison Service Instruction 29/2009. London: NOMS.

HM Prison Service (2009b) 'Generic Parole Process', Prison Service Order 6010. London: HM Prison Service.

HM Prison Service (2010a) *Female Prisoners*. Available at: www.hmprisonservice.gov.uk/adviceandsupport/prison_life/femaleprisoners (accessed 18 July 2010).

HM Prison Service (2010b) *Locate a Prison*. Available at: www.hmprisonservice.gov.uk/prisoninformation/locateaprison/index.asp?frmAction=search&pl1category=57&x=15&y=15 (accessed 14 November 2010).

HM Prison Service (2010c) 'Use of Force', Prison Service Order 1600. London: HM Prison Service.

Hobson, J. and Shine, J. (1998) 'Measurements of Psychopathy in a UK Prison Population Referred for Long Term Psychopathy', *British Journal of Criminology*, 38(3): 139–54.

Hogue, T. (2009) 'The Peaks: Assessing Sex Offenders in a Dangerous and Severe Personality Disorders Unit', in A. Beech, L. Craig and K. Browne (eds) *Assessment and Treatment of Sex Offenders. A Handbook*. Chichester: Wiley-Blackwell.

Hollin, C. and Palmer, E. (2006) 'Criminogenic Need and Women Offenders: A Critique of the Literature', *Legal and Criminological Psychology*, 11: 179–95.

Hollis, V. (2007) *Reconviction Analysis of Programme Data using Interim Accredited Programmes. Software (IAPS)*. London: RDS NOMS Research and Evaluation.

Holmes, S. and Soothill, K. (2008) 'Dangerousness', in Y. Jewkes and J. Bennett (eds) *Dictionary of Prisons and Punishment*. Cullompton: Willan Publishing.

Home Affairs Committee (2008) *Home Affairs – Sixth Report*. Available at: www.parliament.the-stationery-office.co.uk/pa/cm200708/cmselect/cmhaff/263/26302.htm (accessed 4 June 2010).

Home Office (1932) *Report of the Departmental Committee on Persistent Offenders*. London: Home Office.

Home Office (1963) 'Preventive Detention', Report of the Advisory Council on the Treatment of Offenders. London: HMSO.

Home Office (1978) 'Sentences of Imprisonment: A Review of Maximum Penalties', Report of the Advisory Council on the Penal System. London: HMSO.

Home Office (1987) *Prison Department Circular Instruction 21/1987*. London: Home Office.

Home Office (1990) 'Provision for Mentally Disordered Offenders', Home Office Circular No. 66/90. London: Home Office.

Home Office (1996) 'Sentencing and Supervision of Sex Offenders: A Consultation Paper', Cm. 3304. London: Home Office.

Home Office (1997) 'No More Excuses – A New Approach to Tackling Youth Crime in England and Wales', Cm. 3809. London: HMSO.

Home Office (1998) 'Effective Practice Initiative. A National Implementation Plan for the Effective Supervision of Offenders', Probation Circular 35/1998. London: Home Office.

Home Office (2002a) 'Justice for All', Cm. 5563. London: HMSO.

Home Office (2002b) 'Protecting the Public', Cm. 5668. London: HMSO.

Home Office (2004) 'Confident Communities in a Secure Society: The Home Office Strategic Plan 2004–2008', Cm. 6287. London: Home Office.

Home Office (2007) *Review of the Protection of Children from Sex Offenders*. London: Home Office.

Home Office (2009a) 'Protecting Children from Sexual Abuse', *Press Release*, 16 March 2009. London: Home Office.

Home Office (2009b) *A Guide to Violent Offender Orders*. London: Home Office.

Home Office (2010) *Protecting Children*. Available at: http://webarchive.nationalarchives.gov.uk/20100418065544/http://www.homeoffice.gov.uk/about-us/news/child-sex-offenders-disclosure.html (accessed 14 May 2010).

Home Office and Department of Health and Social Security (1975) 'Report of the Committee on Mentally Abnormal Offenders', Cm. 6244. London: HMSO.

Home Office/Scottish Executive (2001) *Consultation Paper on the Review of Part 1 of the Sex Offenders Act 1997*. London: Home Office.

Hood, R., Shute, S., Feilzer, M. and Wilcox, A. (2002) 'Sex Offenders Emerging from Long-Term Imprisonment. A Study of Their Long-Term Reconviction Rates and of Parole Board Members' Judgements of Their Risk', *British Journal of Criminology*, 42: 371–94.

Howard, P. (2006). 'The Offender Assessment System: An Evaluation of the Second Pilot', Home Office Research Findings 278. London: Home Office.

Howard, P. (2009a) 'Predictive Validity of OASys – Improving Prediction of Violent and General Reoffending', in M. Debidin (ed.) 'A Compendium of Research and Analysis on the Offender Assessment System (OASys) 2006–2009', Ministry of Justice Research Series 16/09. London: Ministry of Justice.

Howard, P. (2009b) 'Improving the Prediction of Re-Offending Using the Offender Assessment System', Ministry of Justice Research Summary 2/09. London: Ministry of Justice.

Howard, P. (2009c) Personal communication dated 16 December 2009.

Howard, P. and Seaton, J. (2008) 'Indicators of Violent Reoffending: The New OASys Violence Predictor'. Available at: www.rmascotland.gov.uk/rmapresentations1.aspx (accessed 30 November 2009).

Howard, P., Clark, D. and Garnham, N. (2006) 'An Evaluation and Validation of the Offender Assessment System (OASys)', OASys Central Research Unit. London: HM Prison Service and National Probation Service.

Howard, P., Francis, B., Soothill, K., and Humphreys, L. (2009) 'OGRS 3: The Revised Offender Group Reconviction Scale', Research Summary 7/09. London: Ministry of Justice.

The Howard League (2008) 'High Security Prisons. Prisoner Perspectives', Prison Information Bulletin 4. London: The Howard League.

The Howard League (2009) *More Prisoners Serving Open Ended Sentences in England and Wales than the 46 Countries in Europe*, Press Release, 13 March 2009. Available at: www.howardleague.org/fileadmin/howard_league/user/pdf/Press_2009/lifers_13_March_2009.pdf (accessed 7 April 2010).

The Howard League for Penal Reform (2007) 'Indeterminate Sentences for Public Protection', Prison Information Bulletin 3. London: The Howard League for Penal Reform.

Hunter, G., Hearnden, I. and Gyateng, T. (2009) *Statistics on Women and the Criminal Justice System, A Ministry of Justice Publication under Section 95 of the Criminal Justice Act 1991*. London: Ministry of Justice.

Icenogle, D. L. (1994) 'Sentencing Male Sex Offenders to the Use of Biological Treatments. A Constitutional Analysis', *The Journal of Legal Medicine*, 15: 279–304.

Independent Monitoring Board (2007) *Annual Report: HMP Send, Woking, Surry, April 2006–March 2007*. London: IMB.

Independent Monitoring Board (2009a) *Annual Report: HMP Send, Woking, Surry, April 2008–March 2009*. London: IMB.

Independent Monitoring Board (2009b) *Annual Report: HMYOI Wetherby June 2008–May 2009*. London: IMB.

Information Governance Unit (2009) *Freedom of Information Request*. Available at: www.gmp.police.uk/mainsite/0/872BE70DCF7E661280257611002FC48C/$file/Potentially%20Dangerous%20Persons.pdf (accessed 12 May 2010).

Inquest (2010) *Death of Young People and Children in Prison*. Available at: www.inquest.org.uk (accessed 19 November 2010).

Johnstone, G. (2002) *Restorative Justice*. Cullompton: Willan Publishing.

Jonah, L. (2009) 'The Case Management Protocol for Difficult to Manage Prisoners: HMP Wormwood Scrubs', *Prison Service Journal*, 181: 29–33.

Jordan, R. and O'Hare, G. (2007) 'The Probation Board for Northern Ireland's Cognitive-Self Change programme: An Overview of the Pilot Programme in the Community', *Irish Probation Journal*, 4(1): 125–36.

Joseph, N. (2010) Personal communication received 18 August 2010.

Judd, T. and Goodchild, S. (2002) 'IoS Investigation: The Forgotten Inmates of Secure Mental Hospitals', *The Independent*, 9 June 2002.

Judicial Studies Board (2010) *Youth Court Bench Book*. London: Judicial Studies Board.

Justice (2007) *Submission to Home Affairs Select Committee Inquiry – Towards Effective Sentencing*. London: Justice.

Kafka, M. P. (1997) 'A Monoamine Hypothesis for the Pathophysiology of Paraphilic Disorders', *Archives of Sexual Behavior*, 26(4): 343–58.

Kemshall, H. (1996) 'Reviewing Risk – A Review of Research on the Assessment and Management of Risk and Dangerousness: Implications for Policy and Practice in the Probation Service', A Report for the Home Office Research and Statistics Department. London: Home Office.

Kemshall, H. (2001) 'Risk Assessment and Management of Known Sexual and Violent Offenders: A Review of Current Issues', Police Research Series Paper 140. London: Home Office.

Kemshall, H. (2002) *Risk Assessment and Management of Serious Violent and Sexual Offenders: A Review of Current Issues*. Edinburgh: Scottish Executive Social Research.

Kemshall, H. (2003) *Understanding Risk in Criminal Justice*. Maidenhead: OUP.

Kemshall, H. (2008) *Understanding the Community Management of High Risk Offenders*. Maidenhead: OUP.

Kemshall, H. (2009) 'Working with Sex Offenders in a Climate of Public Blame and Anxiety: How to Make Defensible Decisions for Risk', *Journal of Sexual Aggression*, 15(3): 331–43.

Kemshall, H. and Wood, J. (2007a) 'Beyond Public Protection: An Examination of Community Protection and Public Health Approaches to High-Risk Offenders', *Criminology & Criminal Justice*, 7(3): 203–22.

Kemshall, H. and Wood, J. (2007b) 'The Operation and Experience of Multi-Agency Public Protection Arrangements (MAPPA)', Home Office Findings 285. London: Home Office.

Kemshall, H. and Wood, J. (2009) 'Community Strategies for Managing High-Risk Offenders: The Contribution of Multi-Agency Public Protection Arrangements', in A. R. Beech, L. Craig, and K. Browne (eds) *Assessment and Treatment of Sex Offenders: A Handbook*. Chichester: Wiley-Blackwell.

Kemshall, H. and Wood, J., with Westwood, S., Stout, B., Wilkinson, B., Kelly, G. and MacKenzie, G. (2010) 'Child Sex Offender Review (CSOR) Public Disclosure Pilots: A Process Evaluation', Home Office Research Report 32, Key Findings. London: Home Office.

Kemshall, H., MacKenzie, G., Wood, J., Bailey, R. and Yates, J. (2005) 'Strengthening Multi-Agency Public Protection Arrangements (MAPPAs)', Home Office Development and Practice Report 45. London: Home Office.

Kettle, M. (2008) 'Dangerous and Severe Personality Disorder', in Y. Jewkes and J. Bennett (eds), *Dictionary on Prisons and Punishment*. Cullompton: Willan Publishing.

King, R. (2007) 'Security, Control and the Problems of Containment', in Y. Jewkes (ed.) *Handbook on Prisons*. Cullompton: Willan Publishing.

King, R. (2008) 'Order and Control', in Y. Jewkes, and J. Bennett (eds) *Dictionary of Prisons and Punishment*. Cullompton: Willan Publishing.

Kisely, S. R., Campbell, L. A. and Preston, N. J. (2005) 'Compulsory Community and Involuntary Outpatient Treatment for People with Severe Mental Disorders', *Cochrane Database of Systematic Reviews*, Issue 3. Art. No.: CD004408.

Knight, L. and Stephens, M. (2009) 'Mentally Disordered Offenders in Prison: A Tale of Neglect', *Internet Journal of Criminology*. Available at: www.internetjournalofcriminology.com/Knight_Stephens_Mentally_Disordered_Offenders.pdf (accessed 18 August 2009).

Kozol, H., Boucher, R. and Garofalo, R. (1972) 'The Diagnosis and Treatment of Dangerousness', *Crime and Delinquency*, 18(4): 371–9.

Krueger, R. B. and Kaplan, M. S. (2001) 'Depot-Leuprolide Acetate for Treatment of Paraphilias: A Report of Twelve Cases', *Archives of Sexual Behaviour*, 30(4): 409–22.

Labour Party (1997) *New Labour – Because Britain Deserves Better*. London: Labour Party.

Laws, D. R. and Marshall, W. L. (2003) 'A Brief History of Behavioral and Cognitive Behavioral Approaches to Sexual Offender Treatment: Part 1. Early Developments', *Sexual Abuse: A Journal of Research and Treatment*, 15(2): 75–92.

Lianos, M. and Douglas, M. (2000) 'Dangerization and the End of Deviance. The Institutional Environment', *British Journal of Criminology*, 40: 261–78.

Liberty (2007) *Liberty's Response to the Home Office Consultation on Violent Offender Orders*. London: Liberty.

Liebmann, M. and Wootton, L. (2008) 'Restorative Justice and Domestic Violence/Abuse', A Report Commissioned by HMP Cardiff. Cardiff: Home Office Crime Reduction Unit for Wales.

Liell, G. (2007) 'The Chromis Programme: Research'. Available at: www.bps.org.uk/downloadfile.cfm?file_uuid=4EDD4241-1143-DFD0-7E1F-ADE038D93012&ext=ppt (accessed 21 September 2010).

Lloyd, A. (1995) *Doubly Deviant, Doubly Damned. Society's Treatment of Violent Women*. London: Penguin Books.

Lloyd, M. (2008) 'Close Supervision Centres', in Y. Jewkes, and J. Bennett (eds) *Dictionary of Prisons and Punishment*. Cullompton: Willan Publishing.

Lockhart, L. L., Saunders, B. E. and Cleveland, P. (1989) 'Adult Male Sexual Offenders: An Overview of Treatment Techniques' in J. S. Wodarski and D. L. Whitaker (eds) *Treatment of Sex Offenders in Social Work and Mental Health Settings*. Philadelphia: Haworth Press.

Long, A. (2009) 'Sex Offender Laws of the United Kingdom and the United States: Flawed Systems and Needed Reforms', *Transnational Law & Contemporary Problems*, 18: 145–68.

Losel, F. and Schmucker, M. (2005) 'The Effectiveness of Treatment for Sexual Offenders: A Comprehensive Meta-Analysis', *Journal of Experimental Criminology*, 1: 117–46.

Madoc-Jones, I. and Roscoe, K. (2010) 'Women's Safety Service within the Integrated Domestic Abuse Programme: Perceptions of Service Users', *Child & Family Social Work*, 15: 155–64.

Madsen, L., Parsons, S. and Grubin, D. (2004) 'A Preliminary Study of the Contribution of Periodic Polygraph Testing to the Treatment and Supervision of Sex Offenders', *The Journal of Forensic Psychiatry & Psychology*, 15(4): 682–95.

Maguire, M. and Kemshall, H. (2003) 'Sex Offenders, Risk Penality and the Problem of Disclosure to the Community', in A. Matravers (ed.) *Sex Offenders in the Community. Managing and Reducing the Risks*. Cullompton: Willan Publishing.

Maguire, M., Kemshall, H., Noaks, L., Wincup, E. and Sharpe, K. (2001) 'Risk Management of Sexual and Violent Offenders: The Work of Public Protection Panels', Police Research Series Paper 139. London: Home Office.

Maletzky, B. M. and Field, G. (2003) 'The Biological Treatment of Dangerous Sexual Offenders: A Review and Preliminary Report of the Oregon Pilot Depo-Provera Program', *Aggression and Violent Behavior*, 8: 391–412.

Mandeville-Norden, R. and Beech, A. (2006) 'Risk Assessment of Sex Offenders: The Current Position in the UK', *Child Abuse Review*, 15: 257–72.

Mann, R. (2009) Personal Communication received 10 December 2009.

Mann, R. and Attrill, G. (2006) 'Assessing, Reducing and Managing Risk in HM Prison Service', paper at *RMA Conference: Towards Effective Risk Management*, 19 May 2006. Available at: www.rmascotland.gov.uk/ViewFile.aspx?id=162 (accessed 15 May 2010).

Mann, R. and Fernandez, Y. (2006) 'Sex Offender Programmes: Concept, Theory, and Practice', in C. Hollin and E. Palmer (eds) *Offending Behaviour Programmes. Development, Application and Controversies*. Chichester: J. Wiley & Sons.

Marshall, P. (1997) 'A Reconviction Study of HMP Grendon Therapeutic Community', Home Office Research Findings No. 53. London: Home Office.

Marshall, P. (1999) 'Restorative Justice: An Overview', A Report by the Home Office Research Development and Statistics Directorate. London: HMSO.

Marshall, W. L. (2008) 'Reducing Risk for Reoffending', paper presented at the *10th International IATSO Conference*, Cape Town, South Africa, 27 August 2008.

Marshall, W. L. and Barbaree, H. E. (1990) 'An Integrated Theory of the Etiology of Sexual Offending', in W. L. Marshall, D. R. Laws and H. E. Barbaree (eds) *Handbook of Sexual Assault: Issues, Theories, and the Treatment of the Offender*. New York: Plenum.

Marshall, W. L. and Laws, D. R. (2003) 'A Brief History of Behavioral and Cognitive Behavioral Approaches to Sexual Offender Treatment: Part 2. The Modern Era', *Sexual Abuse: A Journal of Research and Treatment*, 15(2): 93–120.

Marshall, W. L. and Serran, G. A. (2000) 'Improving the Effectiveness of Sexual Offender Treatment', *Trauma, Violence and Abuse*, 1(3): 203–22.

Marshall, W. L., Anderson, D. and Fernandez, Y. (1999) *Cognitive Behavioural Treatment of Sex Offenders*. Chichester: J. Wiley & Sons.

Marshall, W. L., Barbaree, H. E. and Fernandez Y. (1995) 'Some Aspects of Social Competence in Sexual Offenders', *Sexual Abuse: A Journal of Research and Treatment*, 7: 113–27.

Marshall, W. L., O'Sullivan, C. and Fernandez, Y. (1996) 'The Enhancement of Victim Empathy among Incarcerated Child Molesters', *Legal and Criminological Psychology*, 1: 95–102.

Matravers, A. (2008) 'Understanding Women who Commit Sex Offences', in G. Letherby, K. Williams, P. Birch and M. Cain (eds) *Sex as Crime?* Cullompton: Willan Publishing.

Matthews, R. (2009) *Doing Time. An Introduction to the Sociology of Imprisonment* (2nd edn). Basingstoke: Palgrave Macmillan.

Matthews, R., Matthews, J. A. and Speltz, K. (1989) *Female Sexual Offenders: An Exploratory Study*. Orwell, VT: Safer Society Press.

May, C. (1999) 'Explaining Reconviction Following a Community Sentence: The Role of Social Factors', Home Office Research Study 192. London: Home Office.

McAlinden, A-M. (2001) 'Indeterminate Sentences for the Severely Personality Disordered', *Crim. L. R.*, Feb: 108–23.

McAlinden, A-M. (2007) *The Shaming of Sexual Offenders. Risk, Retribution and Reintegration*. Oxford: Hart.

McDiarmid, C. (2000) 'Children who Murder: What is Her Majesty's Pleasure?', *Crim L.R.*, July: 547–63.

McGuire, J. (2007) 'Programmes for Probationers', in G. McIvor and P. Raynor (eds) *Developments in Social Work with Offenders*. London: Jessica Kingsley Publishers.

McLaughlin, E., Fergusson, R., Hughes, G. and Westmarland, L. (eds) (2004) *Restorative Justice: Critical Issues*. London: Sage Publications.

Medlicott, D. (2007) 'Women in Prison', in Y. Jewkes (ed.) *Handbook on Prisons*. Cullompton: Willan Publishing.

Megargee, E. I. (1976) 'The Prediction of Dangerous Behaviour', *Criminal Justice and Behaviour*, 3: 3–22.

Menzies, R., Webster, C. D., McMain, S., Staley, S. and Scaglione, R. (1994) 'The Dimensions of Dangerousness Revisited: Assessing Forensic Predictions about Violence', *Law and Human Behaviour*, 18: 1–28.

Mercer, R., Brooks, M. and Bryan, P. T. (2000) 'Global Positioning Satellite System: Tracking Offenders in Real Time', *Corrections Today*, July: 77–80.

Mersey Care NHS Trust (2010a) *The Formation of Ashworth Hospital*. Available at: www.merseycare.nhs.uk/services/clinical/high_secure/Formation_Ashworth.asp (accessed 21 September 2010).

Mersey Care NHS Trust (2010b) *The High Secure Service – Ashworth Hospital*. Available at: www.merseycare.nhs.uk/services/clinical/high_secure/Ashworth_Hospital.asp (accessed 21 September 2010).

Mersey Care NHS Trust (2010c) *Rehabilitation Service*. Available at: www.merseycare.nhs.uk/services/clinical/high_secure/Rehabilitation_Services.asp (accessed 21 September 2010).

Middleton, D., Mandeville-Norden, R. and Hayes, E. (2009) 'Does Treatment Work with Internet Sex Offenders? Emerging Findings from the Internet Sex Offender Treatment Programme (i-SOTP)', *Journal of Sexual Aggression*, 15(1): 5–19.

Miller, R. D. (1998) 'Forced Administration of Sex-Drive Reducing Medications to Sex Offenders: Treatment or Punishment?', *Psychology, Public Policy and Law*, 4(1/2): 175–99.

Mind (2010a) *Statistics 8: The Criminal Justice System*. Available at: www.mind.org.uk/help/rights_and_legislation/statistics_8_the_criminal_justice_system (accessed 17 August 2010).

Mind (2010b) *Dangerousness and Mental Health: The Facts*. Available at: www.mind.org.uk/help/research_and_policy/dangerousness_and_mental_health_the_facts (accessed 17 August 2010).

Mind (2010c) *Briefing 2: Supervised Community Treatment*. Available at: www.mind.org.uk/help/rights_and_legislation/briefing_2_supervised_community_treatment (accessed 21 September 2010).

Ministry of Justice (2007) *Publication of Reports on the Management of Serious Offenders*. Available at: www.justice.gov.uk/news/newsrelease221007a.htm (accessed 15 May 2010).

Ministry of Justice (2008a) *Consultation – Rules for Mandatory Polygraphy for Sex Offenders*, London: Ministry of Justice.

Ministry of Justice (2008b) 'The Governments' Response to the Report by Peter Smallbridge and Andrew Williamson of a Review of the Use of Restraint in Juvenile Secure Settings', Cm. 7501. London: Ministry of Justice.

Ministry of Justice (2009a) *Offender Management Caseload Statistics 2008*. London: Ministry of Justice.

Ministry of Justice (2009b) 'The Future of the Parole Board', Consultation paper 14/09. London: Ministry of Justice.

Ministry of Justice (2009c) *Rules for Mandatory Polygraphy for Sex Offenders. Response to Consultation*. London: Ministry of Justice.

Ministry of Justice (2009d) *A Report on the Government's Strategy for Diverting Women Away from Crime*. London: Ministry of Justice.

Ministry of Justice (2009e) *The Correctional Services Accreditation Panel Report 2008–2009*. London: Ministry of Justice.

Ministry of Justice (2009f) *Jack Straw Launches First Mental Health Courts*. Available at: www.justice.gov.uk/news/newsrelease020709a.htm (accessed 15 September 2009).

Ministry of Justice (2010a) *Offender Management Caseload Statistics 2009*. London: Ministry of Justice.

Ministry of Justice (2010b) *'Parole Board Members Appointed', Ministry of Justice News Release*, 28 July 2010. Available at: www.justice.gov.uk/news/newsrelease280710a.htm?utm_source=feedburner&utm_medium=email&utm_campaign=Feed%3A+gov%2FWfFX+%28Latest+news+-+Ministry+of+Justice%29 (accessed 28 July 2010).

Ministry of Justice (2010c) *National Statistics for Multi-Agency Public Protection Arrangements Annual Reports 08/09*. Available at: www.justice.gov.uk/news/docs/mappa-figures-2009.pdf (accessed 6 May 2010).

Ministry of Justice (2010d) 'Multi-Agency Public Protection Arrangements Annual Report 2009/10', Ministry of Justice Statistic Bulletin. London: Ministry of Justice.

Ministry of Justice (2010e) *About Us*. Available at: www.justice.gov.uk/about.htm (accessed 12 July 2010).

Ministry of Justice (2010f) *Mental Health Courts Featured on Radio 4*. Available at: www.justice.gov.uk/news/announcement230910c.htm?utm_source=feedburner&utm_medium=email&utm_campaign=Feed%3A+gov%2FWfFX+%28Ministry+of+Justice+latest+news+alerts%29 (accessed 27 September 2010).

Ministry of Justice (2010g) *Physical Control in Care Training Manual*. London: Ministry of Justice.

Ministry of Justice (2010h) 'Offender Management Caseload Statistics 2009', Ministry of Justice Statistics Bulletin. London: Ministry of Justice.

Ministry of Justice, Department of Health (2008) *Forensic Personality Disorder Medium Secure and Community Pilot Services. Planning & Delivery Guide*. London: Department of Health and Ministry of Justice.

Monahan, J. (1981) 'Predicting Violent Behaviour. An Assessment of Clinical Techniques' (Volume 114), Sage Library of Social Research. London: Sage.

Morris, A. and Gelsthorpe, L. (2000) 'Re-Visioning Men's Violence against Female Partners', *Howard Journal*, 39(4) 412–28.

Morris, G. H. (1999a) 'Defining Dangerousness: Risking a Dangerous Definition', *Journal of Contemporary Legal Issues*, 10: 61–102.

Morris, M. (1999b) 'Introducing HMP Grendon: A Therapeutic Community Prison', *IAFP Newsletter 3*. Available at: www.psyctc.org/iafp/nl_3_1/grendon.html (accessed 23 September 2010).

Morris, M. (2006) 'The UK Prison Service Close Supervision Centres', in D. Jones (ed.) *Humane Prisons*. Abingdon: Radcliffe Publishing.

Myers, S. (2001) 'The Registration of Children and Young People Under the Sex Offenders Act (1997): Time for a Change?', *Youth Justice*, 1: 40–8.

NACRO (2005) 'Dangerousness and the Criminal Justice Act 2003', Youth Crime Briefing. London: NACRO.

Nash, M. (1992) 'Dangerousness Revisited', *International Journal of the Sociology of Law*, 20: 337–49.

Nash, M. (2006) *Public Protection and the Criminal Justice Process*. Oxford: Oxford University Press.

National Offender Management Service (2007a) 'Assessment and Management of Sex Offenders', Probation Circular 17/07. London: NOMS.

National Offender Management Service (2007b) 'Medical Treatment for Sex Offenders', Probation Circular 35/2007. London: NOMS.

National Offender Management Service (2009) *MAPPA Guidance 2009*. London: NOMS.

National Policing Improvement Agency (2009) *Business Plan 2009/10*. London: Home Office.

National Policing Improvement Agency (2010) *Dangerous Persons Database – ViSOR*. Available at www.npia.police.uk/en/10510.htm (accessed 12 May 2010).

National Probation Service (2002) *The Treatment and Risk Management of Sexual Offenders in Custody and in the Community*. London: Home Office.

National Probation Service (2003) 'Pilot Project Working With High Risk Male Sex Offenders', Probation Circular 31/2005. London: Home Office.

National Probation Service (2004) 'Piloting of Satellite Tracking Technology', National Probation Service Briefing, Issue 21. London: Home Office.

National Probation Service (2005a) 'Launch of New Internet Sex Offender Treatment Programme (i-SOTP)', Probation Circular 92/2005. London: National Probation Service.

National Probation Service (2005b) 'Public Protection: Cognitive Self-Change Programme', Probation Circular 36/2005. London: National Probation Service.

National Probation Service (2005c) 'Dangerous and Severe Personality Disorder (DSPD) Programme', Probation Circular 40/2005. London: National Probation Service.

National Probation Service (2006) 'Implementation Plans for Internet Sex Offender Treatment programme (i-SOTP)', Probation Circular 18/2006. London: National Probation Service.

National Probation Service (2010) *Community Sex Offender Groupwork Programme. A National Treatment Programme for Sex Offenders*. West Mercia: National Probation Service. Available at: www.westmerciaprobation.org.uk/publications/leaflets/SexOffendSentencers.pdf (accessed 1 June 2010).

National Probation Service – South West (2010) *Integrated Domestic Abuse Programme (IDAP)*. Available at: www.probationsouthwest.org.uk/Main/sd10idap.asp (accessed 1 June 2010).

Nee, C. (1999) 'Surviving Electronic Monitoring in England and Wales: Lessons Learnt from the First Trials', *Legal and Criminological Psychology*, 4(1): 33–43.

Nellis, M. (2005a) 'Out of this World: The Advent of the Satellite Tracking of Offenders in England and Wales', *Howard Journal*, 44(2): 125–50.

Nellis, M. (2005b) 'Electronic Monitoring, Satellite Tracking, and the New Punitiveness in England and Wales', in J. Pratt, D. Brown, M. Brown, S. Hallsworth, and W. Morrison (eds) *The New Punitiveness. Trends, Theories, Perspectives*. Cullompton: Willan Publishing.

Nellis, M. (2007) 'Tracking Offenders by Satellite – Progress or Cost-Cutting?', *Criminal Justice Matters*, 68(1): 10–11.

Nellis, M. (2009) 'Circles of Support and Accountability for Sex Offenders in England and Wales: Their Origins and Implementation between 1999–2005', *British Journal of Community Justice*, 7: 23–44.

Newton, M, (1971) 'Reconviction after Treatment at Grendon', CP Report Series B, No. 1, Prison Department. London: Home Office.

Nichols, C. and Stewart, C. (2008) 'Female Sexual Offending', *Prison Service Journal*, 178: 50–5.

Northamptonshire Probation Trust (2010) *Controlling Anger and Learning to Manage It (CALM). Information for Sentencers*. Available at: www.northants-probation.org.uk/prog_calm.htm (accessed 7 June 2010).

Nottinghamshire Healthcare NHS Trust (2010a) *Rampton Hospital*. Available at: www.nottinghamshirehealthcare.nhs.uk/our-services/forensic-services/rampton-hospital (accessed 21 September 2010).

Nottinghamshire Healthcare NHS Trust (2010b) *Mental Health Directorate*. Available at: www.nottinghamshirehealthcare.nhs.uk/our-services/forensic-services/rampton-hospital/mental-health-directorate (accessed 21 September 2010).

Nottinghamshire Healthcare NHS Trust (2010c) *National High Secure Healthcare Service for Women*. Available at: www.nottinghamshirehealthcare.nhs.uk/our-services/forensic-services/rampton-hospital/womens-directorate (accessed 21 September 2010).

Ogloff, J. R. P. and Davis, M. R. (2004) 'Advances in Offender Assessment and Rehabilitation: Contributions of the Risk–Needs–Responsivity Approach', *Psychology, Crime & Law*, 10: 229–42.

O'Hare, G., McAuley, W., Owens, V. and Reade, A. (2008) 'Dynamic Risk Assessment', paper presented at the *NOTA Conference*, 13 March 2008.

Onyejeli, M. (2010) Personal communication received 21 July 2010.

Orbis Partners (2009) *CALM - Controlling Anger and Learning to Manage It: A Group Program for Male Offenders*. Available at: www.orbispartners.com/wp-content/uploads/2009/02/CALM-program-description-2009.pdf (accessed 7 June 2010).

Ortmann, J. (1980) 'The Treatment of Sexual Offenders: Castration and Anti-Hormone Therapy', *International Journal of Law and Psychiatry*, 3: 443–51.

Oxford English Dictionary (2009a) *Dangerous*. Available at: http://dictionary.oed.com/cgi/entry/50057489?query_type=word&queryword=dangerous&first=1&max_to_show=10&single=1&sort_type=alpha (accessed on 4 March 2009).

Oxford English Dictionary (2009b) *Danger*. Available at: http://dictionary.oed.com/cgi/entry/50057485?query_type=word&queryword=dangerous&first=1&max_to_show=10&single=1&sort_type=alpha (accessed 4 March 2009).

Oxford English Dictionary (2009c) *Chav*. Available at: http://dictionary.oed.com/cgi/entry/20002434?single=1&query_type=word&queryword=chav&first=1&max_to_show=10 (accessed 1 June 2009).

Padfield, N. (2008) *Text and Materials on the Criminal Justice Process*. Oxford: Oxford University Press.

Padfield, N. (2009) 'Parole and Early Release: The Criminal Justice and Immigration Act 2008 Changes in Context', *Crim L.R.*, 3: 166–87.

Pakes, F., Winstone, J., Haskins, J. and Guest, J. (2010) 'Mental Health Court Pilot: Feasibility of an Impact Evaluation', Research Summary 7/10. London: Ministry of Justice.

Parole Board (2010a) *About the Parole Board*. Available at: www.paroleboard.gov.uk/about/http://www.paroleboard.gov.uk/about (accessed 11 May 2010).

Parole Board (2010b) *Management Board Briefing*. Available at: www.paroleboard.gov.uk/about/http://www.paroleboard.gov.uk/about/ (accessed 11 May 2010).

Peay, J. (2007) 'Mentally Disordered Offenders, Mental Health, and Crime', in M. Maguire, R. Morgan and R. Reiner (eds) *The Oxford Handbook of Criminology* (4th edn). Oxford: Oxford University Press.

Pemberton, C. (2009) 'Wetherby YOI and its Keppel Unit are Changing Perceptions of Prison', *communitycare.co.uk*, 9 December 2009. Available at: www.communitycare.co.uk/Articles/2009/12/09/113369/Wetherby-YOI-and-its-Keppel-Unit-are-changing-perceptions-of.htm (accessed 14 November 2010).

Penrose, J. (2009) 'Britain's 35 Serial Killers Who Will Never Be Released from Jail', *The Sunday Mirror*, 15 February 2009.

Plotnikoff, J. and Woolfson, R. (2000) 'Where Are They Now? An Evaluation of Sex Offender Registration in England and Wales', Police Research Series Paper 126. London: Home Office.

Polasckek, D. (2006) 'Violent Offender Programmes: Concept, Theory, and Practice', in C. Hollin and E. Palmer (eds) *Offending Behaviour Programmes. Development, Application and Controversies*. Chichester: J. Wiley & Sons.

Pollock, N., McBain, I. and Webster, C. D. (1989) 'Clinical Decision Making the Assessment of Dangerousness', in K. Howells and C. R. Hollin (eds) *Clinical Approaches to Violence*. Chichester: J. Wiley & Sons.

Powis, B. (2002) 'Offenders' Risk of Serious Harm: A Literature Review', Home Office RDS Occasional Paper 81. London: Home Office.

Pratt, J. (1996a) 'Governing the Dangerous: An Historical Overview of Dangerous Offender Legislation', *Social & Legal Studies*, 5: 21–36.

Pratt, J. (1996b) 'Reflections on Recent Trends towards the Punishment of Persistence', *Crime, Law & Social Change*, 25: 243–64.

Pratt, J. (1997) *Governing the Dangerous: Dangerousness, Law and Social Change*. Sydney: Federation Press.

Pratt, J. (2000) 'Dangerousness and Modern Society', in M. Brown and J. Pratt (eds) *Dangerous Offenders: Punishment and Social Order*. London: Routledge.

Prentky, R. A. (1997) 'Arousal Reduction in Sexual Offenders. A Review of Antiandrogen Interventions', *Sexual Abuse: A Journal of Research and Treatment*, 9(4): 335–47.

Prentky, R. A., Harris, B., Frizzell, K. and Righthand, S. (2000) 'An Actuarial Procedure for Assessing Risk with Juvenile Sex Offenders', *Sexual Abuse: A Journal of Research and Treatment*, 12: 71–93.

Prison Service News (2006) 'CALM after the Storm', *Prison Service News*, 245. Available at: www.hmprisonservice.gov.uk/prisoninformation/prisonservicemagazine/index.asp?id=5237,18,3,18,0,0 (accessed 1 June 2010).

Quinsey, V. L., Rice, M. E. and Harris, G. T. (1995) 'Actuarial Prediction of Sexual Recidivism', *Journal of Interpersonal Violence*, 10: 85–105.

Radzinowicz, L. (1939) 'The Persistent Offender', *The Cambridge Law Journal*, 7: 68–79.

Radzinowicz, L. (1966) *Ideology and Crime. A Study of Crime in its Social and Historical Context*. London: Heinemann Educational Books.

Radzinowicz, L. and Hood, R. (1980) 'Incapacitating the Habitual Criminal: The English Experience', *Michigan Law Review*, 78, 1305–89.

Rainey, B. (2010) 'Dignity and Dangerousness: Sex Offenders and the Community – Human Rights in the Balance?' in K. Harrison (ed.) *Managing High-Risk Sex Offenders in the Community. Risk Management, Treatment and Social Responsibility*. Cullompton: Willan Publishing.

Rennie, Y. (1978) *The Search for Criminal Man. The Dangerous Offender Project*. Lexington: Lexington Books.

Rieber, I. and Sigusch, V. (1979) 'Psychosurgery on Sex Offenders and Sexual "Deviants" in West Germany', *Archives of Sexual Behavior*, 8(6): 523–7.

Roberts, J. and Hough, M. (2005) *Understanding Public Attitudes to Criminal Justice*. Maidenhead: Open University Press.

Robinson, G. (1999) 'Risk Management and Rehabilitation in the Probation Service: Collision and Collusion', *Howard Journal*, 38(4): 421–33.

Roe, S., Coleman, K. and Kazia, P. (2009) 'Violent and Sexual Crime', in A. Walker, J. Flatley, C. Kershaw and D. Moon (eds) *Crime in England and Wales 2008/2009*, Home Office Statistical Bulletin. London: Home Office.

Rose, N. (1992) 'Governing the Enterprising Self', in P. Heelas and P. Morris (eds) *The Values of the Enterprise Culture*. London: Routledge.

Rose, N. (2007) *Psychology as a Social Science*. Available at: www.lse.ac.uk/collections/socialPsychology/pdf/Psychology%20as%20a%20Social%20Science%20-%20LSE%20-%20February%2007.pdf (accessed 3 December 2009).

Rubin, D. (1972) 'Predictions of Dangerousness in Mentally Ill Criminals', *Archives of General Psychiatry*, 27: 397–407.

Russell, S. (1997) 'Castration of Repeat Sexual Offenders: An International Comparative Analysis', *Houston Journal of International Law*, 19: 425–59.

Rutherford, A. (2006) 'Dangerous People: Beginnings of a New Labour Proposal', in T. Newburn and P. Rock (eds) *The Politics of Crime Control. Essays in Honour of David Downes*. Oxford: Oxford University Press.

Sainsbury Centre for Mental Health (2008) *In the Dark. The Mental Health Implications of Imprisonment for Public Protection*. London: Sainsbury Centre for Mental Health.

Saleh, F. M., Niel, T. and Fishman, M. J. (2004) 'Treatment of Paraphilia in Young Adults with Leuprolide Acetate: A Preliminary Case Report Series', *J. Forensic Sci.*, 49(6): 1343–8.

Sandler, J. and Freeman, N. (2007) 'Typology of Female Sex Offenders: A Test of Vandiver and Kercher', *Sex Abuse*, 19: 73–89.

Sano, K. and Mayanagi, Y. (1988) 'Posteromedial Hypothalamotomy in the Treatment of Violent, Aggressive Behaviour', *Acta Neurochir Suppl (Wien)*, 44: 145–51.

Saradjian, J. (2010) 'Understanding the Prevalence of Female-Perpetrated Sexual Abuse and the Impact of that Abuse on Victims', in T. Gannon and F. Cortoni (eds) *Female Sexual Offenders. Theory, Assessment and Treatment.* Chichester: Wiley-Blackwell.

Saradjian, J., Murphy, N. and Casey, H. (2010) 'Report on the First Cohort of Prisoners that Completed Treatment in the Fens Unit, Dangerous and Severe Personality Disorder Unit at HMP Whitemoor', *Prison Service Journal*, 192: 45–54.

Sarbin, T. R. (1967) 'The Dangerous Individual: An Outcome of Social Identity Transformations', *British Journal of Criminology*, 7(3): 285–95.

Saunders, R. (2004) 'Havens in a Hostile World', *Safer Society*, Autumn: 22.

Savidge, K. (2005a) 'Care in the Community', Prison Service News, 236. Available at: www.hmprisonservice.gov.uk/prisoninformation/prisonservicemagazine/index.asp?id=3274,18,3,18,0,0 (accessed 28 July 2010).

Savidge, K. (2005b) 'All-Staff Approach Key to New Psychopathy Programme', Prison Service News, 240. Available at: www.hmprisonservice.gov.uk/prisoninformation/prisonservicemagazine/index.asp?print=1&id=4302,18,3,18,0,0 (accessed 21 September 2010).

Scharff Smith, P. (2006) 'The Effects of Solitary Confinement on Prison Inmates: A Brief History and Review of the Literature, *Crime and Justice*, 34: 441–528.

Schladale, J. (2010) 'Enhancing Community Collaboration to Stop Sexual Harm by Youth', in K. Harrison (ed.) *Managing High-Risk Sex Offenders in the Community. Risk Management, Treatment and Social Responsibility*. Cullompton: Willan Publishing.

Scott, P. D. (1977) 'Assessing Dangerousness in Criminals', *British Journal of Psychiatry*, 131: 127–42.

Scottish Council on Crime (1975) *Crime and Prevention of Crime: A Memorandum by the Scottish Council on Crime*. Edinburgh: HMSO.

Sentencing Guidelines Council (2008) *Dangerous Offenders. Guide for Sentencers and Practitioners*. London: Sentencing Guidelines Council.

Sentencing Guidelines Council (2009) *Overarching Principles – Sentencing Youths*. London: Sentencing Guidelines Council.

Seymour, L. and Rutherford, M. (2008) *The Community Order and the Mental Health Treatment Requirement*. London: The Sainsbury Centre for Mental Health.

Shapland, J., Atkinson, A., Atkinson, H., Chapman, B., Colledge, E., Dignan, J., Howes, M., Johnstone, J., Robinson, G. and Sorsby, A. (2006) 'Restorative Justice in Practice – Findings from the Second Phase of the Evaluation of Three Schemes', Home Office Findings 274, London: Home Office.

Shapland, J., Atkinson, A., Atkinson, H., Chapman, B., Dignan, J., Howes, M., Johnstone, J., Robinson, G. and Sorsby, A. (2007) 'Restorative Justice: The Views of Victims. The Third Report from the Evaluation of Three Schemes', Ministry of Justice Research Series 3/07. London: Ministry of Justice.

Shapland, J., Atkinson, A., Atkinson, H., Dignan, J., Edwards, L., Hibbert, J., Howes, M., Johnstone, J., Robinson, G. and Sorsby, A. (2008) 'Does Restorative Justice Affect Reconviction? The Fourth Report from the Evaluation of Three Schemes', Ministry of Justice Research Series 10/08. London: Ministry of Justice.

Shapland, J., Atkinson, A., Colledge, E., Dignan, J., Howes, M., Johnstone, J., Pennant, R., Robinson, G. and Sorsby, A. (2004) 'Implementing Restorative Justice Schemes (Crime Reduction Programme) A Report on the First Year', Home Office Online Report 32/04. Available at: www.homeoffice.gov.uk/rds/pdfs04/rdsolr3204.pdf (accessed 14 June 2010).

Shaw, S. H. (1973) 'The Dangerousness of Dangerousness', *Medicine, Science, and the Law*, 13(4): 269–71.

Sheldon, K. and Krishnan, G. (2009) 'The Clinical and Risk Characteristics of Patients Admitted to a Secure Hospital-Based Dangerous and Severe Personality Disorder Unit', *British Journal of Forensic Practice*, 11(3): 19–27.

Sheldon, K., Howells, K. and Patel, G. (2010) 'An Empirical Evaluation of Reasons for Non-Completion of Treatment in a Dangerous and Severe Personality Disorder Unit', *Criminal Behaviour and Mental Health*, 20: 129–43.

Sherman, L. (2000) 'Domestic Violence and Restorative Justice: Answering Key Questions', *Virginia Journal of Social Policy & the Law*, 8(1): 263–89.

Shine, J. and Newton, M. (2000) 'Damaged, Disturbed and Dangerous: A Profile of Receptions to Grendon Therapeutic Prison, 1995–2000', in J. Shine (ed.) *A Compilation of Grendon Research*. Leyhill: PES.

Shute, S. (2004) 'The Sexual Offences Act 2003: (4) New Civil Preventative Orders – Sexual Offences Prevention Orders; Foreign Travel Orders; Risk of Sexual Harm Orders', *Crim L.R.*, Jun: 417–40.

Shute, S. (2007) 'Satellite Tracking of Offenders: A Study of the Pilots in England and Wales', Ministry of Justice Research Summary 4. London: Ministry of Justice.

Silverman, J. and Wilson, D. (2002) *Innocence Betrayed: Paedophilia, The Media and Society*. Cambridge: Polity.

Sim, J. (1990) *Medical Power in Prisons: The Prison Medical Service in England 1774–1989*. Buckingham: Open University Press.

Simon, J. (1998) 'Managing the Monstrous: Sex Offenders and the New Penology', *Psychology, Public Policy and Law*, 4(1/2): 452–67.

Smallbridge, P. and Williamson, A. (2008) *Independent Review of Restraint on Juvenile Secure Settings*. London: Ministry of Justice and Department for Children, Schools and Families.

Smartt, U. (2001) *Grendon Tales*. Hook: Waterside Press.

Solomon, E. (2008) 'Life-Sentenced Prisoners', in Y. Jewkes, and J. Bennett (eds) *Dictionary of Prisons and Punishment*. Cullompton: Willan Publishing.

Sony Pictures Television (1998) *Dawson's Creek. The Complete First Season*. Sony Pictures Television.

Steen, C. (2010) 'Female Sex Offenders', paper given at the *11th IATSO Conference*, Oslo, Norway 1–4 September 2010.

Stewart, C. and Parker, M. (2006) 'Send: The Women's Democratic Therapeutic Community in Prison', in M. Parker (ed.) *Dynamic Security. The Democratic Therapeutic Community in Prison*. London: Jessica Kingsley Publishers.

Sutton, A. (2000) 'Drugs and Dangerousness – Perception and Management of Risk in the Neo-Liberal Era', in M. Brown and J. Pratt (eds) *Dangerous Offenders: Punishment and Social Order*. London: Routledge.

Taylor, M. (2008) *Family Group Conferences and Restorative Practices. Working Together to Address Domestic Violence*. Available at: www.restorativejustice.org.uk/.../RJ%20Conf%20London%20Oct%2008%20RJ%20and%20FGCs.ppt (accessed 14 June 2010).

Taylor, R. (2000) 'A Seven-Year Reconviction Study of HMP Grendon Therapeutic Community', Home Office Research Findings No. 115. London: Home Office.

Taylor, R. (2003) 'An Assessment of Violent Incident Rates in the Dangerous Severe Personality Disorder Unit at HMP Whitemoor', Home Office Research Findings No. 210. London: Home Office.

This is Bristol (2009) *Bristol Dad Speaks out after Alleged Sex Attack on Son*. Available at: www.thisisbristol.co.uk/news/Bristol-dad-speaks-alleged-sex-attack-son/article-1341614-detail/article.html (accessed 4 November 2010).

Thomas, D. (2008a) 'IPP amended', *Arch. News*, 5: 7–9.

Thomas, T. (2001) 'Sex Offenders, the Home Office and the Sunday Papers', *Journal of Social Welfare and Family Law*, 23(1): 103–8.

Thomas, T. (2003) 'Sex Offender Community Notification: Experiences from America', *Howard Journal*, 42(3): 217–28.

Thomas, T. (2005) *Sex Crime. Sex Offending and Society* (2nd edn). Cullompton: Willan Publishing.

Thomas, T. (2008b) 'The Sex Offender Register. A Measure of Public Protection or a Punishment in its own Right?', *British Journal of Criminology*, 8: 85–96.

Thomas, T. (2009) 'Children and Young People on the UK Sex Offender Register', *International Journal of Children's Rights*, 17: 491–500.

Thomas, T. (2010) 'The Sex Offender Register, Community Notification and some Reflections on Privacy' in K. Harrison (ed.) *Managing High-Risk Sex Offenders in the Community. Risk Management, Treatment and Social Responsibility*. Cullompton: Willan Publishing.

Thompson, J. (2007) 'Dangerousness', in R. Canton and D. Hancock (eds) *Dictionary of Probation and Offender Management*. Cullompton: Willan Publishing.

Thornton, D. (2002) 'Constructing and Testing a Framework for Dynamic Risk Assessment', *Sexual Abuse: A Journal of Research and Treatment*, 14(2): 139–53.

Thornton, D. (2007) *Scoring Guide for Risk Matrix 2000.9/SVC*. Available at: www.cfcp.bham.ac.uk/Extras/SCORING%20GUIDE%20FOR%20RISK%20MATRIX%202000.9-%20SVC%20-%20(ver.%20Feb%202007).pdf (accessed 6 January 2010).

Thornton, D., Beech, A. and Marshall, W. L. (2004) 'Pre-Treatment Self-Esteem and Post-Treatment Sexual Recidivism', *International Journal of Offender Therapy and Comparative Criminology*, 48: 587–99.

Thornton, D., Mann, R., Webster, S., Blud, L., Travers, R. and Friendship, C. (2003) 'Distinguishing and Combining Risks for Sexual and Violent Recidivism', *Annals of the New York Academy of Sciences*, 89: 225–35.

Tonry, M. (2004) *Punishment and Politics: Evidence and Emulation in the Making of English Crime Control Policy*. Cullompton: Willan Publishing.

Towl, G. and Crighton, D. (1997) 'Risk Assessment with Offenders', *International Review of Psychiatry*, 9: 187–93.

Tribunals Service Mental Health (2010a) *About us. What does the First-Tier Tribunal (Mental Health) Do?* Available at: www.mhrt.org.uk/AboutUs/aboutUs.htm (accessed 11 August 2010).

Tribunals Service Mental Health (2010b) *About us. Roles of the Tribunal Members*. Available at: www.mhrt.org.uk/AboutUs/membersRoles.htm (accessed 11 August 2010).

Turner, K. (2010) Personal communication received 4 March 2010.

Tyrer, P., Duggan, C., Cooper, S., Crawford, M., Seivewright, H., Rutter, D., Maden, T., Byford, S. and Barrett, B. (2010) 'The Successes and Failures of the DSPD Experiment: The Assessment and Management of Severe Personality Disorder', *Medicine, Science and the Law*, 50: 95–9.

Ullrich, S., Yang, M. and Coid, J. (2010) 'Dangerous and Severe Personality Disorder: An Investigation of the Construct', *International Journal of Law and Psychiatry*, 33: 84–8.

UN Committee on the Rights of the Child (2008) *Consideration of Reports Submitted by States Parties under Article 44 of the Convention: Convention on the Rights of the Child: Concluding Observations: United Kingdom of Great Britain and Northern Ireland*. Available at: www.unhcr.org/refworld/docid/4906d1d72.html (accessed 11 November 2010).

Urbas, G. (2000) 'The Age of Criminal Responsibility', *Trends and Issues in Crime and Criminal Justice*, 181. Canberra: Australian Institute of Criminology.

van Dine, S., Dinitz, S. and Conrad, J. (1977) 'The Incapacitation of the Dangerous Offender: A Statistical Experiment', *Journal of Research in Crime and Delinquency*, 22–34.

Vandiver, D. and Kercher G. (2004) 'Offender and Victim Characteristics of Registered Female Sexual Offenders in Texas: A Proposed Typology of Female Sexual Offenders', *Sexual Abuse: A Journal of Research and Treatment*, 16(2) 121–37.

Viki, G., Massey, K and Masser, B. (2005) 'When Chivalry Backfires: Benevolent Sexism and Attitudes towards Myra Hindley', *Legal and Criminological Psychology*, 10: 109–20.

von Hirsch, A. (1976) *Doing Justice: The Choice of Punishments*. New York: Hill & Wong.

von Hirsch A. (2001) 'Proportionate Sentences for Juveniles. How Different than for Adults', *Punishment & Society*, 3: 221–36.

von Hirsch, A., Bottoms, A., Burney, E. and Wikstrom, P-O. (2000) *Criminal Deterrence and Sentence Severity. An Analysis of Recent Research*. Oxford: Hart Publishing.

Walls, S-A. (2010) Personal communication received 16 March 2010.

Walker, A., Flatley, J., Kershaw, C. and Moon, D. (2009) 'Crime in England and Wales 2008/09', Home Office Statistical Bulletin. London: Home Office.

Walker, N. (1982) 'Unscientific, Unwise, Unprofitable or Unjust? The Anti-Protectionist Arguments', *British Journal of Criminology*, 22(3): 276–84.

Walker, N. (1996) *Dangerous People*. London: Blackstone Press.

Walker, S. and Worrall, A. (2000) 'Life as a Woman: The Gendered Pains of Indeterminate Imprisonment', *Prison Service Journal*, 132: 27–37.

Walmsley, R. (1989) 'Special Security Units', Home Office Research Study 109. London: HMSO.

Walmsley, R. (1991) 'Managing Difficult Prisoners: The Parkhurst Special Unit', Home Office Research Study 122. London: HMSO.

Webster, C. and Hucker S. (2007) *Violence Risk. Assessment and Management*. Chichester: John Wiley & Sons.

Webster, C. D., Douglas K. S., Eaves, D. and Hart, S. D. (1997) *HCR-20: Assessing Risk for Violence, Version 2*. Burnaby, British Columbia: Mental Health, Law, and Policy Institute, Simon Fraser University.

Webster, S., Mann, R., Carter, A., Long, J., Milner, R., O'Brien, M., Wakeling, H. and Ray, N. (2006) 'Inter-Rater Reliability of Dynamic Risk Assessment with Sexual Offenders', *Psychology, Crime & Law*, 12(4): 439–52.

Webster's New World College Dictionary (2009a) *Dangerous*. Available at: www.yourdictionary.com/dangerous (accessed 4 March 2009).

Webster's New World College Dictionary (2009b) *Danger*. Available at: www.yourdictionary.com/danger (accessed 4 March 2009).

Weiss, P. (1999) 'Assessment and Treatment of Sex Offenders in the Czech Republic and in Eastern Europe', *Journal of Interpersonal Violence*, 14(4): 411–21.

West London Mental Health NHS Trust (2010) *Broadmoor Hospital*. Available at: www.wlmht.nhs.uk/services/b/broadmoor_hospital.html (accessed 21 September 2010).

West Mercia Probation (2010a) *Integrated Domestic Abuse Programme (IDAP), Information for victims*. Available at: www.westmerciaprobation.org.uk/publications/leaflets/IDAP Victims.pdf (accessed 4 June 2010).

West Mercia Probation (2010b) *Integrated Domestic Abuse Programme (IDAP), Information for Offenders*. Available at: www.westmerciaprobation.org.uk/publications/leaflets/IDAP offenders.pdf (accessed 4 June 2010).

West Yorkshire Probation Trust (2010) *Integrated Domestic Abuse Programme (IDAP)*. Available at: www.westyorksprobation.org.uk/content.php?pageid=218 (accessed 4 June 2010).

White, M. (2010) 'Sarah's Law Alert Scheme Goes Nationwide', *Sky News*. Available at: http://news.sky.com/skynews/Home/UK-News/Sarahs-Law-Sex-Offender-Alert-Scheme-Rolls-Out-Across-UK-Sara-Payne-Welcomes-Move/Article/201003115565451?f=rss (accessed 20 April 2010).

Wilcox, D. T. and Sosnowski, D. E. (2005) 'Polygraph Examination of British Sexual Offenders: A Pilot Study on Sexual History Disclosure Testing', *Journal of Sexual Aggression*, 11(1): 3–25.

Wilcox, D. T., Sosnowski, D. and Middleton, D. (1999) 'The Use of the Polygraph in the Community Supervision of Sex Offenders', *Probation Journal*, 46: 234–40.

Wille, R. and Beier, K. (1989) 'Castration in Germany', *Annals of Sex Research*, 2: 103–33.

Wilson, D. (1992) 'HMP Grendon: A Maverick Prison', *Prison Service Journal*, 87: 20–3.

Wilson, D. (2010) 'Grendon: A Prison in Danger', *Tribune Magazine*, Thursday, 23 September 2010. Available at: www.tribunemagazine.co.uk/2010/09/grendon-a-prison-in-danger (accessed 17 October 2010).

Wilson, D. and McCabe, S. (2002) 'How HMP Grendon "Works" in the Words of Those Undergoing Therapy', *Howard Journal*, 41(3): 279–91.

Wilson, D., Caulfield, L. and Atherton, S. (2009) 'Good Vibrations: The Long-Term Impact of a Prison-Based Music Project', *Prison Service Journal*, 182: 27–32.

Wilson, R., McWhinnie, A. and Wilson, C. (2008) 'Circles of Support and Accountability: An International Partnership in Reducing Sexual Offender Recidivism', *Prison Service Journal*, 178: 26–36.

Winstone, J. and Pakes, F. (2010) 'Process Evaluation of the Mental Health Court Pilot', Ministry of Justice Research Series 18/10. London: Ministry of Justice.

Wood, J. and Kemshall, H. (2010) 'Effective Multi-Agency Public Protection: Learning from the Research', in K. Harrison (ed.) *Managing High Risk Sex Offenders in the Community: Risk Management, Treatment and Social Responsibility*. Cullompton: Willan Publishing.

Wood, T. (2007) 'We Used to Make a Football out of a Goat Head: Working with Young Offenders in a Prison Therapeutic Community', in M. Parker (ed.) *Dynamic Security. The Democratic Therapeutic Community in Prison*. London: Jessica Kingsley Publishers.

Worling, J. and Curwen, T. (2001) 'The ERASOR Estimate of Risk if Adolescent Sexual Offense Recidivism', in M. Calder (ed.) *Juveniles and Children who Sexually Abuse: Frameworks for Assessment*. Lyme Regis: Russell House.

Yorkshire and Humberside Circles of Support and Accountability (2010) Personal communication received 27 July 2010.

Youth Justice Board (2006a) *Criminal Justice Act 2003, 'Dangerousness' and the New Sentences for Public Protection. Guidance for Youth Offending Teams*. London: Youth Justice Board.

Youth Justice Board (2006b) *Managing the Behaviour of Children and Young People in the Secure Estate, Code of Practice*. London: Youth Justice Board.

Youth Justice Board (2008a) *Corporate Plan 2008–11, Business Plan 2008/09: Supporting Young People, Making Communities Safer*. London: Youth Justice Board.

Youth Justice Board (2008b) *Young People who Sexually Abuse*. London: Youth Justice Board.

Youth Justice Board (2009) *Developing a Restraint Minimisation Strategy. Guidance for Secure Establishments on the Development of Restraint Minimisation Strategies*. London: Youth Justice Board.

Youth Justice Board (2010a) *Youth Justice System, Custody Figures*. Available at: www.yjb.gov.uk/en-gb/yjs/Custody/Custodyfigures (accessed 7 November 2010).

Youth Justice Board (2010b) *Young Women in Custody*. Available at: www.yjb.gov.uk/en-gb/yjs/Custody/Youngwomen (accessed 18 November 2010).

Youth Justice Board (2010c) *Secure Training Centres*. Available at: www.yjb.gov.uk/en-gb/yjs/Custody/Securetrainingcentres (accessed 12 November 2010).

Youth Justice Board (2010d) *Secure Children's Homes*. Available at: www.yjb.gov.uk/en-gb/yjs/Custody/Securechildrenshomes (accessed 12 November 2010).

Youth Justice Board (2010e) *Young Offender Institutions*. Available at: www.yjb.gov.uk/en-gb/yjs/Custody/Youngoffenderinstitutions (accessed 12 November 2010).

Youth Justice Board (2010f) *Young Offender Institutions, Contract Details*. Available at: www.yjb.gov.uk/en-gb/yjs/Custody/Secureestatecontactdetails/YOIcontactdetails (accessed 12 November 2010).

Youth Justice Board (2010g) *Behaviour Management*. Available at: www.yjb.gov.uk/en-gb/practitioners/Custody/Behaviourmanagement (accessed 18 November 2010).

Youth Justice Board (2010h) *Anson Unit*. Available at: www.yjb.gov.uk/en-gb/practitioners/Custody/Specialistresources/AnsonUnit (accessed 18 November 2010).

Youth Justice Board (2010i) *HMYOI Wetherby – Anson Unit. Placement Protocol*. London: Youth Justice Board.

Youth Justice Board (2010j) *Young People Convicted of Sexual Offences*. Available at: www.yjb.gov.uk/en-gb/practitioners/Custody/Specialistresources/Youngpeopleconvictedofsexualoffences (accessed 18 November 2010).

Youth Justice Board (2010k) *Placement Protocol: Lucy Faithfull Foundation*. London: Youth Justice Board.

Youth Justice Board and the Ministry of Justice (2010) 'Youth Justice Annual Workload Data 2008/09 England and Wales', Youth Justice Board/Ministry of Justice Statistics Bulletin. London: Youth Justice Board/Ministry of Justice.

INDEX

Note: Page references in *italics* indicate illustrations.